THE ECCLESIAS⅂
OF THE ENGL

BEDE was probably born in Bernicia, the northern component of the Kingdom of the Northumbrians, around the year 673. Nothing is known of his parents. At the age of 7 he entered the recently founded monastery of St Peter at Wearmouth, and was ordained a priest c.703. By about 710 he had begun writing a series of commentaries on various books of the Old and New Testaments, and he undertook his first hagiographical commissions in the same period. His work as historian began with his compilation of chronicle sections to form part of works that he wrote on the divisions of time. He completed writing his best-known book, *The Ecclesiastical History of the English People*, in 731. His last known work was the letter that he sent to Bishop Egbert of York in 734. He died on 25 May 735. After his death his fame in Britain was matched by the interest in him shown by the Anglo-Saxon missionaries on the Continent, for or by whom many of the surviving early manuscripts of his works were written. The Viking attacks on Northumbria in the ninth century cut short a growing cult of Bede, which was revived in a more limited way after the Norman Conquest.

JUDITH MCCLURE is Head of St George's School for Girls in Edinburgh and is the author of articles on Bede and on the Latin Bible in the Early Middle Ages. She is married to her co-editor.

ROGER COLLINS has taught at the University of Liverpool and is currently Research Fellow in the Department of History in the University of Edinburgh. He is the author of several books on early medieval European history. He and Judith McClure are currently writing the first volume of the *Oxford History of Medieval Europe*.

OXFORD WORLD'S CLASSICS

*For over 100 years Oxford World's Classics have brought
readers closer to the world's great literature. Now with over 700
titles—from the 4,000-year-old myths of Mesopotamia to the
twentieth century's greatest novels—the series makes available
lesser-known as well as celebrated writing.*

*The pocket-sized hardbacks of the early years contained
introductions by Virginia Woolf, T. S. Eliot, Graham Greene,
and other literary figures which enriched the experience of reading.
Today the series is recognized for its fine scholarship and
reliability in texts that span world literature, drama and poetry,
religion, philosophy and politics. Each edition includes perceptive
commentary and essential background information to meet the
changing needs of readers.*

OXFORD WORLD'S CLASSICS

BEDE

The Ecclesiastical History of the English People
The Greater Chronicle
Bede's Letter to Egbert

Edited with an Introduction and Notes by
JUDITH McCLURE
and
ROGER COLLINS

OXFORD
UNIVERSITY PRESS

OXFORD
UNIVERSITY PRESS

Great Clarendon Street, Oxford OX2 6DP

Oxford University Press is a department of the University of Oxford.
It furthers the University's objective of excellence in research, scholarship,
and education by publishing worldwide in

Oxford New York

Athens Auckland Bangkok Bogotá Buenos Aires Calcutta
Cape Town Chennai Dar es Salaam Delhi Florence Hong Kong Istanbul
Karachi Kuala Lumpur Madrid Melbourne Mexico City Mumbai
Nairobi Paris São Paulo Singapore Taipei Tokyo Toronto Warsaw

with associated companies in Berlin Ibadan

Oxford is a registered trade mark of Oxford University Press
in the UK and in certain other countries

Published in the United States
by Oxford University Press Inc., New York

Text of The Ecclesiastical History © Oxford University Press 1969
Editorial matter and Translation of The Greater Chronicle and Letter to
Egbert © Judith McClure and Roger Collins

First published as a World's Classics paperback 1994
Reissued as an Oxford World's Classics paperback 1999
Reissued 2008

British Library Cataloguing in Publication Data

Data available

Library of Congress Cataloging in Publication Data

Bede, the Venerable, Saint, 673–735.
[Historica ecclesiastica gentis Anglorum, English]
The ecclesiastical history of the English people; The greater
chronicle; Bede's letter to Egbert / Bede; edited with an
introduction by Judith McClure and Roger Collins.
(Oxford world's classics)
Includes bibliographical references and index.
1. England—Church history—449–1066. 2. Civilization, Anglo-
Saxon. I. McClure, Judith. II. Collins, Roger, 1949–
III. Title: Ecclesiastical history of the English people.
IV. Title: Greater Chronicle. V. Title: Bede's letter to Egbert.
VI. Series.
BR746.B5 1994 274.2'02—dc20 96–3926

ISBN 978-0-19-953723-5

20

Printed and bound in Great Britain by
Clays Ltd, Elcograf S.p.A.

CONTENTS

CONTENTS

ABBREVIATIONS

	Antiquissimi
MGH SRG	Monumenta Germaniae Historica, Scriptores Rerum Germanicarum
MGH SRM	Monumenta Germaniae Historica, Scriptores Rerum Merovingicarum
P	Plummer's edition of *HE: Venerabilis Baedae Historiam Ecclesiasticam Gentis Anglorum*, ed. C. Plummer, 2 vols. (Oxford 1896)
PL	*Patrologia Latina*
PLC	Bede's prose *Life of Cuthbert*, tr. B. Colgrave, in id. (ed.), *Two Lives of St Cuthbert* (Cambridge, 1940)
S	P. H. Sawyer, *Anglo-Saxon Charters* (London, 1968)
SLH	*Scriptores Latini Hiberniae*
TRHS	*Transactions of the Royal Historical Society*
VLC	Bede's verse *Life of Cuthbert*, in W. Jaager (ed.), *Bedas metrische Vita sancti Cuthberti* (Leipzig, 1935); never translated
WH	J. M. Wallace-Hadrill, *Bede's Ecclesiastical History of the English People: A Historical Commentary* (Oxford, 1988)

INTRODUCTION

THE MAN AND HIS MONASTERY

Whether as 'the Venomous Bead' of *1066 and All That* or
through more serious appreciation of his life and work, Bede
may fairly be called the best known of all medieval historians
who wrote in Britain. His *Ecclesiastical History of the English
People*, which he completed in 731, has been enjoyed either in
its original Latin or in numerous English translations for
centuries. It has been seen as the first attempt at a national
history, and although this would not have been Bede's real
aim, it certainly provides us with most of what can be used
to compile a narrative history of the early Anglo-Saxon
kingdoms, from the fifth to the mid-eighth centuries. Sites
associated with Bede's life have also aroused considerable
interest, not least through the growing appeal of popular
archaeology, both in books and on television. The church of
St Paul's at Jarrow, whose chancel contains much of a building dating from Bede's time, receives frequent visitors, and
their number will probably expand in the light of the recent
development of the site as a museum of early Anglo-Saxon life
and culture. It is with Bede's monastery, his home for all but
seven years of his life, that it is best to begin a consideration
of his work, not least because he has left us considerably more
direct information relating to it than he has to himself.

Wearmouth and Jarrow

Between completing his Chronicle in 725 and commencing
the *Ecclesiastical History* of 731, Bede wrote an account of the
foundation and subsequent history of his own monastery. It is
largely thanks to this work, the *History of the Abbots of
Wearmouth and Jarrow*, that we know as much as we do of the
setting of Bede's life, and can also understand how such a
wealth of resources, especially books, was available for him to
draw on throughout his scholarly career. His narrative can

ix

occasionally be supplemented by references in other sources, and these indicate that his *History of the Abbots* is perhaps not always impartial. As will also be seen in the case of his *Ecclesiastical History*, let alone the *Letter to Egbert*, the image of Bede as a detached and saintly scholar does less than justice to the complexity of his personality and of his work.

Combining Bede's account in the *History of the Abbots* with other sources, notably a shorter, anonymous work known as the *Life of Ceolfrid*, written *c*.716/17, the history of the foundation of Wearmouth and Jarrow can be described as follows.[1] At the age of 25 a Northumbrian noble called Biscop Baducing (later also known as Benedict) received a gift of land from king Oswy (642–70), probably following a period of personal and military service in the royal household. He then began a series of journeys to Rome that continued almost until his death. The first of these took place around 653, and Biscop was accompanied as far as Lyons by the future bishop Wilfrid, a detail that Bede does not include.[2] The second visit occurred in the 660s, and after some time in Rome Biscop returned to southern France where he became a monk in the once celebrated island monastery of Lérins. After two years he returned to Rome, where he was present at the arrival and death of Wigheard, who had been sent from England to be consecrated archbishop of Canterbury.[3] When pope Vitalian chose Theodore to replace Wigheard, he also sent Biscop to accompany him on the journey to England. On their arrival in 669, Biscop took over the vacant abbacy of St Augustine's monastery in Canterbury, but relinquished it on the arrival of the African abbot Hadrian in 670. Soon afterwards Biscop was back in Rome, where he began amassing an impressive collection of books. He eventually returned to England and to Northumbria in 674, when he founded the monastery of

---

[1] For consideration of the possibility that the *Life of Ceolfrid* was actually written by Bede, as an anniversary sermon, see J. McClure, 'Bede and the Life of Ceolfrid', *Peritia*, 3 (1984), 71–84.

[2] *LW* ch. 3, p. 8. Only this source adds the detail of Biscop's family name. For the view that Bede was hostile to the influence of Wilfrid and of his supporters, see W. Goffart, *The Narrators of Barbarian History* (Princeton, NJ, 1988), ch. iv: 'Bede and the Ghost of Bishop Wilfrid', 235–328. *EH* v. 19 mentions Wilfrid's presence.

[3] On these events, see *EH* iii. 29 and iv. 1.

Wearmouth on land given him for the purpose by king Ecgfrith (670–85).

To embellish his new foundation he crossed the Channel again in 675 to hire stonemasons in Francia, and he later sent for glaziers, traces of whose work can still be seen at Jarrow. A fourth visit to Rome in the company of Ceolfrid, in the time of pope Agatho (678–81), led to the acquisition for the monastery of more books and of some relics and icons. Biscop also brought back with him the papal cantor John, one of whose tasks in England was to give instruction in the performance of the liturgy. A gift of more estates from king Ecgfrith enabled Biscop to found a sister monastery to Wearmouth at Jarrow in 680/1. The church there was dedicated on 23 April 685, as recorded in the inscription that may still be seen in St Paul's church at Jarrow. Biscop placed Ceolfrid, formerly a monk in Wilfrid's monastery at Ripon, in charge of Jarrow, while entrusting Wearmouth to his own cousin Eosterwine. The latter, another Northumbrian noble turned monk, had been involved with the monastery since its inception in 674. Biscop himself returned to Rome for more books and pictures soon after, not returning until 686. By this time Eosterwine had died (7 March 686) from the plague that had just swept Britain, and Ceolfrid and the Wearmouth monks had elected Sigfrid to succeed him. The failing health of both Sigfrid and Biscop led to the latter appointing Ceolfrid as abbot of both houses on 12 May 688. Sigfrid died on 22 August that year, and Biscop followed on 12 January 689. Ceolfrid remained in office until renouncing the abbacy in 716, to go on a pilgrimage to Rome. Despite the fact that a civil war was raging in northern Francia, he got as far as Langres, where he died. His chosen successor Hwætberct, a former pupil of abbot Sigfrid, was still in office when Bede himself died in 735.

The fragmentary remains of the churches at Wearmouth and Jarrow give an impression of the central feature of the two monasteries, and excavations on the site of Jarrow have revealed something of its domestic layout.[4] Bede's own writ-

---

[4] R. Cramp, 'Monkwearmouth and Jarrow: The Archaeological Evidence' in G. Bonner (ed.), *Famulus Christi: Essays in Commemoration of the Thirteenth Centenary of the Birth of the Venerable Bede* (London, 1976), 5–18.

ings, when analysed for the sources which he drew upon, give an indication of the enormous range of books available in the monastic library in his day, the fruits of Biscop's Continental journeys.[5] Whether this library was divided between the two sites or concentrated in one of them is unknown. Equally tangible are some of the products of the scriptorium of the monastery, including at least one manuscript of Bede's own *Ecclesiastical History*, and the quality of the script and of the vellum on which most were written gives a striking impression both of the wealth of the house and of the calibre of those teaching the arts of the scribe in it.[6] Some of these manuscripts hint at the presence of artists from the Mediterranean, making brief or permanent stays in the monastery, and thus indicate something of the cultural ties linking Northumbria to the Continent and even to the Byzantine or Eastern Roman empire of Constantinople.[7]

Bede's Life

For most of the details known of Bede's life, and there are all too few of them, his own writings are our only source. When composing the final section of his *Ecclesiastical History* (v. 24), he included a short account of himself. He implies that he was aged 59 at the time. Of the significant events of his life he singles out his entry into the monastery of Wearmouth and Jarrow at the age of 7, and his ordination, firstly as deacon and then as priest, at the ages of 19 and 30 respectively. From information he gives in Book V, it is clear that he finished the work sometime after 10 June 731, but before the end of that year.[8] It may be assumed that Bede had entered has fifty-ninth year by this time, though his actual fifty-ninth birthday could have fallen in the early months of 732. Therefore, his birth must have occurred in 672/3. This would date his

[5] M. L. W. Laistner, 'The Library of the Venerable Bede' in A. Hamilton Thompson (ed.), *Bede: His Life, Times and Writings* (Oxford, 1935), pp. 237–66.

[6] M. B. Parkes, *The Scriptorium of Wearmouth-Jarrow* (Jarrow Lecture, 1982).

[7] P. J. Nordhagen, *The Codex Amiatinus and the Byzantine Element in the Northumbrian Renaissance* (Jarrow Lecture, 1977).

[8] *EH* v. 23; see D. P. Kirby, *Bede's 'Historia Ecclesiastica Gentis Anglorum': Its Contemporary Setting* (Jarrow Lecture, 1992), 2–3.

admission to Wearmouth-Jarrow to 679/80, and his ordination as priest to 702/3. The more precise date of his death,
on Wednesday 25 May 735, can be deduced from the account
of his last days given in the letter written by his pupil, the
deacon Cuthbert.

Inevitably, historians have sought to add some more flesh,
however meagre, to the bare bones of Bede's own testimony.
In particular, a story in the *Life of Ceolfrid* has been thought to
refer to an episode in Bede's early life. In 685/6, as mentioned
above, plague devastated the monastic community to which
he had been entrusted a few years earlier. The effects were
particularly severe in Jarrow, where only the abbot Ceolfrid
and a 'young boy' (*puerulus*) survived. Because it is normally
assumed that Bede lived at Jarrow rather than Wearmouth, he
must, it is maintained, be the boy in question. In fact the
association of Bede with Jarrow in particular is poorly
grounded. In his writings, particularly the *History of the Abbots*, he provides physical descriptions of Wearmouth but
never of Jarrow. As the latter was founded only after he had
been admitted to the monastery in 679/80, it can only have
been at Wearmouth that he was received, and he never indicates that he was moved to the new site. While stressing the
unity of the foundation, he always makes it clear that
Wearmouth was the senior of the two components, and it was
there that the abbots of the joint monastery were buried.
Indeed, the story of the boy and the plague helps confirm that
Bede did not live at Jarrow, in that the word used, *puerulus* or
'little boy', would not be applicable to the 12- or 13-year-old
Bede, who, approaching his legal age of majority at 14, would
not have qualified for that diminutive form of the word.

The reasons why Bede has been normally associated with
Jarrow rather than with Wearmouth are probably twofold.
First, his statement that he was educated by the abbots
Benedict Biscop and Ceolfrid could be taken to imply that he
lived at Jarrow, in that Bede here omits reference to abbots
Eosterwine and Sigfrid, who were in charge of Wearmouth for
most of the 680s. However, Bede himself makes it clear in his
History of the Abbots that these two were deputies for Benedict
Biscop, who although often absent and then ill, remained the

sole abbot of the house until his death in 689. His primatial authority then passed to Ceolfrid (d. 716). There were thus only two full abbots of both houses in the period from the foundation of Wearmouth in 674 up to 716: Benedict Biscop and Ceolfrid. The second possible indicator that Bede lived at Jarrow rather than Wearmouth comes from the claim that his bones were discovered in the church of Jarrow in the mid-eleventh century and thence translated (by theft) to Durham cathedral.[9] As little or nothing is known of the history of either house between the late eighth century and the mid-eleventh, and as most medieval 'discoveries' of relics require to be treated with a fair degree of scepticism, this claim cannot be taken as proving that Bede spent most of his life at Jarrow rather than in its sister house at Wearmouth. His own words would place the probability in the opposite direction, though it is important to note that he always stressed the fundamental unity of the two. Despite the geographical distance between them, he, like their founders, wanted them always to be considered as a single institution.

Few other things can be said with certainty about Bede's life. He does not seem to have travelled much. He certainly visited Lindisfarne, where he obtained information for the two versions of his *Life of Cuthbert*, and in his *Letter to Egbert* of 734 he reveals that he had studied at the bishop's monastery (in York?) the previous year. He had also spent some time in the monastery of an otherwise unknown priest called Wicthed, to whom he sent a letter on the subject of the dating of Easter and on Anatolius' calculation of the equinox.[10] Despite the number and wide geographical distribution of his friends and contacts, and, as the *Letter to Egbert* shows, the ability to speak his mind very freely to a bishop who was the cousin of one king and brother of another, it is notable that Bede never rose beyond the rank of priest. While, as was customary, his family will have given the monastery an endowment at the time of his entry, his own resources were few,

---

[9] Symeon of Durham, *History of the Church of Durham*, III. 7, ed. T. Arnold (Rolls Series, vol. lxxv, pt. 1, 1882), 88; written 1104/9.

[10] For the text and discussion, see C. W. Jones (ed.), *Bedae Opera de Temporibus* (Cambridge, Mass., 1943), 168–9, 318–25.

as the *Letter of Cuthbert* indicates. Bede himself gives no clue as to the members or the status of his family, and makes no reference to any named relative.

A cult of Bede clearly developed after his death. In the normal fashion of the period his body would have been left buried for a decade or more. In some cases, such as that of Cuthbert, when the tomb was then opened for the washing of the bones, the body inside was found to be in an unusually good state of preservation—probably due to the composition of the soil or the dryness of the site. Such a phenomenon was taken, not least by Bede himself, to be a sign of particular holiness, and this helps to explain Lindisfarne's particular veneration for Cuthbert and interest in promoting his cult. In the case of Bede the more usual decomposition would seem to have occurred, but his bones would have been washed—a procedure he himself describes in the case of King Oswald[11]—and were subsequently venerated as relics. That this did take place is known from the letter sent by abbot Cuthbert of Wearmouth-Jarrow in 764 to Lul, the Anglo-Saxon bishop of Mainz, thanking him for the gift of a silk sheet which he had sent for the wrapping of Bede's relics. At least one miracle is reported to have been performed through these relics. The Northumbrian deacon Alcuin, in his *Poem on the Bishops, Kings and Saints of York* of c.781/2, records that 'when a sick man was surrounded by the relics of that blessed father he was completely cured from his illness'.[12] There is intrinsically no reason why the cult of Bede should not have developed further, but this would have depended upon the continued survival of his own monastic community. Both Wearmouth and Jarrow seem to have been abandoned around the year 800, probably in consequence of Viking raids. The community, unlike that of Lindisfarne, was unable to relocate itself and so the cults associated with it fell into abeyance. Not until the eleventh century were Wearmouth and Jarrow restored, and they were quickly brought under the control of the monks of Durham, who already believed they had possession of Bede's

[11] *EH* III. 11.
[12] Alcuin, *Bishops, Kings and Saints of York*, ed. and tr. P. Godman (Oxford, 1982), lines 1317–18, p. 105.

relics. Whatever the truth of that claim, the cult of Bede was neither allowed nor could hope to compete with that of Cuthbert, the patron saint of the Durham monks and their church.[13]

WRITINGS

The greater part of Bede's writings consist of commentaries on a variety of books of the Bible, from both Old and New Testaments. As with most other early medieval exegetes, his method of work was largely one of making extracts from the writings of such recognized earlier authorities as Ambrose (d. 397), Jerome (d. 419), Augustine (d. 430), and Gregory the Great (d. 604), whom he was the first to call the four 'Fathers of the Church'. There is little that is truly personal in such compositions, though his stated objectives and methods of work can prove revealing of aspects of his thinking and of his society.[14] Few of his works give precise indications of their dates of composition; but some of these have been deduced, however roughly, on the basis of internal indicators. The following list is divided up generically, and indicates current views on dating.

1. Biblical commentaries

Commentary on the Apocalypse: c.703–9; dedicated to Hwætberct before he became abbot (716).

Commentary on Acts: c.709; dedicated to Acca, bishop of Hexham; later, c.725–31, Bede wrote a *Retraction* to accompany this work.

Commentary on the Catholic Epistles: date unknown; in terms of extant manuscripts, the most popular of Bede's exegetical works.

Commentary on Luke: c.709–15.

Commentary on Mark: after 716.

---

[13] See A. J. Piper, *The Durham Monks at Jarrow* (Jarrow Lecture, 1986).
[14] See e.g. J. McClure, 'Bede's *Notes on Genesis* and the Training of the Anglo-Saxon Clergy', in K. Walsh and D. Wood (eds.), *The Bible in the Medieval World* (Oxford, 1985), 17–30; also B. Ward, *The Venerable Bede* (London, 1990), 41–87.

Commentary on Samuel: books 1–3 were finished before Ceolfrid's departure from Wearmouth in 716; book 4 was begun just after. Acca encouraged Bede to write this work.

Commentary on Genesis: after 721? It was dedicated to Acca.

Commentary on Proverbs: 720s?

Commentary on the Song of Songs: 720s?

On the Tabernacle: c.720–5.

30 Questions on the Books of Kings: c.725; dedicated to Nothhelm.

On the Temple of Solomon: c.729–31?[15]

Commentary on Tobit: date unknown.

Commentary on Ezra and Nehemiah: c.725–31.

Commentary on the Prayer of Habakkuk: 720s? It was dedicated to an unnamed nun.

2. Hagiography

Life of St Anastasius: date unknown, but possibly pre-725.

Life of St Felix: date unknown.

Verse Life of St Cuthbert: 705–16.

Prose Life of St Cuthbert: c.721.

The Martyrology: 725–31.

3. History

Ecclesiastical History: 731 (with additions 732/3?).

History of the Abbots of Wearmouth and Jarrow: c.730.

4. Homilies and liturgical works

50 Homilies on the Gospels: date unknown.

Hymns: at least sixteen genuine ones known.

5. Scientific and educational texts

On the Art of Metre and *On Figures of Speech*: c.701/2

On Orthography: 690s.

On Nature: pre-703.

On Time: 703 (with the *Lesser Chronicle*).

On the Computation of Time 725 (with the *Greater Chronicle*).

---

[15] This has been dated by the reference to it in Bede's letter to Albinus; however, that may well be spurious. See p. 359 below.

The Ecclesiastical History

For all those elements that go to make Bede seem accessible to us, as the founding father of a national historiography whom we also might like to visualize in the relatively well-preserved remains of buildings that would have been familiar to him, there are other features that distance him from us. These were important to him, and should not be overlooked or explained away. As the preceding list shows, most of his life and his scholarly activity was directed towards the study of the Bible and the arts of the *computus*, or the calculation of dates and time. History was far from being his sole or even prime preoccupation, and that the *Ecclesiastical History* proved to be his last major composition was due more to accident than design. As the account of his death given by his pupil Cuthbert shows (pp. 300–303 below) he was engaged on a scriptural project, the translation of John's Gospel into Old English, at the time of his death. His interest in and knowledge of the Bible helped shape both the purposes and the literary style that he used in writing the *Ecclesiastical History*.[16] As his Chronicle indicates, he had no sense of the discontinuity of history. The world of the Old Testament, above all as described in its historical books, was not so remote from him in time as to seem irrelevant; those books provided him with models, both for the description of such secular events as battles and the making and unmaking of kings, of which he had no first-hand knowledge, and for the appreciation of how divine purposes might be worked out in the apparent randomness of the events of human history. He had learned too from the first great historian of the coming of Christianity to the Roman world, bishop Eusebius of Caesarea (*c*.260–339/40), whose *Ecclesiastical History* influenced his view of the purpose of historical writing, and in its use of sources and inclusion of documents lent him a methodology.

The tendency to make Bede an honorary inhabitant of the twentieth century has sometimes also led to the downplaying

---

[16] This is explained in greater detail in J. McClure, 'Bede's Old Testament Kings', in P. Wormald, D. Bullough, and R. Collins (eds.), *Ideal and Reality in Frankish and Anglo-Saxon Society* (Oxford, 1983), 76–98.

or rationalizing of two other major elements of his thought. The first, and this is something he shared with most early medieval authors, was his interest in the miraculous. His careful and critical approach to the selecting of material for his *History* has seemed to some to be at variance with his interest in seeking out stories of miraculous events, and above all those worked through the relics of the various monks and bishops who people his pages. Modern approaches to such elements in the history and hagiography of the Early Middle Ages have enabled us to understand the role such phenomena played in the thought-world of most other authors of this period.[17]

Equally liable to be understated is Bede's interest in the disputes about the correct way to calculate the date of Easter. No reader of the *Ecclesiastical History* can fail to be struck by the frequency with which this topic occurs, and the detail in which it is discussed. Apart from the initial papal letters relating to the conversion of the kingdoms of Kent and of the Northumbrians, the only documents that Bede quotes verbatim in the text of the *EH* are ones relating to the dating of Easter. The longest chapter in the whole work is taken up with a letter on this from Bede's abbot Ceolfrid to the Pictish king Nechtan. On the other hand, he was capable of omitting sections from such letters where their arguments did not suit or might contradict his purpose, and he may well have been aware that the actual practices of the Roman Church in this area did not always correspond with his version of them.[18] He would also have us believe that the whole of the important Synod of Whitby of 664 was devoted almost exclusively to the discussion of this issue, and he all but hides from sight the equally contentious subject of differences of monastic tonsure. By the time that Bede was writing the *EH* in 731 the issue was hardly a living one, yet he gives it an extraordinary

[17] See e.g. P. Brown, 'Relics and Social Status in the Age of Gregory of Tours', in his *Society and the Holy in Late Antiquity* (London, 1982), 222–50, and id., *The Cult of Saints* (Chicago, 1981).

[18] W. Stevens, 'Sidereal Time in Anglo-Saxon England' in C. B. Kendall and P. S. Wells (eds.), *Voyage to the Other World: The Legacy of Sutton Hoo* (Minneapolis, 1992), 125–52. See the same author's *Bede's Scientific Achievement* (Jarrow Lecture, 1985) for an assessment of Bede's own contributions in this and related areas.

prominence, which is also matched in his Chronicle by references to the subject and to those who wrote about it. Whereas his interest in the miraculous was common, his interest in Easter-dating must appear somewhat idiosyncratic.

Only relatively recently has it come to be appreciated that some explanation is needed for Bede's undertaking of his *Ecclesiastical History*; one, moreover, that takes account of his particular methods of working and of the special concerns which he displays for various themes, topics, and personalities.[19] This in turn involves the settling of a number of preliminary arguments. One such obvious area of debate concerns the question of whom Bede was actually writing about. Who are his *Angli*: are they the Angles, as opposed to the Saxons, Jutes, and others whose arrival in Britain he describes in Book I of *EH*; or has he extended the meaning of this previously specific ethnic term to embrace all of the inhabitants of the kingdoms ruled by Anglo-Saxon dynasties? The former theory may help to explain why he says relatively so little about the various Saxon kingdoms in the south and about the Mercians, and would accord with his usage in his *Letter to Egbert*, in which 'our people' are clearly the Angles living north of the Humber. On the other hand, in his Chronicle he uses Angles and Saxons as synonyms, and he had the authority of Gregory the Great for depicting all of the inhabitants of the former Roman provinces of Britain as Angles.[20] It cannot be said, though, that even this issue has been resolved. As with other elements in this rich text, questions exceed answers.

In preparing the edition of the Latin text of the *Ecclesiastical History* on which the translation by Bertram Colgrave was based, Sir Roger Mynors followed the late-nineteenth-century editor Charles Plummer in detecting the existence of two distinct classes of manuscripts. These Plummer had desig-

---

[19] Goffart, in *The Narrators of Barbarian History*, has led the way here; although his thesis, that Bede was reacting to the posthumous influence of Wilfrid, may seem a little narrow.

[20] See M. Richter, 'Bede's *Angli*: Angles or English?', *Peritia*, 3 (1984), 99–114, and P. Wormald, 'Bede, the *Bretwaldas* and the Origins of the *Gens Anglorum*', in Wormald *et al.*, *Ideal and Reality*, 99–129.

nated as 'C' and 'M', and Mynors called them *c* and *m*. The differences between the two classes are neither numerous nor substantial. Thus, a short prayer is found added to the Preface to the whole work in manuscripts of class *m* but at the end of Book V in those of class *c*. One of the miracle stories associated with king Oswald (v. 14) is omitted in *c*. A reference in IV. 18 to a non-existent previous mention of Benedict Biscop is found only in *m*. There is a small textual difference in one sentence in IV. 30. One of the works of Bede, his *Capitula* on the Prophets, is omitted from the list of his writings in v. 24 in *c*; which class also includes the annals for 733 and 734 in the chronological synopsis in the same chapter. Manuscripts in class *m* here add a phrase lacking in *c* but end with the annal for 731.[21] To these six differences noted by Mynors should be added another: in the list of Bede's works, v. 24 *c* rightly describes his *Commentary on the Song of Songs* as being divided into six books, while *m* erroneously makes it seven.

The two classes of manuscripts also seem to have enjoyed very different transmissions. Manuscripts in *c* class are exclusively linked to Britain. All extant manuscripts of this class, even if now found in Continental libraries, were written in Anglo-Saxon England. It was on the basis of the *c*-class text that an Old English vernacular translation was made, probably in Mercia in the ninth century.[22] On the other hand, the *m* text appears to have been the one first sent to the Continent, from the mid-eighth century onwards, where it became the dominant form. Of this class two manuscripts are particularly important for their closeness in date to the original composition of the *EH*. The first of these, Cambridge University Library Kk. 5, known from its donor as 'the Moore Bede', is thought to have been written in Northumbria soon after 737, which is the last date mentioned in the brief annalistic continuation added at the end of the *EH*.[23] Signs of haste in the copying and its lack of decoration have led to the

---

[21] C&M, pp. xxxix–xli.

[22] D. Whitelock, 'The Old English Bede', *Proceedings of the British Academy*, 48 (1962), 57–90.

[23] *CLA*, ii, no. 139; C&M, pp. xliii–xliv.

suggestion that this was transcribed by someone visiting Wearmouth-Jarrow. For an actual product of the monastery's scriptorium, one made with more care and attention to detail, it is possible to turn to Leningrad Public Library MS lat. Q. v. I. 18.[24] This manuscript was not known to Plummer, which is why the Mynors text is now taken as the standard. It was written no later than 747.[25] Neither it nor the Cambridge manuscript were Bede's own work, and what was thought to be the author's own signature in the Leningrad manuscript has been shown to be a medieval forgery.[26] However, it is exceedingly rare to have one, let alone two, manuscripts so close in time to the authorial composition of any early medieval work, and the existence of this pair has made the task of establishing an authoritative version of the text of the *m* class of manuscripts remarkably easy.

The *c* class is much less well represented than the *m*, which as well as in the two manuscripts just mentioned can be found in several others of eighth- and ninth-century date. For *c* the best extant representatives are, first, Kassel Landesbibliothek 4° MS theol. 2, which was written in Northumbria in the late eighth century.[27] Unfortunately, only Books IV and V of the *HE* have survived in this manuscript. Secondly, there is London, British Library MS Cotton Tiberius C. II, written probably in Canterbury in the late eighth or early ninth century.[28] Sir Roger Mynors argued on the basis of the textual differences between *c* and *m*, listed above, that priority should be given to the latter class, and this was made the basis for his edition. He was particularly struck by the addition of the miracle story in IV. 14 to the *m*-class manuscripts. It might, however, be argued that the presence of annals for 732 and 733 in the body of the text of *EH* indicates that the archetype of class *c* was written *c*.733/4, in other words, a few months

[24] *CLA* xi, no. 1621; C&M, p. xliv.

[25] D. H. Wright, 'The Date of the Leningrad Bede', *Revue bénédictine*, 71 (1961), 265–73.

[26] P. Meyvaert, 'The Bede "Signature" in the Leningrad Colophon', ibid. 274–86.

[27] *CLA* viii, no. 1140; C&M, p. xlii.

[28] *CLA* ii, no. 191; C&M, p. xlii. L. Webster and J. Backhouse (eds.), *The Making of England: Anglo-Saxon Art and Culture AD 600–900* (London, 1991), no. 170.

before Bede's death. It is also clear that the story retold in IV. 14 was known to Bede long before he wrote the *EH*, and that it was not inserted in *m* just because it had recently been brought to his attention. Ultimately, though, it is unwise to see one class having more 'authority' than another. The original versions of both will have been written by or for Bede in Wearmouth-Jarrow in the years 731–4, and the differences between them are too slight to suggest that one or other represented a more definitive form of the author's intentions.

It is regrettable that the few surviving eighth-century letters referring to works of Bede do not include any references to his *EH*. In two letters the Anglo-Saxon missionary and archbishop of Mainz, Boniface (d. 754), asked abbot Hwætberct of Wearmouth-Jarrow to send him some of Bede's exegetical writings and his lectionary. It is understandable enough that in the Saxon and Frisian mission fields, the *EH* might have seemed less necessary than some scriptural commentaries. It is clear, though, that at least one manuscript of *EH* made its way to the monastery of Fulda, which Boniface had founded; though this cannot be dated precisely. A manuscript that certainly left England at an early date, although it later returned, is the 'Moore Bede' of Cambridge University Library, described above. This has been shown to have been located in the palace library of Charlemagne by about 800, and via a lost intermediary seven extant ninth-century western Carolingian copies of it were made. Library lists and provenanced manuscripts dating from the same century indicate that copies of the *EH* were also to be found in many of the principal eastern Carolingian monasteries and episcopal churches, notably Lorsch, Murbach, Reichenau, St Gallen, Würzburg, and St Hubert. On the other hand, circulation of the *EH* in Italy at this time appears to have been very limited, and it was apparently entirely unknown in Spain.[29] An Old Irish translation, now found only in the

---

[29] For a fuller, though not comprehensive, discussion of the circulation of the manuscripts of *HE*, see C&M, pp. xlvi–lxx. See also M. L. W. Laistner, *A Hand-List of Bede Manuscripts* (New York, 1943), 93–112, for a listing of medieval manuscripts of the work.

fifteenth-century 'Book of the White Earl' (Oxford, Bodleian Library, MS Laud. misc. 610) was made in the tenth century.[30]

Although it is normally assumed that only the earliest manuscripts of a work such as *EH* need to be consulted to produce a critical text and to work out the first stages of its transmission, in this case there is a possible exception. The set of annals that continue the narrative from 732 to 766, and provide an important source for the history of the Northumbrian kingdom in those years, survive only in a group of seven very late medieval manuscripts. They seem all to be associated with the Low Countries and northern Germany, having provenances in such places as Gouda, Kampen, Utrecht, and Pegau (near Leipzig), but their precise interrelationships have never been worked out. It is usually assumed that they must all ultimately share an ancestor in a lost Northumbrian manuscript of *EH* written in or soon after 766. However, possible use of *ASC* (see p. 421) for one entry would date this lost archetype at the late ninth century at the earliest.

The Greater Chronicle

Having finished the *Ecclesiastical History*, a reader would be pardoned for thinking of Bede as living isolated on the very edge of civilization, and possessing only small sources of illumination, like bonfires seen across a valley, for the wider world. To plot on a map the places that he mentions in the work only confirms such a view. They dwindle in number and decrease in geographical concentration the further south the gaze moves; just extending across the Channel and with only Rome as the most distant point on a dark horizon. However, such an impression is totally misleading: the *Greater Chronicle*, written in 725 as part of Bede's most elaborate work on the divisions of time, shows just how widely his interest and his knowledge extended. His geographical range expands from Britain and northern France to embrace Spain, North Africa,

---

[30] On this see P. Ní Chatáin, 'Bede's Ecclesiastical History in Irish', *Peritia*, 3 (1984), 115–30. The MS contains only Books I and II of *HE*.

and the eastern provinces of the Byzantine empire. Rome, from being on the periphery of his vision in *EH*, becomes the centre of it in the Chronicle.

As in Book I of the *EH*, it is a question not so much of what Bede includes in his work, as of what he obviously knew about but decided not to include. His intentions dictated his selections: he was far from just stuffing into his historical writing all the scraps of information that came to hand. In the Chronicle, as in the first book of *EH*, it is possible to identify the works that he used for much of his information; this provides further testimony to the wealth of the library that he had at his disposal in Wearmouth-Jarrow. Not only is it possible to see what particularly interested him and what he thought the purposes of his own works might be, by comparing what he selected with the complete works from which he made his choices; it is also instructive to contrast his use of these materials with those of others who also employed them. In comparison, for example, with Isidore of Seville (d. 636), who wrote a comparable work in the mid-620s, the texture of Bede's Chronicle is very dense and complex. He used the widest possible variety of sources that were available to him, including ones that were not historical in character, to put together his account. He also adopted a critical approach to the literary merits of what he read. Thus, of his main sources, the one most likely to be quoted verbatim was the Spanish priest Orosius, whose seven-book history was completed in 418. On the other hand, neither in the Chronicle nor in *EH* did Bede ever fail to alter the wording of the passages that he cited from the British monk Gildas' *On the Ruin of Britain*. In contrast, Isidore in his Chronicle tended to use a much more limited range of sources and to allow one to predominate in each period that he covered, and he made hardly any stylistic alterations to the texts he borrowed.

A full discussion of the sources that Bede drew on in compiling his Chronicle would not be practicable here.[31] However, one specific debt is particularly interesting, in that

---

[31] All of the identified borrowings can be found in the apparatus to the *CCSL* edition that is used as the basis for this translation: *CCSL* cxxiiiA, ed. C. W. Jones (Turnhout, 1977), 495–535.

it also sheds some light on the composition of *EH*. For
the Roman Church, a variety of theological issues, and
aspects of the political history of both Italy and the Eastern
Roman empire, Bede made considerable use of a manuscript
of the *Liber Pontificalis*. This is a collection of papal biographies, probably initially compiled in the first half of the
sixth century, and kept up pontificate by pontificate from
the mid-seventh century onwards. Bede used information
from this source throughout the section of the Chronicle
translated here, and with the fading of alternatives it becomes
his dominant fount of information for the later seventh and
early eighth centuries. While it is reasonable to assume that
most of the books that Bede used throughout his career came
from the nucleus of the monastic library of Wearmouth-
Jarrow, which was endowed with the works that Benedict
Biscop brought back from Francia and from Rome in his
visits in the 670s and 680s, Bede's manuscript of the *Liber
Pontificalis* was a more recent arrival. This can be deduced
from the fact that Bede was using material from it to describe
events as late as 716. This includes items relating to the
pontificate of Gregory II (715–31). As Bede was writing in
725 and the final version of the biography of Gregory II could
not have been compiled until 731, it seems that some form
of annual record was being kept in Rome. Furthermore, the
only known point of contact between Bede and Rome,
where an up-to-date version of the *Liber Pontificalis* would
have to be found, was the visit of Nothhelm, referred to in the
Preface to *EH*. Nothhelm was sent by abbot Albinus of St
Augustine's in Canterbury, not least to find copies of papal
letters relating to the conversion of England. These he
brought up to Bede in Wearmouth-Jarrow after his return.
The visit to Rome should, therefore, be dated to the year 717
or immediately after. If so, it may be that Nothhelm also gave
Bede an oral account of the events in Constantinople and
Italy in that year, which form the final items in the Chronicle.
These items, amongst others, made Bede's work a primary
source for the history of the contemporary Lombard kingdom
in Italy, and Paul the Deacon, writing his *History of the
Lombards* in southern Italy in the late 780s, depended on it for
part of his narrative.

This literary debt is itself useful evidence for the transmission of the work, *De Temporum Ratione*, or *On the Computation of Time*, in which the Chronicle appears. It is most probable that Paul found it, as well as the *EH*, in Francia during his attendance at the court of Charlemagne in the years 782–*c*.786. By the end of the century it had been copied in many of the principal Carolingian scriptoria, and had also appeared in northern Italy, where an abbreviated version of it was written in Verona. At the time of the publication in 1943 of the first and only critical edition of the *DTR* nothing was known of the very earliest history of the transmission of this text. The subsequent discovery of some fragments of the work in Northumbrian script, which have been dated to *c*.746–50, shows that like so many of Bede's writings it first crossed the Channel as a result of the interest of the Anglo-Saxon monks evangelizing Saxony and Frisia in acquiring his works.[32] Another recently discovered fragment in Germany may even date from Bede's own lifetime. Of its purely English circulation virtually nothing is known, as no manuscript of British provenance predates the Norman conquest.[33] By the end of the eighth century at the latest, the Chronicle was also circulating separately from its parent, and appears without the rest of the *DTR* in collections of historical works. Conversely, from the ninth century onwards some manuscripts of the *DTR* omit the Chronicle. Although less numerous than manuscripts of the complete *DTR*, those containing the Chronicle by itself continue to be found throughout the Middle Ages, and from all over western Europe, other than Spain. It was as a separate work that the Chronicle received its first critical edition, that of Theodor Mommsen for the MGH in 1898. The *DTR* itself had to wait until 1943 to receive the same treatment. For reasons of length its editor C. W. Jones there omitted the Chronicle, though subsequently incorporating it in the reprint of the 1943 edition published in the *CCSL* series in 1977. It is this text which has been translated here. Although only partial, this is the first English translation of it.

---

[32] J. Petersohn, 'Neue Bedafragmente in northumbrischer Unziale saec. VIII', *Scriptorium*, 20 (1966), 215–47.

[33] For the manuscripts, see W. M. Stevens, *Bede's Scientific Achievement* (Jarrow Lecture, 1985), 39–42.

The *DTR* was a substantial expansion of one of Bede's earliest works, his *De Temporibus* or *On Time*, completed in 703. The Chronicle section of the later work is very considerably longer and more substantial than that found in the *De Temporibus*, which is normally referred to as Bede's *Lesser Chronicle*; although one or two items in the latter were not incorporated into the former. These include a reference to the early sixth-century African bishop Fulgentius of Ruspe and to the forced conversion of the Spanish Jews in the time of king Sisebut (612–21). Both works were probably initially intended for the use of Bede's pupils in Wearmouth-Jarrow.[34] Although very different in scale, both works adopt a similar structure, progressing from a discussion of the smallest units of time, through hours, days, months, years to the largest linear divisions of history. These were the Six Ages, the principal events of which are briefly described in the two versions of the Chronicle.

This, in its two very differently proportioned forms, takes the birth of Adam as its chronological starting-point, dividing the rest of time into the Six Ages: the First from Adam to the Flood, the Second from Noah to Abraham, the Third from Abraham to David, the Fourth from David until the Captivity of the Jews in Babylon, the Fifth extending thence to the birth of Christ. In the *Greater Chronicle* the Sixth Age, the section which is translated here, takes up just over half of the total length. This for Bede and his readers was both the current and the last Age before the Second Coming, and would be terminated by the appearance of Antichrist. Ever since the formulation of the idea of the Six Ages by Augustine of Hippo (354–430), and the application to it of the chronological information to be found in Jerome's Latin version of the great Chronicle of Eusebius of Caesarea (*c*.260–339/40), there had been speculation as to how long the Sixth Age would last. One popular view was that its duration would be a thousand years. Bede, following both Augustine and Isidore of Seville, resolutely stated that there was no way of knowing; as he ends the

[34] See Jones, *Bedae Opera de Temporibus*, 130–9.

De Temporibus: 'The remainder of the Sixth Age is open only to God.'

One reason that led him to doubt the popular view that the first five Ages covered 5,000 years was that his own calculations, based on the Bible and the Jewish historian Josephus, led him to assign a total of 3,952 years to the period from Adam to the birth of Christ. Such deviations from received opinion led in 708 to his being accused of heresy in the presence of bishop Wilfrid by a certain David. When informed of this he wrote a letter to one of the monks of Hexham, called Plegwine, both defending himself and ridiculing the scholarly weaknesses of his detractors. This episode may have coloured his view of Wilfrid, and help to explain the critical tone of some of the comments on him in *EH* and the omission of any references to his relations with Benedict Biscop.[35] Bede's anger and touchiness on the subject lasted long after Wilfrid's death in 709, and he remained very sensitive to the possibilities of criticism when composing the *DTR* and its Chronicle in 725.

Unlike the language of *EH* and of the *Letter to Egbert*, that of the Chronicle is highly compressed. This was a feature of this particular literary genre, and Bede was able to adapt to it in those sections of the work that were entirely of his own composing. In translating such texts it is usually necessary to be more verbose than the original and to insert words or phrases not in the Latin, if the full meaning is to be brought out. Such additions are here signalled by the use of square brackets.

Bede's Letter to Egbert

This is very probably Bede's last surviving work. It is only to be found in three manuscripts, the earliest of which dates to the tenth century, and clearly had a very limited dissemination.[36] It was first edited by Sir James Ware in Dublin in 1664.

---

[35] Jones, *Bedae Opera de Temporibus*, 132–5; Goffart, *The Narrators of Barbarian History*.

[36] MS Hague Koningklijke Bibl. 70 H 7: Laistner *A Hand-List of Bede Manuscripts*, 120. P used the 12th-c. London BL MS Harley 4688.

The most recent edition, that of Charles Plummer (P), is used for this translation. However, he used the twelfth-century London BL MS Harley 4688 for his text, being unaware of the existence of an earlier manuscript; this has yet to be embodied in a modern edition. Despite its title of 'Letter' and the very circumstantial details given in the opening section to explain why Bede has had to commit his thoughts to writing rather than express them more discretely to Egbert in private conversation, there is no doubt that this was intended as a free-standing treatise in its own right and as a very radical manifesto. Its complex rhetorical style and extensive use of biblical quotations were used to support some hard-hitting criticisms of the contemporary state of the Church in Northumbria and to promote a very idiosyncratic remedy that Bede wished to propose.

Bede's primary targets for complaint were the episcopate and monasteries founded and directed by those untrained in and unsuited for the monastic life, as he would have defined it. Although sometimes thought to apply to the Church in England more widely, it is clear from his arguments that Bede's criticisms of the bishops applied to the kingdom of the Northumbrians. He wanted more bishoprics created, at least to try to bring into existence the pattern of twelve northern sees, subordinate to the metropolitan authority of York, which Gregory the Great had envisaged in one of his letters to Augustine of Canterbury. Bede expected that such new sees would have to be based on monasteries; York was anyway the only approximation to a functioning town that would have been found in Northumbria at this time. As well as wanting more bishops, he made clear in the *Letter* that he wanted a higher standard of episcopal behaviour and more assiduous attention to the pastoral responsibilities of that office. It is interesting to note that at the time he was writing there were three episcopal sees in Bernicia, all based on monasteries, and only one in Deira, that of York. Of the former, two of the holders were singled out for praise in *HE*, and the third had become bishop after its completion. The criticisms raised in the *Letter* might apply to the latter, but would seem most suited to the recipient of the work itself, bishop Egbert.

The radical nature of Bede's solution to the problem of the proliferation of what he regarded as unsatisfactory monasteries has hardly been commented on. His proposal that written and witnessed deeds of gift made by previous kings should be annulled by their successors on the grounds of the lack of moral worth of the recipients or of their intentions is truly extraordinary. If adopted it would have undermined the whole principle of security of tenure based on possession of documentary proof of ownership. This tradition, manifested in the use of charters, deriving from Roman legal practice, and established throughout western Europe at this time, was introduced into Anglo-Saxon England early in the seventh century.[37] Admittedly, Bede does not go very far in defining the practical programme that he wished to see implemented. How was the quality of the monastic life to be assessed by those here called upon to annul gifts of land made to founding abbots? Whatever the personal merits of the individuals concerned, Bede's own monastery of Wearmouth-Jarrow, founded by a family of nobles withdrawing from royal service and from military activity, originated in the very way that he condemns in the *Letter*. In his last message to posterity Bede's .words remain enigmatic and problematic.

Cuthbert's Letter on the Death of Bede

This short work, probably composed as part of Wearmouth-Jarrow's promotion of the cult of Bede in the years following his death, has survived in a variety of English and continental contexts. It was incorporated into Symeon's *History of the Church of Durham*, written 1104/9, and is often found appended to manuscripts of the *EH* from the twelfth century onwards. A ninth century manuscript of it from St. Gallen places it after selections from Jerome on Isaiah, wrongly

---

[37] See the various studies in W. Davies and P. Fouracre (eds.), *The Settlement of Disputes in Early Medieval Europe* (Cambridge, 1986), and P. Wormald, *Bede and the Conversion of England: The Charter Evidence* (Jarrow Lecture, 1984).

attributed to Bede. It appears later in a number of hagiographical collections, notably in Austrian monastic libraries.[38]

[38] For a full study of its transmission see E. van K. Dobbie, *The Manuscripts of Cædmon's hymn and Bede's Death Song* (New York, 1937).

NOTE ON THE TRANSLATIONS

The translation of the *Ecclesiastical History* is that produced by the late Bertram Colgrave for the Oxford Medieval Texts edition of the work, first published in 1969. It is reprinted here without the footnotes which originally accompanied it. Improvements to the translation suggested by J. M. Wallace-Hadrill in his *Bede's Ecclesiastical History: A Historical Commentary*, published in 1988 in the same series to accompany the Colgrave and Mynors edition, have been included in the notes in this volume, together with other corrections that now seem necessary.

The translation of the 'Sixth Age' section of the *Greater Chronicle* has been made by us, following C. W. Jones's edition of the *De Temporum Ratione*, of which the Chronicle text originally formed a part. This was published as vol. cxxiiiA of the *Corpus Christianorum Series Latina* in 1977, pp. 495–535, but was originally prepared in 1943 and not subsequently revised.

For the *Letter to Egbert* the edition in C. Plummer, *Baedae Opera Historica* (Oxford, 1896), i. 405–23, which has been followed here, remains the most recent and most critical, although Plummer, who used two later manuscripts of the work, was unaware of the existence of a third, the tenth-century MS Hague Koningklijke Bibl. 70 H 7.

This manuscript from the Hague was used as the basis for the edition of Cuthbert's *Letter on the Death of Bede* included in Colgrave and Mynors's OMT volume. The translation by Bertram Colgrave is reprinted here.

SELECT BIBLIOGRAPHY

ANDERSON, A. O., and M. O. (eds.), *Adamnán's Life of Columba* (revised edn.; Oxford, 1991).

ARNOLD, C. J., *An Archaeology of the Early Anglo-Saxon Kingdoms* (London, 1988).

ATTENBOROUGH, F. L., *The Laws of the Earliest English Kings* (Cambridge, 1922).

BASSETT, S. (ed.), *The Origins of Anglo-Saxon Kingdoms* (Leicester, 1989).

BATTISCOMBE, C. F. (ed.), *The Relics of St Cuthbert* (Oxford, 1956).

BLAIR, P. HUNTER, *The World of Bede* (Cambridge, 1970; rev. edn., 1990).

BONNER, G. (ed.), *Famulus Christi: Essays in Commemoration of the Thirteenth Centenary of the Birth of the Venerable Bede* (London, 1976).

—— ROLLASON, D., and STANCLIFFE, C. (eds.), *St Cuthbert: His Cult and his Community* (Woodbridge, 1989).

BROOKS, N., *The Early History of the Church of Canterbury* (Leicester, 1984).

BRUCE-MITFORD, R. (ed.), *The Sutton Hoo Ship Burial*, i (London, 1975).

CAMPBELL, J. (ed.), *The Anglo-Saxons* (Oxford, 1982).

—— *Essays in Anglo-Saxon History* (London and Ronceverte, W. Va., 1986).

CARVER, M., *The Age of Sutton Hoo* (Woodbridge, 1992).

COLGRAVE, B., *The Earliest Life of Gregory the Great* (Kansas City, Kan., 1968).

DORNIER, A. (ed.), *Mercian Studies* (Leicester, 1977).

FARRELL, R., and NEUMAN DE VEGVAR, C. (eds.), *Sutton Hoo: Fifty Years After* (Oxford, Oh., 1992).

GOFFART, W., *The Narrators of Barbarian History* (Princeton, NJ, 1988), ch. 4: 'Bede and the Ghost of Bishop Wilfrid', 235–328.

HENDERSON, G., *From Durrow to Kells: The Insular Gospel-Books 650–800* (London, 1987).

HIGHAM, N. J., *The Kingdom of Northumbria 350–1100* (Stroud, 1993).

HILL, D., *An Atlas of Anglo-Saxon England* (Oxford, 1981).

HOLLIS, S., *Anglo-Saxon Women and the Church* (Woodbridge, 1992).

HOPE-TAYLOR, B., *Yeavering* (London, 1977).

Select Bibliography

JONES, C. W. (ed.), *Bedae Opera de Temporibus* (Cambridge, Mass., 1943).

KENDALL, C. B., and WELLS, P. S. (eds.), *Voyage to the Other World: The Legacy of Sutton Hoo* (Minneapolis, 1992).

KIRBY, D. P., *The Earliest English Kings* (London, 1991).

LAISTNER, M. L. W., *A Hand-List of Bede Manuscripts* (New York, 1943).

LEVISON, W., *England and the Continent in the Eighth Century* (Oxford, 1946).

MAYR-HARTING, H., *The Coming of Christianity to Anglo-Saxon England* (London, 1972).

MEYVAERT, P., *Benedict, Gregory, Bede and Others* (London, 1977).

ROLLASON, D., *Saints and Relics in Anglo-Saxon England* (Oxford, 1989): pt. II, 'The Age of Bede', 23–129.

SIMS-WILLIAMS, P., *Religion and Literature in Western England, 600–800* (Cambridge, 1990).

SMYTH, A. P., *Warlords and Holy Men* (London, 1984).

TAYLOR, H. M., and J., *Anglo-Saxon Architecture*, 3 vols. (Cambridge, 1965–78).

THOMAS, A. C., *Christianity in Roman Britain to AD 500* (London, 1981).

THOMPSON, A. Hamilton (ed.), *Bede: His Life, Times and Writings* (Oxford, 1935).

VINCE, A. (ed.), *Pre-Viking Lindsey* (Lincoln, 1993).

WEBSTER, L., and BACKHOUSE, J. (eds.), *The Making of England: Anglo-Saxon Art and Culture AD 600–900* (London, 1991).

WELCH, M., *Anglo-Saxon England* (London, 1992).

WORMALD, P., BULLOUGH, D., and COLLINS, R. (eds.), *Ideal and Reality in Frankish and Anglo-Saxon Society* (Oxford, 1983).

WILSON, D., *Anglo-Saxon Paganism* (London, 1993).

YORKE, B., *Kings and Kingdoms of Early Anglo-Saxon England* (London, 1990).

The England of Bede, c.731. Place-names from *The Ecclesiastical History*.
Source: David Hill, *An Atlas of Anglo-Saxon England* (Oxford, 1981), 30.

THE ECCLESIASTICAL
HISTORY OF
THE ENGLISH PEOPLE

PREFACE

To the most glorious King Ceolwulf,* Bede, servant of Christ
and priest.

Your Majesty has asked to see the *History of the English
Church and Nation** which I have lately published.* It was
with pleasure, sire, that I submitted it for your perusal and
criticism on a former occasion; and with pleasure I now send
it once again, for copying and fuller study, as time may
permit. I gladly acknowledge the unfeigned enthusiasm with
which, not content merely to lend an attentive ear to hear the
words of Holy Scripture, you devote yourself to learn the
sayings and doings of the men of old, and more especially
the famous men of our own race. Should history tell of good
men* and their good estate, the thoughtful listener is spurred
on to imitate the good; should it record the evil ends of
wicked men, no less effectually the devout and earnest listener
or reader is kindled to eschew what is harmful and perverse,
and himself with greater care pursue those things which he
has learned to be good and pleasing in the sight of God. This
you perceive, clear-sighted as you are; and therefore, in your
zeal for the spiritual well-being of us all, you wish to see my
History more widely known, for the instruction of yourself and
those over whom divine authority has appointed you to rule.
Now, in order to remove all occasions of doubt about those
things I have written, either in your mind or in the minds of
any others who listen to or read this history, I will make it my
business to state briefly from what sources* I have gained my
information.

My principal authority and helper in this modest work has
been the revered Abbot Albinus,* a man of universal learning
who was educated in the Kentish Church by Archbishop
Theodore* and Abbot Hadrian* of blessed memory, both
venerable and learned men. There he carefully ascertained,
from written records or from the old traditions,* all that the
disciples of St Gregory* had done in the kingdom of Kent or
in the neighbouring kingdoms. He passed on to me whatever

seemed worth remembering through Nothhelm, a godly priest of the Church in London, either in writing or by word of mouth. Afterwards Nothhelm* went to Rome and got permission from the present Pope Gregory* to search through the archives of the holy Roman church and there found some letters of St Gregory and of other popes. On the advice of Father Albinus he brought them to us on his return to be included in our *History*.

So, from the period at which this volume begins to the time when the English race accepted the faith of Christ, I have obtained my material from here and there, chiefly from the writings of earlier writers.* From then to the present time I have learned what the disciples of St Gregory or their successors did in the Kentish church and under what kings these events happened, through the efforts of Abbot Albinus, Nothhelm, as I said, acting as intermediary. Some of my information about the East and West Saxons, as well as East Anglia and Northumbria, was provided by them, especially under what bishops and in whose reigns they received the grace of the gospel. In short, it was chiefly through the encouragement of Albinus that I ventured to undertake this work. Daniel,* the esteemed bishop of the West Saxons who still survives, communicated to me in writing something of the history of the church of his own kingdom, as well as of the neighbouring kingdoms of Sussex and the Isle of Wight. Further I learned from the brethren of the monastery known as Lastingham* which was founded by Cedd and Chad* how, through the ministry of these devoted priests of Christ, the kingdom of Mercia achieved the faith of Christ which it had never known, and how the kingdom of Essex recovered the faith which it had formerly rejected. I also learned from the monks of Lastingham about the life and death of these two fathers. Further, I learned the history of the church of East Anglia, partly from the writings or the traditions of men of the past, and partly from the account of the esteemed Abbot Esi.* As to the kingdom of Lindsey, I learned of the growth of their faith in Christ and of the succession of bishops, either through a letter from the reverend Bishop Cyneberht* or from the lips of other trustworthy men. But what happened in the church

4

in the various parts of the kingdom of Northumbria, from the time when they received the faith of Christ up to the present, apart from those matters of which I had personal knowledge, I have learned not from any one source but from the faithful testimony of innumerable witnesses, who either knew or remembered these things. In this respect it is to be noted that what I have written about the most holy father Bishop Cuthbert,* either in this volume or in his biography, I took partly from what I had previously found written about him by the brethren of the church at Lindisfarne, accepting the story I read in simple faith; but in part I also made it my business to add with care what I was able to learn myself from the trustworthy testimony of reliable witnesses. So I humbly beg the reader, if he finds anything other than the truth set down in what I have written, not to impute it to me. For, in accordance with the principles of true history,* I have simply sought to commit to writing what I have collected from common report, for the instruction of posterity.

Furthermore I humbly beseech all who either read this history of our nation or hear it read, that they will not forget frequently to ask for God's mercy upon my weaknesses both of mind and body; and that in their various kingdoms they will repay me with good measure. Since I have diligently sought to put on record concerning each of the kingdoms and the more important places, those events which I believe to be worthy of remembrance and likely to be welcome to the inhabitants, let me reap among them all, the harvest of their charitable intercessions.

END OF PREFACE   BEGINNING OF CHAPTER HEADINGS

BOOK I

These are the contents of the first book of the history of the Church of the English people.

6

END OF CHAPTER HEADINGS   BEGINNING OF BOOK I

CHAPTER 1

BRITAIN,* once called Albion, is an island of the ocean and lies to the north-west, being opposite Germany, Gaul, and Spain, which form the greater part of Europe, though at a considerable distance from them. It extends 800 miles to the north, and is 200 miles broad, save only where several promontories stretch out further and, counting these, the whole circuit of the coastline covers 4,875 miles.* To the south lies Belgic Gaul, from which the city called *Rutubi Portus* (which the English now corruptly call *Reptacæstir* (Richborough)) is the nearest port for travellers. Between this and the closest point in the land of the Morini, *Gessoriacum* (Boulogne), is a crossing of fifty miles or, as some writers have it, 450 *stadia*. Behind the island, where it lies open to the boundless ocean, are the Orkney islands. The island is rich in crops and in trees, and has good pasturage for cattle and beasts of burden. It also produces vines in certain districts, and has plenty of both land- and waterfowl of various kinds. It is remarkable too for its rivers, which abound in fish, particularly salmon and eels, and for copious springs. Seals as well as dolphins are frequently captured and even whales; besides these there are various kinds of shellfish, among which are mussels, and enclosed in these there are often found excellent pearls of every colour, red and purple, violet and green, but mostly white. There is also a great abundance of whelks, from which a scarlet-coloured dye is made, a most beautiful red which neither fades through the heat of the sun nor exposure to the rain; indeed the older it is the more beautiful it becomes. The land possesses salt springs and warm springs and from them flow rivers which supply hot baths, suitable for all ages and both sexes, in separate places and adapted to the needs of each. For water, as St Basil* says, acquires the quality of heat when it passes through certain metals, so that it not only becomes warm but even scalding hot. The land also has rich veins of metal, copper, iron, lead, and silver. It produces a great deal of excellent jet, which is glossy black and burns when put into the fire and, when kindled, it drives away serpents; when it is warmed by rubbing it attracts whatever is applied to it, just as amber does. The country was once famous for its twenty-eight noble cities as well as innumerable fortified places equally well guarded by the strongest of walls and towers, gates and locks. Because Britain lies almost under the North Pole, it has short nights in summer, so that often at midnight it is hard for those who are watching to say whether it is evening twilight which still lingers, or whether morning dawn has come, since the sun at night returns to the east through the regions towards the north without passing far below the horizon. For this reason the summer days are extremely long. On the other hand the winter nights are also of great length, namely eighteen hours, doubtless because the sun has then departed to the region of Africa. In summer too the nights are extremely short; so are the days in winter, each consisting of six standard equinoctial hours, while in Armenia, Macedonia, Italy, and other countries in the same latitude the longest day or night consists of fifteen hours and the shortest of nine.

At the present time, there are five languages* in Britain, just as the divine law is written in five books, all devoted to seeking out and setting forth one and the same kind of wisdom, namely the knowledge of sublime truth and of true sublimity. These are the English, British, Irish, Pictish, as well as the Latin languages; through the study of the scriptures, Latin is in general use among them all. To begin with, the inhabitants of the island were all Britons,* from whom it receives its name; they sailed to Britain, so it is said, from the land of Armorica,* and appropriated to themselves the southern part of it. After they had got possession of the greater part of the island, beginning from the south, it is related that the Pictish race* from Scythia sailed out into the ocean in a few warships and were carried by the wind beyond the furthest bounds of Britain, reaching Ireland* and landing on its northern shores. There they found the Irish race and asked permission to settle among them but their request was refused. Now Ireland is the largest island of all next to Britain, and lies to the west of it. But though it is shorter than Britain to the north, yet in the south it extends far beyond the limits of that island and as far as the level of North Spain, though a great expanse of sea divides them. The Picts then came to this island, as we have said, by sea and asked for the grant of a place to settle in. The Irish answered that the island would not hold them both; 'but', said they, 'we can give you some good advice as to what to do. We know of another island not far from our own, in an easterly direction, which we often see in the distance on clear days. If you will go there, you can make a settlement for yourselves; but if any one resists you, make use of our help.' And so the Picts went to Britain and proceeded to occupy the northern parts of the island, because the Britons had seized the southern regions. As the Picts had no wives, they asked the Irish for some; the latter consented to give them women, only on condition that, in all cases of doubt, they should elect their kings from the female royal line rather than the male; and it is well known that the custom has been observed among the Picts to this day. In course of time Britain received a third tribe in addition to the Britons and the Picts, namely the Irish. These came from Ireland under their leader Reuda, and won lands among the Picts either by friendly treaty or by the sword. These they still possess. They are still called Dalreudini* after this leader, *Dal* in their language signifying a part.

Ireland* is broader than Britain, is healthier and has a much milder climate, so that snow rarely lasts there for more than three days. Hay is never cut in summer for winter use nor are stables built for their beasts. No reptile is found there nor could a serpent survive; for although serpents have often been brought from Britain, as soon as the ship approaches land they are affected by the scent of the air and quickly perish. In fact almost everything that the island produces is efficacious against poison. For instance we have seen how, in the case of people suffering from snake-bite, the leaves of manuscripts from Ireland were scraped, and the scrapings put in water and given to the sufferer to drink. These scrapings at once absorbed the whole violence of the spreading poison and assuaged the swelling. The island abounds in milk and honey, nor does it lack vines, fish, and birds. It is also noted for the hunting of stags and roe-deer. It is properly the native land of the Irish; they emigrated from it as we have described and so formed the third nation in Britain in addition to the Britons and the Picts. There is a very wide arm of the sea which originally divided the Britons from the Picts. It runs far into the land from the west. Here there is to this day a very strongly fortified British town called Alcluith (Dumbarton). The Irish whom we have mentioned settled to the north of this arm of the sea and made their home there.

CHAPTER 2

Now Britain* had never been visited by the Romans and was unknown to them until the time of Gaius Julius Caesar who, in the year of Rome 693,* that is, in the year 60 before our Lord, was consul with Lucius Bibulus. When he was waging war against the Germans and the Gauls, who were divided only by the river Rhine, he came to the Morini, from whose land is the nearest and shortest crossing to Britain. He prepared about eighty transport ships and light vessels and sailed across to Britain, where first of all he was roughly handled in a severe battle and then caught by a contrary gale, so that he lost a great part of his fleet and no small number of his soldiers, including almost all his cavalry. He returned to Gaul, sent the legions into winter quarters, and then gave orders for the construction of 600 ships of both types. With these he sailed to Britain again in early spring. But while he was marching against the enemy with his army, the ships riding at anchor were caught by a storm and either dashed against each other or cast up on the sands and broken up. Forty of them were lost and the rest were only repaired with great difficulty. At the first encounter Caesar's cavalry were defeated by the Britons and there the tribune Labienus was killed. In the second battle, though his men incurred heavy risks, he conquered the Britons and put them to flight. Thence he marched to the river Thames. An immense multitude of the enemy was established on the further bank under the leadership of Cassobellaunus (Cassivelaunus). The bank of the river and almost all the ford beneath the water had been blocked with sharp stakes. The traces of these stakes are visible even today; each of them, on inspection, is seen to be about the thickness of a man's thigh encased in lead and fixed immovably in the river bed. The Romans saw and avoided these, so the barbarians, being unable to resist the charge of the legions, hid themselves in the woods, from which they made constant sallies and frequently did the Romans great damage. Meanwhile the strongest city of the Trinovantes with its leader Androgeus surrendered to Caesar and gave him forty hostages. Several other towns followed their example and made terms with the Romans. With their guidance Caesar, at length, after heavy fighting, captured the town of Cassivelaunus, which was situated between two marshes and further fortified by a belt of woodland and provided with ample stores of every kind. After this Caesar returned from Britain to Gaul, but no sooner had he sent his legions to their winter quarters than he was surrounded and assailed on every hand by sudden wars and tumults.

CHAPTER 3

IN the year of Rome* 798 the Emperor Claudius, fourth after* Augustus, wishing to prove that he was a benefactor to the State, sought to make war everywhere and to gain victories on every hand. So he made an expedition to Britain, which had apparently been roused to rebellion because of the refusal of the Romans to give up some deserters. He crossed to the island which no one either before or after Julius Caesar had dared to invade until then, and without any fighting or bloodshed he received the surrender of the greater part of the island within a very few days. He even annexed to the Roman empire the Orkneys, some islands which lie in the Ocean beyond Britain. He returned to Rome only six months after he had set out and gave his son the title of Britannicus. He brought the war to an end in the fourth year* of his reign, that is in the year of our Lord 46, the year in which occurred the very severe famine throughout Syria, which, as is recorded in the Acts of the Apostles, was foretold by the prophet Agabus.

Vespasian,* who became emperor after Nero, was sent to Britain by Claudius and brought the Isle of Wight also under Roman rule. It is close to the south coast of Britain, and is about thirty miles in length from east to west and twelve from north to south. At its eastern end it is six miles and at its western end three miles from the southern coast of Britain. Nero, who succeeded Claudius as emperor, undertook no military campaigns of any kind. Consequently he brought countless other disasters upon the Roman empire, and nearly lost Britain as well. For two very noble cities were captured and destroyed there during his reign.

CHAPTER 4

IN the year of our Lord 156 Marcus* Antoninus Verus was made emperor together with his brother Aurelius Commodus. He was the fourteenth after Augustus. In their time, while a holy man called Eleutherius was bishop of the church at Rome, Lucius,* a king of Britain, sent him a letter praying him that he might be made a Christian by a rescript from him. His pious request was quickly granted and the Britons preserved the faith which they had received, inviolate and entire, in peace and quiet, until the time of the Emperor Diocletian.

CHAPTER 5

IN the year of our Lord 189 Severus,* an African by race, of the town of Leptis in the province of Tripoli, became emperor. He was the seventeenth after Augustus and reigned for seventeen years. He was harsh by nature and harassed by continual wars; he ruled the State firmly but with great difficulty. Having been victorious in the very grievous civil wars which happened in his time, he was drawn into Britain by the defection of almost all the federate tribes there. After fighting many great and hard battles, he decided to separate the part of the island over which he had regained control, from the other unconquered tribes, not by a wall as some think, but by a rampart. For a wall is made of stones but a rampart, with which the forts are strengthened to resist the violence of the enemy, is made of sods cut from the earth and is raised high above the ground like a wall. In front is the ditch from which the sods have been lifted and above it are fixed stakes made of the strongest wood. So Severus constructed a great ditch from sea to sea and a very strong rampart fortified by numerous towers upon it. He fell ill and died at York and left two sons, Bassianus and Geta. Of these Geta perished, having been judged an enemy of the state, while Bassianus, who assumed the surname of Antoninus, gained the empire.

CHAPTER 6

In the year* of our Lord 286 Diocletian, the thirty-third after Augustus, was elected emperor by the army and reigned twenty years. He made Maximianus, whose surname was Herculius, his co-emperor. In their time a certain Carausius, a man of mean birth but able and energetic, had been appointed to guard the shores of the Ocean, which were then infested by Franks and Saxons. This man acted rather to the prejudice than to the benefit of the body politic, in that, when he took booty from the robbers, he restored none of it to its owners but kept it all himself. Thus he gave rise to the suspicion that he even allowed the enemy to invade the territories through intentional neglect. For this reason Maximianus gave orders for him to be put to death, but instead Carausius assumed the purple and occupied Britain. He seized and held it for seven years with great daring but was finally killed by the treachery of his colleague Allectus. The latter afterwards held the island which he had seized from Carausius for three years after which Asclipiodotus, the commander of the imperial bodyguard, overthrew him and, ten years later, restored Britain to the Empire.

Meanwhile Diocletian in the east and Maximianus Herculius in the west ordered the churches to be laid waste and the Christians persecuted and slain, the tenth persecution after Nero. This one lasted longer and was more cruel than almost any of the previous ones; it continued without ceasing for ten years accompanied by the burning of churches, the outlawry of innocent people, and the slaughter of the martyrs. In fact Britain also attained to the great glory of bearing faithful witness to God.

CHAPTER 7

DURING this persecution St Alban suffered. Fortunatus* in his *Praise of the Virgins*, in which he mentions the blessed martyrs, who came to the Lord from every quarter of the globe, calls him 'Illustrious Alban, fruitful Britain's child'.

When infidel rulers were issuing violent edicts against the Christians, Alban,* though still a heathen at the time, gave hospitality to a certain cleric who was fleeing from his persecutors. When Alban saw this man occupied day and night in continual vigils and prayers, divine grace suddenly shone upon him and he learned to imitate his guest's faith and devotion. Instructed little by little by his teaching about salvation, Alban forsook the darkness of idolatry and became a wholehearted Christian. When this cleric had been staying with him for some days, it came to the ears of the evil ruler that a man who confessed Christ, though not yet destined to be a martyr, was hiding in Alban's house. He at once ordered his soldiers to make a thorough search for him there. When they came to the martyr's dwelling, St Alban at once offered himself to the soldiers in place of his guest and teacher, and so, having put on the garment, that is to say the cloak, which the cleric was wearing, he was brought in bonds to the judge.

Now it happened that, when Alban was brought in to him, the judge was standing before the devils' altars and offering sacrifices to them. Seeing Alban, he immediately flew into a rage because this man of his own accord had dared to give himself up to the soldiers and to run so great a risk on behalf of the guest whom he had harboured. He ordered Alban to be dragged before the images of the devils in front of which he was standing and said, 'You have chosen to conceal a profane rebel rather than surrender him to my soldiers, to prevent him from paying a well-deserved penalty for his blasphemy in despising the gods; so you will have to take the punishment he has incurred if you attempt to forsake our worship and religion.' St Alban had of his own accord declared himself a Christian before the enemies of the faith, and was not at all afraid of the ruler's threats; arming himself for spiritual warfare, he openly refused to obey these commands. The judge said to him, 'What is your family and race?' Alban answered, 'What concern is it of yours to know my parentage? If you wish to hear the truth about my religion, know that I am now a Christian and am ready to do a Christian's duty.' The judge said, 'I insist on knowing your name, so tell me at once.' The saint said, 'My parents call me Alban and I shall ever adore and worship the true and living God who created all things.' The judge answered very angrily, 'If you wish to enjoy the happiness of everlasting life, you must sacrifice at once to the mighty gods.' Alban answered, 'The sacrifices which you offer to devils cannot help their votaries nor fulfil the desires and petitions of their suppliants. On the contrary, he who has offered sacrifices to these images will receive eternal punishment in hell as his reward.' When the judge heard this he was greatly incensed and ordered the holy confessor of God to be beaten by the torturers, thinking that he could weaken by blows that constancy of heart which he could not affect by words. Alban, though he was subjected to the most cruel tortures, bore them patiently and even joyfully for the Lord's sake. So when the judge perceived that he was not to be overcome by tortures nor turned from the Christian faith, he ordered him to be executed.

As he was being led to his execution, he came to a rapid river whose stream ran between the town wall and the arena where he was to suffer. He saw there a great crowd of people of both sexes and of every age and rank, who had been led (doubtless by divine inspiration) to follow the blessed confessor and martyr. They packed the bridge over the river so tightly that he could hardly have crossed it that evening. In fact almost everyone had gone out so that the judge was left behind in the city without any attendants at all. St Alban, whose ardent desire it was to achieve his martyrdom as soon as possible, came to the torrent and raised his eyes towards heaven. Thereupon the river-bed dried up at that very spot and he saw the waters give way and provide a path for him to walk in. The executioner who was to have put him to death was among those who saw this. Moved by a divine prompting, he hastened to meet the saint as he came to the place appointed for his execution; then he threw away his sword which he was carrying ready drawn and cast himself down at the saint's feet, earnestly praying that he might be judged worthy to be put to death either with the martyr whom he himself had been ordered to execute, or else in his place.

So while he was turned from a persecutor into a companion in the true faith, and while there was a very proper hesitation among the other executioners in taking up the sword which lay on the ground, the most reverend confessor ascended the hill with the crowds. This hill lay about five hundred paces from the arena, and, as was fitting, it was fair, shining and beautiful, adorned, indeed clothed, on all sides with wild flowers of every kind; nowhere was it steep or precipitous or sheer but Nature had provided it with wide, long-sloping sides stretching smoothly down to the level of the plain. In fact its natural beauty had long fitted it as a place to be hallowed by the blood of a blessed martyr. When he reached the top of the hill, St Alban asked God to give him water and at once a perpetual spring bubbled up, confined within its channel and at his very feet, so that all could see that even the stream rendered service to the martyr. For it could not have happened that the martyr who had left no water remaining in the river would have desired it on the top of the hill, if he had not realized that this was fitting. The river, when it had fulfilled its duty and completed its pious service, returned to its natural course, but it left behind a witness of its ministry. And so in this spot the valiant martyr was beheaded and received the crown of life which God has promised to those who love him. But the one who laid his unholy hands on that holy neck was not permitted to rejoice over his death; for the head of the blessed martyr and the executioner's eyes fell to the ground together.

The soldier who had been constrained by the divine will to refuse to strike God's holy confessor was also beheaded there. In his case it is clear that though he was not washed in the waters of baptism, yet he was cleansed by the washing of his own blood and made worthy to enter the kingdom of heaven. Then the judge, who was astonished by these strange heavenly miracles, ordered the persecution to cease and began to respect the way in which the saints met their death, though he had once believed that he could thereby make them forsake their devotion to the Christian faith. The blessed Alban suffered death on 22 June near the city of Verulamium which the English now call either *Uerlamacæstir* or *Uæclingacæstir* (St Albans). Here when peaceful Christian times returned, a church of wonderful workmanship was built, a worthy memorial of his martyrdom. To this day sick people are healed in this place and the working of frequent miracles continues to bring it renown.

About this time Aaron and Julius,* both citizens of the city of the Legions (Caerleon), suffered, and many others of both sexes in various other places. They were racked by many kinds of torture and their limbs were indescribably mangled but, when their sufferings were over, their souls were carried to the joys of the heavenly city.

CHAPTER 8

WHEN the storm* of persecution had ceased, the faithful Christians who in the time of danger had hidden themselves in woods and deserts and secret caverns came out of hiding. They rebuilt the churches which had been razed to the ground; they endowed and built shrines to the holy martyrs. Everywhere, they displayed them as tokens of victory, celebrating festal days and performing their sacred rites with pure heart and voice. The churches of Britain remained at peace until the time of the Arian madness* which corrupted the whole world and even infected this island, sundered so far from the rest of mankind, with the poison of its error. This quickly opened the way for every foul heresy from across the Ocean to pour into an island which always delights in hearing something new and holds firmly to no sure belief.

At this time Constantius* died in Britain, a man of great clemency and courtesy, who had governed Gaul and Spain while Diocletian was alive. He left a son Constantine,* who was made emperor of Gaul, being the child of his concubine Helena. Eutropius* writes that Constantine was created emperor in Britain and succeeded to his father's kingdom. In his time arose the Arian heresy which was exposed and condemned by the Council of Nicaea.* Nevertheless, the deadly poison of its evil doctrine, as has been said, tainted the churches of the whole world, including those of our own islands.

CHAPTER 9

IN the year of our Lord 377* Gratian, the fortieth after Augustus, ruled the empire alone for six years after the death of Valens. He had already reigned for a long time previously with his uncle Valens and his brother Valentinian. Seeing that the body politic was in a disordered state and on the point of collapse, and faced with the need of restoring it, he invested Theodosius, a Spaniard, with the purple at Syrmium and at the same time made him emperor of Thrace and the east. At this moment, an energetic and upright man named Maximus, one worthy of the title of Augustus had he not risen to the rank of dictator by breaking his oath of allegiance, was elected emperor by the army in Britain almost against his will, and crossed to Gaul. There he treacherously murdered the Emperor Gratian, who had been terrified by the sudden incursion and was intending to cross into Italy. Maximus also drove from Italy Gratian's brother, the Emperor Valentinian, who thereupon fled to the east, where Theodosius received him with fatherly affection and soon restored him to the empire. The dictator Maximus was trapped within the walls of Aquileia, where he was caught and killed.

CHAPTER 10

IN the year of our Lord 394 Arcadius, son of Theodosius, became joint-emperor with his brother Honorius and ruled for thirteen years. He was the forty-third from Augustus. In his time the Briton Pelagius* spread his treacherous poison far and wide, denying our need of heavenly grace. He had as his supporter Julianus* of Campania, who had long been stirred by an intemperate desire to get back his lost bishopric. St Augustine and the rest of the orthodox fathers answered them by quoting many thousands of catholic authorities against them but failed to correct their folly; and, what was worse, the madness which should have been healed by turning to the truth was rather increased by rebuke and contradiction. The rhetorician Prosper* expresses it well in telling couplets* when he says:

> Some hack, 'tis said, of envy long the prey,
> Against Augustine crawls his serpent way.
> Who made this piteous worm raise from the ground
> A head once rightly sunk in caves profound?
> Sure, sea-girt Britain's porridge bred this twaddle—
> Or else Campania's groats have turned his noddle.

CHAPTER 11

IN the year of our Lord 407,* when Honorius Augustus, son of Theodosius the second was emperor, being the forty-fourth from Augustus, two years before the invasion of Rome by Alaric, king of the Goths, Gratian, a citizen, was set up here in Britain as dictator and killed. It was the year when the Alani, Suevi, Vandals, and many other races defeated the Franks, crossed the Rhine, and ravaged all Gaul. In his place Constantine, a worthless soldier of the lowest rank, was elected in Britain solely on account of the promise of his name and with no virtue to recommend him. As soon as he had seized power he crossed over to Gaul. There he was often deluded by the barbarians into making doubtful treaties and so inflicted great harm on the body politic. Soon afterwards, on the orders of Honorius, his officer Constantius marched into Gaul with an army, besieged Constantine in the city of Arles, captured and killed him. Constans his son whom he had created Caesar, though a monk, was also put to death at Vienne by Gerontius, his own officer.

Now Rome was taken by the Goths in the eleven hundred and sixty-fourth year after its foundation; after this the Romans ceased to rule in Britain, almost 470 years after Gaius Julius Caesar had come to the island. They had occupied the whole land south of the rampart already mentioned, set up across the island by Severus, an occupation to which the cities, lighthouses, bridges, and roads which they built there testify to this day. Moreover they possessed the suzerainty over the further parts of Britain as well as over the islands which are beyond it.

CHAPTER 12

FROM that time* Britain, or the British part of it, which had been stripped of all its armed men, its military supplies, and the whole flower of its active youth, who by the rashness of the dictators, had been led away never to return, lay wholly exposed to plunderers and the more so because the people were utterly ignorant of the practice of warfare. For instance, they were rapidly reduced to a state of terror and misery by two extremely fierce races from over the waters, the Irish from the west and the Picts from the north; and this lasted many years. We call* them races from over the waters, not because they dwelt outside Britain but because they were separated from the Britons by two wide and long arms of the sea, one of which enters the land from the east, the other from the west, although they do not meet. Half way along the eastern branch is the city of *Giudi*,* while above the western branch, that is on its right bank, is the town of *Alcluith* (Dumbarton), a name which in their language means 'Clyde Rock' because it stands near the river of that name.

As a result of these invasions, the Britons sent messengers to Rome bearing letters with tearful appeals for aid, promising to be their subjects for ever, if only they would drive away their threatening foes. An armed legion was quickly dispatched to them which duly reached the island, attacked the enemy, destroying a great number of them and driving the rest from the territories of their allies. When the Romans had freed them from their dire distress, they urged the Britons to build a wall across the island from sea to sea, as a protection against their foes. And so the legion returned home in great triumph. The islanders built the wall,* as they had been bidden to do, but they made it, not of stone, since they had no skill in work of this kind, but of turves, so that it was useless. They built many miles of it between the two channels or arms of the sea already mentioned, so that where there was no water to shield them, the protecting wall might defend their borders from enemy incursions. The clearest traces of the work constructed there, in the form of a very wide and high wall, can be seen to this day. It starts almost two miles west of the monastery at *Aebbercurnig* (Abercorn) in the place which the Picts all *Peanfahel*, while in English it is called *Penneltun* (Kinneil). It stretches westward as far as *Alcluith* (Dumbarton).

But as soon as their former foes saw the Roman soldiers depart, they took ship and broke into their borders, felling, trampling, and treading down everything they met, like reapers mowing ripe corn. Once more envoys were sent to Rome with pitiful appeals for help so that their wretched country might not be utterly destroyed, and the name of a Roman province, long renowned amongst them, might not be obliterated and disgraced by the barbarity of foreigners. Once again a legion was sent, which arrived unexpectedly in the autumn and did great destruction amongst the enemy, while all who succeeded in escaping were driven across the waters; before this they had been accustomed to carry off their booty every year across the same waters without any opposition. Then the Romans informed the Britons that they could no

longer be burdened with such troublesome expeditions for
their defence; they advised them to take up arms themselves
and make an effort to oppose their foes, who would prove too
powerful for them only if they themselves were weakened
by sloth. Moreover, thinking that it might be some help to
the allies whom they were compelled to abandon, they built
a strong wall of stone from sea to sea in a straight line
between the fortresses which had been built there for fear of
the enemy, on the site which Severus had once made his
rampart.* So, at public and private expense and with the help
of the Britons, they made a famous wall which is still to be
seen. It is eight feet wide and twelve feet high, running in a
straight line from east to west, as is plain for all to see even to
this day. When it was complete they gave some heartening
advice to this sluggish people and showed them how to make
themselves weapons. In addition they built lookout towers at
intervals along the shores of the Ocean to the south, where
their ships plied and where there was fear of barbarian attacks.
And so they took leave of their allies never to return.

   After the Romans had gone back to their own land, the
Irish and Picts, who knew they were not to return, immediately came back themselves and, becoming bolder than ever,
captured the whole of the northern and farthest portion of
the island as far as the wall, driving out the natives. There the
Britons deployed their dispirited ranks along the top of the
defence and, day and night, they moped with dazed and
trembling hearts. On the other hand the enemy with hooked
weapons* never ceased from their ravages. The cowardly
defenders were wretchedly dragged from the walls and dashed
to the ground. In short, they deserted their cities, fled from
the wall, and were scattered. The enemy pursued and there
followed a massacre more bloodthirsty than ever before. The
wretched Britons were torn in pieces by their enemies like
lambs by wild beasts. They were driven from their dwellings
and their poor estates; they tried to save themselves from the
starvation which threatened them by robbing and plundering
each other. Thus they increased their external calamities by
internal strife until the whole land was left without food and
destitute except for such relief as hunting brought.

CHAPTER 13

IN the year of our Lord 423 Theodosius* the younger became emperor after Honorius, being the forty-fifth from Augustus, and ruled twenty-six years. In the eighth year of his reign Palladius* was sent by Celestinus the pontiff of the Roman church to the Irish believers in Christ to be their first bishop. In the twenty-third year of his reign Aetius,* a man of high rank, who was also a patrician, held his third consulship* together with Symmachus. The wretched remnant of the Britons sent him a letter which began: 'To Aetius, thrice consul, come the groans of the Britons.' In the course of the letter they unfolded their sorrows: 'The barbarians drive us to the sea: the sea drives us back on the barbarians; between them two kinds of death face us: we are either slaughtered or drowned.' In spite of all this they were unable to obtain any help from him, seeing that he was at that time engaged in a deadly struggle* with Blædla and Attila, the kings of the Huns; and although in the previous year Blædla had been murdered by the treachery of his own brother Attila, nevertheless Attila continued to be so dangerous an enemy to the state that he devastated almost the whole of Europe, attacking and destroying cities and strongholds alike. At that time too, Constantinople was attacked by a famine, which was followed immediately by the plague. Moreover most of the walls of the city fell, together with fifty-seven towers. Many cities also fell into ruins, while hunger and a pestiferous stench which filled the air destroyed many thousands more men and cattle.

CHAPTER 14

MEANWHILE* this famine, which left to posterity a lasting memory of its horrors, afflicted the Britons more and more. It compelled many of them to surrender to the plundering foe; others, trusting in divine aid when human help failed them, would never give in but continued their resistance, hiding in mountains, caves, and forests. At last they began to inflict severe losses on the enemy who had been plundering their land for many years. So the shameless Irish robbers returned home, intending to come back before long, while the Picts, from that time on, settled down in the furthest part of the island, though they did not cease to plunder and harass the Britons occasionally.

After the enemy's depredations had ceased, there was so great an abundance of corn in the island as had never before been known. With this affluence came an increase of luxury, followed by every kind of foul crime; in particular, cruelty and hatred of the truth and love of lying increased so that if anyone appeared to be milder than the rest and somewhat more inclined to the truth, the rest, without consideration, rained execrations and missiles upon him as if he had been an enemy of Britain. Not only were laymen guilty of these offences but even the Lord's own flock and their pastors. They cast off Christ's easy yoke and thrust their necks under the burden of drunkenness, hatred, quarrelling, strife, and envy and other similar crimes. In the meantime a virulent plague suddenly fell upon these corrupt people which quickly laid low so large a number that there were not enough people left alive to bury the dead. Yet those who survived could not be awakened from the spiritual death which their sins had brought upon them either by the death of their kinsmen or by fear of their own death. For this reason a still more terrible retribution soon afterwards overtook this sinful people for their fearful crimes. They consulted as to what they should do and where they should seek help to prevent or repel the fierce and very frequent attacks of the northern nations; all, including their king Vortigern,* agreed that they should call the Saxons to their aid from across the seas. As events plainly showed, this was ordained by the will of God so that evil might fall upon those miscreants.

CHAPTER 15

IN the year of our Lord 449 Marcian,* forty-sixth from Augustus, became emperor with Valentinian and ruled for seven years. At that time* the race of the Angles or Saxons, invited by Vortigern, came to Britain in three warships and by his command were granted a place of settlement in the eastern part of the island, ostensibly to fight on behalf of the country, but their real intention was to conquer it. First they fought against the enemy* who attacked from the north and the Saxons won the victory. A report of this as well as of the fertility of the island and the slackness of the Britons reached their homes and at once a much larger fleet was sent over with a stronger band of warriors; this, added to the contingent already there, made an invincible army. The newcomers received from the Britons a grant of land in their midst on condition that they fought against their foes for the peace and safety of the country, and for this the soldiers were also to receive pay.

They came from three very powerful Germanic tribes, the Saxons, Angles, and Jutes.* The people of Kent* and the inhabitants of the Isle of Wight are of Jutish origin and also those opposite the Isle of Wight, that part of the kingdom of Wessex which is still today called the nation of the Jutes. From the Saxon country, that is, the district now known as Old Saxony,* came the East Saxons, the South Saxons, and the West Saxons. Besides this, from the country of the Angles, that is, the land between the kingdoms of the Jutes and the Saxons, which is called *Angulus*, came the East Angles, the Middle Angles, the Mercians, and all the Northumbrian race (that is those people who dwell north of the river Humber) as well as the other Anglian tribes. *Angulus* is said to have remained deserted from that day to this. Their first leaders are said to have been two brothers, Hengist and Horsa.* Horsa was afterwards killed in battle by the Britons, and in the eastern part of Kent there is still a monument bearing his name. They were the sons of Wihtgisl,* son of Witta, son of Wecta, son of Woden,* from whose stock the royal families of many kingdoms claimed their descent.

It was not long* before hordes of these peoples eagerly crowded into the island and the number of foreigners began to increase to such an extent that they became a source of terror to the natives who had called them in. Then suddenly they made a temporary treaty with the Picts whom they had already driven far away and began to turn their weapons against their allies. First they made them provide a greater quantity of food; then, seeking an occasion for a quarrel, they insisted that unless they received still greater supplies, they would break the treaty and lay waste every part of the island. Nor were they at all slow in carrying out their threats. To put it briefly, the fire kindled by the hands of the heathen executed the just vengeance of God on the nation for its crimes. It was not unlike that fire once kindled by the Chaldeans which consumed the walls and all the buildings of Jerusalem. So here in Britain the just Judge ordained that the fire of their brutal conquerors should ravage all the neighbouring cities and countryside from the east to the western sea, and burn on, with no one to hinder it, until it covered almost the whole face of the doomed island. Public and private buildings fell in ruins, priests were everywhere slain at their altars, prelates and people alike perished by sword and fire regardless of rank, and there was no one left to bury those who had died a cruel death. Some of the miserable remnant were captured in the mountains and butchered indiscriminately; others, exhausted by hunger, came forward and submitted themselves to the enemy, ready to accept perpetual slavery for the sake of food, provided only they escaped being killed on the spot: some fled sorrowfully to lands beyond the sea, while others remained in their own land and led a wretched existence, always in fear and dread, among the mountains and woods and precipitous rocks.

CHAPTER 16

WHEN the army* of the enemy had exterminated or scattered the native peoples, they returned home and the Britons slowly began to recover strength and courage. They emerged from their hiding-places and with one accord they prayed for the help of God that they might not be completely annihilated. Their leader at that time was a certain Ambrosius Aurelianus,* a discreet man, who was, as it happened, the sole member of the Roman race who had survived this storm in which his parents, who bore a royal and famous name, had perished. Under his leadership the Britons regained their strength, challenged their victors to battle, and, with God's help, won the day. From that time on, first the Britons won and then the enemy were victorious until the year of the siege of Mount Badon, when the Britons slaughtered no small number of their foes about forty-four years* after their arrival in Britain. But more of this hereafter.

CHAPTER 17

A FEW years* before their arrival, the Pelagian heresy* introduced by Agricola,* the son of the Pelagian bishop Severianus, had corrupted the faith of Britain with its foul taint. The Britons had no desire at all to accept this perverse teaching and so blaspheme the grace of Christ, but could not themselves confute by argument the subtleties of the evil belief; so they wisely decided to seek help in this spiritual warfare from the Gaulish bishops. For this reason a great synod was called to consult together as to who should be sent thither to support the faith; by unanimous consent the apostolic bishops, Germanus of Auxerre and Lupus of Troyes, came to Britain to confirm their belief in heavenly grace. These, with ready zeal, complied with the requests and commands of the holy Church and embarked on the Ocean. The ship sped along safely with favouring winds and had reached half-way across the channel between Britain and Gaul, when suddenly they were met on their way by the hostile fury of devils; these were enraged that men of such quality should be sent to restore salvation to the people. They raised storms, they darkened the sky, turning day into night with clouds; the sails could not resist the fury of the winds; the sailors toiled in vain; the ship was supported by prayers rather than by their efforts. As it happened, their leader, the bishop, was worn out and fell asleep. Their champion having thus deserted his post (or so it seemed), the storm increased in fury and the ship, overwhelmed by the waves, was about to sink.

Then St Lupus and all the rest in their dismay awakened their leader so that he might oppose the fury of the elements. More resolute than they in the face of frightful danger, Germanus called on Christ and in the name of the Holy Trinity took a little water and sprinkled it on the raging billows. At the same time he admonished his colleague and encouraged them all, whereupon with one consent and one voice they offered up their prayers. Divine help was forthcoming, the adversaries were put to flight, peace and calm followed, and the contrary winds veered round and helped them on their way; after a quick and peaceful crossing they reached the land they sought. There, great crowds gathered together from all quarters to meet the bishops, whose arrival had been foretold even by their enemies. The evil spirits proclaimed that what they feared had come to pass; and when driven out by the bishops' commands from the bodies of those possessed, they owned up to the nature of the tempest and the dangers which they had brought about, confessing that they had been vanquished by the merits and the power of these men.

In the meantime the island of Britain was soon filled with the fame of the preaching and the miracles of these apostolic bishops. They preached the word of God daily not only in the churches but also in the streets and in the fields, so that the faithful and the catholic were everywhere strengthened and the perverted recognized the true way; like the apostles, they acquired honour and authority for themselves through a good conscience, their learning through the scriptures, and the power of working miracles through their merits. And so the whole country readily turned to their way of thinking, while the authors of the false doctrine went into hiding and, like evil spirits, grieved over the loss of the people who had escaped destruction at their hands. At last, after long deliberation, they ventured to join battle. They came, ostentatiously displaying their wealth in their gorgeous robes and surrounded by a multitude of their supporters, preferring to risk a contest rather than be put to shame by their own silence before the people whom they had subverted, lest by saying nothing they should appear to admit defeat. An immense multitude had been attracted thither with their wives and children. The crowds were present, ready to act as judges, but the contestants differed widely one from the other: on the one side was divine faith, on the other side, human presumption: on the one side piety, on the other pride: on the one side Pelagius the founder of their faith, on the other Christ. The holy bishops gave their adversaries the opportunity of speaking first; these occupied their time and attention for a long period with nothing but empty words. Then the venerable bishops showered upon them the words of the apostles and evangelists in torrents of eloquence. They mingled their own words with the word of God, supporting their most trenchant arguments by the testimony of the scriptures. Falsehood was overcome, deceit unmasked, so that their opponents, as every argument was presented, could not reply but had to confess their errors. The people who were judging found it hard to refrain from violence but nevertheless signified their verdict by applause.

CHAPTER 18

IMMEDIATELY after this, a man who held the rank of tribune* came into the midst with his wife bringing to the bishops his blind daughter, a child of ten, to be healed. They bade the parents take her to their adversaries but the latter, rebuked by their consciences, joined in the prayers of the parents and begged the bishop to heal the child. Seeing their opponents yield, they uttered a short prayer and then Germanus, full of the Holy Spirit, invoked the Trinity. He tore from his neck the little bag which hung down close to his side, containing relics of the saints. Grasping it firmly, he pressed it in the sight of all on the girl's eyelids; her eyes were immediately delivered from darkness and filled with the light of truth. The parents rejoiced while the people were overawed by the miracle. From that day the evil doctrine was so utterly banished from the minds of them all that they thirsted eagerly after the teaching of the bishops.

So when this damnable heresy had been suppressed and its authors confuted and the minds of all had been built up again on the pure faith, the bishops visited the martyr St Alban* to give thanks to God through him. Germanus had with him relics of all the apostles and various martyrs; and, after praying, he ordered the tomb to be opened so that he might place his precious gifts in it. He thought it fitting that the limbs of saints which had been gathered from near and far should find lodging in the same tomb, seeing that they had all entered heaven equal in merits. When these were honourably bestowed and placed side by side, he collected a heap of soil from the place where the blood of the blessed martyr had been shed, to take away with him. In it the blood still showed, pointing the contrast between the scarlet tide of martyrdom and the pale visage of the persecutor. After these incidents a countless number of men turned to the Lord on the same day.

CHAPTER 19

WHILE they were returning, the treacherous foe, setting his chance snares, caused Germanus to fall and bruise his foot, not knowing that his merits like those of Job would be increased by bodily affliction. While he was necessarily confined to one building because of the accident, a neighbouring cottage caught fire; the other dwellings which were thatched with reeds were destroyed and the fire, fanned by the wind, approached the house where he lay. All the people flocked to the bishop intending to lift him up in their arms and rescue him from the danger which threatened; but in the fulness of his faith, he rebuked them and would not allow himself to be moved. So the whole crowd in despair ran to fight the fire. That the power of God might be made more manifest, whatever the crowds sought to preserve was destroyed; but, sick and prostrate as he was, he proved a sure defence. The saint's dwelling was wide open, yet the flames avoided and leapt over it though they raged hither and thither; and amid the masses of blazing fire, his shelter remained unharmed, preserved by the man who lay within. The crowd rejoiced at the miracle, glad to be outdone by the power of God. Day and night a countless multitude watched before the poor man's hut, some desiring to have their souls healed and some their bodies.

All that Christ wrought by his servant cannot be told, for though sick himself, he performed miracles; nor did he allow any remedy to be applied to his own injury. But one night he saw a person standing by him, clad in snow-white garments, who with outstretched hand seemed to raise him as he lay and bade him stand firm upon his feet. From that hour his pain departed and he was restored to his former health, so that when day returned he set out on his toilsome journey full of confidence.

CHAPTER 20

MEANWHILE the Saxons and Picts* had joined forces and were making war upon the Britons, who were forced to take up arms. Fearing they were no match for their foes, they besought the help of the holy bishops. These came at once to fulfil their promise and inspired such confidence in the timid people that one would have thought that a large army had come to their support. Indeed, with such apostolic leaders, it was Christ Himself who fought in their camp. Now the holy season of Lent had come round and was made more sacred by the presence of the bishops, so much so that the people, instructed by their daily teaching, flocked eagerly to receive the grace of baptism. Vast numbers of the army were baptized. A church of wattle was built in preparation for Easter Day and set up for the army in the field as though it were in a city. So, still soaked in the waters of baptism, the army set out. The people's faith was fervent and putting no trust in their arms they expectantly awaited the help of God. The disposition and arrangement of the army was reported to the enemy; they were as sure of victory as though they were attacking an unarmed foe and hastened forward with renewed eagerness; but their approach was observed by the British scouts. So when the Easter solemnities had been celebrated and the greater part of the army, still fresh from the font, were beginning to take up arms and prepare for war, Germanus himself offered to be their leader. He picked out the most active and, having explored the surrounding country, he saw a valley surrounded by hills of moderate height lying in the direction from which the enemy was expected to approach. In this place he stationed his untried army and himself took command. The fierce enemy forces approached, plainly visible as they drew near to the army which was lying in ambush. Germanus who was bearing the standard, thereupon ordered his men to repeat his call in one great shout; as the enemy approached confidently, believing that their coming was unexpected, the bishops shouted 'Alleluia' three times. A universal shout of 'Alleluia' followed, and the echoes from the surrounding hills multiplied and increased the sound. The enemy forces were smitten with dread, fearing that not only the surrounding rocks but even the very frame of heaven itself would fall upon them. They were so filled with terror that they could not run fast enough. They fled hither and thither casting away their weapons and glad even to escape naked from the danger. Many of them rushed headlong back in panic and were drowned in the river which they had just crossed. The army, without striking a blow, saw themselves avenged and became inactive spectators of the victory freely offered to them. They gathered up the spoils lying ready to hand and the devout soldiery rejoiced in this heaven-sent triumph. The bishops thus overcame the enemy without the shedding of blood; they won a victory by faith and not by might.

So a widespread peace was restored to the island and foes visible and invisible were overcome; and the bishops prepared to return home. Their own merits and the intercession of the blessed martyr Alban won them a quiet voyage and their vessel prosperously brought them back in peace to their beloved people.

CHAPTER 21

NOT long afterwards news came from Britain that a small number of people were again spreading abroad the Pelagian heresy. Again all the clergy sent to St Germanus, begging him to defend the cause of God which he had maintained before. He hastened* to grant their request and, taking with him Severus, a man of great sanctity, put to sea and reached Britain after a good voyage with favouring winds. Severus was a disciple of St Lupus, Bishop of Troyes; he was afterwards consecrated Bishop of Trier, preaching the word to the tribes in Germany west of the Rhine.

Meanwhile the evil spirits sped through the whole island, prophesying, though against their will, that Germanus was coming. So a certain Elafius, a chief of that district, hastened to meet the holy men, though no visible messenger had announced their coming. He took with him his son, who, while in the flower of his youth, had been smitten by a painful disease. His knee was wasted and the sinews shrunk so that he was unable to walk because the leg had withered. The whole population of the district followed Elafius. The bishops arrived and were met by the ignorant multitude, on whom they at once bestowed their blessing, giving them instruction in the Word of God. They recognized that the people as a whole had remained true to the faith from the time Germanus had left them; but on learning of the guilt of the few, they searched out the authors of the evil and condemned them. Then Elafius threw himself at the bishop's feet and presented his son, whose infirmity proclaimed his need louder than words. All were grieved but especially the bishops, who were moved by pity to invoke the mercy of God. St Germanus at once told the boy to sit down and then stroked the knee which had been twisted by the disease. He passed his healing hand over all the afflicted parts and recovery quickly followed his health-giving touch. The withered knee regained its strength and the sinews were renewed; in the presence of them all, health was restored to the son and the son was restored to his father. The people were amazed at the miracle, and the catholic faith, already implanted in the hearts of them all, was further strengthened. Thereupon Germanus turned to the people and warned them in a sermon to correct their error. The teachers of the heresy, who had been expelled from the island, were brought by common consent before the bishops, who banished them into the marchlands, so that the country might be rid of them and they might be rid of their error. Thus it came to pass that the faith remained untainted in those parts for a very long time.

So when everything had been settled, the holy bishops returned as successfully as they had come. After this Germanus went to Ravenna to obtain peace for the people of Armorica. He was received with the greatest reverence by Valentinian and his mother Placidia and there he departed to be with Christ. His body was carried to his own town with a splendid retinue and miracles took place on the way. Not long after, in the sixth year of the reign of Marcian, Valentinian was murdered by the followers of the patrician Aetius whom he had put to death, and with Valentinian the western empire fell.*

CHAPTER 22

MEANWHILE* Britain had rest for a time from foreign though not from civil wars. The ruins of the cities destroyed and abandoned by the enemy still remained, while the citizens who had escaped from the foe fought against each other. Nevertheless, so long as the memory of the calamity and bloodshed was still fresh, somehow the kings, priests, nobles, and private citizens kept within bounds. But, when they died, a generation succeeded which knew nothing of all these troubles and was used only to the present state of peace. Then all restraints of truth and justice were so utterly destroyed and abandoned that, not merely was there no trace of them to be found, but only a small, a very small minority even remembered their existence. To other unspeakable crimes,* which Gildas their own historian describes in doleful words, was added this crime, that they never preached the faith to the Saxons or Angles who inhabited Britain with them. Nevertheless God in His goodness did not reject the people whom He foreknew, but He had appointed much worthier heralds of the truth to bring this people to the faith.

CHAPTER 23

In the year of our Lord 582 Maurice,* the fifty-fourth from Augustus, became emperor; he ruled for twenty-one years. In the tenth year of his reign, Gregory,* a man eminent in learning and in affairs, was elected pontiff of the apostolic see of Rome; he ruled for thirteen years, six months, and ten days. In the fourteenth year* of this emperor and about 150 years after the coming of the Angles to Britain, Gregory, prompted by divine inspiration, sent a servant of God named Augustine* and several more God-fearing monks with him to preach the word of God to the English race. In obedience to the pope's commands, they undertook this task and had already gone a little way on their journey when they were paralysed with terror. They began to contemplate returning home rather than going to a barbarous, fierce, and unbelieving nation whose language they did not even understand. They all agreed that this was the safer course; so forthwith they sent home Augustine whom Gregory had intended to have consecrated as their bishop if they were received by the English. Augustine was to beg St Gregory humbly for permission to give up so dangerous, wearisome, and uncertain a journey. Gregory, however, sent them an encouraging letter in which he persuaded them to persevere with the task of preaching the Word and trust in the help of God. The letter* was in these terms:

Gregory, servant of the servants of God, to the servants of our Lord.

My dearly beloved sons, it would have been better not to have undertaken a noble task than to turn back deliberately from what you have begun: so it is right that you should carry out with all diligence this good work which you have begun with the help of the Lord. Therefore do not let the toilsome journey nor the tongues of evil speakers deter you. But carry out the task you have begun under the guidance of God with all constancy and fervour. Be sure that, however great your task may be, the glory of your eternal reward will be still greater. When Augustine your prior returns, now, by our appointment, your abbot, humbly obey him in all things, knowing that whatever you do under his direction will be in all respects profitable to your souls. May Almighty God protect you by His grace and grant that I may see the fruit of your labours in our heavenly home. Though I cannot labour with you, yet because I should have been glad indeed to do so, I hope to share in the joy of your reward. May God keep you safe, my dearly loved sons.

Given on the 23 July, in the fourteenth year of the reign of our most religious emperor Maurice Tiberius, and the thirteenth year after his consulship, and the fourteenth indiction.*

CHAPTER 24

THE venerable pontiff at the same time also sent a letter to Etherius,* archbishop of Arles, asking him to receive Augustine kindly on his return to Britain. This is the text:

To his most reverend and holy brother and fellow bishop Etherius, Gregory, servant of the servants of God. Although religious men stand in need of no recommendation with those bishops who have that love which is pleasing to God, yet because a suitable occasion for writing presents itself, we think fit to send this letter to you our brother, informing you that we have directed thither the bearer of this document, Augustine, the servant of God, of whose zeal we are assured, together with other servants of God devoted to winning souls with the Lord's help. It is essential that your holiness should assist him with episcopal zeal and hasten to provide him with what he needs. And in order that you may be the more prompt with your help, we have specially enjoined him to tell you of his mission. We are sure that when you know this you will be prepared with all zeal to afford him your help for the Lord's sake as the occasion requires. We also commend to your charity the priest Candidus,* a son of both of us, whom we have sent to take charge of a small patrimony of our church. God keep you safe, most reverend brother.

Given on the 23 July, in the fourteenth year of the reign of our most religious emperor, Maurice Tiberius, and the thirteenth year after his consulship and the fourteenth indiction.

CHAPTER 25

So Augustine, strengthened by the encouragement of St Gregory, in company with the servants of Christ, returned to the work of preaching the word, and came to Britain. At that time Æthelberht,* king of Kent, was a very powerful monarch. The lands over which he exercised his suzerainty stretched as far as the great river Humber, which divides the northern from the southern Angles. Over against the eastern districts of Kent there is a large island called Thanet which, in English* reckoning, is 600 hides* in extent. It is divided from the mainland by the river Wantsum, which is about three furlongs wide, can be crossed in two places only, and joins the sea at either end. Here Augustine, the servant of the Lord, landed with his companions, who are said to have been nearly forty in number. They had acquired interpreters* from the Frankish race according to the command of Pope St Gregory. Augustine sent to Æthelberht to say that he had come from Rome bearing the best of news, namely the sure and certain promise of eternal joys in heaven and an endless kingdom with the living and true God to those who received it. On hearing this the king ordered them to remain on the island where they had landed and be provided with all things necessary until he had decided what to do about them. Some knowledge about the Christian religion had already reached him because he had a Christian wife of the Frankish royal family whose name was Bertha.* He had received her from her parents on condition that she should be allowed to practise her faith and religion unhindered, with a bishop named Liudhard* whom they had provided for her to support her faith.

Some days afterwards the king came to the island and, sitting in the open air, commanded Augustine and his comrades to come thither to talk with him. He took care that they should not meet in any building, for he held the traditional superstition that, if they practised any magic art, they might deceive him and get the better of him as soon as he entered. But they came endowed with divine not devilish power and bearing as their standard a silver cross and the image of our Lord and Saviour painted on a panel. They chanted litanies and uttered prayers to the Lord for their own eternal salvation and the salvation of those for whom and to whom they had come. At the king's command they sat down and preached the word of life to himself and all his *gesiths** there present. Then he said to them: 'The words and the promises you bring are fair enough, but because they are new to us and doubtful, I cannot consent to accept them and forsake those beliefs which I and the whole English race* have held so long. But as you have come on a long pilgrimage and are anxious, I perceive, to share with us things which you believe to be true and good, we do not wish to do you harm; on the contrary, we will receive you hospitably and provide what is necessary for your support; nor do we forbid you to win all you can to your faith and religion by your preaching.' So he gave them a dwelling in the city of Canterbury, which was the chief city* of all his dominions; and, in accordance with his promise, he granted them provisions and did not refuse them freedom to preach. It is related that as they approached the city in accordance with their custom carrying the holy cross and the image of our great King and Lord, Jesus Christ, they sang this litany in unison: 'We beseech Thee, O Lord, in Thy great mercy, that Thy wrath and anger may be turned away from this city and from Thy holy house, for we have sinned. Alleluia.'

CHAPTER 26

As soon as they had entered the dwelling-place allotted to them, they began to imitate the way of life of the apostles and of the primitive church. They were constantly engaged in prayers, in vigils and fasts; they preached the word of life to as many as they could; they despised all worldly things as foreign to them; they accepted only the necessaries of life from those whom they taught; in all things they practised what they preached and kept themselves prepared to endure adversities, even to the point of dying for the truths they proclaimed. To put it briefly, some, marvelling at their simple and innocent way of life and the sweetness of their heavenly doctrine, believed and were baptized. There was nearby, on the east of the city, a church built in ancient times in honour of St Martin,* while the Romans were still in Britain, in which the queen who, as has been said, was a Christian, used to pray. In this church they first began to meet to chant the psalms, to pray, to say mass, to preach, and to baptize, until, when the king had been converted to the faith, they received greater liberty to preach everywhere and to build or restore churches.

At last* the king, as well as others, believed and was baptized, being attracted by the pure life of the saints and by their most precious promises, whose truth they confirmed by performing many miracles. Every day more and more began to flock to hear the Word, to forsake their heathen worship, and, through faith, to join the unity of Christ's holy Church. It is related that the king, although he rejoiced at their conversion and their faith, compelled no one to accept Christianity; though none the less he showed greater affection for believers since they were his fellow citizens in the kingdom of heaven. But he had learned from his teachers and guides in the way of salvation that the service of Christ was voluntary and ought not to be compulsory. It was not long before he granted his teachers a place to settle in, suitable to their rank, in Canterbury, his chief city, and gave them possessions of various kinds for their needs.

CHAPTER 27

MEANWHILE Augustine, the man of God, went to Arles* and, in accordance with the command of the holy father Gregory, was consecrated archbishop of the English race by Etherius, the archbishop of that city. He returned to Britain and at once sent to Rome the priest Laurence and the monk Peter* to inform the pope St Gregory that the English race had received the faith of Christ and that he himself had been made their bishop. At the same time he asked his advice about certain

questions which seemed urgent. He received fitting answers*
to his inquiry without delay, and we have thought proper to
insert them in our *History*.

I. The first question of St Augustine, bishop of the Kentish
church. How should bishops live with their clergy? How are
the offerings which the faithful bring to the altar to be appor-
tioned, and how ought a bishop to act in the church?

Pope Gregory, bishop of the city of Rome answered: The
sacred scriptures with which you are doubtless very familiar
bear witness to this and especially the epistles of St Paul to
Timothy, in which he took pains to instruct him how he ought
to behave himself in the house of God. It is a custom of the
apostolic see to give instruction to those who have been
consecrated bishops that all money received should be
divided into four portions: that is, one for the bishop and his
household for purposes of hospitality and entertainment, a
second for the clergy, a third for the poor, and a fourth for the
repair of churches. But because you, brother, are conversant
with monastic rules, and ought not to live apart from your
clergy in the English Church, which, by the guidance of God,
has lately been converted to the faith, you ought to institute
that manner of life which our fathers followed in the earliest
beginnings of the Church: none of them said that anything he
possessed was his own, but they had all things in common. If,
however, there are any who are clerics but in minor orders
and who cannot be continent, they should marry and receive
their stipends outside the community; for we know that it is
written concerning those fathers whom we have mentioned
that division was to be made to each according to his need.
Care must also be taken and provision made for their stipends
and they must be kept under ecclesiastical rule, living a moral
life and attending to the chanting of the psalms and, under
God's guidance, keeping their heart, their tongue, and their
body from all things unlawful. And what need we say to those
who lead a common life about assigning portions or dispens-
ing hospitality or giving alms? For all that is over is to be spent
for holy and religious purposes as the Lord and Master of all

teaches: 'Give alms of what you have over and behold all things are clean unto you.'

II. Augustine's second question. Even though the faith is one are there varying customs in the churches? and is there one form of mass in the Holy Roman Church and another in the Gaulish churches?

Pope Gregory answered: My brother, you know the customs of the Roman Church in which, of course, you were brought up. But it is my wish that if you have found any customs in the Roman or the Gaulish church or any other church which may be more pleasing to Almighty God, you should make a careful selection of them and sedulously teach the Church of the English, which is still new in the faith, what you have been able to gather from other churches. For things are not to be loved for the sake of a place, but places are to be loved for the sake of their good things. Therefore choose from every individual Church whatever things are devout, religious, and right. And when you have collected these as it were into one bundle, see that the minds of the English grow accustomed* to it.

III. Augustine's third question. I beg you to tell me how one who robs a church should be punished.

Gregory answered: My brother, you must judge from the thief's circumstances what punishment he ought to have. For there are some who commit theft though they have resources, while others transgress in this matter through poverty. So some must be punished by fines, some by a flogging, some severely and others more leniently. And when the punishment is more severe, it must be administered in love and not in anger, for it is bestowed on the one who is punished so that he shall not be delivered up to hell-fire. We ought to maintain discipline among the faithful as good fathers do with their children according to the flesh; they beat them with stripes for their faults and yet the very ones they chastise, they intend to make their heirs; and they keep whatever they possess for those whom they appear to persecute in their anger. So we must always keep love in mind and love must dictate the method of correction, so that we do not decide on anything unreasonable. You should also add that they ought to restore whatever they have stolen from a church. But God forbid that the Church should make a profit out of the earthly things it seems to lose and so seek to gain from such vanities.

IV. Augustine's fourth question. May two brothers marry two sisters provided they belong to a family not related to them?

Gregory answered: This is entirely permissible, for there is nothing in the sacred writings on this point which seems to forbid it.

V. Augustine's fifth question. Within what degree may the faithful marry their kindred; and is it lawful to marry a stepmother or a sister-in-law?

Gregory answered: A certain secular law in the Roman State allows that the son and daughter of a brother and sister, or of two brothers or two sisters may be married. But we have learned from experience that the offspring of such marriages cannot thrive. Sacred law forbids a man to uncover the nakedness of his kindred; hence it is necessary that the faithful should only marry relations three or four times removed, while those twice removed must not marry in any case, as we have said. It is a grave sin to marry one's stepmother, because it is written in the law: 'Thou shalt not uncover thy father's nakedness.' Now the son cannot uncover his father's nakedness, but because it is written, 'They twain shall be one flesh', he who presumes to uncover his stepmother's nakedness who was one flesh with his father at the same time uncovers his father's nakedness. So also it is forbidden to marry a brother's wife, because by a former union she had become one flesh with his brother. For this reason also John the Baptist was beheaded and won holy martyrdom. He was not bidden to deny Christ nor was he executed for his confession of Christ. But since our Lord Jesus Christ said, 'I am the truth', and John was killed for the sake of the truth, therefore he shed his blood for Christ.

Now because there are many of the English race who, while they were unbelievers, are said to have contracted these unlawful marriages, when they accept the faith, they should be warned that they must abstain, because such marriages are a grave sin. Let them fear the heavy judgement of God, lest, for the gratification of their carnal desires, they incur the pains of eternal punishment. Nevertheless they are not to be deprived of the communion of the sacred Body and Blood of the Lord for this cause, lest they seem to be punished for sins which they committed through ignorance, before they received the washing of baptism. For in these days the holy Church corrects some things with zeal and tolerates some things with gentleness, while in her wisdom she connives at other things and so by forbearance and connivance often succeeds in checking the evil which she resists. But all who come to the faith must be warned not to perpetrate any such crime. If any do so, then they shall be deprived of the communion of the Body and Blood of the Lord; for as the sin is in some measure to be tolerated in those who did it through ignorance, so it must be strenuously prosecuted in those who presume to sin knowingly.

VI. Augustine's sixth question. Whether a bishop may be consecrated without other bishops being present, if they are at so great a distance from one another that they cannot easily meet.

Gregory answered: In the English Church of which you are as yet the only bishop, it is not possible for you to consecrate a bishop otherwise than alone. For how often do bishops come from Gaul who can assist as witnesses at the consecration of a bishop? But, my brother, we wish you to consecrate bishops in order that they may not be separated by long distances, and thus there will be no lack, so that at the consecration of a bishop, other pastors also may easily be present: for their presence is extremely useful. When therefore, by God's help, bishops have been consecrated in places near to one another, no consecration of a bishop should take place under any circumstances, except in the presence of three or four bishops. For even in spiritual affairs we may take example from things of the flesh in order that they may be conducted wisely and discreetly. When marriages are celebrated in the world, certain married people are invited so that those who have preceded them in the path of matrimony may also share in the joy of the union of those who follow them. Why then, in the spiritual consecration too in which a man is joined to God in the sacred ministry, should not such persons meet together so that they may rejoice in the elevation of the newly consecrated bishop and also pour out their prayers to Almighty God for his preservation?

VII. Augustine's seventh question. How ought we to deal with the bishops of Gaul and Britain?

Gregory answered: We give you no authority over the bishops of Gaul because the bishop of Arles* received the pallium long ago in the days of my predecessors and we must on no account deprive him of the authority he has received. So, my brother, if you chance to cross over to the province of Gaul, you must consult with the bishop of Arles as to how such faults as are found among the bishops may be amended. If he should happen to be slack in his discipline he must be kindled by your zeal. We have also sent letters to him bidding him profit by the presence of your Holiness in Gaul, to use his utmost efforts to check whatever is contrary to our Creator's commands in the conduct of the bishops. You have no right to judge the bishops of Gaul, who are outside your jurisdiction; but, by persuading and winning them and by showing them a good example to imitate, you may restore the minds of the depraved to a zeal for holiness. It is written in the Law: 'When you pass through the standing corn of another, you shall not put a sickle into it: but you may rub the ears with your hands and eat.' You cannot put the sickle of judgement into that harvest which you see has been entrusted to another: but by the influence of good works you may clear the Lord's wheat from the chaff of its vices and by warning and persuasion transform it into the Church's body as though by eating it. But whatever has to be done by the exercise of authority is to be done in collaboration with the bishop of Arles, lest a rule should be neglected which was established by the ancient disposition of the fathers, but we commit to you, my brother, all the bishops of Britain that the unlearned may be instructed, the weak strengthened by your counsel, and the perverse corrected by your authority.

VIII. Augustine's eighth question. Should a pregnant woman be baptized? And when the child has been born how much time should elapse before she can enter the church? And after how many days may the child receive the sacrament of holy baptism so as to forestall its possible death; and after what length of time may her husband have intercourse with her; and is it lawful for her to enter the church if she is in her periods or to receive the sacrament of holy communion? Or may a man who has had intercourse with his wife enter the church before he has washed; or approach the mystery of the holy communion? All these things the ignorant English people need to know.

Gregory answered: I do not doubt, my brother, that you have been asked such questions and I think I have already given you the answer. But I believe that you merely wish that what you yourself may have thought and felt should be confirmed by my answer. Why indeed should a pregnant woman not be baptized, since the fruitfulness of the body is no sin in the eyes of Almighty God? For when our first parents had sinned in Paradise they forfeited by God's just judgement that immortality which they had received. And so because Almighty God had no desire to wipe out the human race entirely on account of its sin, He deprived man of immortality because of his transgression and yet in his loving-kindness and mercy He preserved man's power of propagating the race after him. For what reason then is that which has been preserved for human nature by the gift of Almighty God a cause for debarring anyone from the grace of holy baptism? In this mystery in which all guilt is utterly blotted out, it would be extremely foolish if a gift of grace could be considered an objection.

When a woman has been delivered, after how many days ought she to enter the church? You know by the teaching of the Old Testament that she should keep away for thirty-three days if the child is a boy and sixty-six days if it is a girl. This, however, must be understood figuratively. For if she enters

47

the church even at the very hour of her delivery, for the purpose of giving thanks, she is not guilty of any sin: it is the pleasure of the flesh, not its pain, which is at fault. But it is in the intercourse of the flesh that the pleasure lies; for in bringing forth the infant there is pain. That is why it was said to the first mother of all: 'In sorrow thou shalt bring forth children.' So if we forbid a woman who has been delivered to enter the church, we reckon her punishment as a sin.

But there is nothing to hinder you from baptizing a woman who has been delivered or her infant either, if there is danger of death, even at the very hour when one is delivered and the other born. For while the grace of the holy mystery is to be discreetly provided for those who are still alive and have understanding, let it be administered without delay to those who are on the point of death for fear that while we are waiting for a suitable time to administer the mystery of redemption, if there should be even a very small interval of delay, the person to be redeemed could no longer be found.

Her husband should not approach his bedfellow until her infant is weaned. But an evil custom has arisen among married people that women scorn to suckle the children they have borne, but hand them over to other women to be suckled; and this presumably has arisen solely as a result of incontinence because, as they will not be continent, they are unwilling to suckle their infants. And so those women who in accordance with this evil custom hand over their children to others to be nourished must not have intercourse with their husbands until the time of purification has passed. For apart from childbirth, women are forbidden from intercourse with their husbands during their ordinary periods: so much so that the sacred law condemned to death anyone who approached a menstruous woman. Nevertheless a woman must not be prohibited from entering a church during her usual periods, for this natural overflowing cannot be reckoned a crime: and so it is not fair that she should be deprived from entering the church for that which she suffers unwillingly. For we know that the woman who was suffering from the issue of blood humbly came behind the Lord's back and touched the hem of his garment and immediately her infirmity left her. So if she, when she had an issue of blood, could touch the Lord's garment and win commendation, why is it not lawful for a woman in her periods to enter the Lord's church? But you will say, 'She was driven by her infirmity; but these we speak of are fettered by the natural order of things.' Consider then, most beloved brother, that all that we suffer in this mortal flesh through the infirmity of nature is ordained by the just judgement of God as a result of sin. For hunger and thirst, heat, cold, and weariness are the result of the infirmity of our nature. And if we seek food when hungry, drink when thirsty, fresh air when hot, clothes when cold, and rest when weary, what else are we doing but seeking a remedy for our sicknesses? So a woman's menstruous flow of blood is an infirmity. Therefore if that woman who, in her infirmity, touched our Lord's garment was justified in her boldness, why is it that what was permitted to one was not permitted to all women who are afflicted through the weakness of their natures?

A woman ought not to be forbidden to receive the mystery of the Holy Communion at these times. If, out of deep reverence she does not venture to receive it, that is praiseworthy; but if she has received it she is not to be judged. It is the part of noble minds to acknowledge their faults to some extent even when no fault exists, for an action is often itself faultless, though it originates in a fault. So when we are hungry it is no sin to eat even though our hunger is the result of the sin of the first man. A woman's periods are not sinful, because they happen naturally. But nevertheless, because our nature is itself so depraved that it appears to be polluted even without the consent of the will, the depravity arises from sin, and human nature itself recognizes its depravity to be a judgement upon it; so mankind having wilfully committed sin must bear the guilt of sin though unwillingly. Let women make up their own minds and if they do not venture to approach the sacrament of the Body and Blood of the Lord when in their periods, they are to be praised for their right thinking: but when as the result of the habits of a religious life, they are carried away by the love of the same mystery, they are not to be prevented, as we said before. For as in the Old Testament

49

it is the outward deeds that are observed, so in the New Testament careful heed is paid not so much to what is done outwardly as to what is thought inwardly, so that the punishment may be rendered on subtler grounds. For as the law forbids the eating of many things as unclean, nevertheless in the gospel the Lord said: 'Not that which goeth into the mouth defileth a man: but that which cometh out of the mouth, that defileth a man.' And shortly afterwards He added in explanation, 'Out of the heart proceed evil thoughts.' Whence it is abundantly clear that that is shown by Almighty God to be polluted indeed which is rooted in a polluted thought. So the Apostle Paul also says: 'Unto the pure all things are pure, but unto them that are defiled and unbelieving nothing is pure.' And further on, declaring the cause of that defilement he adds: 'For even their mind and conscience is defiled.' Therefore if no food is impure to him whose mind is pure, why should that which a pure-minded woman endures from natural causes be imputed to her as uncleanness?

A man who has had intercourse with his wife ought not to enter the church unless he has washed himself; and even when washed he ought not to enter immediately. Now the law commanded the ancient people that when a man had intercourse with a woman he ought to wash himself and should not enter the church before sunset; but this can be explained in a spiritual sense. A man has intercourse with a woman when his mind is united with her in thought in the delights of illicit concupiscence, so unless the fire of concupiscence is first quenched in his mind he should not consider himself worthy of the company of his brethren while he sees himself burdened by the sinfulness of depraved desire. Although different nations think differently in this matter and appear to observe different rules, yet it has always been the custom of the Romans from ancient times, after intercourse with one's own wife to seek purification by washing and reverently to abstain from entering the church for a brief period. In saying this we do not reckon marriage as a sin; but because even lawful intercourse cannot take place without fleshly desire, it is right to abstain from entering a sacred place, for the desire itself can by no means be without sin. The man who said,

'Behold I was conceived in iniquity and in sin my mother brought me forth' was not born of adultery or fornication but of lawful wedlock. He knew himself to have been conceived in iniquity and lamented that he was born of sin: for, like a tree, he bears in the branch the sap of evil which he drew from the root: in these words, however, he does not declare the intercourse of married people to be a sin, but only the desire for intercourse. There are indeed many things which are right and lawful and yet we are to some extent defiled in doing them; thus often by being angry we censure the faults of others and disturb our own peace of mind; though what we do is right, it is nevertheless not to be approved that in so doing our peace of mind is disturbed. He who said, 'My eye was disturbed with anger', had been roused to wrath against the vices of sinners. Since it is only a calm mind that can bask in the light of contemplation, so he was grieved because his eye was disturbed with anger. For while he was censuring evil deeds here below, he was compelled to be confused and disturbed in the contemplation of the highest things. And so anger against sin is praiseworthy and none the less harmful, seeing that he thought that by being perturbed in mind he had incurred some guilt. And so fleshly copulation is lawful when it is for the sake of producing offspring and not of desire; and the fleshly intercourse must be for the sake of producing children and not the satisfaction of vicious instincts. So if anyone approaches his wife, not carried away by lustful desire but only for the sake of getting children, such a man is by all means to be left to his own judgement both in the matter of entering the church and of receiving the mystery of the Lord's Body and Blood; for one who is placed in the fire and yet cannot burn ought not to be hindered by us from receiving. But when it is not the love of getting children but desire which dominates in the act of coition, the couple have cause to lament. Though the holy word of prophecy concedes this, yet the very concession gives them cause to fear. For when the Apostle Paul said, 'Let him who cannot contain himself have his own wife', he took care to add forthwith, 'But this I say by way of indulgence, not of commandment'. For that which is lawful is not granted by way of indulgence, so because he said it was an indulgence he proved it to be an offence. It should be considered carefully that when the Lord was about to speak to the people from Mount Sinai he first commanded them to abstain from women. And if such a standard of bodily purity was demanded when the Lord spoke to men through a creature as his substitute, that those who received the words of the Lord were not to approach women, how much more carefully should women who are receiving the Body of the omnipotent Lord preserve the purity of the flesh lest they be weighed down by the greatness of that inestimable Mystery. For this reason also the priest instructed David that if his followers had not approached women, they might receive the shewbread, which they would by no means have received if David had not first declared that they were pure in this respect. A man then who, after intercourse with his wife, has washed, is able to receive the mystery of the Holy Communion, since it is lawful for him, according to what has been said, to enter the church.

IX. Augustine's ninth question. Can anyone receive the Body of the Lord after an illusion such as is wont to occur in a dream; and if he is a priest can he celebrate the holy mysteries?

Gregory answered: The Old Testament, as we have said in an earlier chapter, declares him to be unclean and, unless he has washed, it does not allow him to enter the church until evening. Spiritual people will accept this law but will interpret it differently as we have already explained; for that man is deceived as it were by a dream who, after being tempted with impurity, is defiled in his waking thoughts by real images; and he must be washed with water in the sense that he should wash away the sins of thought with his tears: and unless the fire of temptation has first departed, let him reckon himself guilty until evening, so to speak. But in this same illusion a very necessary distinction must be carefully made as to the reason why it enters into the sleeper's mind; sometimes it happens through gluttony, sometimes through a natural superfluity or weakness, sometimes through the thoughts. And indeed when it happens through a natural superfluity or weakness, the illusion is not in any way to be feared; for though it is a matter of regret that the mind unwittingly suffered it, it did not bring it about. But when a gluttonous appetite carries one away into immoderate eating and the receptacles of the humours are overburdened, then the mind contracts some guilt but not enough to prevent him from partaking of the holy mystery or celebrating the solemn rites of the mass, when perhaps either a feast day demands it or necessity compels him to administer the mystery because there is no other priest in the place. If others are present who can fulfil the ministry, an illusion caused by gluttony ought not to prevent one from receiving the sacred mystery, provided that the mind of the sleeper has not been overcome by vile imaginations. I think, however, that he ought humbly to abstain from offering the sacrifice of the holy mystery. There are some whose mind, when it experiences such an illusion even when the body is asleep, is not contaminated by base imaginations. Here one thing is plain, that the mind is guilty and not even cleared by its own judgement, since even though it has no memory of having seen anything while the body was asleep, nevertheless remembers that while the body was awake it fell into gluttony. But if the sleeper's illusion arises from evil thoughts while awake, then the guilt is clear to the mind; for he sees from what root this defilement sprang because what he thought of wittingly, he experienced unwittingly. But it must be considered whether the thought was the result of a mere suggestion or of pleasure, or what is much more serious, of consent to sin. For all sin is committed in three ways, namely by suggestion, pleasure, and consent. The devil makes the suggestion, the flesh delights in it and the spirit consents. It was the serpent who suggested the first sin, Eve representing the flesh was delighted by it, and Adam representing the spirit consented to it: and when the mind sits in judgement on itself it is necessary to make careful distinction between suggestion and delight, between delight and consent. For when an evil spirit suggests a sin to the mind, if no delight in the sin follows then the sin is not committed in any form; but when the flesh begins to delight in it then sin begins to arise. But if the mind deliberately consents, then the sin is seen to be complete. So the seed of sin is in suggestion, the nourishment of sin is in delight, and the maturity is in consent. It often happens that what an evil spirit sows in the thought, the flesh finds delight in, but the spirit nevertheless does not consent to that delight. And since the flesh cannot get delight without the mind, the mind, struggling against the desires of the flesh, is in some ways unwillingly bound down by carnal delight, so that through reason it refuses to give its consent: and yet it is bound by carnal delight, but vehemently bewails its fetters. It was for this reason that that chief soldier in the heavenly army uttered his complaint saying, 'I see another law in my members warring against the law of my mind and bringing me into captivity to the law of sin, which is in my members.' Now if he was a captive he would not fight; but he did fight: therefore he was both a captive and at the same time fought against the law of the mind to which the law that was in his members was opposed: but if he fought he was not a captive. And so here is a man who so to speak is both captive and free: free on account of his love of right, and captive because of the delight which he unwillingly experiences.

CHAPTER 28

SUCH were the answers of the blessed Pope Gregory to the questions of the most reverend Bishop Augustine. The letter which he says he had written to the bishop of Arles was directed to Vergilius,* the successor of Etherius. This is the substance of it:

To the most reverend and holy brother Vergilius, my fellow bishop, Gregory, servant of the servants of God.

The fact that we usually invite our brethren because we love them shows how much affection ought to be lavished on those brethren who come uninvited. And so if the brother of us both, Bishop Augustine, should happen to come to you, receive him, beloved, as is fitting, with such kindness and affection that he may be refreshed by your kindness and goodwill and that others may be taught how brotherly love should be practised. And because it very often happens that those who are watching from a distance recognize sooner than

54

those implicated what matters need to be emended, if he should bring to your notice, my brother, the sins committed by bishops and others, you will, in counsel with him, inquire into such affairs with elaborate investigation, showing yourself strict and careful in those matters which offend God and provoke Him to wrath, that the guilty may be punished, the innocent cleared, and others amend their ways. May God keep you safe, most reverend brother.

Given on the 22 June in the nineteenth year* of the reign of our most religious emperor Maurice Tiberius and the eighteenth year after his consulship and in the fourth indiction.

CHAPTER 29

SINCE Bishop Augustine had advised him that the harvest was great and the workers were few, Pope Gregory sent more colleagues and ministers of the word together with his messengers. First and foremost among these were Mellitus, Justus, Paulinus, and Rufinianus; and he sent with them all such things as were generally necessary for the worship and ministry of the Church, such as sacred vessels, altar cloths and church ornaments, vestments for priests and clerks, relics of the holy apostles and martyrs, and very many manuscripts. He also sent a letter in which he announced that he had despatched the pallium* to him and at the same time directed how he should organize the bishops in Britain. Here is the text of this letter:

To the most reverend and holy brother Augustine, our fellow-bishop, Gregory, servant of the servants of God.

While it is certain that untold rewards in the eternal kingdom are laid up for those who labour for Almighty God, nevertheless it is necessary that we should bestow rewards and honours upon them, so that they may be encouraged by this recognition to toil more abundantly in their spiritual work. And because the new church of the English has been brought into the grace of Almighty God, through the bounty of the Lord and by your labours, we grant to you the use of the pallium in the church but only for the performance of the solemn rites of the mass: so that you may ordain twelve bishops in various places who are to be subject to your jurisdiction: the bishop of London* shall however, for the future, always be consecrated by his own synod and receive the honour of the pallium from that holy and apostolic see which, by the guidance of God, I serve. We wish to send as bishop to the city of York one whom you yourself shall decide to consecrate; yet, always provided that if this city together with the neighbouring localities should receive the Word of the Lord, he is also to consecrate twelve bishops and enjoy the honourable rank of a metropolitan: for it is our intention, God willing, if we live, to give him the pallium too; nevertheless, brother, we wish him to be subject to your authority: but, after your death, he should preside over the bishops he has consecrated, being in no way subject to the authority of the bishop of London. There is, however, to be this distinction in honour, in future, between the bishops of London and York, that he who was first consecrated is to be reckoned senior. But let them agree to do whatever has to be done, taking counsel together and acting out of zeal for Christ. Let them judge rightly and with one mind and so carry out their decisions without disagreement.

You, brother, are to have under your subjection those bishops whom you have consecrated as well as those who shall be consecrated by the bishop of York, and not those only but also all the bishops of Britain, under the guidance of our Lord God, Jesus Christ: so that they may see from the words and actions of your Holiness what true faith and good living are like and so, fulfilling their office in faith and righteousness, may attain to the heavenly kingdom when it shall please the Lord. May God keep you safe, most reverend brother.

Given the 22 June in the nineteenth year of the reign of our most religious emperor Maurice Tiberius, the eighteenth year after his consulship and in the fourth indiction.

CHAPTER 30

WHEN these messengers had departed, St Gregory sent after them a letter which is worth recording, in which he plainly showed his eager interest in the salvation of our race. This is what he wrote:

To my most beloved son, Abbot Mellitus, Gregory, servant of the servants of God.

Since the departure of our companions and yourself I have felt much anxiety because we have not happened to hear how your journey has prospered. However, when Almighty God has brought you to our most reverend brother Bishop Augustine, tell him what

I have decided after long deliberation about the English people, namely that the idol temples of that race should by no means be destroyed, but only the idols in them. Take holy water and sprinkle it in these shrines, build altars and place relics in them. For if the shrines are well built, it is essential that they should be changed from the worship of devils to the service of the true God. When this people see that their shrines are not destroyed they will be able to banish error from their hearts and be more ready to come to the places they are familiar with, but now recognizing and worshipping the true God. And because they are in the habit of slaughtering much cattle as sacrifices to devils, some solemnity ought to be given them in exchange for this. So on the day of the dedication or the festivals of the holy martyrs, whose relics are deposited there, let them make themselves huts from the branches of trees around the churches which have been converted out of shrines, and let them celebrate the solemnity with religious feasts. Do not let them sacrifice animals to the devil, but let them slaughter animals for their own food to the praise of God, and let them give thanks to the Giver of all things for His bountiful provision. Thus while some outward rejoicings are preserved, they will be able more easily to share in inward rejoicings. It is doubtless impossible to cut out everything at once from their stubborn minds: just as the man who is attempting to climb to the highest place, rises by steps and degrees and not by leaps. Thus the Lord made Himself known to the Israelites in Egypt; yet he preserved in his own worship the forms of sacrifice which they were accustomed to offer to the devil and commanded them to kill animals when sacrificing to him. So with changed hearts, they were to put away one part of the sacrifice and retain the other, even though they were the same animals as they were in the habit of offering, yet since the people were offering them to the true God and not to idols, they were not the same sacrifices. These things then, dearly beloved, you must say to our brother so that in his present position he may carefully consider how he should order all things. May God keep you in safety, most beloved son.

Given the 18 July in the nineteenth year of the reign of our most religious emperor Maurice Tiberius, and in the eighteenth year after his consulship and in the fourth indiction.

CHAPTER 31

AT the same time Pope Gregory heard that Augustine had been performing miracles and sent him a letter on the subject, in which he exhorts Augustine not to incur the danger of being elated by their great number:

I know, most beloved brother, that Almighty God, out of love for you has worked great miracles through you for the race which it was his will to have among the chosen. It is therefore necessary that you should rejoice with trembling over this heavenly gift and fear as you rejoice. You will rejoice because the souls of the English are drawn by outward miracles to inward grace: but you will fear lest among these signs which are performed, the weak mind may be raised up by self-esteem and so the very cause by which it is raised to outward honour may lead through vainglory to its inward fall. We ought to remember that when the disciples were returning from their preaching full of joy, they said to their heavenly Master, 'Lord, even the devils are subject to us through thy name.' And forthwith they received the reply, 'In this rejoice not, but rather rejoice that your names are written in heaven.' They had set their minds on personal and temporal joys when they rejoiced over their own miracles: but they are recalled from private to common joys and from temporal to eternal joys by his words, 'Rejoice in this that your names are written in heaven.' For not all the elect work miracles, but nevertheless all their names are written in heaven. Therefore those who are true disciples ought not to rejoice except in that good thing which they have in common with all the elect and which they will enjoy for ever. So it remains, most dear brother, that amidst those outward deeds which you perform through the Lord's power you should always judge your inner self carefully and carefully note within yourself what you are and how great is the grace shown to that people for whose conversion you have received the gift of working miracles. And if you remember that you have at any time sinned against your Creator either in word or deed, always call this to mind in order that the memory of your guilt may suppress the vainglory which arises in your heart. And whatever power of working miracles you have received or shall receive, consider that these gifts have been conferred not on you, but on those for whose salvation they have been granted you.

CHAPTER 32

POPE GREGORY, at the same time also sent a letter to King Æthelberht, as well as numerous gifts of every kind. He was anxious to glorify the king with temporal honours, while at the same time he rejoiced to think that Æthelberht had attained to the knowledge of heavenly glory by Gregory's own labour and industry. This is a copy of the letter:

Bishop Gregory to his most worthy son, the glorious lord Æthelberht, king of the English.*

Almighty God raises up certain good men to be rulers over nations in order that he may by their means bestow the gifts of his righteousness upon all those over whom they are set. We realize that this has happened to the English race over whom your Majesty is placed, so that, by means of the blessings granted to you, heavenly benefits may also be bestowed upon your subjects. So, my most illustrious son, watch carefully over the grace you have received from God and hasten to extend the Christian faith among the people who are subject to you. Increase your righteous zeal for their conversion; suppress the worship of idols; overthrow their buildings and shrines; strengthen the morals of your subjects by outstanding purity of life, by exhorting them, terrifying, enticing, and correcting them, and by showing them an example of good works; so that you may be rewarded in heaven by the One whose name and knowledge you have spread on earth. For He whose honour you seek and maintain among the nations will also make your glorious name still more glorious even to posterity.

It was thus that Constantine,* the most religious emperor, converted the Roman State from the false worship of idols and subjected it and himself to Almighty God, our Lord Jesus Christ, turning to Him with all his heart, together with the nations under his rule. So it came about that he transcended in renown the reputation of former princes and surpassed his predecessors as much in fame as he did in good works. And now let your Majesty hasten to instil the knowledge of the one God, Father, Son, and Holy Spirit, into the kings and nations subject to you, that you may surpass the ancient kings of your race in praise and merit, and since you have caused others among your subjects to be cleansed from their sins, so you yourself may become less anxious about your own sins before the dread judgement of Almighty God.

Our most reverend brother Bishop Augustine, who was brought up under a monastic Rule, is filled with the knowledge of the holy scriptures and endowed with good works through the grace of God; so whatever counsel he gives you, listen to it gladly, follow it earnestly and keep it carefully in mind. If you listen to him as he speaks on behalf of Almighty God, that same Almighty God will listen to him more readily as he prays for you. But if, which God forbid, you neglect his words, how can Almighty God listen to him when he speaks on your behalf, seeing that you fail to listen to him when he speaks on God's behalf? So ally yourself to him with all your heart in fervent faith and aid his efforts with that vigour which God has bestowed on you, so that He may make you share in His kingdom, if you cause His faith to be accepted in your kingdom.

Besides, we would wish your Majesty to know that the end of the world is at hand, as we learn from the words of Almighty God in the holy scriptures; and the kingdom of the saints which knows no end is near. As the end of the world approaches,* many things threaten which have never happened before; these are changes in the sky and terrors from the heavens, unseasonable tempests, wars, famine, pestilence, and earthquakes in divers places. Not all these things will come about in our days, but they will all follow after our days. So if you see any of these things happening in your land, do not be troubled in mind; for these signs of the end of the world are sent in advance to make us heedful about our souls, watching for the hour of death, so that when the Judge comes we may, through our good works, be found prepared. I have said these things briefly, my distinguished son, but when the Christian faith increases in your kingdom, our discourses to you will become more abundant and we shall be ready to speak more fully in proportion as the joys of our heart are multiplied by the complete conversion of your race.

I am sending you some small gifts which will not be small to you, because you will receive them with the blessing of St Peter the Apostle. And may Almighty God fulfil the grace which He has begun in you and prolong your life here for many years, and in due time receive you into the fellowship of the heavenly country. May the grace of God keep your excellency in safety, my lord and son.

Given the 22 June, in the nineteenth year of the reign of our most religious emperor, Maurice Tiberius Augustus, the eighteenth year after his consulship and in the fourth indiction.

CHAPTER 33

AFTER Augustine had, as we said before, received his episcopal see in the royal city, he with the help of the king restored a church* in it, which, as he was informed, had been built in ancient times by the hands of Roman believers. He dedicated it in the name of the holy Saviour, our Lord and

God, Jesus Christ; and there he established a dwelling for himself and all his successors. He also founded a monastery* not far from the city, to the east, in which Æthelberht, encouraged by him, built from its foundations the church of the Apostles St Peter and St Paul and endowed it with various gifts, so that the bodies of Augustine himself and all the bishops of Canterbury and the kings of Kent might be placed in it. The church was consecrated, not by Augustine but by his successor Laurence.

The first abbot of this monastery was the priest Peter, who was sent on a mission to Gaul and was drowned in a bay of the sea known as *Amfleat* (Ambleteuse). He was given an unworthy burial by the inhabitants of the place but, in order that Almighty God might show how worthy a man he was, a heavenly light appeared every night above his grave until at last the people of the neighbourhood noticed it. They saw that it was a saint who had been buried there; so, after making inquiries as to who he was and whence he came, they removed his body and put it in a church in Boulogne with all the honour due to so great a man.

CHAPTER 34

AT this time Æthelfrith,* a very brave king and most eager for glory, was ruling over the kingdom of Northumbria. He ravaged the Britons more extensively than any other English ruler. He might indeed be compared with Saul who was once king of Israel, but with this exception, that Æthelfrith was ignorant of the divine religion. For no ruler or king had subjected more land to the English race or settled it, having first either exterminated or conquered the natives. To him, in the character of Saul, could fittingly be applied the words which the patriarch said when he was blessing his son, 'Benjamin shall ravin as a wolf; in the morning he shall devour the prey and at night shall divide the spoil.'* For this reason Aedan,* king of the Irish living in Britain, aroused by his successes, marched against him with an immensely strong army; but he was defeated and fled with few survivors. Indeed, almost all his army was cut to pieces in a very famous place called *Degsastan*, that is the stone of Degsa.* In this fight Theobald,* Æthelfrith's brother, was killed together with all his army. Æthelfrith brought this war to an end in the year of our Lord 603, and the eleventh year of his reign, which lasted for twenty-four years. It was also the first year of the reign of Phocas* who was then Roman emperor. From that time no Irish king in Britain has dared to make war on the English race to this day.

BOOK II

Here are the contents of the second book of the history of the Church of the English people.

BEGINNING OF BOOK II   GOOD LUCK TO THE READER!

CHAPTER 1

ABOUT this time, in the year of our Lord 605,* Pope St Gregory, who had reigned in great glory over the apostolic Roman see for thirteen years, six months, and ten days, died and was taken up to reign for ever in the kingdom of heaven. Well indeed may we, the English nation converted by his efforts from the power of Satan to the faith of Christ, give a somewhat full account* of him in our *History of the Church*. We can and should by rights call him our apostle, for though he held the most important see in the whole world and was head of Churches which had long been converted to the true faith, yet he made our nation, till then enslaved to idols, into a Church of Christ, so that we may use the apostle's words about him, 'If he is not an apostle to others yet at least he is to us, for we are the seal of his apostleship in the Lord.'

He was of Roman race, his father's name being Gordianus. He traced his descent from ancestors who were not only noble but also devout. Felix,* for example, who was once bishop of the apostolic see and a man of great reputation both in Christ and in the Church, was his forefather. That ancestral tradition of religion he followed with the same religious devotion as his parents and kinsmen, while the noble position which was accounted his, according to the standards of the world, was by God's grace entirely sacrificed to winning glory and honour of a higher kind. He promptly renounced his secular habit and entered a monastery,* in which he proceeded to live with such grace and perfection—as he used afterwards to declare with tears—that his soul was then above all transitory things; and that he rose superior to all things subject to change. He used to think nothing but thoughts of heaven, so that, even though still imprisoned in the body, he was able to pass in contemplation beyond the barriers of the flesh. He loved death, which in the eyes of almost everybody is a punishment, because he held it to be the entrance to life and the reward of his labours. He used to relate all this, not boasting over his progress towards moral perfection, but rather bewailing the loss which he seemed to have incurred as the result of his pastoral cares. Once, for instance, when he was talking privately with his deacon Peter and enumerating the former virtues of his soul, he added mournfully that now on account of his pastoral cares, he had to trouble himself with the business of men of this world, and after the enjoyment of peace so lovely, he was soiled by the dust of earthly activities. After dissipating his strength on outward things by descending to the affairs of all and sundry, even when he sought the things of the spirit, he inevitably returned to them impaired. 'I realize', he said, 'what I endure and what I have lost; and when my mind turns to what I have lost, then what I endure becomes so much the more burdensome.'

The holy man said all this in a spirit of great humility. We need not believe, however, that he had lost any of his monastic perfection by reason of his pastoral cares. It would appear that he profited more by his efforts over the conversion of many than he had done from the quiet retirement of his earlier way of life. This was largely because, while fulfilling his pontifical duties, he turned his own house into a monastery; and when he was first taken from the monastery and was ordained to the ministry of the altar, having been sent to Constantinople as delegate of the apostolic see, he never ceased from his heavenly manner of life, though he had to live in an earthly palace. He even used some of the brothers from his monastery who had followed him out of brotherly love to the royal city to protect him in his observance of the Rule. Thus, as he himself writes, through their unremitting example he could bind himself, as it were by an anchor cable, to the calm shores of prayer, while he was being tossed about on the ceaseless tide of secular affairs. So his mind, shaken by worldly business, could be strengthened by the encouragement derived from daily reading and contemplation in their company. By their fellowship he was thus not only defended against worldly assaults, but was also encouraged more and more to the activities of the heavenly life.

They urged him to unfold by spiritual interpretation the book of Job, a work which is shrouded in great obscurity. Nor could he refuse the task imposed on him by his loving brethren, seeing that it was likely to be of great use to many. So in thirty-five books* of exposition he taught in a marvellous manner the literal meaning of the book, its bearing on the mysteries of Christ and the Church, and the sense in which it applies to each of the faithful. He began this work while he was delegate in the royal city (Constantinople) and finished it after he was made pope at Rome. While he was still in the royal city, helped by the grace of the catholic truth, he crushed at its birth a new heresy which arose there concerning our state at the resurrection. Eutychius, the bishop of the city, taught that our body in its resurrection glory, would be impalpable and more subtle than wind or air. When Gregory heard this he proved both by sound reasoning and by the example of our Lord's resurrection that this dogma was contrary in every particular to the orthodox belief. For the catholic faith maintains that our body, while it is indeed exalted by the glory of immortality and made subtle by the effectual working of the spirit, is palpable by the reality of its nature as was our Lord's body, concerning which he said to his disciples, when it had been raised from the dead, 'Handle me and see, for a spirit has not flesh and bones as you see me have.' The venerable father Gregory strove so earnestly in his declaration of the faith against this newborn heresy and, with the help of the most religious emperor Tiberius Constantine,* suppressed it with such resolution, that no one has since been found to resuscitate it.

He composed another remarkable book called the *Pastoral Care*, in which he set forth in the clearest manner what sort of persons should be chosen to rule the Church and how these rulers ought to live; with how much discrimination they should instruct different types of listeners and how earnestly they ought each day to reflect on their own frailty. He composed forty *Homilies on the Gospel*, which he divided into two volumes of equal size, and made four books of *Dialogues* in which, at the request of Peter his deacon, he collected the virtues of the most famous saints he knew or could learn of in Italy, as an example of life to posterity: as in his expository works he taught what virtues men ought to strive after, so, by describing the miracles of the saints, he showed how glorious those virtues are. He also showed in twenty-two homilies how much inner light is to be found within the most obscure sections of the prophet Ezekiel, namely the first part and the last. There is also a useful Synodal book which he composed in collaboration with the bishops of Italy, dealing with some of the Church's vital problems, together with familiar letters to certain individuals, not to mention the book of answers to the questions of St Augustine, the first bishop of the English race, which I have described above and of which the whole is included in this *History*. It is all the more wonderful that he was able to produce so many books and of such length since almost continually throughout his early manhood he had been, to use his own words, tortured with frequent pains in the bowels and every moment of the day he was exhausted by a weakness of the internal organs, and his breathing was affected by a low but unremitting fever. Yet always amid these troubles, when he carefully reflected on the testimony of the scriptures that, 'He scourgeth every son whom he receiveth', the more severely he was oppressed by present evils, the more surely he was refreshed by eternal hope.

This much may be said of his immortal spirit, which could not be quenched by so much bodily pain. Other popes applied themselves to the task of building churches and adorning them with gold and silver, but he devoted himself entirely to winning souls. Whatever money he had, he took diligent care to distribute it and give to the poor, that his righteousness might endure for ever and his horn be exalted with honour, so that the words of the blessed Job might truly be said of him: 'When the ear heard me, then it blessed me and when the eye saw me it gave witness to me because I delivered the poor that cried and the fatherless also that had none to help him. The blessing of him that was ready to perish came upon me and I consoled the widow's heart. I put on righteousness and I clothed myself with my judgement as with a robe and a diadem. I was eyes to the blind and feet was I to the lame. I was a father to the poor and the cause which I knew not, I diligently searched out. I broke the jaws of the wicked and plucked the spoil out of his teeth.' And again a little further on he says, 'If I have withheld their desire from the poor or have caused the eyes of the widow to fail; if I have eaten my morsel myself alone and the fatherless has not eaten thereof; for from my youth my compassion grew up with me and from my mother's womb it came forth with me.'

To his works of piety and justice this also belongs, that he snatched our race from the teeth of the ancient foe and made them partakers of everlasting freedom by sending us preachers. Rejoicing in their faith and commending them with worthy praise he says in his commentary on the blessed Job: 'Lo, the mouth of Britain, which once only knew how to gnash its barbarous teeth, has long since learned to sing the praises of God with the alleluia of the Hebrews. See how the proud Ocean has become a servant, lying low now before the feet of the saints, and those barbarous motions, which earthly princes could not subdue with the sword, are now, through the fear of God, repressed with a simple word from the lips of priests; and he who, as an unbeliever, did not flinch before troops of warriors, now, as a believer, fears the words of the humble. For having received the heavenly Word and being enlightened by miracles as well, he is filled with the grace and the knowledge of God. He is restrained by the fear of God so that he dreads to do evil and with all his heart he longs to attain to everlasting grace.' In these words St Gregory also declares that St Augustine and his companions led the English race to the knowledge of the truth, not only by preaching the Word but also by showing heavenly signs.

Amongst other things Pope St Gregory arranged that masses should be celebrated in the churches of the apostles St Peter and St Paul over their bodies. And in the celebration of the mass, he added three quite perfect petitions, 'Dispose our days in peace, and command that we be saved from eternal damnation, and that we be numbered among the flock of thine elect'.

He ruled the Church during the days of the Emperors Maurice* and Phocas. He departed this life in the second year of Phocas and passed to the true life in heaven. His body was buried in the church of St Peter the Apostle, before the sanctuary, on 12 March; and in that body he will one day rise

again in glory together with the other pastors of the Church.
His epitaph written on his tomb runs as follows:

> Earth, take this corse—'tis dust of thine own dust:
> When God shall give new life, restore thy trust.
> Star-bound his soul: for Death's writ does not run
> Where grave's but gateway to life new-begun.
> A great high-priest this sepulchre inherits,
> Who lives for ever by uncounted merits;
> Hunger with meat, winter with clothes he ended,
> Souls with sound learning from the foe defended;
> Whate'er he taught, himself fulfilled in act—
> Mystic his words, but his example fact.
> Anglia to Christ at piety's dictation
> He turned, won thousands from an unknown nation.
> Thus that great shepherd laboured, thus he wrought;
> To increase his Master's flock was all his thought.
> Take thy reward in triumph and in joy,
> Who in God's council sit'st eternally!

We must not fail to relate the story about St Gregory which
has come down to us as a tradition of our forefathers. It
explains the reason why he showed such earnest solicitude for
the salvation of our race. It is said that one day, soon after
some merchants had arrived in Rome, a quantity of merchandise was exposed for sale in the market-place. Crowds came
to buy and Gregory too amongst them. As well as other
merchandise he saw some boys put up for sale, with fair
complexions, handsome faces, and lovely hair. On seeing
them he asked, so it is said, from what region or land they had
been brought. He was told that they came from the island of
Britain, whose inhabitants were like that in appearance. He
asked again whether those islanders were Christians or still
entangled in the errors of heathenism. He was told that they
were heathen. Then with a deep-drawn sigh he said, 'Alas
that the author of darkness should have men so bright of face
in his grip, and that minds devoid of inward grace should bear
so graceful an outward form.' Again he asked for the name of
the race. He was told that they were called *Angli*. 'Good', he
said, 'they have the face of angels, and such men should be
fellow-heirs of the angels in heaven'. 'What is the name', he

asked, 'of the kingdom from which they have been brought?'
He was told that the men of the kingdom were called *Deiri*.
'*Deiri*', he replied, '*De ira!* good! snatched from the wrath of
Christ and called to his mercy. And what is the name of the
king of the land?' He was told that it was Ælle;* and playing
on the name, he said, 'Alleluia! the praise of God the Creator
must be sung in those parts.' So he went to the bishop of
Rome and of the apostolic see, for he himself had not yet been
made pope, and asked him to send some ministers of the
word to the race of the Angles in Britain to convert them to
Christ. He added that he himself was prepared to carry out
the task with the help of the Lord provided that the pope was
willing. But he was unable to perform this mission, because
although the pope was willing to grant his request, the citizens
of Rome could not permit him to go so far away from the city.
Soon after he had become pope, he fulfilled the task which he
had long desired. It is true that he sent other preachers, but he
himself helped their preaching to bear fruit by his encouragement and prayers. I have thought it proper to insert this story*
into this Church *History*, based as it is on the tradition which
we have received from our ancestors.

CHAPTER 2

MEANWHILE Augustine, making use of the help of King
Æthelberht, summoned the bishops and teachers of the
neighbouring British kingdom to a conference at a place
which is still called in English *Augustinæs Ác*, that is Augustine's oak, on the borders of the Hwicce* and the West
Saxons. He proceeded to urge them with brotherly admonitions, that they should preserve catholic peace with him and
undertake the joint labour of evangelizing the heathen for the
Lord's sake. They did not keep Easter Sunday* at the proper
time, but from the fourteenth to the twentieth day of the lunar
month; this reckoning is based on an 84-year cycle. They did
other things too which were not in keeping with the unity of
the Church. After a long dispute they were unwilling, in spite
of the prayers, exhortations, and rebukes of Augustine and his

companions to give their assent, preferring their own traditions to those in which all the churches throughout the world agree in Christ. The holy father Augustine brought the long and wearisome struggle to an end by saying, 'Let us pray God who makes men to be of one mind in his Father's house to vouchsafe to show us by heavenly signs which tradition is to be followed and by what paths we must hasten to enter his kingdom. Let some sick man be brought, and let the faith and practice of him by whose prayers he is healed be considered as in accordance with God's will and proper for us all to follow.' His adversaries agreed unwillingly and a man of English race was brought forward who was blind. He was presented to the British bishops, but no healing or benefit was obtained from their ministry. Then Augustine, compelled by genuine necessity, prayed, bowing his knees to the Father of our Lord Jesus Christ, that he would restore his lost sight to the blind man and, through the bodily enlightenment of one man, would bring the grace of spiritual light to the hearts of many believers. At once the blind man's sight was restored and all acknowledged Augustine to be a true herald of the heavenly light. Then the Britons confessed that they realized that it was the true way of righteousness which Augustine preached but that they could not disown their former customs without the consent and approval of their own people. They therefore asked that a conference should be held for a second time and that more should attend.

When this had been decided upon, it is related that seven British bishops and many learned men came, chiefly from their most famous monastery which the English call *Bancornaburg** (Bangor Iscoed). At that time it is said to have been ruled over by Abbot Dinoot. As they were about to set out for the conference, they went first to a certain holy and prudent man who lived as a hermit among them to consult him as to whether they ought to forsake their own traditions at the bidding of Augustine. He answered, 'If he is a man of God, follow him.' They replied, 'But how can we tell?' He answered, 'The Lord said: Take my yoke upon you and learn of me, for I am meek and lowly of heart. If this Augustine is meek and lowly of heart, it is to be supposed that he himself bears the yoke of Christ and is offering it to you to bear; but if he is harsh and proud, it follows that he is not from God and we have no need to regard his words.' Once more they said, 'But how can we know even this?' He said, 'Contrive that he and his followers arrive first at the meeting place and, if he rises on your approach, you will know that he is a servant of Christ and will listen to him obediently; but if he despises you and is not willing to rise in your presence, even though your numbers are greater, you should despise him in return.' They did as he had said. Now it happened that Augustine remained seated while they were coming in; when they saw this, they forthwith became enraged and, setting him down as a proud man, strove to contradict everything he said. Then he said to them, 'You do many things which are contrary to our customs or rather to the customs of the universal Church; nevertheless, if you are willing to submit to me in three points, we will gladly tolerate all else that you do, even though it is contrary to our customs. The three points are: to keep Easter at the proper time; to perform the sacrament of baptism, whereby we are born again to God, according to the rites of the holy Roman and apostolic Church; and to preach the word of the Lord to the English people in fellowship with us.' They answered that they would do none of these things nor would they accept him as their archbishop, saying between themselves that if he was even unwilling to rise at their approach now, he would despise them much more if they were to begin to give way to him. It is said that Augustine, the man of God, warned them with threats that, if they refused to accept peace from their brethren, they would have to accept war from their enemies; and if they would not preach the way of life to the English nation, they would one day suffer the vengeance of death at their hands. This, through the workings of divine judgement, came to pass in every particular as he had foretold.

For later on, that very powerful king of the English, Æthelfrith, whom we have already spoken of, collected a great army against the city of the legions which is called *Legacæstir* by the English and more correctly *Caerlegion* (Chester) by the Britons, and made a great slaughter of that nation of heretics.

When he was about to give battle and saw their priests, who had assembled to pray to God on behalf of the soldiers taking part in the fight, standing apart in a safer place, he asked who they were and for what purpose they had gathered there. Most of them were from the monastery of Bangor, where there was said to be so great a number of monks that, when it was divided into seven parts with superiors over each, no division had less than 300 men, all of whom were accustomed to live by the labour of their hands. After a three days' fast, most of these had come to the battle in order to pray with the others. They had a guard named Brocmail, whose duty it was to protect them against the barbarians' swords while they were praying. When Æthelfrith heard why they had come he said, 'If they are praying to their God against us, then, even if they do not bear arms, they are fighting against us, assailing us as they do with prayers for our defeat.' So he ordered them to be attacked first and then he destroyed the remainder of their wicked host, though not without heavy losses. It is said that in this battle about twelve hundred men were slain who had come to pray and only fifty escaped by flight. Brocmail and his men at the first enemy attack turned their backs on those whom they should have defended, leaving them unarmed and helpless before the swords of their foes. Thus the prophecy of the holy Bishop Augustine was fulfilled, although he had long been translated to the heavenly kingdom, namely that those heretics would also suffer the vengeance of temporal death because they had despised the offer of everlasting salvation.

CHAPTER 3

IN the year of our Lord 604 Augustine, archbishop of Britain, consecrated two bishops, namely Mellitus and Justus. He consecrated Mellitus to preach in the province of the East Saxons, which is divided from Kent by the river Thames and borders on the sea to the east. Its chief city is London, which is on the banks of that river and is an emporium* for many nations who come to it by land and sea. At that time Sæberht, nephew of Æthelberht and son of his sister Ricule, ruled over the nation although he was under the dominion of

Æthelberht's who, as already said, held sway over all the English nations as far as the Humber. After this race had accepted the word of truth through the preaching of Mellitus, King Æthelberht built the church of the apostle St Paul in the city of London, in which Mellitus and his successors were to have their episcopal seat. Augustine consecrated Justus in Kent itself, in the city of *Dorubrevis* which the English call *Hrofæscæstræ* (Rochester), after one of their former chiefs whose name was Hrof. It is about twenty-four miles west of Canterbury and in it King Æthelberht built the church of the apostle St Andrew;* he later bestowed many gifts on the bishops of each of these churches and that of Canterbury; and he also added both lands and possessions for the maintenance of the bishops' retinues.

On the death* of our father Augustine, a man beloved of God, his body was buried outside but close to the church of the apostles St Peter and St Paul mentioned already, for it was not yet either finished or consecrated. But as soon as it was consecrated, the body was carried inside and honourably buried in the chapel on the north side. In it the bodies of all succeeding archbishops have been buried with the exception of two, Theodore and Berhtwald, whose bodies were placed in the church itself because there was no more room in the chapel. Almost in the middle of the chapel is an altar dedicated in honour of the pope St Gregory, at which a priest of that place celebrates a solemn mass in their memory every Saturday. This is the epitaph inscribed on Augustine's tomb: 'Here lies the most reverend Augustine, first archbishop of Canterbury, who was formerly sent hither by St Gregory, bishop of Rome; being supported by God in the working of miracles, he led King Æthelberht and his nation from the worship of idols to faith in Christ and ended the days of his office in peace; he died on the twenty-sixth day of May during the reign of the same king.'

CHAPTER 4

AUGUSTINE was succeeded in the episcopate by Laurence, whom he had consecrated during his lifetime* lest, when he was dead, the church, being in so raw a condition, might begin to falter if deprived of its shepherd even for an hour. Herein he followed the example of the first pastor of the Church, St Peter, chief of the apostles, who, when the Church of Christ was founded at Rome, is said to have consecrated Clement to help him in evangelistic work and at the same time to be his successor. When Laurence had acquired the rank of archbishop, he strove to build up the foundations of the church which had been so magnificently laid and to raise it to its destined height; this he did by frequent words of holy exhortation and by continually setting a pattern of good works. For example, he not only undertook the charge of the new Church which had been gathered from among the English, but he also endeavoured to bestow his pastoral care upon the older inhabitants of Britain as well as upon those Irish who live in Ireland, which is an island close to Britain. He came to realize that in Ireland, as well as in Britain, the life and profession of the people was not in accordance with church practice in many things. He noticed especially that they did not celebrate the festival of Easter at the proper time but, as we have said before, held that the day of the Lord's resurrection should be observed from the fourteenth to the twentieth day of the paschal moon. So he wrote a letter of exhortation in conjunction with his fellow bishops, beseeching and warning them to keep the unity of peace and of catholic observance with the Church of Christ which is scattered over the whole world. This is the beginning of the letter:

To our most beloved brethren the bishops and abbots throughout the whole realm of Ireland, Bishops Laurence, Mellitus, and Justus, servants of the servants of God.

The apostolic see, according to its custom in all parts of the world, directed us to preach to the heathen in these western regions, and it was our lot to come to this island of Britain; before we knew them we held the holiness both of the Britons and of the Irish in great esteem, thinking that they walked according to the customs of the universal Church: but on becoming acquainted with the Britons, we still thought that the Irish would be better. But now we have learned from Bishop Dagan* when he came to this island and from Abbot

Columban* when he came to Gaul that the Irish did not differ from
the Britons in their way of life. For when Bishop Dagan came to us
he refused to take food, not only with us but even in the very house
where we took our meals.

This Laurence with his fellow bishops also sent a letter, of a
sort befitting his rank, to the British priests, striving to bring
them into catholic unity. But the present state of affairs shows
how little he succeeded.

About this time Mellitus, bishop of London, went to Rome
to confer with Pope Boniface* about the needs of the English
Church. The holy father had summoned a synod of the
bishops of Italy to draw up regulations concerning monastic
life and harmony. Mellitus himself took his place among them
in the eighth year of the Emperor Phocas, on 27 February and
in the thirteenth indiction in order that he might subscribe to
the formal decisions and ratify them by his authority, bringing
them back with him to Britain for the information of the
English Churches and for their observance. The pope also
sent with them letters written to Archbishop Laurence, the
beloved of God, and to all the clergy, as well as a letter to
King Æthelberht and to the English people. St Boniface was
the fourth bishop of Rome after St Gregory. He obtained for
the Church of Christ from the Emperor Phocas the gift of the
temple at Rome anciently known as the Pantheon because it
represented all the gods. After he had expelled every abomi-
nation from it, he made a church of it dedicated to the holy
Mother of God and all the martyrs of Christ, so that, when
the multitudes of devils had been driven out, it might serve as
a shrine for a multitude of saints.

CHAPTER 5

In the year of our Lord 616, the twenty-first year after
Augustine and his companions had been sent to preach to the
English nation, King Æthelberht of Kent, after ruling his
temporal kingdom gloriously for fifty-six years, entered upon
the eternal joys of the heavenly kingdom. He was the third
English king to rule over all the southern kingdoms,* which

are divided from the north by the river Humber and the surrounding territory; but he was the first to enter the kingdom of heaven. The first king to hold the like sovereignty was Ælle,* king of the South Saxons; the second was Cælin, king of the West Saxons, known in their own language as Ceawlin;* the third, as we have said, was Æthelberht, king of Kent; the fourth was Rædwald, king of the East Angles, who even during the lifetime of Æthelberht was gaining the leadership* for his own race; the fifth was Edwin, king of the Northumbrians, the nation inhabiting the district north of the Humber. Edwin had still greater power and ruled over all the inhabitants of Britain, English and Britons alike, except for Kent only. He even brought under English rule the Mevanian Islands (Anglesey and Man) which lie between England and Ireland and belong to the Britons. The sixth to rule within the same bounds was Oswald, the most Christian king of the Northumbrians, while the seventh was his brother Oswiu who for a time held almost the same territory. The latter overwhelmed and made tributary even the tribes of the Picts and Irish who inhabit the northern parts of Britain; but of this more later.

King Æthelberht died on 24 February, twenty-one years after he had accepted the faith, and was buried in the chapel of St Martin, within the church of the Apostles St Peter and St Paul, where his queen, Bertha, also lies. Among other benefits which he conferred upon the race under his care, he established with the advice of his counsellors a code of laws* after the Roman manner. These are written in English and are still kept and observed by the people. Among these he set down first of all what restitution must be made by anyone who steals anything belonging to the church or the bishop or any other clergy; these laws were designed to give protection to those whose coming and whose teaching he had welcomed. Now Æthelberht was the son of Eormenric, the son of Octa, the son of Oeric whose surname was Oisc, whence the kings of Kent were known as *oiscingas*.* Oisc's father was Hengest who with his son Oisc first entered Britain at the invitation of Vortigern, as related above.

But after the death of Æthelberht, when his son Eadbald had taken over the helm of state, there followed a severe setback to the tender growth of the Church. Not only had he refused to receive the faith of Christ but he was polluted with such fornication as the apostle declares to have been not so much as named among the Gentiles, in that he took his father's wife. By both of these crimes he gave the occasion to return to their own vomit to those who had accepted the laws of faith and continence during his father's reign either out of fear of the king or to win his favour. The apostate king, however, did not escape the scourge of divine punishment in chastisement and correction; for he was afflicted by frequent fits of madness and possessed by an unclean spirit.

On the death of Sæberht, king of the East Saxons, the tempest of troubles became yet more violent, for when he departed to the eternal kingdom he left three sons* as heirs to his temporal kingdom who had all remained heathen. They quickly began to practise openly the idolatry which, during their father's lifetime, they had apparently given up to some extent and they allowed their subjects to worship idols. There is a story that when they saw the bishop, who was celebrating solemn mass in church, give the Eucharist to the people, they said to him, puffed up as they were with barbarian pride, 'Why do you not offer us the white bread which you used to give to our father Saba' (for so they used to call him) 'and yet you still give it to the people in church?' The bishop answered them, 'If you are willing to be cleansed in the same font of salvation as your father was, you may also partake of the holy bread as he did. But if you despise its life-giving waters, you certainly shall not receive the bread of life.' They answered, 'We will not enter the font because we know that we have no need of it, but all the same we wish to be refreshed by the bread.' In vain were they warned earnestly and often that this could not be done and that without that holy cleansing no one could share in the sacred oblation; at last in their rage they exclaimed, 'If you will not oblige us in so trifling a matter as this, you cannot remain in our kingdom.'

So they expelled him and ordered him and his companions to leave the realm. After he had been driven out, he went to Kent to consult with his fellow bishops Laurence and Justus as to what ought to be done in these circumstances. It was decided by common consent that they should all return to their own country and serve God with a free conscience, rather than remain fruitlessly among these barbarians who had rebelled against the faith. So first of all Mellitus and Justus departed to Gaul, there to await the outcome of events. But not for long did the kings who had driven away the herald of truth worship their devils unpunished. They went out to fight against the Gewisse* and they and all their army perished together. But thought the instigators perished, the people, once they had been encouraged to do evil, could not be converted and recalled to the simplicity of faith and love which is in Christ.

CHAPTER 6

Now when Laurence was about to follow Mellitus and Justus and to leave Britain, he ordered a bed to be prepared for him that night in the church of the Apostles St Peter and St Paul, which we have frequently mentioned. After he had poured forth many prayers and tears to God for the state of the Church, he lay down to rest and slept. As he slept the blessed prince of the apostles appeared to him and in the dead of night scourged him hard* and long. Then St Peter asked him with apostolic severity why he had left the flock which he himself had entrusted to him; or to what shepherd he would commit the sheep of Christ when he ran away and left them in the midst of wolves. Then he added, 'Have you forgotten my example? For the sake of the little ones whom Christ himself entrusted to me as a token of his love, I endured chains, blows, imprisonment, and every affliction. Finally I suffered death, even the death of the cross, at the hands of infidels and enemies of Christ that I might be crowned with Him.' Deeply moved by the scourgings and exhortations of St Peter, Christ's servant Laurence went to the king as soon as morning had come, drew back his robe and showed him the marks of his stripes. The king was amazed and asked who had dared to inflict such injuries on so great a man. When he heard that it was for the sake of his salvation that the bishop had suffered such torments and wounds at the hands of the apostle of Christ, he was greatly afraid. So he banned all idolatrous worship, gave up his unlawful wife, accepted the Christian faith, and was baptized; and thereafter he promoted and furthered the interests of the Church to the best of his ability.

He also sent to Gaul and recalled Mellitus and Justus, bidding them return and govern their churches in freedom. They came back one year after they had left, Justus returning to Rochester over which he had formerly ruled. But the people of London refused to receive Mellitus, preferring to serve idolatrous high priests. For King Eadbald had less royal power than his father had and was unable to restore the bishop to his church against the will and consent of the heathen. Nevertheless after he and his race had turned to the Lord, they strove to follow God's commandments, and in the monastery of the blessed chief of the apostles he built a church dedicated to the holy Mother of God, which was afterwards consecrated by Archbishop Mellitus.

CHAPTER 7

DURING this king's reign, the blessed Archbishop Laurence entered the heavenly kingdom* and was buried on 2 February in the church and monastery of St Peter the Apostle near to his predecessor Augustine. Thereupon Mellitus who was bishop of London succeeded to the see of Canterbury, the third after Augustine. Justus, who was still living, ruled over the church at Rochester. While guiding the English Church with great care and energy they received letters of exhortation from Rome from Pope Boniface,* who had succeeded Deusdedit* in the year of our Lord 619. Now Mellitus suffered from a bodily infirmity, the gout, yet in mind he was sound and active enough; indeed he leapt lightly over all earthly affairs and flew towards those heavenly concerns which he had always loved, pursued, and sought after. He was noble by birth but nobler still in loftiness of spirit.

I will relate, for example, one instance of his power from which the rest may be inferred. On a certain occasion the city of Canterbury had been carelessly set on fire and was rapidly being consumed by the growing blaze. It could not be quenched by throwing water on it and no small part of the city had already been destroyed, while the raging fire was spreading towards the bishop's house. Mellitus, trusting in divine help since human aid had failed, ordered them to carry him into the path of the furious flames where tongues of fire were flying about hither and thither. The church of the Four Crowned Martyrs* stood just where the fury of the flames was at its height; the bishop was carried to this spot by his followers, and, weak as he was, proceeded to avert by his prayers the peril which had defeated strong men in spite of all their efforts. Immediately the south wind, which had spread the conflagration over the city, veered round to the north and first of all prevented the fury of the flames from destroying those places which were in its path; then it soon ceased entirely and there was a calm, while the flames also sank and died out. So brightly did the man of God burn with the fire of divine love, so often had he repelled the stormy powers of the air from harming him and his people by his prayers and exhortations, that it was right for him to be able to prevail over earthly winds and flames and to ensure that they should not injure him or his people.

He, too, after ruling over the church for five years went to heaven during Eadbald's reign and was buried with his fathers in the monastery and church of the blessed chief of the apostles so often mentioned, on 24 April in the year of our Lord 624.

CHAPTER 8

JUSTUS, bishop of the church of Rochester, immediately succeeded Mellitus in the archbishopric. He consecrated

Romanus, bishop of Rochester, in his own place, having been granted licence to consecrate bishops by Pope Boniface whom we have referred to above as the successor to Deusdedit. This is the form of the licence:

Boniface to our most beloved brother Justus.

The devotion and indeed the vigilance, my dear brother, with which you have toiled for the gospel of Christ are known to us not only from the contents of your letter but still more from the successful fruition which heaven has bestowed upon your work. Almighty God has not failed either to uphold the honour of his name or to grant fruit to your labours, in accordance with his faithful promise to those who preach the gospel, 'Lo, I am with you always, even unto the end of the world.' This promise he has in his mercy specially fulfilled in the ministry he has given you, opening the hearts of the Gentiles to receive the wondrous mystery of the gospel you preach. For by his grace and favour he has crowned the gratifying progress of your toils with a great reward, and he has prepared an abundant harvest for the faithful employment of those talents entrusted to you, having bestowed on you what you can hand back to him in the form of a multitude of souls born again. This is conferred upon you in compensation for the praiseworthy patience with which you have awaited the redemption of that nation, continually persevering in your appointed mission: and salvation has been bestowed upon them so that they too might profit by your merits. For our Lord says, 'He that endureth to the end shall be saved.' You have been saved by your patient hope and courageous endurance in the work of cleansing the hearts of unbelievers from their inherent disease of superstition, so that they might win the mercy of the Saviour. We have learnt from the letters received from our son King Eadbald* how you, brother, by your learning and holy eloquence have guided his soul to the assurance of true conversion and a state of real faith. For this reason and because we have complete faith in the long-suffering mercy of God, we are certain that the result of your ministry will be the complete conversion not only of the peoples subject to him, but also of their neighbours. In this way, as it is written, you will receive the reward of a finished task from the Lord and Giver of all good things: and indeed all nations will confess having received the mystery of the Christian faith and will declare in truth that 'their sound is gone out into all the earth, and their words unto the end of the world.' Moved by your zeal we are sending you a pallium by the bearer of this present letter and confer upon you permission to use it only when celebrating the sacred mysteries. We also grant you the privilege of consecrating bishops as occasion demands and as the Lord in his mercy guides you: so that the gospel of Christ may be spread abroad by the preaching of many among all those peoples who are not yet converted. And, my brother, see to it that with unimpaired integrity of heart you preserve what you have received through the favour of the apostolic see, remembering the significance of this honourable vestment which you have been given to wear on your shoulders. Seek God's mercy and study to show yourself such that, before the tribunal of the great Judge who is to come, you may display this honour which has been granted you, not only without stain or guilt, but also enriched by your reward of souls converted. May God keep you safe, most beloved brother.

CHAPTER 9

AT this time the Northumbrian race, that is the English race which dwelt north of the river Humber, together with their king Edwin,* also accepted the word of faith through the preaching of Paulinus already mentioned. The king's earthly power had increased as an augury that he was to become a believer and have a share in the heavenly kingdom. So, like no other English king before him, he held under his sway the whole realm of Britain, not only English kingdoms but those ruled over by the Britons as well. He even brought the islands of Anglesey and Man under his power as we have said before. The former of these, which is to the south, is larger in size and more fruitful, containing 960 hides* according to the English way of reckoning, while the latter has more than 300.

The occasion of the conversion of this race was that Edwin became related* to the kings of Kent, having married King Æthelberht's daughter Æthelburh, who was also called Tate. When he first sent ambassadors to ask her in marriage from her brother Eadbald, who was then king of Kent, the answer was that it was not lawful for a Christian maiden to be given in marriage to a heathen for fear that the faith and mysteries of the heavenly King might be profaned by a union with a king who was an utter stranger to the worship of the true God. When Edwin heard the messengers' reply he promised that he would put no obstacles of any kind in the way of the Christian worship which the maiden practised; on the other hand, he would allow her and all who came with her, men and women, priests or retainers, to follow the faith and worship of their religion after the Christian manner; nor did he deny the possibility that he might accept the same religion himself if, on examination, it was judged by his wise men to be a holier worship and more worthy of God.

Thereupon the maiden was betrothed and sent to Edwin and, in accordance with the agreement, Paulinus, a man beloved of God, was consecrated bishop to accompany her and to make sure by daily instruction and the celebration of the heavenly sacraments that she and her companions were not polluted by contact with the heathen.

Paulinus was consecrated bishop by Archbishop Justus, on 21 July in the year of our Lord 625, and so in the princess's train he came to Edwin's court, outwardly bringing her to her marriage according to the flesh. But more truly his whole heart was set on calling the people to whom he was coming to the knowledge of the truth; his desire was to present it, in the words of the apostle, as a pure virgin to be espoused to one husband, even Christ. On his arrival in the kingdom he set vigorously to work, not only, with the Lord's help, to prevent those who had come with him from lapsing from the faith, but also to convert some of the heathen, if he could, to grace and faith by his preaching. But although he toiled hard and long in preaching the word, yet as the apostle says, 'The god of this world blinded the minds of them that believed not, lest the light of the glorious gospel of Christ should shine unto them.'

The following year there came to the kingdom an assassin whose name was Eomer, who had been sent by Cwichelm,* king of the West Saxons, hoping to deprive King Edwin of his kingdom and his life. He carried a short sword, double-edged and smeared with poison, to ensure that if the sword wound was not enough to kill the king, the deadly poison would do its work. He came on Easter Day to the king's hall which then stood by the river Derwent. He entered the hall on the pretence of delivering a message from his lord, and while the cunning rascal was expounding his pretended mission, he suddenly leapt up, drew the sword from beneath his cloak, and made a rush at the king. Lilla, a most devoted thegn,* saw this, but not having a shield in his hand to protect the king from death, he quickly interposed his own body to receive the blow. His foe thrust the weapon with such force that he killed the thegn and wounded the king as well through his dead body. Swords were drawn and the assassin was at once attacked from every quarter, but in the tumult he slew with his hideous weapon yet another of the king's retainers named Forthhere.

On the same night, the holy night of Easter Day, the queen had borne the king a daughter named Eanflæd. The king, in the presence of Bishop Paulinus, gave thanks to his gods for the birth of his daughter; but the bishop, on the other hand, began to thank the Lord Christ and to tell the king that it was in answer to his prayers to God that the queen had been safely delivered of a child, and without great pain. The king was delighted with his words, and promised that if God would grant him life, and victory over the king who had sent the assassin who wounded him, he would renounce his idols and serve Christ; and as a pledge that he would keep his word, he gave his infant daughter to Bishop Paulinus to be consecrated to Christ. She was baptized on the holy day of Pentecost, the first of the Northumbrian race to be baptized, together with eleven others of his household.

When in due course the king had been healed of his wound, he summoned his army and marched against the West Saxons. During the course of the campaign he either slew all whom he discovered to have plotted his death or forced them to surrender. So he returned victorious to his own country; but he was unwilling to accept the mysteries of the Christian faith at once and without consideration, even though he no longer worshipped idols after he had promised that he would serve Christ. But first he made it his business, as opportunity occurred, to learn the faith systematically from the venerable Bishop Paulinus, and then to consult with the counsellors whom he considered the wisest, as to what they thought he ought to do. He himself being a man of great natural sagacity would often sit alone for long periods in silence, but in his innermost thoughts he was deliberating with himself as to what he ought to do and which religion he should adhere to.

CHAPTER 10

AT that time he received a letter* from Boniface, bishop of the apostolic see, exhorting him to accept the faith. It ran as follows:

Copy of the letter of the most blessed and apostolic pope of the Church of the city of Rome, Boniface, addressed to the most illustrious Edwin, king of the English.

To Edwin, the illustrious king of the English, Bishop Boniface, servant of the servants of God.

Human speech can never explain the power of the most high God, consisting as it does in its own invisible, unsearchable, and eternal greatness, so that no wisdom can comprehend or express how great it is. Yet, in His goodness, He opens the doors of the heart so that He Himself may enter, and by His secret inspiration pours into the human heart a revelation of Himself. So we have undertaken to extend our pastoral responsibilities so far as to declare to you the fullness of the Christian faith, so that we may bring to your notice the Gospel of Christ, which our Saviour has bidden us preach to all the nations, and so that the means of salvation may be put before you. Thus the goodness of the Divine Majesty who, by his word of command alone, made and created all things, both heaven and earth, the sea and all that is in them, ordaining the orders in which they subsist, and who, by the counsel of the co-eternal Word in the unity of the Holy Spirit, has made man in His own image and likeness, fashioning him out of clay, has also granted him the high privilege and distinction of placing him over all things, so that if he keeps within the bounds of God's commands, he may be granted eternal life. This God, the Father, Son, and Holy Spirit, an undivided Trinity, is adored and worshipped through faith and confession unto salvation by all the human race, from the rising to the setting of the sun, as the Maker of all things and its own Creator. To Him also the greatest empires and the powers of the world are subject, because it is by His disposition that all rule is bestowed. It has pleased Him therefore, in His mercy and loving-kindness towards all His creation to melt, by the fire of His Holy Spirit, the frozen hearts of races even in the far corners of the earth to knowledge of Himself, and that in a marvellous manner.

We suppose that your Majesty is fully aware of what has been accomplished by the mercy of the Redeemer in the enlightenment of our illustrious son King Eadbald and the nations which are subject to him, for your lands are close to one another. We confidently trust that, through the mercy of heaven, this wonderful gift will also be conferred upon you and more especially as we learn that your illustrious consort, who is indeed one flesh with you, has been enlightened by the gift of eternal life through the regeneration of holy baptism. So we have undertaken in this letter to exhort your Majesty with all affection and deepest love, to hate idols and idol worship, to spurn their foolish shrines and the deceitful flatteries of their soothsaying, and to believe in God the Father Almighty and in his Son Jesus Christ and the Holy Spirit, so that you may be freed from the devil's fetters and, by the power of the holy and undivided Trinity, become a partaker of eternal life.

The great guilt of those who cling to the pernicious superstitions of idolatrous worship is seen in the damnable form of their gods. Of these the psalmist says, 'All the gods of the nations are devils; but the Lord made the heavens.' And again, 'Eyes have they but they see not; they have ears but they hear not; noses have they but they smell not; they have hands but they handle not; feet have they but they walk not; and those who put their trust in them therefore become like them.' How can they have power to help anyone, when they are made from corruptible material by the hands of your own servants and subjects and, by means of such human art, you have provided them with the inanimate semblance of the human form? They cannot walk unless you move them, but are like a stone fixed in one place, and, being so constructed, have no understanding, are utterly insensible, and so have no power to harm or help. We cannot understand in any way how you can be so deluded as to worship and follow those gods to whom you yourselves have given the likeness of the human form.

So you should take upon you the sign of the holy cross, by which the human race has been redeemed, and cast out of your hearts the accursed wiles and cunning of the devil, who is the jealous foe of the works of God's goodness. Then set your hand vigorously to the task of breaking and destroying the gods which up till now you have fashioned from material substances. In fact the very destruction and decay of those things which have never had the breath of life nor could by any means acquire understanding from their makers, should show you clearly the worthless nature of what you have worshipped up to now. You may certainly consider yourselves who have received the breath of life from the Lord to be better made than they. For

Almighty God has appointed your descent through many ages and countless generations, from the first man he created. So come to the knowledge of Him who created you and breathed into you the breath of life, who sent His only-begotten Son for your redemption and to save you from original sin, so that He might deliver you from the power of the devil's perversity and wickedness, and bestow heavenly rewards upon you.

Accept the teaching of the preachers and the gospel of God which they proclaim to you, so that, as we have often said, you may believe in God the Father Almighty and in Jesus Christ His Son and the Holy Spirit, the indivisible Trinity. Then when you have put to flight devilish thoughts and driven from you the temptations of the venomous and deceitful foe, having been born again by water and the Holy Spirit, may you through his bountiful aid dwell with Him in whom you have believed, in the splendour of eternal glory.

We are sending you the blessing of your protector, St Peter, chief of the apostles, in the form of a robe embroidered with gold and a garment from Ancyra, asking your Majesty to accept these gifts in the same spirit of goodwill as that in which they were sent by us.

CHAPTER 11

THE Pope also sent a letter to King Edwin's consort Æthelburh to this effect:

Copy of the letter of the most blessed and apostolic pope of the church of the city of Rome, Boniface, addressed to Æthelburh, King Edwin's queen.

To his daughter the most illustrious lady, Queen Æthelburh, Bishop Boniface, servant of the servants of God.

Our Redeemer, in His goodness, has here furnished providential means of salvation for the human race, freeing us from the bonds of enslavement to the devil, by shedding His precious blood: so that when He had made his name known in various ways to the Gentiles, they might acknowledge their Creator by accepting the mystery of the Christian faith. And this has plainly been conferred on your Majesty's own soul, by the gift of God in your mystical purification and regeneration. Our heart has been greatly rejoiced by the goodness and bounty of the Lord, because He has deigned to kindle by your conversion the spark of orthodox religion; that thereby He could the more easily inflame with His love not only the mind of your illustrious husband but of all the nation that is subject to you.

We have been informed by those who came to tell us of the happy conversion of our illustrious son King Eadbald, that your Majesty, who had also accepted the wondrous mystery of the Christian faith, continually shines in pious works pleasing to God and diligently avoids the worship of idols and the enticements of shrines and soothsaying; that, with unimpaired devotion, you occupy yourself so much with the love of your Redeemer that you never cease from lending your aid in spreading the Christian faith. But when, in our fatherly love, we inquired earnestly about your illustrious husband, we learned that he was still serving abominable idols and hesitated to hear and obey the words of the preachers. This caused us no small grief, that he who is one flesh with you should remain a stranger to the knowledge of the supreme and undivided Trinity. Therefore we do not hesitate, in accordance with our fatherly duty, to send a warning to your Christian Highness; we urge you that, being imbued with the Holy Spirit, you should not hesitate, in season and out of season, to labour so that, through the power of our Lord and Saviour Jesus Christ, he may be added to the number of the Christians, so that you may thereby enjoy the rights of marriage in undefiled union. For it is written, 'They twain shall be one flesh': how then can it be said that there is unity between you if he continues a stranger to your shining faith, seeing that the darkness of detestable error remains between you?

So, applying yourself continually to prayer, do not cease to pray to God to grant him, in His long-suffering mercy, the benefits of His illumination: so that those who have been united by the bonds of earthly marriage may also, when this life has passed, be for ever united in the bonds of faith. Therefore, my illustrious daughter, persevere with all your might to soften his hard heart as soon as possible, by piously teaching him God's commandments. Pour into his mind a knowledge of the greatness of the mystery in which you have believed and the wonder of the reward which, by the new birth, you have been accounted worthy to receive. Inflame his cold heart by teaching him about the Holy Spirit, so that he may lose that numbness which an evil religion produces and so that the warmth of divine faith may, through your frequent exhortations, kindle his understanding. Then the testimony of holy scripture will be clearly and abundantly fulfilled in you: 'The unbelieving husband shall be saved by the believing wife.' For this reason you have obtained the mercy of the Lord, in order that you might restore to your Redeemer an abundant harvest of faith in return for the benefits bestowed upon you. We never cease to pray that, with God's merciful help, you may fulfil this task. We have mentioned these matters, prompted by our duty and our fatherly love for you: now we urge you that as soon as a messenger is available you should, with all speed, comfort us with the good news of the wonders which the Almighty has seen fit to work through you, in the conversion of your husband and of the peoples subject to him; so that our anxiety for the salvation of the souls of you all may be set at rest by your letter. Then, as we see the enlightenment of God's redemption more widely spread among you, we may give our abundant thanks, as is right, in joyful acknowledgement to God the giver of all good things and to St Peter, chief of the apostles.

As well as the blessing of St Peter, chief of the apostles and your protector, we send a silver mirror and an ivory comb adorned with gold. We beseech your Majesty to accept it in the same kindly spirit as that in which it is sent.

CHAPTER 12

SUCH was the letter Pope Boniface wrote concerning the salvation of King Edwin and his race. But a heavenly vision which God in His mercy had deigned to reveal to Edwin when he was once in exile at the court of Rædwald, king of the Angles, helped him in no small measure to understand and accept in his heart the counsels of salvation. Paulinus saw how difficult it was for the king's proud mind to turn humbly to the way of salvation and accept the mystery of the life-giving cross; yet he continued to labour for the salvation of the king and also the people he ruled, uttering words of exhortation to men as well as words of prayer to the merciful Lord. At length, as seems most probable, he was shown in spirit the nature of the vision which God had once revealed to the king. Nor did he lose any time in warning the king to fulfil the vows which, when he saw the vision, he had undertaken to perform if he should be delivered from the trouble he was then in and should ascend the royal throne.

This was his vision: when he was being persecuted by his predecessor Æthelfrith,* he wandered secretly as a fugitive for many years through many places and kingdoms, until at last he came to Rædwald and asked him for protection against the plots of his powerful persecutor. Rædwald received him gladly, promising to do what he asked. But when Æthelfrith learned that he had been seen in that kingdom and was living on intimate terms with the king among his retainers, he sent messengers offering Rædwald large sums of money to put Edwin to death. But it had no effect. He sent a second and third time, offering even larger gifts of silver and further threatening to make war on him if Rædwald despised his offer. The king, being either weakened by his threats or corrupted by his bribes, yielded to his request and promised either to slay Edwin or to give him up to the messengers. A very faithful friend of Edwin's found this out and entered his room where he was preparing to sleep, for it was the first hour of the night. He called him outside and told him what the king had promised to do with him, adding, 'If you are willing I will take you from this kingdom this very hour and guide you to a place where neither Rædwald nor Æthelfrith will ever be able to find you.' Edwin answered, 'I thank you for your goodwill, but I cannot do what you say, as I should have to be the first to break the compact which I made with this great king; he has done me no wrong nor shown any enmity towards me so far. If I am to die, let me rather die by his hand than at the hands of some meaner person. Whither am I now to fly seeing that I have been wandering for long years throughout all the kingdoms of Britain, trying to avoid the snares of my enemies?' So his friend went away, but Edwin remained alone outside, sitting sadly in front of the palace with his mind in a tumult, not knowing what to do or which way to turn.

He remained long in silent anguish of spirit and 'consumed with inward fire', when suddenly at dead of night, he saw a man silently approach him whose face and attire were strange to him. When he saw this unexpected stranger, he was not a little alarmed. But the stranger approached and greeted him, asking why he was sitting so sadly upon a stone, watchful and alone, when everyone else was resting and fast asleep. Edwin asked in return what concern it was of his, whether he passed the night indoors or out. The stranger replied, 'Do not think I am unaware of the cause of your sorrow and sleeplessness and why you sit alone outside, for I know quite well who you are and why you grieve and the ills which you fear will soon come upon you. But tell me what reward you are willing to give to anyone who would free you from these troubles and persuade Rædwald not to do you any wrong himself nor give you over to your enemies to perish.' Edwin answered that he would give such a person all that he was able in return for such a service. 'And what', said the stranger, 'if he assured you that your enemies would be destroyed and that you would be a king who surpassed in power not only all your ancestors, but also all who have reigned before you over the English?' Edwin, encouraged by his questions, did not hesitate to promise that he would be suitably grateful to anyone who offered him such benefits. Then he asked him a third time, 'If the one who truly foretold all these great and wonderful benefits could also give you better and more useful counsel as to your salvation and your way of life than any of your parents and kinsmen ever heard, would you consent to obey him and to accept his saving advice?' Edwin did not hesitate to promise at once that he would follow in every particular the teaching of that one who could rescue him from so many troubles and raise him to the throne. Upon this answer the one who was speaking to him immediately laid his right hand on Edwin's head and said, 'When this sign shall come to you, remember this occasion and our conversation, and do not hesitate to fulfil what you are now promising.' On these words it is related* that he suddenly disappeared so that Edwin might realise that it was not a man but a spirit who had appeared to him.

The young prince continued to sit there alone, rejoicing in the consolation he had received but much concerned and anxiously wondering who the person might be who had conversed with him and whence he came. Meanwhile his friend already mentioned returned, joyfully greeted him, and said, 'Rise and come inside; put away your anxieties and let both your mind and your body rest in peace. The king has changed his mind and intends to do you no wrong but to keep faith with you. When he secretly revealed to the queen the plan I told you of, she dissuaded him from it, warning him that it was in no way fitting for so great a king to sell his best friend for gold when he was in such trouble, still less to sacrifice his own honour, which is more precious than any ornament, for the love of money.' To be brief, the king did as he had said and not only did he not betray the exile to the enemy messengers but he even assisted Edwin to gain the throne. As soon as the messengers had returned home, he raised a large army to overthrow Æthelfrith. Not giving him time to summon and assemble his whole army, Rædwald met him with a much greater force and slew him on the Mercian border on the east bank of the river Idle.* In this battle Rædwald's son, Regenhere, was killed. Thus Edwin, in accordance with the vision he had received, not only avoided the snares of the king his enemy but after he was killed succeeded him on the throne.

King Edwin hesitated to accept the word of God which Paulinus preached but, as we have said, used to sit alone for hours at a time, earnestly debating within himself what he ought to do and what religion he should follow. One day Paulinus came to him and, placing his right hand on the king's head, asked him if he recognized this sign. The king began to tremble and would have thrown himself at the bishop's feet but Paulinus raised him up and said in a voice that seemed familiar, 'First you have escaped with God's help from the hands of the foes you feared; secondly you have acquired by His gift the kingdom you desired; now, in the third place, remember your own promise; do not delay in fulfilling it but receive the faith and keep the commandments of Him who rescued you from your earthly foes and raised you to the honour of an earthly kingdom. If from henceforth you are willing to follow His will which is made known to you through me, He will also rescue you from the everlasting torments of the wicked and make you a partaker with Him of His eternal kingdom in heaven.'

CHAPTER 13

WHEN the king had heard his words, he answered that he was both willing and bound to accept the faith which Paulinus taught. He said, however, that he would confer about this with his loyal chief men and his counsellors so that, if they agreed with him, they might all be consecrated together in the waters of life. Paulinus agreed and the king did as he had said. A meeting of his council* was held and each one was asked in turn what he thought of this doctrine hitherto unknown to them and this new worship of God which was being proclaimed.

Coifi, the chief of the priests, answered at once, 'Notice carefully, King, this doctrine which is now being expounded to us. I frankly admit that, for my part, I have found that the religion which we have hitherto held has no virtue nor profit in it. None of your followers has devoted himself more earnestly than I have to the worship of our gods, but nevertheless there are many who receive greater benefits and greater honour from you than I do and are more successful in all their undertakings. If the gods had any power they would have helped me more readily, seeing that I have always served them with greater zeal. So it follows that if, on examination, these new doctrines which have now been explained to us are found to be better and more effectual, let us accept them at once without any delay.'

Another of the king's chief men agreed with this advice and with these wise words and then added, 'This is how the present life of man on earth, King, appears to me in comparison with that time which is unknown to us. You are sitting feasting with your ealdormen and thegns in winter time; the fire is burning on the hearth in the middle of the hall and all inside is warm, while outside the wintry storms of rain and snow are raging; and a sparrow flies swiftly through the hall. It enters in at one door and quickly flies out through the other. For the few moments it is inside, the storm and wintry tempest cannot touch it, but after the briefest moment of calm, it flits from your sight, out of the wintry storm and into it again. So this life of man appears but for a moment; what follows or indeed what went before, we know not at all. If this new doctrine brings us more certain information, it seems right that we should accept it.' Other elders and counsellors of the king continued in the same manner, being divinely prompted to do so.

Coifi added that he would like to listen still more carefully to what Paulinus himself had to say about God. The king ordered Paulinus to speak, and when he had said his say, Coifi exclaimed, 'For a long time now I have realized that our religion is worthless; for the more diligently I sought the truth in our cult, the less I found it. Now I confess openly that the truth shines out clearly in this teaching which can bestow on us the gift of life, salvation, and eternal happiness. Therefore I advise your Majesty that we should promptly abandon and commit to the flames the temples and the altars which we have held sacred without reaping any benefit.' Why need I say more? The king publicly accepted the gospel which Paulinus preached, renounced idolatry, and confessed his faith in Christ. When he asked the high priest of their religion which of them should be the first to profane the altars and the shrines of the idols, together with their precincts, Coifi answered, 'I will; for through the wisdom the true God has given me no one can more suitably destroy those things which I once foolishly worshipped, and so set an example to all.' And at once, casting aside his vain superstitions, he asked the king to provide him with arms and a stallion; and mounting it he set out to destroy the idols. Now a high priest of their religion was not allowed to carry arms or to ride except on a mare. So, girded with a sword, he took a spear in his hand and mounting the king's stallion he set off to where the idols were. The common people who saw him thought he was mad. But as soon as he approached the shrine, without any hesitation he profaned it by casting the spear which he held into it; and greatly rejoicing in the knowledge of the worship of the true God, he ordered his companions to destroy and set fire to the shrine and all the enclosures. The place where the idols once stood is still shown, not far from York, to the east, over the river Derwent. Today it is called Goodmanham,* the place where the high priest, through the inspiration of the true God, profaned and destroyed the altars which he himself had consecrated.

CHAPTER 14

So King Edwin, with all the nobles of his race and a vast number of the common people, received the faith and regeneration by holy baptism* in the eleventh year of his reign, that is in the year of our Lord 627 and about 180 years after the coming of the English to Britain. He was baptized at York on Easter Day, 12 April, in the church of St Peter the Apostle, which he had hastily built of wood while he was a catechumen and under instruction before he received baptism. He established an episcopal see for Paulinus, his instructor and bishop, in the same city. Very soon after his baptism, he set about building a greater and more magnificent church of stone,* under the instructions of Paulinus, in the midst of which the chapel which he had first built was to be enclosed. The foundations were laid and he began to build this square church surrounding the former chapel. But before the walls were raised to their full height, the king was slain by a cruel death and the work left for his successor Oswald to finish. Paulinus continued to preach the word of the Lord in that kingdom for six years, that is, until the end of the king's reign, with his consent and favour. As many as were foreordained to eternal life believed and were baptized, among whom were Osfrith and Eadfrith, sons of King Edwin, their mother being Cwenburh, daughter of Ceorl,* king of the Mercians; they were born while he was in exile.

Other children of his by Queen Æthelburh were baptized later on, namely Æthelhun and a daughter Æthelthryth and a second son Uscfrea; the first two were snatched from this life while they were still wearing the chrisom* and are buried in the church at York. Yffi, son of Osfrith, was also baptized and not a few others of noble and royal stock. So great is said to have been the fervour of the faith of the Northumbrians and their longing for the washing of salvation, that once when Paulinus came to the king and queen in their royal palace at Yeavering,* he spent thirty-six days there occupied in the task of catechizing and baptizing. During these days, from morning till evening, he did nothing else but instruct the crowds who flocked to him from every village and district in the teaching of Christ. When they had received instruction he washed them in the waters of regeneration in the river Glen, which was close at hand. This palace was left deserted in the time of the kings who followed Edwin, and another was built instead in a place called *Mælmin*.

All this happened in the kingdom of Bernicia; but also in the kingdom of Deira where he used to stay very frequently with the king, he baptized in the river Swale which flows beside the town of Catterick. For they were not yet able to build chapels or baptistries there in the earliest days of the church. Nevertheless in *Cambodonum* where there was also a royal dwelling, he built a church which was afterwards burnt down, together with the whole of the buildings, by the heathen who slew King Edwin. In its place, later kings built a dwelling for themselves in the region known as *Loidis*. The altar escaped from the fire because it was of stone, and is still preserved in the monastery of the most reverend abbot and priest Thrythwulf, which is in the forest of Elmet.*

CHAPTER 15

So great was Edwin's devotion to the true worship, that he also persuaded Eorpwald,* son of Rædwald* and king of the East Angles, to abandon his idolatrous superstitions and, together with his kingdom, to accept the Christian faith and sacraments. Indeed his father Rædwald had long before been initiated into the mysteries of the Christian faith in Kent, but in vain; for on his return home, he was seduced by his wife and by certain evil teachers and perverted from the sincerity of his faith, so that his last state was worse than his first. After the manner of the ancient Samaritans, he seemed to be serving both Christ and the gods whom he had previously served; in the same temple he had one altar for the Christian sacrifice and another small altar on which to offer victims to devils. Ealdwulf, who was ruler of the kingdom up to our time, used to declare that the temple lasted until his time and that he saw it when he was a boy. Rædwald, who was noble by birth though ignoble in his deeds, was the son of Tytil, whose father was Wuffa, from whom the kings of the East Angles are called Wuffings.*

Eorpwold was killed not long after he had accepted the faith, by a heathen called Ricberht. Thereupon the kingdom remained in error for three years, until Eorpwold's brother Sigeberht* came to the throne. The latter was a devout Christian and a very learned man in all respects; while his brother was alive he had been in exile in Gaul, where he had been initiated into the mysteries of the Christian faith. As soon as he began to reign he made it his business to see that the whole kingdom shared his faith. Bishop Felix* most nobly supported his efforts. This bishop, who had been born and consecrated in Burgundy, came to Archbishop Honorius, to whom he expressed his longings; so the archbishop sent him to preach the word of life to this nation of the Angles. Nor were his wishes in vain, for the devoted husbandman reaped an abundant harvest of believers in this spiritual field. Indeed, as his name signified, he freed the whole of this kingdom from long-lasting evil and unhappiness, brought it to the faith and to the works of righteousness and bestowed on it the gift of everlasting felicity. He received the seat of his bishopric in the city of *Dommoc* (Dunwich);* and when he had ruled over the kingdom as bishop for seventeen years, he ended his life there in peace.

CHAPTER 16

Now Paulinus also preached the word in the kingdom of Lindsey,* the first land on the south bank of the river Humber, bordering on the sea. His first convert was the reeve of the city of Lincoln called Blæcca,* he and his household. In this city he built a stone church* of remarkable workmanship; its roof has now fallen either through long neglect or by the hand of the enemy, but its walls are still standing and every year miracles of healing are performed in this place, for the benefit of those who seek them in faith. After Justus had departed to Christ, in his place Paulinus consecrated

Honorius bishop in this church, as we shall relate in due course.

A priest and abbot of the monastery of Partney,* named Deda, a most truthful man, told me this, regarding the faith of the kingdom; a certain old man told him that he had been baptized at noon by Bishop Paulinus, in the presence of King Edwin together with a great crowd of people, in the river Trent, near a city which the English call *Tiowulfingacæstir* (Littleborough). He also used to describe the appearance of Paulinus: he was tall, with a slight stoop, black hair, a thin face, a slender aquiline nose, and at the same time he was both venerable and awe-inspiring in appearance. He had also a deacon named James associated with him in the ministry, a man of zeal* and great reputation with both Christ and the church, who survived right up to our days.

It is related that there was so great a peace in Britain, wherever the dominion of King Edwin reached, that, as the proverb still runs, a woman with a newborn child could walk throughout the island from sea to sea and take no harm.* The king cared so much for the good of the people that, in various places where he had noticed clear springs near the highway, he caused stakes to be set up and bronze drinking cups to be hung on them for the refreshment of travellers. No one dared to lay hands on them except for their proper purpose because they feared the king greatly nor did they wish to, because they loved him dearly. So great was his majesty in his realm that not only were banners carried before him in battle, but even in time of peace, as he rode about among his cities, estates, and kingdoms with his thegns, he always used to be preceded by a standard-bearer. Further, when he walked anywhere along the roads, there used to be carried before him the type of standard which the Romans call a *tufa* and the English call a *thuf*.*

CHAPTER 17

At that time Honorius,* the successor of Boniface, was bishop of the apostolic see. When he heard that the Northumbrian race and its king had been converted to the faith and the confession of Christ by the preaching of Paulinus, he sent the latter a pallium. He also sent King Edwin letters of exhortation encouraging him and his people with fatherly love, to persevere and increase in the true faith which they had accepted. This is the tenor of the letter:

To my most excellent lord and noble son, Edwin, king of the English, Bishop Honorius, servant of the servants of God, sends greeting.

The zeal of your Christian Majesty in the worship of your Creator burns so brightly with the fire of faith that it shines far and wide and the report of it, carried throughout the world, tells of an abundant fruit for your labours. You know that you are a king, only on condition that you have faith in your King and Creator (as you have been instructed by orthodox teaching to do) and, by offering worship to God, pay Him, so far as human conditions allow, the sincere devotion of your heart. For what more can we offer to God than a hearty desire to persevere in good deeds, to worship Him and pay Him our vows, confessing Him to be the Creator of the human race? And therefore, most excellent son, we exhort you with fatherly love, as is fitting, that you labour in every way with earnest intention and constant prayer to preserve the privilege you have had of being called by divine mercy to receive His grace, so that He who has deigned to free you from all error and lead you to a knowledge of ·His name in this present world may prepare a mansion for you in the heavenly fatherland. So employ yourself in frequent readings from the works of Gregory, your evangelist and my lord, and keep before your eyes the love of that teaching which he gladly gave you for the sake of your souls: so his prayers may exalt both your kingdom and your people and present you faultless before Almighty God. We are preparing to concede you willingly and without delay those rights which you hoped we should grant your bishops: we do this on account of the sincerity of your faith which has been abundantly declared to us in terms of praise by the bearers of this letter. We are also sending a pallium for each of the two metropolitans, that is for Honorius and Paulinus, so that when either of them is summoned from the world into the presence of his Creator, the other may put a bishop in his place by this our authority. This we have been led to do, not only for the sake of our love and affection for you, but also because of the great extent of the kingdoms which, as we are aware, lie between us and you, so that in all things we may show our readiness to accept your love and to fulfil your desires.

May the grace of heaven preserve your Excellency in safety.

CHAPTER 18

MEANWHILE Archbishop Justus was translated to the heavenly kingdom on 10 November* and Honorius was elected to the archbishopric in his place. He came to Paulinus to be consecrated, meeting him at Lincoln, and there was consecrated bishop of the church at Canterbury, the fifth from Augustine. Pope Honorius sent a pallium to him also, with a letter in which he prescribes what he had already previously laid down in the letter sent to King Edwin, namely that when the archbishop of Canterbury or York* departed this life, the survivor, being his colleague and of the same rank, should have the right to consecrate another bishop in the place of the one who had passed away; so that it should be unnecessary always to make a toilsome journey to Rome, over great distances of land and sea, for the purpose of consecrating an archbishop. We have thought it proper to insert the text of the letter into our *History*:

Honorius to his most beloved brother Honorius.

Among the many good gifts which the Redeemer in His mercy deigns to bestow upon His servants, His munificent bounty and kindness has granted us this special gift that we are permitted to show our mutual love by brotherly intercourse, even as if it were face to face. For this gift we continually offer thanks to God's Majesty; and we humbly beseech Him perpetually to strengthen you, beloved brother, as you labour in preaching the gospel, bearing much fruit and following the rule of your master and head, St Gregory; praying also that, through you, He may bring forth more abundant fruit for the increase of the Church; so, through faith and works, in the fear and love of God, the increase which you and your predecessors have already gained from the seeds sown by our lord Gregory may grow in strength and extend still further; so too may the promises spoken by our Lord be fulfilled in you so that these words of His may summon you to eternal happiness, 'Come unto Me all ye that labour and are heavy laden and I will refresh you'; and again, 'Well done, good and

102

faithful servant; because thou hast been faithful over few things, I will make thee ruler over many things; enter into the joy of thy Lord.' And we, most beloved brethren, sending you first these words of exhortation out of our enduring love, do not fail to grant those things which again we realize may befit the privileged position of your Churches.

So in accordance with your request and that of the kings our sons, we grant you authority by these presents, in the name of St Peter, the prince of the apostles, that when God in His divine grace shall summon one of you to His presence, the one who remains may consecrate another bishop in place of the dead man. For this reason we have sent a pallium to each of you, beloved, so that you may carry out the consecration as God wills, by our authority and command. It is a long distance by sea and land which lies between us and you, which has compelled us to grant you this so that no loss may befall your church on any pretext whatever; but rather that the devotion of the people committed to your charge may be increased. May God keep you safe beloved brother.

Given on 11 June in the 24th year of the reign of our most religious emperor Heraclius* and the 23rd year after his consulship, the 23rd year of his son Constantine and the 3rd year after his consulship; in the 3rd year of the most illustrious Caesar his son Heraclius, in the 7th indiction.

That was in the year of our Lord 634.

CHAPTER 19

POPE HONORIUS also wrote a letter to the Irish race, whom he had found to have erred over the keeping of Easter, as we explained above, urging them with much shrewdness not to consider themselves, few as they were and placed on the extreme boundaries of the world, wiser than the ancient and modern Churches of Christ scattered throughout the earth; nor should they celebrate a different Easter contrary to the paschal tables and the decrees of the bishops of all the world met in synod.

But John* who succeeded Severinus,* the successor of Honorius, while he was yet pope-elect, sent them a letter* of great authority and learning to correct the error; he showed clearly that Easter Sunday ought to be looked for between the

fifteenth and twenty-first day of the moon, as was approved in
the Synod of Nicaea. He took care to warn them, in the same
letter, to guard against the Pelagian heresy and reject it, for he
had been informed that there was a revival of it in their midst;
this is the beginning of the letter:

> To our well-beloved and holy Tómíne, Columban, Crónán, Díma
> and Baetán, bishops; to Crónán, Ernene, Laisréne, Sillan and
> Ségéne, priests; to Saran and the other Irish teachers and abbots;*
> Hilarus the archpriest and vicegerent of the holy apostolic see; also
> John the deacon and pope-elect in the name of the Lord, and John,
> chief secretary and vicegerent of the holy apostolic see, and John,
> servant of God and counsellor of the same.

> The writings which were brought by envoys to Pope Severinus of
> holy memory, were left with the questions contained in them unan-
> swered when he departed this life. These we re-opened so that no
> obscurity should remain uncleared in questions of such import and
> we discovered that certain men of your kingdom were attempting to
> revive a new heresy out of an old one and, befogged with mental
> blindness, to reject our Easter in which Christ was sacrificed for us,
> contending with the Hebrews that it should be celebrated on the
> fourteenth day of the moon.

At the beginning of this letter it is clearly asserted that this
heresy had sprung up among them very recently and that not
all the race but only certain of them were implicated in it.

After they had explained the method of observing Easter
they added this in the same letter about the Pelagians:

> And this also we have learnt that the poison of the Pelagian heresy*
> has of late revived amongst you; we therefore exhort you utterly to
> put away this kind of poisonous and criminal superstition from
> your minds. You cannot be unaware that this execrable heresy has
> been condemned; and not only has it been abolished for some two
> hundred years but it is daily condemned by us and buried beneath
> our perpetual ban. We exhort you then not to rake up the ashes
> amongst you of those whose weapons have been burnt. For who can
> fail to execrate the proud and impious attempt of those who say that
> a man can live without sin and that, not by the grace of God, but by
> his own will? In the first place it is foolish and blasphemous to say
> that any man is without sin: it is impossible except for that one
> mediator between God and men, the man Christ Jesus, who was
> conceived and brought forth without sin. For all other men were

born with original sin and are known to bear the mark of Adam's transgression, even though they are without actual sin, in accordance with the prophet's words: 'Behold, I was shapen in iniquity and in sin did my mother bring me forth.'

CHAPTER 20

EDWIN had reigned most gloriously over the English and the British race for seventeen years, for six of which, as we have said, he was also a soldier in the kingdom of Christ, when Cædwalla,* king of the Britons, rebelled against him. He was supported by Penda,* a most energetic member of the royal house of Mercia, who from that date ruled over that nation for twenty-two years with varying success. A fierce battle was fought on the plain called *Hæthfelth* (Hatfield Chase) and Edwin was killed on 12 October in the year of our Lord 633, in his forty-eighth year. The whole of his army was either slain or scattered. In this war too, one of his sons, Osfrith, a warlike youth, fell before him while the other, Eadfrith, was compelled to desert to King Penda; the latter, in spite of an oath, afterwards murdered him, during the reign of Oswald.

At this time there was a great slaughter both of the Church and of the people of Northumbria, one of the perpetrators being a heathen and the other a barbarian who was even more cruel than the heathen. Now Penda and the whole Mercian race were idolaters and ignorant of the name of Christ; but Cædwalla, although a Christian by name and profession, was nevertheless a barbarian in heart and disposition and spared neither women nor innocent children. With bestial cruelty he put all to death by torture and for a long time raged through all their land, meaning to wipe out the whole English nation from the land of Britain. Nor did he pay any respect to the Christian religion which had sprung up amongst them. Indeed to this very day it is the habit of the Britons to despise the faith and religion of the English and not to co-operate with them in anything any more than with the heathen. The head of King Edwin* was brought to York and afterwards placed in the church of the apostle St Peter, which he himself had begun to build and his successor Oswald completed, as we have said before. It was placed in the chapel of the holy Pope Gregory from whose disciples he himself had received the word of life.

As the affairs of Northumbria had been thrown into confusion at the time of this disaster and as there seemed no safety except in flight, Paulinus took with him Queen Æthelburh, whom he had previously brought thither, and returned by boat to Kent, where he was most honourably received by Archbishop Honorius and King Eadbald. He came thither in the charge of Bass, a very brave thegn of King Edwin. He had with him also Edwin's daughter, Eanflæd, and his son Uscfrea, and Yffi, the son of Osfrith, Edwin's son. Æthelburh, fearing Kings Eadbald and Oswald, afterwards sent these children to Gaul to be brought up by King Dagobert,* who was her friend. Both children died there in infancy and were buried in the church with the honour due to royal children and Christian innocents. Paulinus also brought with him much precious treasure belonging to King Edwin, including a great golden cross and a golden chalice, consecrated to the service of the altar. These are still preserved and are to be seen in the church of the Kentish people.

At that time the Church at Rochester had no pastor because its bishop, Romanus, who had been sent on an embassy to Pope Honorius by Archbishop Justus, had been drowned in the Italian sea. Paulinus therefore took charge of it at the invitation of Bishop Honorius and King Eadbald and held it until his time came to ascend to the heavenly kingdom, bearing with him the fruits of his glorious labours. When he died he left in the church the pallium which he had received from the pope at Rome.

Now Paulinus had left in the church at York a certain James, a deacon, a true churchman and a saintly man; he remained for a long time in the church and, by teaching and baptizing, rescued much prey from the ancient foe. There is a village near Catterick in which he often used to dwell, which is still called by his name. He was very skilful in church music and when peace was restored to the kingdom and the number of believers grew, he also began to instruct many in singing, after the manner of Rome and the Kentish people; and when he was old and full of days, as the Scripture says, he went the way of his fathers.

END OF THE SECOND BOOK

BOOK III

These are the contents of the third book of the history of the Church of the English people.

16. How, by his prayers, he drove away the fire which had been started by enemies to destroy the royal city.

17. How the buttress of the church against which he was leaning when he died could not be consumed by fire when the rest of the church was burning; and about his spiritual life.

18. About the life and death of the devout King Sigeberht.

19. How Fursa built a monastery among the East Angles; about his visions and his holiness and how, after his death, his uncorrupt body bore testimony to him.

20. How, when Honorius died, Deusdedit became archbishop; and who were the bishops of the East Angles and of the church at Rochester at the time.

21. How the kingdom of the Middle Angles became Christian under King Peada.

22. How the East Saxons, who had long rejected the faith, under King Sigeberht were reconverted through the preaching of Cedd.

23. How Bishop Cedd, who had received the site from King Oethelwald on which to build a monastery, consecrated it to the Lord with prayer and fasting; and about his death.

24. How the kingdom of Mercia received the Christian faith after the slaying of Penda; and how Oswiu, as a thank-offering for victory, gave possessions and lands to God for building monasteries.

25. How the question about the date of keeping Easter arose with those who had come from Ireland.

26. How Colman was defeated and returned home; and how Tuda became bishop in his place; and about the state of the church under these teachers.

27. How Egbert, a holy Englishman, lived as a monk in Ireland.

28. How, when Tuda was dead, Wilfrid was consecrated in Gaul and Chad in Wessex as bishops of the kingdom of Northumbria.

29. How the priest Wigheard was sent to Rome from Britain to be made archbishop, and how a letter sent by the pope told of his death.

30. How the East Saxons turned to idolatry in the time of plague, but were at once restored from their errors by the zeal of Bishop Jaruman.

BEGINNING OF BOOK III

CHAPTER 1

AFTER Edwin had been killed in battle, the kingdom of the Deiri, the cradle of his race and the foundation of his royal power, passed to a son of his uncle Ælfric whose name was Osric; he had received the mysteries of the faith through the preaching of Paulinus. But the Northumbrian race was originally divided into two portions,* and the other kingdom, that of the Bernicians, went to a son of Æthelfrith named Eanfrith, who derived from it both his lineage and his claim to the throne. During the whole of Edwin's reign the sons of King Æthelfrith his predecessor, together with many young nobles, were living in exile among the Irish or the Picts where they were instructed in the faith as the Irish taught it and were regenerated by the grace of baptism. On the death of their enemy King Edwin they were allowed to return to their own land, and the eldest of them, Eanfrith, as we have said, became king of the Bernicians. But no sooner had these two kings gained the sceptres of their earthly kingdom than they abjured and betrayed the mysteries of the heavenly kingdom to which they had been admitted and reverted to the filth of their former idolatry, thereby to be polluted and destroyed.

Very soon* afterwards, Cædwalla, the king of the Britons, killed them both, executing a just vengeance upon them, though with unrighteous violence. First, in the following summer he killed Osric, who had rashly besieged him in a fortified town; he broke out suddenly with all his forces, took Osric by surprise, and destroyed him and all his army. After this he occupied the Northumbrian kingdoms for a whole year, not ruling them like a victorious king but ravaging them like a savage tyrant, tearing them to pieces with fearful bloodshed. Finally when Eanfrith* came to him unadvisedly to make peace, accompanied only by twelve chosen thegns, he destroyed him as well. To this day that year is still held to have been ill-omened and hateful to all good men, not only on account of the apostasy of the English kings who cast aside the mysteries of their faith, but also because of the outrageous tyranny of the British king. So all those who compute the dates of kings have decided to abolish the memory of those perfidious kings and to assign this year to their successor Oswald, a man beloved of God. After his brother Eanfrith was killed, Oswald came with an army, small in numbers but strengthened by their faith in Christ, and destroyed the abominable leader of the Britons together with the immense force which he boasted was irresistible, at a place which is called in the English tongue, *Denisesburn*,* that is the brook of the *Denise*.

CHAPTER 2

THE place is still shown today and is held in great veneration* where Oswald, when he was about to engage in battle, set up the sign of the holy cross and, on bended knees, prayed God to send heavenly aid to His worshippers in their dire need. In fact it is related that when a cross had been hastily made and the hole dug in which it was to stand, he seized the cross himself in the ardour of his faith, placed it in the hole, and held it upright with both hands until the soldiers had heaped up the earth and fixed it in position. Thereupon he raised his voice and called out to the whole army, 'Let us all kneel together and pray the almighty, everliving, and true God to defend us in His mercy from the proud and fierce enemy; for He knows that we are fighting in a just cause* for the preservation of our whole race.' They all did as he commanded, advanced against the enemy just as dawn was breaking, and gained the victory that their faith merited. Innumerable miracles of healing are known to have been wrought in the place where they prayed, doubtless as a token and memorial of the king's faith. And even to this day many people are in the habit of cutting splinters from the wood of this holy cross and putting them in water which they then give to sick men or beasts to drink or else they sprinkle them with it; and they are quickly restored to health.

This place is called in English Heavenfield,* and in Latin *Caelestis campus*, a name which it certainly received in days of old as an omen of future happenings; it signified that a heavenly sign was to be erected there, a heavenly victory won, and that heavenly miracles were to take place there continuing to this day. The place, on its north side, is close to the wall with which the Romans once girded the whole of Britain from sea to sea, to keep off the attacks of the barbarians as already described. To this place the brethren of the church at Hexham, not far away, have long made it their custom to come every year, on the day before* that on which King Oswald was killed, to keep vigil there for the benefit of his soul, to sing many psalms of praise, and, next morning, to offer up the holy sacrifice and oblation on his behalf. And since that good custom has spread, a church has lately been built there so that the place has become still more sacred and worthy of honour in the eyes of all. And rightly so: for, as far as we know, no symbol of the Christian faith, no church, and no altar had been erected in the whole of Bernicia before that new leader of the host, inspired by his devotion to the faith, set up the standard of the holy cross when he was about to fight his most savage enemy. It is not irrelevant to narrate one of the many miracles which have taken place at the cross.

One of the brothers of the church of Hexham who is still living, named Bothelm, a few years ago was walking incautiously on the ice by night when he suddenly fell and broke his arm. He suffered such anguish from the fractured limb that he could not raise his hand to his mouth because of the pain. Hearing one morning that one of the brothers was proposing to go up to the site of the holy cross, he asked him to bring him back some part of the revered wood, saying he believed that the Lord would grant him healing by its means. The brother did as he was asked, returning that evening when all the others were seated at table. He gave the sick man some of the ancient moss with which the surface of the wood was covered. Bothelm was sitting at the table and, as he had nowhere at hand to keep the proffered gift in safety, he placed it in his bosom. When he went to bed he forgot to take it out and allowed it to remain where it was. At midnight he awoke feeling something cold close to his side and, putting his hand

down to find out what it was, he discovered that his arm and
hand were as sound as if they had never pained him.

CHAPTER 3

OSWALD, as soon as he had come to the throne, was anxious
that the whole race under his rule should be filled with the
grace of the Christian faith of which he had had so wonderful
an experience in overcoming the barbarians. So he sent to the
Irish elders* among whom he and his thegns had received the
sacrament of baptism when he was an exile. He requested
them to send a bishop by whose teaching and ministry the
English race over whom he ruled might learn the privileges
of faith in our Lord and receive the sacraments. His request
was granted without delay. They sent him Bishop Aidan,* a
man of outstanding gentleness, devotion, and moderation,
who had a zeal for God though not entirely according to
knowledge. For after the manner of his race, as we have very
often mentioned, he was accustomed to celebrate Easter
Sunday between the fourteenth and the twentieth day of the
moon. The northern province of the Irish and the whole
nation of the Picts were still celebrating Easter Sunday according to this rule right up to that time, thinking that in this
observance they were following the writings of the esteemed
and holy father, Anatolius.* Every instructed person can very
easily judge whether this is true or not. But the Irish peoples
who lived in the southern part of Ireland had long before
learned to observe Easter according to canonical custom,
through the teaching of the pope.

On the bishop's arrival, the king gave him a place for his
episcopal see on the island of Lindisfarne, in accordance with
his wishes. As the tide ebbs and flows, this place is surrounded twice daily by the waves of the sea like an island and
twice, when the shore is left dry, it becomes again attached to
the mainland. The king humbly and gladly listened to the
bishop's admonitions in all matters, diligently seeking to build
up and extend the Church of Christ in his kingdom. It was
indeed a beautiful sight when the bishop was preaching the

gospel, to see the king acting as interpreter of the heavenly word for his ealdormen* and thegns, for the bishop was not completely at home in the English tongue, while the king had gained a perfect knowledge of Irish during the long period of his exile.

From that time, as the days went by, many came from the country of the Irish* into Britain and to those English kingdoms over which Oswald reigned, preaching the word of faith with great devotion. Those of them who held the rank of priest administered the grace of baptism to those who believed. Churches were built in various places and the people flocked together with joy to hear the Word; lands and property of other kinds were given by royal bounty to establish monasteries, and English children, as well as their elders, were instructed by Irish teachers in advanced studies and in the observance of the discipline of a Rule.

Indeed they were mostly monks who came to preach. Bishop Aidan was himself a monk; he was sent from the island known as Iona, whose monastery was for a very long time chief among all the monasteries of the northern Irish and the Picts, exercising supervision over their communities. The island itself belongs to Britain and is separated from the mainland by a narrow strait, but the Picts who inhabit those parts of Britain gave it to the Irish monks long ago, because they had received the faith of Christ through the monks' preaching.

CHAPTER 4

In the year of our Lord 565, when Justin the second* took over the control of the Roman Empire after Justinian, there came from Ireland to Britain a priest and abbot named Columba,* a true monk in life no less than habit; he came to Britain to preach the word of God to the kingdoms of the northern Picts* which are separated from the southern part of their land by steep and rugged mountains. The southern Picts who live on this side of the mountains had, so it is said, long ago given up the errors of idolatry and received the true faith through the preaching of the Word by that reverend and holy man Bishop Ninian,* a Briton who had received orthodox instruction at Rome in the faith and the mysteries of the truth. His episcopal see is celebrated for its church, dedicated to St Martin* where his body rests, together with those of many other saints. The see is now under English rule. This place which is in the kingdom of Bernicia is commonly called Whithorn,* the White House, because Ninian built a church of stone there, using a method unusual among the Britons.

Columba came to Britain when Bridius the son of Malcolm,* a most powerful king, had been ruling over the Picts for over eight years. Columba turned them to the faith of Christ by his words and example and so received the island of Iona from them in order to establish a monastery there. It is not a large island, being only about five hides in English reckoning. His successors hold it to this day and he himself was buried there at the age of seventy-seven, about thirty-two years after he came to Britain to preach. Before this he had founded a famous monastery in Ireland called Dearmach (Durrow), the Field of the Oaks, on account of the great number of oaks there. From both of these sprang very many monasteries which were established by his disciples in Britain and Ireland, over all of which the island monastery in which his body lies held pre-eminence.

This island always has an abbot for its ruler who is a priest, to whose authority the whole kingdom, including even bishops,* have to be subject. This unusual arrangement follows the example of their first teacher, who was not a bishop but a priest and monk. Some written records of his life and teachings are said to have been preserved by his disciples. Whatever he was himself, we know this for certain about him, that he left successors distinguished for their great abstinence, their love of God, and their observance of the Rule. It is true that they used tables of doubtful accuracy in fixing the date of the chief festival, since they were so far away at the ends of the earth that there was none to bring them the decrees of the synods concerning the observance of Easter; but they diligently practised such works of religion and chastity as they were able to learn from the words of the prophets, the evangelists, and the apostles. This reckoning of Easter persisted among them for a very long time, no less than 150 years, up to the year of our Lord 715.

At that time the greatly revered and holy father and priest Egbert,* an Englishman, came to them. He had long lived in exile in Ireland for the sake of Christ and was most learned in the scriptures, being famous for his long and holy life; he set them right and brought them to observe the true and canonical Easter Day. They did not always observe it on the fourteenth day of the moon, with the Jews, as some believe,* but they celebrated it always on the Sunday, though not in the proper week. Being Christians they knew that the resurrection of our Lord, which happened on the first day after the sabbath, must always be celebrated on that day; but, rude barbarians as they were, they had never learned when that particular first day after the sabbath, which we now call the Lord's Day, should come. But because they were not lacking in grace and fervent love, they were accounted worthy to gain full knowledge on this subject also, even as the apostle had promised, saying, 'And if in anything ye be otherwise minded, God shall reveal it unto you.' But we must speak more fully about this matter later on in its proper place.

CHAPTER 5

SUCH was the island, such the community, from which Aidan was sent to give the English people instruction in Christ after he had been consecrated bishop during the abbacy of the priest Ségéne.* Aidan taught the clergy many lessons about the conduct of their lives but above all he left them a most salutary example of abstinence and self-control; and the best recommendation of his teaching to all was that he taught them no other way of life than that which he himself practised among his fellows. For he neither sought after nor cared for worldly possessions but he rejoiced to hand over at once, to any poor man he met, the gifts which he had received from kings or rich men of the world. He used to travel everywhere, in town and country, not on horseback but on foot, unless compelled by urgent necessity to do otherwise, in order that, as he walked along, whenever he saw people whether rich or poor, he might at once approach them and, if they were unbelievers, invite them to accept the mystery of the faith; or, if they were believers, that he might strengthen them in the faith, urging them by word and deed to practise almsgiving and good works.

Aidan's life was in great contrast to our modern sloth-fulness;* all who accompanied him, whether tonsured or lay-men, had to engage in some form of study, that is to say, to occupy themselves either with reading the scriptures or learn-ing the psalms. This was the daily task of Aidan himself and of all who were with him, wherever they went. And if it happened, as it rarely did, that he was summoned to feast with the king, he went with one or two of his clergy, and, after taking a little food, he hurried away either to read with his people or to pray. At that time a number of men and women, instructed by his example, formed the habit of prolonging their fast on Wednesdays and Fridays throughout the year, until the ninth hour, with the exception of the period between Easter and Pentecost. Neither respect nor fear made him keep silence about the sins of the rich, but he would correct them with a stern rebuke. He would never give money to powerful men of the world, but only food on such occasions as he entertained them; on the contrary he distributed gifts of money which he received from the rich, either, as we have said, for the use of the poor or for the redemption of those who had been unjustly sold into slavery.* In fact, many of those whom he redeemed for a sum of money he afterwards made his disciples and, when he had trained and instructed them, he ordained them priests.

The story goes that when King Oswald asked the Irish for a bishop to minister the word of faith to him and his people, another man of harsher disposition was first sent. But he preached to the English for some time unsuccessfully and seeing that the people were unwilling to listen to him, he returned to his own land. At a meeting of the elders he reported that he had made no headway in the instruction of the people to whom he had been sent, because they were intractable, obstinate, and uncivilized. It is related that there was a long discussion at the conference as to what ought to be done; for they were anxious to give that people the help it asked for and regretted that the preacher they had sent had not been accepted. Then Aidan, who was present at the conference, said to the priest in question, 'It seems to me, brother, that you have been unreasonably harsh upon your ignorant hearers: you did not first offer them the milk of simpler teaching, as the apostle recommends, until little by little, as they grew strong on the food of God's word, they were capable of receiving more elaborate instruction and of carrying out the more transcendent commandments of God.' All eyes were turned on Aidan when they heard these words and all present carefully considered what he had said. They agreed that he was worthy to be made a bishop and that he was the man to send to instruct those ignorant unbelievers, since he had proved himself to be pre-eminently endowed with the grace of discretion, which is the mother of all virtues.* So he was consecrated and sent to preach to them. As time went on he proved himself to be remarkable not only for the moderation and good sense which they had first observed in him, but for many other virtues as well.

CHAPTER 6

WITH such a man as bishop to instruct them, King Oswald, together with the people over which he ruled, learned to hope for those heavenly realms which were unknown to their forefathers; and also Oswald gained from the one God who made heaven and earth greater earthly realms than any of his ancestors had possessed. In fact he held under his sway all the peoples* and kingdoms of Britain, divided among the speakers of four different languages, British, Pictish, Irish, and English.

Though he wielded supreme power over the whole land, he was always wonderfully humble, kind, and generous to the poor and to strangers. For example, the story is told that on a certain occasion, one Easter Day, when he had sat down to dinner with Bishop Aidan, a silver dish was placed on the table before him full of rich foods. They had just raised their hands to ask a blessing on the bread when there came in an officer of the king, whose duty it was to relieve the needy, telling him that a very great multitude of poor people from every district were sitting in the precincts and asking alms of the king. He at once ordered the dainties which had been set in front of him to be carried to the poor, the dish to be broken up, and the pieces divided amongst them. The bishop, who was sitting by, was delighted with this pious act, grasped him by the right hand, and said, 'May this hand never decay.' His blessing and his prayer were fulfilled in this way: when Oswald was killed in battle, his hand and arm were cut off from the rest of his body, and they have remained uncorrupt until this present time; they are in fact preserved in a silver shrine in St Peter's church, in the royal city which is called after Queen Bebba* (Bamburgh) and are venerated with fitting respect by all.

By the efforts of this king the kingdoms of Deira and Bernicia, which had up to this time been at strife with one another, were peacefully united and became one people. Now Oswald was the nephew of Edwin through his sister Acha,* and it was fitting that so great a predecessor should have so worthy a kinsman to inherit both his religion and his kingdom.

CHAPTER 7

ABOUT this time the West Saxons, who in early days were called the Gewisse, received the faith of Christ during the reign of Cynegisl* through the preaching of Bishop Birinus.* The latter had come to Britain on the advice of Pope Honorius, having promised in the pope's presence that he would scatter the seeds of the holy faith in the remotest regions of England, where no teacher had been before. For this reason he was consecrated bishop at the pope's command by Asterius, bishop of Genoa. So he came to Britain and visited the race of the Gewisse first of all; finding that they were all completely heathen, he decided that it would be more useful to preach the word there rather than go further seeking for others to evangelize.

While he was preaching the gospel in this kingdom, the king himself, after receiving instruction, was cleansed from his sins in the waters of baptism together with all his people. It so happened* that at the time Oswald, the saintly and victorious king of the Northumbrians, was present and stood godfather for him. Lovely indeed and well-pleasing to God was their relationship; that same man whose daughter* Oswald was later to receive as his wife, that day, after his new birth and dedication to God, was received by Oswald as his son. The two kings gave the bishop a city called Dorchester* in which to establish his episcopal see. After he had built and dedicated churches and brought many to the Lord by his pious labours, he went to be with the Lord and was buried in the same city. Many years afterwards, when Hædde* was bishop, his body was translated thence to the city of Winchester and was deposited in the church of the apostles St Peter and St Paul.

On the death of Cynegisl, his son Cenwealh* came to the throne. He refused to receive the faith and the mysteries of the heavenly kingdom and not long afterwards lost his earthly kingdom also. Now he had repudiated his wife who was sister of Penda, king of the Mercians, and had married another woman; for this he was attacked by Penda and deprived of his kingdom, retiring to the court of the East Anglian king, whose name was Anna. During his three years of exile he acknowledged and accepted the true faith, for the king with whom he lived in exile was a good man and blessed with a good and saintly family as we shall learn later.

When Cenwealh had been restored to his kingdom there came to his land from Ireland a bishop named Agilbert,* a Gaul by birth, who had spent a long time in Ireland for the purpose of studying the Scriptures. He now attached himself to the king and voluntarily undertook the task of preaching. When the king saw his learning and industry, he asked him to accept an episcopal see in that place and to remain as bishop of his people. Agilbert complied with his request and presided over the nation as bishop for a number of years. But at last the king, who knew only the Saxon language, grew tired of his barbarous speech* and foisted upon the kingdom a bishop named Wine* who had also been consecrated in Gaul but who spoke the king's own tongue. He divided his kingdom into two dioceses and gave Wine an episcopal seat in the city of *Venta* which the Saxons call *Wintancæstir* (Winchester). Agilbert was deeply offended because the king had done this without consulting him and returned to Gaul, where he accepted the bishopric of Paris and there died 'being old and full of days'. Not many years after his departure from Britain, Wine was also expelled from the bishopric by the king; he took refuge with Wulfhere, king of Mercia, and bought the see of the city of London from him for a sum of money, remaining its bishop to the end of his life. So for a considerable time the kingdom of the West Saxons remained without a bishop.

Meanwhile King Cenwealh, who was continually suffering heavy losses in his kingdom at the hands of his enemies, at length called to mind that it was unbelief that had once driven him from his kingdom and his acknowledgement of faith in Christ which had restored him; he realized equally that a kingdom which was without a bishop was, at the same time, justly deprived of divine protection. So he sent messengers to Agilbert in Gaul, offering to make amends and praying him to return again to the diocese. But Agilbert excused himself, declaring that he could not come because he was pledged to the bishopric of his own city and diocese. However, rather than refuse to give any help when the king sought it so eagerly, he sent his nephew, the priest Leuthere,* in his place to be consecrated bishop if the king were willing, adding that he considered him worthy of a bishopric. Leuthere was honourably received by the king and the people, and they asked Theodore who was then archbishop of Canterbury to consecrate him bishop. He was accordingly consecrated at Canterbury and for many years governed the whole see of the Gewisse with industry and moderation, ruling alone by the authority of the council.

CHAPTER 8

IN the year of our Lord 640 Eadbald, king of Kent, departed this life and left the government of his kingdom to his son Eorcenberht,* who ruled with distinction for twenty-four years and some months. He was the first English king to order idols to be abandoned and destroyed throughout the whole kingdom. He also ordered the forty days fast of Lent to be observed by royal authority. And so that his commands might not be too lightly neglected, he prescribed suitably heavy punishments for offenders. His daughter Eorcengota, a child worthy of her parent, was a most virtuous maiden who served the Lord in a monastery founded in the land of the Franks by a noble abbess named Fara in a place called Brie.* At that time, because there were not yet many monasteries founded in England, numbers of people from Britain used to enter the monasteries of the Franks or Gauls to practise the monastic life; they also sent their daughters to be taught in them and to be wedded to the heavenly bridegroom. They mostly went to the monasteries at Brie, Chelles,* and Andelys-sur-Seine; among these was Sæthryth, stepdaughter of Anna, king of the East Angles mentioned above, and Æthelburh,* his own daughter. Both of these though foreigners were, by the merit of their virtues, made abbesses of the monastery at Brie. The eldest daughter of the king was Seaxburh,* wife of King Eorcenberht of Kent, whose daughter Eorcengota deserves special mention.

Many wonders and miraculous signs associated with this dedicated virgin are related even to this day by the people who live in that place. It will be enough for us to speak, and that briefly, of her departure from this world to the heavenly kingdom. When the day of her summons was imminent, she went round the monastery visiting the cells of Christ's infirm handmaidens and especially of those who were of great age or distinguished for their virtuous lives. She humbly commended herself to their prayers, not concealing from them that it had been revealed to her that her own death was near. She explained that the revelation she had received was in this form: she saw a crowd of men dressed in white enter the monastery; on being asked what they were looking for or what they wanted, they answered that they had been sent to take back with them the golden coin which had been brought thither from Kent. At the very end of the same night, just as the dawn was breaking, she passed from the darkness of the present world into the light of heaven. Many of the brothers of the monastery who were in other buildings related that they clearly heard choirs of angels singing, as well as the sound of what seemed to be a mighty throng entering the monastery. Hurrying out to discover what was the matter, they saw a very great light coming down from heaven, which bore away the holy soul, now freed from the bonds of the flesh, to the eternal joys of the heavenly country. They also relate other miracles which were divinely manifested in the monastery on the same night; but as we must turn to other matters, we will leave them to be related by her own people. The holy body of the virgin and bride of Christ was buried in the church of the blessed protomartyr Stephen; it was decided, three days after, to take up the stone which covered her sepulchre and raise it higher in the same place; while they were doing this, so sweet a fragrance arose from the depths of the sepulchre that it seemed to all the brothers and sisters who were standing by as if stores of balsam had been unsealed.

Her aunt Æthelburh already mentioned, lived a life of great self-denial, also preserving the glory of perpetual virginity which is well pleasing to God. But after her death the greatness of her virtue was more clearly revealed. While she was abbess, she had begun to build a church in her monastery dedicated to all the apostles, in which she wished her body to be buried. But when the work was less than half finished, she was cut off by death and so unable to complete it; she was nevertheless buried in that part of the church which she had chosen. After her death the brothers were more concerned with other things, so that the building was left for seven years. At the end of this time they decided to abandon completely the attempt to build the church which had proved too great a task. They resolved to raise the bones of the abbess from their resting place and translate them to another church which was already finished and dedicated. On opening her sepulchre they found her body as untouched by decay as it had also been immune from the corruption of fleshly desires. They washed it again, clothed it in other garments, and translated it to the church of St Stephen the Martyr. Her festival is celebrated there with great honour on 7 July.

CHAPTER 9

OSWALD, the most Christian king of Northumbria, ruled for nine years if we include that year* which the brutal wickedness of the British king and the mad apostasy of the English kings rendered detestable. But, as we have explained previously, it was decided by the unanimous consent of all that the name and memory of those apostates ought to be utterly blotted out from the list of Christian kings and that no year should be assigned to their reign. At the end of this period, Oswald was killed in a great battle by the same heathen people and the same heathen Mercian king as his predecessor Edwin in a place called in the English tongue *Maserfelth*,* on 5 August in the thirty-eighth year of his age.

His great faith in God and his devotion of heart were also made clear after his death by certain miracles. Indeed in that place where he was slain by the heathen fighting for his fatherland, sick men and beasts are healed to this day. It has happened that people have often taken soil from the place where his body fell to the ground, have put it in water, and by its use have brought great relief to their sick. This custom became very popular and gradually so much earth was removed that a hole was made, as deep as a man's height. Nor is it to be wondered at that the sick are cured in the place where he died, for while he was alive he never ceased to care for the sick and the poor, to give them alms, and offer them help. Many miracles are related which took place either at that site or through the soil taken from it. But we think that it is enough to relate two only which we have heard our elders tell.

It happened that not long after his death a man was travelling on horseback past this place. The horse suddenly began to tire; next it stopped, bending its head to the ground and foaming at the mouth and then, as the pain became unbearable, it fell to the earth. The rider alighted, took off its saddle-cloth, and waited to see whether it would recover or whether he would have to leave it for dead. The beast was long tortured by the agonizing pain and twisted about from place to place, until as it turned over, it came upon the very spot where the famous king had fallen. Forthwith the pain ceased, and the horse stopped its frantic struggles; then, as horses do, after they have been resting, it rolled from side to side, stood up completely cured and began to crop the grass greedily.

When the rider, who was an intelligent man, saw this, he realized that there must be some special sanctity associated with the place in which the horse was cured. He put up a sign to mark the site, shortly afterwards mounted his horse, and reached the inn where he intended to lodge. On his arrival, he found a girl there, niece of the patron, who had long suffered from paralysis. When he heard the members of the household lamenting the girl's grievous infirmity, he told them of the place where his horse had been cured. Why need I say more? They put her in a cart, brought her to the place and laid her down there. In a short time she fell asleep and when she woke up she found that she was healed of her infirmity. She asked for water, washed her face, arranged her hair, and covered her head with a linen kerchief, returning home on foot in perfect health, with those who had brought her.

CHAPTER 10

THE story is told that about this time another man, a Briton, was travelling near that place where the battle had been fought, when he noticed that a certain patch of ground was greener and more beautiful than the rest of the field. He very wisely conjectured that the only cause for the unusual greenness of that part must be that some man holier than the rest of the army had perished there. So he took some of the soil with him wrapped up in a cloth, thinking that it might prove useful, as was indeed to happen, as a cure for sick persons. He went on his way and came in the evening to a certain village, entering a house where the villagers were enjoying a feast. He was received by the owners of the house and sat down to the feast with them, hanging up the cloth containing the dust he had brought on one of the wall-posts. They lingered long over their feasting and tippling, while a great fire burned in the midst of the dwelling. It happened that the sparks flew up to the roof which was made of wattles and thatched with hay, so that it suddenly burst into flames. As soon as the guests saw this, they fled outside in terror and confusion, quite unable to save the burning house which was on the point of destruction. So the whole house was burnt down with the single exception that the post on which the soil hung, enclosed in its bag, remained whole and untouched by the fire. Those who saw it were greatly amazed by this miracle. After careful inquiries they discovered that the soil had been taken from that very place where Oswald's blood had been spilt. The fame of these miracles spread far and wide and as the days went by many began to frequent the place and there obtained the grace of healing for themselves and their friends.

CHAPTER 11

AMONG these stories, I think I ought not to pass over in silence the miracles and heavenly signs which were shown when his bones were discovered and translated to the church in which they are now preserved. This came about through the efforts of Osthryth,* queen of Mercia, who was the daughter of Oswald's brother Oswiu, who reigned after him as we shall relate in due course.

There is a famous monastery in the kingdom of Lindsey called Bardney,* which was greatly loved, venerated, and enriched by the queen and her husband Æthelred and in which she wished to place her uncle's honoured bones.* The carriage on which the bones were borne reached the monastery toward evening. But the inmates did not receive them gladly. They knew that Oswald was a saint but, nevertheless, because he belonged to another kingdom and had once conquered them, they pursued him even when dead with their former hatred.* So it came about that the relics remained outside all night with only a large tent erected over the carriage in which the bones rested. But a sign from heaven revealed to them how reverently the relics should have been received by all the faithful. All through the night a column of light stretched from the carriage right up to heaven and was visible in almost every part of the kingdom of Lindsey. In the morning, the brothers in the monastery who had refused the relics of God's beloved saint the day before, now began to pray earnestly that the relics might be lodged with them. The bones were washed, laid in a shrine constructed for the purpose, and placed in the church with fitting honours; and in order that the royal saint might be perpetually remembered, they placed above the tomb his banner of gold and purple, pouring out the water in which the bones had been washed in a corner of the sanctuary. Ever afterwards the soil which had received that holy water had the power and saving grace of driving devils from the bodies of people possessed.

Some time afterwards, when Queen Osthryth was staying in the monastery, a certain reverend abbess named Æthelhild, who is still living, came to visit her. The abbess was the sister of two holy men, Æthelwine* and Ealdwine, the former of whom was bishop of Lindsey, while the other was abbot in the monastery known as Partney, not far from which Æthelhild's monastery stood. As the abbess talked with the queen, the conversation amongst other subjects turned on Oswald, and Æthelhild told how on that memorable night she herself had seen the light over his relics reaching up to the very heavens. The queen in her turn told her that many sick people had been healed by the soil of the floor on which the water, used for washing his bones, had been poured out. Thereupon the abbess begged for some of this health-giving soil; she took it, wrapped it up in a cloth, put it in a casket, and returned home. Some time afterwards, when she was in her monastery, there came a guest who used very often to be greatly troubled in the night, without warning, by an unclean spirit. This guest was hospitably received and, after supper, had lain down on his bed, when he was suddenly possessed by the devil and began to gnash his teeth and foam at the mouth, while his limbs were twisted by convulsive movements. As he could neither be held down nor bound, a servant ran and knocked at the abbess's gate and told her. She opened the monastery door and went out with one of the nuns to the men's dwelling, where she called a priest and asked him to come with her to the patient. When they reached the place they found a crowd there, all trying in vain to hold the possessed man down and to restrain his convulsive movements. The priest pronounced exorcisms and did all he could to soothe the madness of the wretched man but, though he toiled hard, he effected nothing. When there seemed to be no means of overcoming his madness, the abbess suddenly remembered this soil; she at once ordered a serving-woman to go and fetch the casket in which it was kept. No sooner had the servant brought the soil as ordered, and entered the porch of the house in which the demoniac was lying in his contortions, than he was suddenly silent and laid his head down as if he were in a relaxed sleep, while his limbs became quiet and composed. 'Hushed were they all and, fixed in silence, gazed', waiting anxiously to see how it would all end. After about an hour the man who had been afflicted sat up and said with a deep sigh, 'Now I feel that I am well and have been restored to my senses.' Thereupon they earnestly inquired how this had happened. He answered, 'As soon as this maid reached the porch of the house with the casket she was carrying, all the evil spirits which were oppressing me left me and departed to be seen no more.' Then the abbess gave him a tiny portion of the soil and, after the priest had prayed, he passed a most peaceful night. From that time onwards he suffered no more night alarms nor afflictions from the ancient foe.

CHAPTER 12

SOME time after this there was a little boy in the same monastery who had long been greatly troubled with recurrent fevers. One day when he was anxiously expecting a return of his trouble, one of the brethren came in and said to him, 'My son, would you like me to tell you how you can be cured of your troublesome sickness? Get up, come to the church, and go up to the tomb of Oswald. Sit down there and remain quietly beside the tomb and see that you do not go out nor move from the spot until the time for the return of your fever has passed. Then I will come in and take you away.' The boy did as he had been told; as he sat by the tomb of the saint the disease did not venture to attack him; indeed it fled away in such terror that it did not dare to touch him either on the second or the third day or at any time afterwards. The brother who told me of the incident and had come from the monastery added that, at the time he was speaking to me, the boy to whom this miracle of healing happened was still at the monastery, though now a grown man. It is not to be wondered at that the prayers of this king who is now reigning with the Lord should greatly prevail, for while he was ruling over his temporal kingdom, he was always accustomed to work and pray most diligently for the kingdom which is eternal.

It is related, for example, that very often he would continue in prayer from mattins until daybreak; and because of his frequent habit of prayer and thanksgiving, he was always accustomed, wherever he sat, to place his hands on his knees with the palms turned upwards. It is also a tradition which has become proverbial, that he died with a prayer on his lips. When he was beset by the weapons of his enemies and saw that he was about to perish he prayed for the souls of his army. So the proverb runs, 'May God have mercy on their souls, as Oswald said when he fell to the earth.'

So Oswald's bones were translated to the monastery we have mentioned and there interred. The king who slew him ordered his head and his hands to be severed from his body and hung on stakes. A year afterwards, his successor Oswiu came thither with an army and took them away. He buried the head in a burial-place in the church at Lindisfarne, but the hands and arms he buried in the royal city of Bamburgh.

CHAPTER 13

NOT only did the fame* of this renowned king spread through all parts of Britain but the beams of his healing light also spread across the ocean and reached the realms of Germany and Ireland. For example, the most reverend Bishop Acca* is accustomed to tell how, when he was on his way to Rome, he and his own Bishop Wilfrid stayed with the saintly Willibrord,* archbishop of the Frisians, and often heard the archbishop describe the miracles which happened in that kingdom at the relics of the most reverend king. He also related how, while he was still only a priest, and living a pilgrim's life in Ireland out of love for his eternal fatherland, the fame of Oswald's sanctity had spread far and wide in that island too. One of these miracle stories which he told I have thought worth including in the present *History*.

'At the time of the plague', he said, 'which caused widespread havoc both in Britain and Ireland one of the many victims was a certain Irish scholar, a man learned in literary studies but utterly careless and unconcerned about his own everlasting salvation. When he realized that he was near death, he trembled to think that, as soon as he was dead, he would be snatched away to the bondage of hell because of his sins. As I happened to be near by, he sent for me and, trembling and sighing in his weakness, tearfully told me his troubles. "You see", he said, "that I am getting worse and have now reached the point of death; nor do I doubt that, after the death of my body, my soul will immediately be snatched to everlasting death to suffer the torments of hell; for in spite of all my study of the scriptures, it has long been my custom to entangle myself in vice rather than obey God's commands. But I have made up my mind, if, by the grace of Heaven I am granted any further term of life, to correct my vicious ways and to devote my whole heart and life to obeying the divine will. I know indeed that it will not be through any merits of my own that I shall receive a new lease of life, nor can I hope to receive it unless perhaps God should deign to grant me forgiveness, wretched and unworthy though I am, through the intercession of those who have served him faithfully. Now we have heard a wide-spread report about an extremely holy king of your race named Oswald, and how since his death the occurrence of frequent miracles has borne witness to his outstanding faith and virtue. So I beg you, if you have any of his relics with you, to bring them to me, so that the Lord may perhaps have mercy upon me through his merits." I answered, "I have some of the wooden stake on which his head was fixed by the heathen after he was killed. If you firmly believe with all your heart, God, in His grace, can grant you a longer term of earthly life through the merits of this man and also fit you to enter into eternal life." He at once answered that he had complete faith in it. Then I blessed some water, put a splinter of the oak into it, and gave it to the sick man to drink. He immediately felt better, recovered from his sickness, and lived for many years. He turned to the Lord in heart and deed and, wherever he went, he proclaimed the goodness of the merciful Creator and the glory of His faithful servant.'

CHAPTER 14

AFTER Oswald had been translated to the heavenly kingdom, his brother Oswiu* succeeded to his earthly kingdom in his place, as a young man of about thirty, and ruled for twenty-eight troubled years. He was attacked by the heathen people, the Mercians, who had slain his brother, and in addition, by his own son Alhfrith* and his nephew Oethelwald,* the son of his brother and predecessor.

In his second year, that is in the year of our Lord 644, the most reverend father Paulinus, once bishop of York and then of Rochester, departed to be with the Lord on 10 October having held the office of bishop for nineteen years, two months, and twenty-one days. He was buried in the sanctuary of the church of the blessed apostle Andrew, which King Æthelberht had built from its foundations at Rochester. In his place Archbishop Honorius consecrated Ithamar,* a man of

131

Kentish extraction but the equal of his predecessors in learning and in holiness of life.

At the beginning of his reign Oswiu had as a partner in the royal dignity a man called Oswine,* of the family of King Edwin, a son of Osric who has already been mentioned. He was a man of great piety and religion and ruled the kingdom of Deira for seven years in the greatest prosperity, beloved by all. But Oswiu, who ruled over the rest of the northern land beyond the Humber, that is the kingdom of Bernicia, could not live at peace with him. The causes of dissension increased so greatly that Oswiu cruelly made an end of him. Each raised an army against the other but Oswine, realizing that he could not fight against an enemy with far greater resources, considered it wiser to give up the idea of war and wait for better times. So he disbanded the army which he had assembled at a place called *Wilfaræsdun*, that is the hill of Wilfare,* about ten miles north-west of the village of Catterick. He went with one faithful thegn named Tondhere and hid in the home of a *gesith* named Hunwold, whom he believed to be his friend. But alas, it was quite otherwise. The *gesith* betrayed him to Oswiu who caused him to be foully murdered, together with his thegn, by a reeve* called Æthelwine. This happened on 20 August, in the ninth year of his reign at a place called Gilling.* There in after days, to atone for his crime, a monastery was built in which prayers were to be offered daily to the Lord for the redemption of the souls of both kings, the murdered king and the one who ordered the murder.

King Oswine was tall and handsome, pleasant of speech, courteous in manner, and bountiful to nobles and commons alike; so it came about that he was beloved by all because of the royal dignity which showed itself in his character, his appearance, and his actions; and noblemen from almost every kingdom flocked to serve him as retainers. Among all the other graces of virtue and modesty with which, if I may say so, he was blessed in a special manner, his humility is said to have been the greatest, as a single example is enough to prove.

He had given Bishop Aidan an excellent horse so that, though he was normally accustomed to walk, he could ride if

he had to cross a river or if any other urgent necessity compelled him. A short time afterwards Aidan was met by a
beggar who asked him for an alms. He at once alighted and
offered the horse with all its royal trappings to the beggar; for
he was extremely compassionate, a friend of the poor and a
real father to the wretched. The king was told of this and,
happening to meet the bishop as they were going to dinner, he
said, 'My lord bishop, why did you want to give a beggar the
royal horse intended for you? Have we not many less valuable
horses or other things which would have been good enough to
give to the poor, without letting the beggar have the horse
which I had specially chosen for your own use?' The bishop at
once replied, 'O King, what are you saying? Surely this son of
a mare is not dearer to you than that son of God?' After these
words they went in to dine. The bishop sat down in his own
place and the king, who had just come in from hunting, stood
warming himself by the fire with his thegns. Suddenly he
remembered the bishop's words; at once he took off his
sword, gave it to a thegn, and then hastening to where the
bishop sat, threw himself at his feet and asked his pardon.
'Never from henceforth', he said, 'will I speak of this again
nor will I form any opinion as to what money of mine or how
much of it you should give to the sons of God.' When the
bishop saw this he was greatly alarmed; he got up immediately
and raised the king to his feet, declaring that he would be
perfectly satisfied if only the king would banish his sorrow
and sit down to the feast. The king, in accordance with the
bishop's entreaties and commands, recovered his spirits, but
the bishop, on the other hand, grew sadder and sadder and at
last began to shed tears. Thereupon a priest asked him in his
native tongue, which the king and his thegns did not understand, why he was weeping, and Aidan answered, 'I know that
the king will not live long; for I never before saw a humble
king. Therefore I think that he will very soon be snatched
from this life; for this nation does not deserve to have such a
ruler.' Not long after, the bishop's gloomy forebodings were
fulfilled in the sad death of the king which we have already
described. Bishop Aidan only lived for twelve days after the
murder of the king whom he loved; for he was taken from the

world on 31 August and received from the Lord the eternal reward of his labours.

CHAPTER 15

HE who judges the heart showed by signs and miracles what Aidan's merits were, and of these miracles it will be enough to set down three, which deserve to be remembered. There was a certain priest named Utta,* a man of great worth and sincerity and accordingly honoured by all, including the secular rulers; he was sent to Kent to bring back Eanflæd* to be Oswiu's queen. She was the daughter of Edwin and had been taken away there when her father was killed. Utta intended to travel to Kent by land but to return with the maiden by sea; so he went to Bishop Aidan and begged him to pray to the Lord for himself and those who were to make the long journey with him. Aidan blessed them, commended them to the Lord, and gave them some holy oil, saying, 'I know that when you board your ship, you will meet storms and contrary winds; but remember to pour the oil I have given you on to the sea; the winds will drop at once, the sea will become calm and serene and will bring you home the way you wish.' All this happened just as the bishop had foretold; at first the sea was stormy and the sailors attempted to hold the ship by throwing out the anchor, but all to no purpose. The waves swept over the ship from all sides; the vessel began to fill and they all realized that death was imminent and that their last hour had come, when the priest, remembering the bishop's words, took out the flask and poured some of the oil into the sea. At once, as Aidan had predicted, the sea calmed down. So it came to pass that the man of God foretold the tempest by the spirit of prophecy, and, by virtue of the same spirit, calmed it when it had arisen, although he was absent in body. I heard the story of this miracle from no dubious source, but from a most trustworthy priest of our church named Cynemund, who declared that he had heard it from the priest Utta on whom and through whom the miracle was wrought.

CHAPTER 16

ANOTHER memorable miracle is related about Aidan by many who were in a position to know. During the time of his episcopate a hostile Mercian army, under the leadership of Penda, which had been cruelly devastating the kingdom of Northumbria far and wide, reached the royal city* called after a former queen Bebba (Bamburgh). As he could not capture it by assault or siege, he attempted to set it on fire. He pulled down all the steadings which he found in the neighbourhood of the town and brought thither a vast heap of beams, rafters, walls of wattles, and thatched roofs, and built them up to an immense height around that side of the city which faced the land; then when a favourable wind arose, he set it on fire in an attempt to burn the town. At that time the reverend Bishop Aidan was staying on Farne Island, which is less than two miles from the city. He often used to retire there to pray in solitude and silence; in fact the site of his solitary habitation is shown on the island to this day. When he saw the tongues of flame and the smoke being carried by the winds right above the city walls, the story goes that he raised his eyes and hands towards heaven and said with tears, 'Oh Lord, see how much evil Penda is doing.' As soon as he had uttered these words, the winds veered away from the city and carried the flames in the direction of those who had kindled them, so that, as some of them were hurt and all of them terrified, they ceased to make any further attempt on the city, realizing that it was divinely protected.

CHAPTER 17

AT the time when death came upon him, after completing seventeen years as bishop, Aidan was on a royal estate, not far away from the city of which we have been speaking. Here he had a church and a cell where he often used to go and stay, travelling about in the neighbourhood to preach. He did the same on the other royal estates; for he had no possessions of his own except the church and a small piece of land around it. They erected a tent for him during his illness, at the west end of the church, the tent itself being attached to the church wall. So it happened that he breathed his last, leaning against the buttress which supported the church on the outside. He died on 31 August, in the seventeenth year of his episcopate. His body was shortly afterwards translated to the island of Lindisfarne and buried in the cemetery of the brothers. Some time afterwards, when a larger church had been built there and dedicated in honour of the most blessed chief of the apostles, his bones were translated to it and buried on the right side of the altar, with the honour due to so great a bishop.

Finan,* who had also been sent from the Irish island monastery of Iona, succeeded him in the bishopric, and remained bishop for no short time. Now it happened a few years afterwards that Penda, king of Mercia, came with a hostile army to these parts destroying everything he could with fire and sword; and the village in which the bishop had died, together with the church just mentioned, was burnt down. But it was astonishing that the buttress alone, against which the bishop had been leaning when he died, could not be devoured by the flames though they destroyed everything around it. When the fame of the miracle spread, the church was speedily restored in the same place and the buttress was placed outside as before to strengthen the walls. Shortly afterwards it happened that the same village and church were again burned down, this time through culpable carelessness. But on this occasion too the flames could not touch the buttress. The miracle was such that, though the flames had entered the very nail holes by which it was attached to the building, yet they could not injure the buttress itself. So when the church was rebuilt for the third time, they put the buttress, not outside as before to support the structure, but inside the church itself as a memorial of the miracle, so that people entering the church could kneel there and ask for God's mercy. Since that time many are known to have obtained the grace of healing at this place; and by cutting splinters from the buttress and putting them into water, they have found the means of curing the sicknesses of themselves and their friends.

I have written these things about the character and work of Aidan, not by any means commending or praising his lack of knowledge in the matter of the observance of Easter; indeed I heartily detest it, as I have clearly shown in the book which I wrote called *De Temporibus*,* but, as a truthful historian, I have described in a straightforward manner those things which were done by him or through him, praising such of his qualities as are worthy of praise and preserving their memory for the benefit of my readers. Such were his love of peace and charity, temperance and humility; his soul which triumphed over anger and greed and at the same time despised pride and vainglory; his industry in carrying out and teaching the divine commandments, his diligence in study and keeping vigil, his authority, such as became a priest, in reproving the proud and the mighty, and his tenderness in comforting the weak, in relieving and protecting the poor. To put it briefly, so far as one can learn from those who knew him, he made it his business to omit none of the commands of the evangelists, the apostles, and the prophets, but he set himself to carry them out in his deeds, so far as he was able. All these things I greatly admire and love in this bishop and I have no doubt that all this was pleasing to God. But I neither praise nor approve of him in so far as he did not observe Easter at the proper time, either because he was ignorant of the canonical time or because, if he knew it, he was compelled by the force of public opinion not to follow it. But, nevertheless, I do approve of this, that in his celebration of Easter he had no other thought in his heart, he reverenced and preached no other doctrine than we do, namely the redemption of the human race by the passion, resurrection, and ascension into heaven of the one mediator between God and men, even the man Christ Jesus. And therefore he always kept Easter, not as some falsely believe, on the fourteenth day of the moon, like the Jews, no matter what the day of the week was, but on the Lord's Day which fell between the fourteenth and the twentieth day of the moon. He did this because of his belief that the resurrection of our Lord took place on the first day of the week and also in hope of our resurrection which he, together with holy Church, believed would undoubtedly happen on this same first day of the week now called the Lord's Day.

CHAPTER 18

ABOUT this time, Sigeberht* came to the throne of East Anglia after the death of his brother Eorpwald,* who was Rædwald's successor. Sigeberht was a good and religious man and had long been in exile in Gaul, while he was fleeing from the enmity of Rædwald.* It was here that he received baptism and, when he returned to his own land to become king, he at once sought to imitate some of the excellent institutions which he had seen in Gaul, and established a school where boys could be taught letters, with the help of Bishop Felix, who had come to him from Kent and who provided him with masters and teachers as in the Kentish school. So greatly did he love the kingdom of heaven that at last he resigned his kingly office and entrusted it to his kinsman Ecgric,* who had previously ruled over part of the kingdom. He thereupon entered a monastery which he himself had founded. He received the tonsure and made it his business to fight instead for the heavenly kingdom. When he had been in the monastery for some considerable time, it happened that the East Anglians were attacked by the Mercians under their King Penda. As the East Anglians realized that they were no match for their enemies, they asked Sigeberht to go into the fight with them in order to inspire the army with confidence. He was unwilling and refused, so they dragged him to the fight from the monastery, in the hope that the soldiers would be less afraid and less ready to flee if they had with them one who was once their most vigorous and distinguished leader. But remembering his profession and surrounded though he was by a splendid army, he refused to carry anything but a staff in his hand. He was killed together with King Ecgric, and the whole army was either slain or scattered by the heathen attacks.

Their successor on the throne was Anna, son of Eni,* an excellent man of royal descent and the father of a distinguished family, whom we must speak of again in the proper place; he also was slain later on, like his predecessors, by the heathen Mercian leader.

CHAPTER 19

WHILE Sigeberht was still ruling, there came a holy man from Ireland called Fursa;* he was renowned in word and deed and remarkable for his singular virtues. He was anxious to live the life of a pilgrim* for the Lord's sake, wherever opportunity offered. When he came to the kingdom of the East Angles, he was honourably received by the king and followed his usual task of preaching the gospel. Thus he converted many both by the example of his virtues and the persuasiveness of his teaching, turning unbelievers to Christ and confirming believers in His faith and love.

Once when he was suffering from an illness, he was counted worthy to enjoy a vision of angels, in which he was directed to maintain diligently the task that he had undertaken of ministering the Word, and to continue to watch and pray and not be weary, because death was certain but the hour of death uncertain, as the Lord said, 'Watch, therefore, for ye know neither the day nor the hour.' After he had been strengthened by the vision, he set himself with all speed to build a monastery on a site which he had received from King Sigeberht and to establish there the observance of a Rule. Now the monastery was pleasantly situated close to the woods and the sea, in a Roman camp which is called in English *Cnobheresburg*, that is the city of Cnobhere* (Burgh Castle). The king of that realm, Anna, and his nobles afterwards endowed it with still finer buildings and gifts.

He was a man of very noble Irish race, but still nobler in spirit than by birth. From his boyhood's days he had devoted all his energy to the study of sacred books and to the monastic discipline; furthermore, as a saint should, he earnestly sought to do whatever he learned to be his duty. What more need be said? As time went on he built a monastery for himself where he could more freely devote himself to his divine studies. On one occasion when he was attacked by illness, as his Life fully describes, he was snatched from the body; he quitted it from evening to cock crow and during that time he was privileged to gaze upon the angelic hosts and to listen to their blessed songs of praise. He used to say that he heard them sing among other songs, 'The saints shall go from strength to strength', and again, 'The God of gods shall be seen in Sion'. He returned to his body and, two days afterwards, was taken out of it a second time and saw not only the very great joys of the blessed but also the fierce onslaughts of the evil spirits who, by their manifold accusations, wickedly sought to prevent his journey to heaven; but they failed utterly for he was protected by angels. If anyone wishes to know more of these matters, let him read the book I have mentioned and I think that he will gain great spiritual benefit from it. There he will learn with what subtlety and deceit the devils reported Fursa's deeds, his idle words, and his very thoughts, just as if they had written them down in a book; and the joyful and sad things that he learned both from the angels and from the righteous men who appeared to him in the company of the angels.

But there is one of these incidents which we have thought it might be helpful to many to include in this history. When Fursa had been taken up to a great height, he was told by the angels who were conducting him to look back at the world. As he looked down, he saw some kind of dark valley immediately beneath him and four fires in the air, not very far from one another. When he asked the angels what these fires were, he was told that they were the fires which were to kindle and consume the world. One of them is falsehood, when we do not fulfil our promise to renounce Satan and all his works as we undertook to do at our baptism; the second is covetousness, when we put the love of riches before the love of heavenly things; the third is discord, when we do not fear to offend our neighbours even in trifling matters; the fourth is injustice, when we think it a small thing to despoil and defraud the weak. Gradually these fires grew together and merged into one vast conflagration. As it approached him, he cried out in fear to the angel, 'Look, sir, the fire is coming near me.' But the angel answered, 'That which you did not kindle will not burn you; for although the conflagration seems great and terrible, it tests each man according to his deserts, and the evil desires of everyone will be burned away in this fire. For just as in the body a man burns with illicit pleasures, so when he is free from the body, he makes due atonement by burning.' Then he saw one of the three angels who had been his guides throughout both visions go forward and divide the flames, while the other two flew on each side of him to defend him from the peril of the conflagration. He also saw devils flying through the flames and stirring up fires of hostility against the righteous. There follow, in the book, the accusations of the evil spirits against himself, the defence of the good spirits, and a fuller vision of the heavenly hosts, as well as of the saints of his own nation, whose names he knew by repute and who had been devoted priests in days gone by. From them he learned many things valuable both to himself and to those who might be willing to listen. When they had finished speaking and had returned to heaven in their turn with the angelic spirits, the three angels we have mentioned remained with Fursa to restore him to his body. When they approached the conflagration, the angel, as before, parted the flames. But when the man of God came to the passage opened up in the midst of the fire, the evil spirits seized one of those who were burning in the flames, hurled him at Fursa, hitting him and scorching his shoulder and jaw. Fursa recognized the man and remembered that on his death he had received some of his clothing. The angel took the man and cast him back at once into the fire. The spiteful foe said, 'Do not reject him whom you once acknowledged; for, since you have received the property of a sinner, you ought to share in his punishment.' The angel withstood him saying, 'He did not receive it out of greed but to save his soul.' The fire then died down and the angel turned to Fursa and said, 'You were burned by the fire you had kindled. For if you had not received the property of this man who died in his sins, you would not have been burned by the fire of his punishment.' He then went on to give helpful advice as to what should be done for the salvation of those who repented in the hour of death. When Fursa had been restored to his body, he bore for the rest of his life the marks of the burns which he had suffered while a disembodied spirit; they were visible to all on his shoulder and his jaw. It is marvellous to think that what he suffered secretly as a disembodied spirit showed openly upon his flesh. He always took care, as he had done before, to encourage all both by his sermons and by his example to practise virtue. But he would only give an account of his visions to those who questioned him about them, because they desired to repent. An aged brother is still living in our monastery who is wont to relate that a most truthful and pious man told him that he had seen Fursa himself in the kingdom of the East Angles and had heard these visions from his own mouth. He added that although it was during a time of severe winter weather and a hard frost and though Fursa sat wearing only a thin garment, yet as he told his story, he sweated as though it were the middle of summer, either because of the terror or else the joy which his recollections aroused.

To return to what we were saying before, he preached the word of God in Ireland for many years until, when he could no longer endure the noise of the crowds who thronged to him, he gave up all that he seemed to have and left his native island. He came with a few companions through the land of the Britons and into the kingdom of the East Angles, where he preached the Word and there, as we have said, built a monastery. Having duly accomplished all this, he longed to free himself from all worldly affairs, even those of the monastery itself; so leaving his brother Foillán* in charge of the monastery and its souls and also the priests Gobán and Dícuill and, being free from all worldly cares, he resolved to end his life as a hermit. He had another brother called Ultán,* who, after a long time of probation in the monastery, had passed on to the life of a hermit. So Fursa sought him out in his solitude and for a whole year lived with him in austerity and prayer, labouring daily with his hands. Then, seeing that the kingdom was disturbed by heathen invasions* and that the monasteries were also threatened with danger, he left all things in order and sailed for Gaul, where he was honourably entertained by Clovis,* king of the Franks, and by the patrician Eorcenwold. He built a monastery in a place called Lagny,* where, not long afterwards, he was taken ill and died.

The patrician Erchinoald took his body and placed it in one of the chapels of the church which he was building in his own town called Péronne, until such time as the church was dedicated. This happened twenty-seven days afterwards, when the body was translated from the chapel and reburied near the altar. It was found as whole as if he had died that very hour. Four years afterwards, when a very beautiful shrine was built for the reception of his body, on the east side of the altar, it was still found without taint of corruption and was translated thither with all due honour. It is well known that through the mediation of God, many miracles have been performed there to show his merits. We have briefly touched on these matters and about the incorruption of his body so that readers may clearly know how eminent a man he was. All these subjects, as well as an account of his fellow warriors, will be found more fully set out in his Life for all those who wish to read it.

CHAPTER 20

MEANWHILE Felix died seventeen years after becoming bishop of the East Angles, and Honorius consecrated in his place his deacon named Thomas* who belonged to the nation of the Gyrwe.* When he died five years afterwards, Honorius put in his place Berhtgisl, also named Boniface,* from the kingdom of Kent. Then Honorius himself, after he had finished his course, departed in the year of our Lord 653, on 30 September. After the see had been vacant for eighteen months, Deusdedit, a West Saxon by race, was elected sixth archbishop of Canterbury. Ithamar, bishop of Rochester, went thither to consecrate him. He was consecrated on 26 March and ruled the church for nine years, four months, and two days. Deusdedit,* on the death of Ithamar, consecrated Damian* in his place, a man of the South Saxon race.

CHAPTER 21

AT this time the Middle Angles,* that is the Angles of the Midlands, accepted the faith and the mysteries of the truth under their chief Peada who was the son of King Penda. As he was a most noble youth, worthy both of the name and office of king, he was placed by his father on the throne of the kingdom of the Middle Angles. He thereupon went to Oswiu, and asked for the hand of his daughter Alhflæd. But his request was granted only on condition that he and his nation accepted the Christian faith and baptism. When Peada heard the truth proclaimed and the promises of the kingdom of heaven, the hope of resurrection and of future immortality, he gladly declared himself ready to become a Christian even though he were refused the hand of the maiden. He was earnestly persuaded to accept the faith by Alhfrith, son of King Oswiu, who was his brother-in-law and friend,* having married Penda's daughter, Cyneburh.*

So Peada was baptized by Bishop Finan together with all the *gesiths* and thegns who had come with him, as well as all their servants, at a famous royal estate called *Ad Murum** (Wallbottle?). He took four priests with him who were considered suitable, by reason of their learning and character, to teach and baptize his people, and so he returned home joyfully. The priests were Cedd,* Adda, Betti, and Diuma,* the last of whom was an Irishman while the others were English. Adda was the brother of the famous priest Utta,* abbot of the monastery at the place called Gateshead, already mentioned. After these priests had come with the king into his kingdom, they preached the Word and were listened to gladly, so that many, both nobles and commons, renounced the filth of idolatry and were washed in the fountain of the faith.

Now King Penda did not forbid the preaching of the Word, even in his own Mercian kingdom, if any wished to hear it. But he hated and despised those who, after they had accepted the Christian faith, were clearly lacking in the works of faith. He said that they were despicable and wretched creatures who scorned to obey the God in whom they believed. All this started two years before Penda's death. When he was killed and the Christian King Oswiu had gained the throne of Mercia, as we shall describe later, Diuma, one of the four priests already mentioned, was consecrated bishop of the Middle Angles and the Mercians by Bishop Finan, since a shortage of bishops made it necessary for one bishop to be set over both nations. After he had won no small number for the Lord in a short space of time, he died in the country of the Middle Angles in a district called *Infeppingum.** Ceollach* became bishop after him, another man of Irish race, who, not long after, left his bishopric and returned to the island of Iona where the Irish monastery was, which was chief and head of many monasteries. Trumhere followed him as bishop, a pious man trained in the monastic life, who though of English race was consecrated bishop by the Irish. This happened in the time of King Wulfhere, of whom we shall have more to say hereafter.

CHAPTER 22

ABOUT this time the East Saxons, at the instance of King Oswiu, received the faith which they had once rejected when they expelled Bishop Mellitus. Now Sigeberht* was king of this people, successor of Sigeberht the Small* and friend of King Oswiu. The latter used to urge Sigeberht, on his frequent visits to the kingdom of Northumbria, to realize that objects made by the hands of men could not be gods. Neither wood nor stone were materials from which gods could be created, the remnants of which were either burned in the fire or made into vessels for men's use or else cast out as refuse, trodden underfoot and reduced to dust. God must rather be looked upon as incomprehensible in His majesty, invisible to human eyes, omnipotent, eternal, Creator of heaven and earth and of mankind, who rules over the world and will judge it in righteousness. We must believe that His eternal abode is in heaven, not in base and perishable metal. It is therefore only right to believe that all those who learn to do the will of

Him by whom they were created will receive from Him an eternal reward. King Oswiu often put forward these and many other similar reasons to King Sigeberht in friendly and brotherly counsel until at last, supported by the consent of his friends, he believed. He took counsel with his followers and, after he had addressed them, they all agreed to accept the faith and so he was baptized with them by Bishop Finan in the royal estate mentioned above called *Ad Murum** (Wallbottle?) because it stands close to the wall which the Romans once built across the island of Britain. It is about twelve miles from the east coast.

So King Sigeberht returned to the seat of his temporal kingdom, having been made a citizen of the eternal kingdom. He asked King Oswiu to send him teachers to convert his people to the faith of Christ and wash them in the fountain of salvation. Oswiu thereupon sent to the kingdom of the Middle Angles and summoned the man of God, Cedd,* to his presence. He gave him another priest as a companion and sent them to preach the Word to the East Saxons. After these priests had traversed the whole kingdom and built up a great Church for the Lord, it happened that on a certain occasion Cedd returned home and came to Lindisfarne to consult with Bishop Finan. Finan, finding that his evangelistic work had prospered, made him bishop of the East Saxons, summoning two other bishops to assist in the consecration. Cedd, having received the rank of a bishop, returned to his kingdom carrying on with greater authority the work he had begun. He established churches in various places and ordained priests and deacons to assist him in preaching the word of faith and in the administration of baptism, especially in the city called *Ythancæstir* in the Saxon tongue (Bradwell-on-Sea) and also in the place called Tilbury. The former is on the river *Penta* (Blackwater) and the latter on the banks of the Thames. In these places he gathered together a multitude of Christ's servants and taught them to observe the discipline of a Rule, so far as these rough people were capable of receiving it.

For a long time the instruction of the people in the heavenly life prospered day by day in the kingdom, to the joy of the king and the whole nation; but it then happened that the king was murdered, at the instigation of the enemy of all good men, by his own kinsmen. It was two brothers who perpetrated the crime. When they were asked why they did it, they could make no reply except that they were angry with the king and hated him because he was too ready to pardon his enemies, calmly forgiving them for the wrongs they had done him, as soon as they asked his pardon. Such was the crime for which he met his death, that he had devoutly observed the gospel precepts. But nevertheless, by this innocent death a real offence was punished in accordance with the prophecy of the man of God. For one of these *gesiths* who murdered him was unlawfully married, a marriage which the bishop had been unable to prevent or correct. So he excommunicated him and ordered all who would listen to him not to enter the man's house nor take food with him. But the king disregarded this command and accepted an invitation of the *gesith* to dine at his house. As the king was coming away, the bishop met him. When the king saw him, he leapt from his horse and fell trembling at the bishop's feet, asking his pardon. The bishop, who was also on horseback, alighted too. In his anger he touched the prostrate king with his staff which he was holding in his hand, and exercising his episcopal authority, he uttered these words, 'I declare to you that, because you were unwilling to avoid the house of this man who is lost and damned, you will meet your death in this very house.' Yet we may be sure that the death of this religious king was such that it not only atoned for his offence but even increased his merit; for it came about as a result of his piety and his observance of Christ's command.

Swithhelm,* the son of Seaxbald, was successor to Sigeberht. He was baptized by Cedd in East Anglia, in the royal village called Rendlesham,* that is, the residence of Rendil. King Æthelwold* of East Anglia, the brother of King Anna, a previous king of the East Angles, was his sponsor.

CHAPTER 23

WHILE Cedd was acting as bishop of the East Saxons, he used very often to revisit his own land, the kingdom of

Northumbria, to preach. Oethelwald,* son of King Oswald who reigned over Deira, seeing that Cedd was a wise, holy, and upright man, asked him to accept a grant of land, on which to build a monastery where he himself might frequently come to pray and hear the Word and where he might be buried; for he firmly believed that the daily prayers of those who served God there would greatly help him. This king had previously had with him Cælin, Cedd's brother, a man equally devoted to God, who had been accustomed to minister the word and the sacraments of the faith to himself and his family; for he was a priest. It was through him chiefly that the king had got to know and had learned to love the bishop. So, in accordance with the king's desire, Cedd chose himself a site for the monastery amid some steep and remote hills which seemed better fitted for the haunts of robbers and the dens of wild beasts than for human habitation; so that, as Isaiah says, 'In the habitations where once dragons lay, shall be grass with reeds and rushes',* that is, the fruit of good works shall spring up where once beasts dwelt or where men lived after the manner of beasts.

The man of God was anxious first of all to cleanse the site which he had received for the monastery from the stain of former crimes by prayer and fasting, before laying the foundations. So he asked the king to grant him permission and opportunity to spend the whole of the approaching season of Lent there in prayer. Every day except Sunday he prolonged his fast until evening as his custom was and then he took nothing but a small quantity of bread, one hen's egg, and a little milk mixed with water. He explained that this was a custom of those from whom he had learned the discipline of a Rule that, when they had received a site for building a monastery or a church, they should first consecrate it to the Lord with prayer and fasting. But ten days before the end of Lent, a messenger came to summon him to the king. Thereupon in order that this holy labour might not be interrupted because of the king's affairs, he asked his own brother Cynebill, who was a priest, to complete the sacred task. The latter gladly agreed and, when the work of fasting and prayer was ended, he built a monastery now called Lastingham and established in it the religious observances according to the usage of Lindisfarne where he had been brought up.

When Cedd had been bishop in the kingdom for many years and had borne the responsibility of this monastery, whose rules he had established,* he happened to come to it while the plague was raging there, fell sick and died. He was first of all buried outside the walls, but in course of time a stone church was built in the monastery in honour of the blessed Mother of God, and his body was buried in it on the right side of the altar.

The bishop left the monastery to be governed after him by his brother Chad who was afterwards consecrated bishop as we shall hear later. There were then four brothers whom we have mentioned, Cedd, Cynebill, Cælin and Chad, who were all famous priests of the Lord, a very rare thing to happen, and two of them reached the rank of bishop. When the brothers who were in his monastery in the kingdom of the East Saxons heard that the bishop was dead and buried in the kingdom of Northumbria, about thirty of them came from that monastery, wishing to live near the body of their father* or, if the Lord so willed, to die and be buried there. They were gladly received by their brothers and fellow soldiers in Christ, but another attack of the pestilence came upon them and they all died, with the exception of one small boy who was preserved from death by the intercession of Cedd his father. After a long time devoted to the reading of the scriptures, a moment came when he realized that he had not been baptized. He was speedily washed in the waters of the font of salvation and afterwards admitted to priest's orders, rendering useful service to many in the church. I do not doubt that he was delivered from the jaws of death by the intercession of his father Cedd, to whose tomb he had come out of love for him; so he himself escaped eternal death and, by his teaching, exercised a ministry of life and salvation for the brethren.

CHAPTER 24

ABOUT this time King Oswiu was exposed to the savage and insupportable attacks of Penda, so often mentioned before, the king of the Mercians who had killed Oswiu's brother. Oswiu was at last forced to promise him an incalculable and incredible store of royal treasures and gifts as the price of peace, on condition that Penda would return home and cease to devastate, or rather utterly destroy, the kingdoms under his rule. But the heathen king would not accept this offer, for he was determined to destroy and exterminate the whole people* from the greatest to the least; as Oswiu turned to God's mercy for help seeing that nothing else could save them from this barbarous and evil enemy. Oswiu therefore bound himself with an oath, saying, 'If the heathen foe will not accept our gifts, let us offer them to Him who will, even the Lord our God.' So he vowed that if he gained the victory he would dedicate his daughter to the Lord as a holy virgin and give twelve small estates to build monasteries. In this spirit he entered the fight with his tiny army. Indeed it is said that the heathens had an army which was thirty times as great. They had thirty legions of soldiers experienced in war and commanded by the most famous ealdormen; King Oswiu and his son Alhfrith,* as we have said, had a very small force but they met the foe trusting in Christ their leader. Oswiu's other son Ecgfrith* was at the time a hostage in the Mercian kingdom with Queen Cynewise.* But Oethelwald, King Oswald's son, who ought to have helped them, was on the side of his foes and was leading the enemies of his own uncle and of his native land; he withdrew, however, in the hour of battle and awaited the outcome in a place of safety. The battle was joined and the heathen were put to flight or destroyed; of the thirty royal ealdormen who had come to Penda's help nearly all were killed. Among them was Æthelhere,* brother and successor to Anna, king of the East Angles and the cause of the war; he was cut down, having suffered the loss of all his thegns and followers. The battle was fought near the river Winwæd* which, owing to heavy rains, had overflowed its channels and its banks to such an extent that many more were drowned in flight than were destroyed by the sword in battle.

Then King Oswiu, in fulfilment of his vow to the Lord, returned thanks to God for the victory granted him and gave his daughter Ælfflæd,* who was scarcely a year old, to be consecrated to God in perpetual virginity. He also gave twelve small estates on which, as they were freed from any concern about earthly military service, a site and means might be provided for the monks to wage heavenly warfare and to pray with unceasing devotion that the race might win eternal peace. Six of the estates which he gave were in Deira and six in Bernicia. Each estate consisted of ten hides* so that there were a hundred and twenty hides altogether. Oswiu's daughter who had been dedicated to God entered the monastery named *Heruteu* (Hartlepool), that is, the island of the hart, over which Hild was then abbess. Two years later she gained possession of ten hides in the place known as *Streanæshealh* (Whitby) and there built a monastery; in it the king's daughter was first a pupil and then she became a teacher, of life under the Rule; then, about the age of sixty, the blessed virgin departed to be united with her heavenly bridegroom. She is buried in this monastery together with her father Oswiu, her mother Eanflæd, her grandfather Edwin, and many other nobles, all in the church of the holy apostle Peter. King Oswiu brought the campaign to a close in the district of *Loidis* (Leeds) on 15 November in the thirteenth year of his reign, to the great benefit of both peoples; for he freed his own subjects from the hostile devastations of the heathen people and converted the Mercians and the neighbouring kingdoms to a state of grace in the Christian faith, having destroyed their heathen ruler.

The first bishop in the kingdom of Mercia, of Lindsey, and the Middle Angles was Diuma: as has already been said, he died and was buried among the Middle Angles. The second bishop was Ceollach, who resigned his bishopric before his death and returned to Ireland, for both he and Diuma were Irish. The third bishop was Trumhere, an Englishman but educated and consecrated by the Irish. He was abbot of the monastery called Gilling, the place where King Oswine was killed, as described above. Queen Eanflæd, his kinswoman, had asked King Oswiu to expiate Oswine's unjust death by granting God's servant Trumhere, also a near relative of the murdered king, a site at Gilling to build a monastery; in it prayer was continually to be said for the eternal welfare of both kings, for the one who planned the murder and for his victim. King Oswiu ruled over the Mercian race, as well as the rest of the southern kingdoms, for three years after King Penda was killed. Oswiu also subjected the greater part of the Pictish race* to the dominion of the English.

At this time Oswiu gave Peada,* the son of King Penda, the kingdom of Southern Mercia because he was his kinsman. It was said to consist of 5,000 hides,* being divided by the river Trent from Northern Mercia, which is 7,000 hides in extent. But Peada was most foully murdered in the following spring by the treachery, or so it is said, of his wife during the very time of the Easter festival. Three years after King Penda's death the ealdormen of the Mercian race, Immin, Eafa, and Eadberht, rebelled against King Oswiu and set up as their king Wulfhere,* Penda's young son, whom they had kept concealed; and having driven out the ealdormen of the foreign king, they boldly recovered their lands and their liberty at the same time. So being free and having their own king, they rejoiced to serve their true king, Christ, for the sake of an everlasting kingdom in heaven. King Wulfhere ruled over the Mercians for seventeen years and had as his first bishop Trumhere,* whom we have already mentioned, his second, Jaruman,* his third, Chad* and his fourth, Winfrith.* All these in succession held the bishopric of the Mercians under King Wulfhere.

CHAPTER 25*

MEANWHILE, after Bishop Aidan's death, Finan succeeded him as bishop, having been consecrated and sent over by the Irish. He constructed a church on the island of Lindisfarne suitable for an episcopal see, building it after the Irish method, not of stone but of hewn oak, thatching it with reeds; later on the most reverend Archbishop Theodore* consecrated it in honour of the blessed apostle Peter. It was Eadberht,* who was bishop of Lindisfarne, who removed the reed thatch and had the whole of it, both roof and walls, covered with sheets of lead.

In those days there arose a great and active controversy about the keeping of Easter. Those who had come from Kent or Gaul declared that the Irish observance of Easter Sunday was contrary to the custom of the universal church. One most violent defender of the true Easter was Ronan* who, though Irish by race, had learned the true rules of the church in Gaul or Italy. In disputing with Finan* he put many right or at least encouraged them to make a more strict inquiry into the truth; but he could by no means put Finan right; on the contrary, as he was a man of fierce temper, Ronan made him the more bitter by his reproofs and turned him into an open adversary of the truth. James, once the deacon of the venerable Archbishop Paulinus, as we have already said, kept the true and catholic Easter with all those whom he could instruct in the better way. Queen Eanflæd and her people also observed it as she had seen it done in Kent, having with her a Kentish priest named Romanus who followed the catholic observance. Hence it is said that in these days it sometimes happened that Easter was celebrated twice in the same year, so that the king had finished the fast and was keeping Easter Sunday, while the queen and her people were still in Lent and observing Palm Sunday. This difference in the observance of Easter was patiently tolerated by all while Aidan was alive, because they had clearly understood that although he could not keep Easter otherwise than according to the manner of those who had sent him, he nevertheless laboured diligently to practise the works of faith, piety, and love, which is the mark of all the saints. He was therefore deservedly loved by all, including those who had other views about Easter. Not only was he respected by the ordinary people but also by bishops, such as Honorius of Kent and Felix of East Anglia.

When Finan, Aidan's successor, was dead and Colman,* who had also been sent from Ireland, had become bishop, a still more serious controversy arose concerning the observance of Easter as well as about other matters of ecclesiastical discipline. This dispute naturally troubled the minds and hearts of many people who feared that, though they had received the name of Christian, they were running or had run in vain. All this came to the ears of the rulers themselves,

Oswiu and his son Alhfrith. Oswiu, who had been educated and baptized by the Irish and was well versed in their language, considered that nothing was better than what they had taught. But Alhfrith had as his instructor in the Christian faith one Wilfrid, a most learned man who had once been to Rome to study church doctrine and had spent much time at Lyons with Dalfinus,* archbishop of Gaul, having received there his ecclesiastical tonsure in the form of a crown; so Alhfrith rightly preferred his teaching to all the traditions of the Irish and had therefore given him a monastery of forty hides in the place called Ripon.* He had presented the site, a short time before, to those who followed Irish ways; but because, when given the choice, they preferred to renounce the site rather than change their customs, he gave it to one who was worthy of the place both by his doctrine and his way of life. At that time there had come to the kingdom of Northumbria Agilbert, bishop of the West Saxons, whom we have mentioned before, a friend of Alhfrith and of Abbot Wilfrid; he stayed some time with them and, at the request of Alhfrith, he ordained Wilfrid priest in his own monastery. Agilbert had with him a priest called Agatho.

When this question of Easter and of the tonsure and other ecclesiastical matters was raised, it was decided to hold a council to settle the dispute at a monastery called *Streanæshealh* (Whitby), a name which means the bay of the lighthouse; at this time Hild, a woman devoted to God, was abbess. There came to the council the two kings, both father and son, Bishop Colman with his Irish clergy, and Agilbert with the priests Agatho and Wilfrid. James and Romanus were on their side while the Abbess Hild and her followers were on the side of the Irish; among these also was the venerable Bishop Cedd, who, as has been mentioned, had been consecrated long before by the Irish and who acted as a most careful interpreter* for both parties at the council.

First King Oswiu began by declaring that it was fitting that those who served one God should observe one rule of life and not differ in the celebration of the heavenly sacraments, seeing that they all hoped for one kingdom in heaven; they ought therefore to inquire as to which was the truer tradition and then all follow it together. He then ordered his bishop Colman to say first what were the customs which he followed and whence they originated. Colman thereupon said, 'The method of keeping Easter which I observe, I received from my superiors who sent me here as bishop; it was in this way that all our fathers, men beloved of God, are known to have celebrated it. Nor should this method seem contemptible and blameworthy seeing that the blessed evangelist John, the disciple whom the Lord specially loved, is said to have celebrated it thus, together with all the churches over which he presided.' When he had said all this and more to the same effect, the king ordered Agilbert to expound the method he observed, its origin and the authority he had for following it. Agilbert answered, 'I request that my disciple, the priest Wilfrid, may speak on my behalf, for we are both in agreement with the other followers of our church tradition who are here present; and he can explain our views in the English tongue better and more clearly than I can through an interpreter.' Then Wilfrid, receiving instructions from the king to speak, began thus: 'The Easter we keep is the same as we have seen universally celebrated in Rome, where the apostles St Peter and St Paul lived, taught, suffered, and were buried. We also found it in use everywhere in Italy and Gaul when we travelled through those countries for the purpose of study and prayer. We learned that it was observed at one and the same time in Africa, Asia, Egypt, Greece, and throughout the whole world, wherever the Church of Christ is scattered, amid various nations and languages. The only exceptions are these men and their accomplices in obstinacy, I mean the Picts and the Britons, who in these, the two remotest islands of the Ocean, and only in some parts of them, foolishly attempt to fight against the whole world.'

Colman answered, 'I wonder that you are willing to call our efforts foolish, seeing that we follow the example of that apostle who was reckoned worthy to recline on the breast of the Lord; for all the world acknowledges his great wisdom.' Wilfrid replied, 'Far be it from me to charge John with foolishness: he literally observed the decrees of the Mosaic law when the Church was still Jewish in many respects, at a time when the apostles were unable to bring to a sudden end the entire observance of that law which God ordained in the same way as, for instance, they made it compulsory on all new converts to abandon their idols which are of devilish origin. They feared, of course, that they might make a stumbling-block for the Jewish proselytes dispersed among the Gentiles. This was the reason why Paul circumcised Timothy, why he offered sacrifices in the temple, and why he shaved his head at Corinth in company with Aquila and Priscilla; all this was of no use except to avoid scandalizing the Jews. Hence James said to Paul, "Thou seest, brother, how many thousands there are among the Jews of them which have believed; and they are all zealous for the law." But in these days when the light of the Gospel is spreading throughout the world, it is not necessary, it is not even lawful for believers to be circumcised or to offer God sacrifices of flesh and blood. So John, in accordance with the custom of the law, began the celebration of Easter Day in the evening of the fourteenth day of the first month, regardless of whether it fell on the sabbath or any other day. But when Peter preached at Rome, remembering that the Lord rose from the dead and brought to the world the hope of the resurrection on the first day of the week, he realized that Easter ought to be kept as follows: he always waited for the rising of the moon on the evening of the fourteenth day of the first month in accordance with the custom and precepts of the law, just as John did, but when it had risen, if the Lord's Day, which was then called the first day of the week, followed in the morning, he proceeded to celebrate Easter as we are accustomed to do at the present time. But if the Lord's Day was due, not on the morning following the fourteenth day of the moon but on the sixteenth or seventeenth or any other day until the twenty-first, he waited for it, and began the holy Easter ceremonies the night before, that is, on the Saturday evening; so it came about that Easter Sunday was kept only between the fifteenth day of the moon and the twenty-first. So this evangelical and apostolic tradition does not abolish the law but rather fulfils it, by ordering the observance of Easter from the evening of the fourteenth day of the moon in the first month up to the twenty-first of the moon in the same month.

All the successors of St John in Asia since his death and also the whole church throughout the world have followed this observance. That this is the true Easter and that this alone must be celebrated by the faithful was not newly decreed but confirmed afresh by the Council of Nicaea as the history of the Church informs us.* So it is plain, Colman, that you neither follow the example of John, as you think, nor of Peter, whose tradition you knowingly contradict; and so, in your observance of Easter, you neither follow the law nor the gospel. For John who kept Easter according to the decrees of the Mosaic law, took no heed of the Sunday; you do not do this, for you celebrate Easter only on a Sunday. Peter celebrated Easter Sunday between the fifteenth and the twenty-first day of the moon; you, on the other hand, celebrate Easter Sunday between the fourteenth and the twentieth day of the moon. Thus you very often begin Easter on the evening of the thirteenth day of the moon, which is never mentioned in the law. This was not the day—it was the fourteenth, in which the Lord, the author and giver of the Gospel, ate the old passover in the evening and instituted the sacraments of the new testament to be celebrated by the church in remembrance of his passion. Besides, in your celebration of Easter you utterly exclude the twenty-first day, which the law of Moses specially ordered to be observed. So, as I have said, in your celebration of the greatest of the festivals you agree neither with John nor Peter, neither with the law nor the Gospel.'

Colman replied, 'Did Anatolius, a man who was holy and highly spoken of in the history of the Church to which you appeal, judge contrary to the law and the Gospel when he wrote that Easter should be celebrated between the fourteenth and the twentieth day of the moon? Or must we believe that our most reverend father Columba and his successors, men beloved of God, who celebrated Easter in the same way, judged and acted contrary to the holy scriptures, seeing that there were many of them to whose holiness the heavenly signs and the miracles they performed bore witness? And as I have no doubt that they were saints, I shall never cease to follow their way of life, their customs, and their teaching.'

Wilfrid replied, 'It is true that Anatolius was a most holy and learned man, worthy of all praise; but what have you to do with him since you do not observe his precepts? He followed a correct rule in celebrating Easter, basing it on a cycle of nineteen years, of which you are either unaware or, if you do know of it, you despise it, even though it is observed by the whole Church of Christ. He assigned the fourteenth day of the moon to Easter Sunday, reckoning after the Egyptian manner that the fifteenth day of the moon began on the evening of the fourteenth. So also he assigned the twentieth day to Easter Sunday, reckoning that after evening it was the twenty-first day. But it appears that you are ignorant of this distinction, in that you sometimes clearly keep Easter Day before full moon, that is on the thirteenth day of the moon. So far as your father Columba* and his followers are concerned, whose holiness you claim to imitate and whose rule and precepts (confirmed by heavenly signs) you claim to follow, I might perhaps point out that at the judgement, many will say to the Lord that they prophesied in His name and cast out devils and did many wonderful works, but the Lord will answer that He never knew them. Far be it from me to say this about your fathers, for it is much fairer to believe good rather than evil about unknown people. So I will not deny that those who in their rude simplicity loved God with pious intent, were indeed servants of God and beloved by Him. Nor do I think that this observance of Easter did much harm to them while no one had come to show them a more perfect rule to follow. In fact I am sure that if anyone knowing the catholic rule had come to them they would have followed it, as they are known to have followed all the laws of God as soon as they had learned of them. But, once having heard the decrees of the apostolic see or rather of the universal Church, if you refuse to follow them, confirmed as they are by the holy Scriptures, then without doubt you are committing sin. For though your fathers were holy men, do you think that a handful of people in one corner of the remotest of islands is to be preferred to the universal Church of Christ which is spread throughout the world? And even if that Columba of yours—yes, and ours too, if he belonged to Christ—was a holy man of mighty works, is he to be preferred to the most blessed chief of the apostles, to whom the Lord said, 'Thou art Peter and upon this rock I will build my Church and the gates of hell shall not prevail against it, and I will give unto thee the keys of the kingdom of heaven'?

When Wilfrid had ended, the king said, 'Is it true, Colman, that the Lord said these words to Peter?' Colman answered, 'It is true, O King.' Then the king went on, 'Have you anything to show that an equal authority was given to your Columba?' Colman answered, 'Nothing.' Again the king said, 'Do you both agree, without any dispute, that these words were addressed primarily to Peter and that the Lord gave him the keys of the kingdom of heaven?' They both answered, 'Yes.' Thereupon the king concluded, 'Then, I tell you, since he is the doorkeeper I will not contradict him; but I intend to obey his commands in everything to the best of my knowledge and ability, otherwise when I come to the gates of the kingdom of heaven, there may be no one to open them because the one who on your own showing holds the keys has turned his back on me.' When the king had spoken, all who were seated there or standing by, both high and low, signified their assent, gave up their imperfect rules, and readily accepted in their place those which they recognized to be better.

CHAPTER 26

WHEN the dispute was ended and the assembly had broken up, Agilbert returned home. Colman saw that his teachings were rejected and his principles despised; he took those who wished to follow him, that is, those who would not accept the catholic Easter and the tonsure in the shape of a crown (for there was no small argument about this too), and returned to Ireland in order to discuss with his own party what he ought to do in the matter. Cedd left the practices of the Irish and returned to his own see, having accepted the catholic method of keeping Easter. This dispute took place in the year of our Lord 664, in the twenty-second year of King Oswiu's reign and after the Irish had held the episcopate in the English kingdom for thirty years: that is to say, Aidan for seventeen years, Finan for ten, and Colman for three.

After Colman had returned to his native land, Tuda, a servant of Christ, who had been educated among the southern Irish and there consecrated bishop, became bishop of the Northumbrian people; he had the ecclesiastical tonsure in the form of a crown,* according to the custom of that kingdom, and also observed the catholic rules for the date of Easter. He was a good and devoted man but only ruled over the church for a very short time. He had arrived from Ireland during Colman's episcopate and diligently taught the true faith to all by word and example. A man named Eata,* gentle and greatly revered, abbot of the monastery called Melrose, was placed as their abbot over the brothers who preferred to remain at Lindisfarne when the Irish departed. It is said that Colman, on his departure, had asked and obtained this favour from King Oswiu, because Eata was one of those twelve boys of English* race whom Aidan, when he first became bishop, had taken and instructed in Christ; for the king greatly loved Bishop Colman on account of his innate prudence. This same Eata, not long afterwards, became bishop of the church at Lindisfarne. Colman, on leaving, took with him some of the bones of the reverend father Aidan. He left some in the church over which he had presided, directing that they should be interred in the sanctuary.

How frugal and austere he and his predecessors had been, the place itself over which they ruled bears witness. When they left, there were very few buildings there except for the church, in fact only those without which the life of a community was impossible. They had no money but only cattle; if they received money from the rich they promptly gave it to the poor; for they had no need to collect money or to provide dwellings for the reception of worldly and powerful men, since these only came to the church to pray and to hear the word of God. The king himself used to come, whenever opportunity allowed, with only five or six thegns, and when he had finished his prayers in the church he went away. If they happened to take a meal there, they were content with the simple daily fare of the brothers and asked for nothing more.

The sole concern of these teachers was to serve God and not the world, to satisfy the soul and not the belly. For this reason the religious habit was held in great respect at that time, so that whenever a cleric or a monk went anywhere he was gladly received by all as God's servant. If they chanced to meet him by the roadside, they ran towards him and, bowing their heads, were eager either to be signed with the cross by his hand or to receive a blessing from his lips. Great attention was also paid to his exhortations, and on Sundays the people flocked eagerly to the church or the monastery, not to get food for the body but to hear the word of God. If by chance a priest came to a village, the villagers crowded together, eager to hear from him the word of life; for the priests and the clerics visited the villages for no other reason than to preach, to baptize, and to visit the sick, in brief to care for their souls. They were so free from all taint of avarice that none of them would accept lands or possessions to build monasteries, unless compelled to by the secular authorities. This practice was observed universally among the Northumbrian churches for some time afterwards. But enough has been said on this subject.

CHAPTER 27

IN this year of our Lord 664 there was an eclipse of the sun on 3 May* about 4 o'clock in the afternoon. In the same year a sudden pestilence first depopulated the southern parts of Britain and afterwards attacked the kingdom of Northumbria, raging far and wide with cruel devastation and laying low a vast number of people. Bishop Tuda was carried off by it and honourably buried in the monastery called *Pægnalæch.** The plague did equal destruction in Ireland.

At this time there were many in England,* both nobles and commons, who, in the days of Bishops Finan and Colman, had left their own country and retired to Ireland either for the sake of religious studies or to live a more ascetic life. In course of time some of these devoted themselves faithfully to the monastic life, while others preferred to travel round to the cells of various teachers and apply themselves to study. The Irish welcomed them all gladly, gave them their daily food, and also provided them with books to read and with instruction, without asking for any payment.

Among these were two young Englishmen of great ability, named Æthelhun and Egbert,* both of noble birth. The former was a brother of Æthelwine,* a man equally beloved of God, who, later on, also went to Ireland to study; when he had been well grounded he returned to his native land and was made bishop in the kingdom of Lindsey, over which he ruled for a long time with great distinction. Æthelhun and Egbert were in a monastery which the Irish call *Rathmelsigi*,* and all their companions were carried off by the plague or scattered about in various places, while they themselves were both stricken by the same disease and were dangerously ill. An aged and venerable priest, a most truthful man, told me this story about Egbert, declaring that he had heard it from his own lips: when Egbert thought he was on the point of death, early in the morning he left the infirmary where all the sick lay and found a convenient spot in which to be alone; there he began earnestly to consider his past life. He was so stricken with remorse at the memory of his sins that he wept bitterly, and prayed God with all his heart that he might not die until he had had time to make amends for all the thoughtless offences of which he had been guilty during infancy and boyhood and to practise good works more abundantly. He also made a vow that he would live in exile and never return to his native island, Britain; that in addition to the solemn psalmody of the canonical offices he would daily recite the whole psalter to the praise of God, unless prevented by illness; and every week he would fast for a day and a night. When he had ended his tears, his prayers, and his vows, he returned home and found his companion asleep; he too lay on his bed and began to settle down to rest. After a short time of quiet, his companion awoke, looked at him, and said, 'Brother Egbert, what have you done? I hoped that we should both enter into eternal life together; but you are to know that your request will be granted.' He had learned in a vision what it was that Egbert had prayed for and also that his prayer had been answered. To put it briefly, Æthelhun died the same night while Egbert threw off his sickness, recovered, and lived for a long time afterwards, gracing the office of priest which he had received by deeds worthy of it. After having lived a virtuous life according to his wish, he recently passed away to the heavenly realms, in the year of our Lord 729, at the age of ninety. He lived a life of great humility, gentleness, temperance, simplicity, and righteousness. He brought much blessing both to his own race and to those among whom he lived in exile, the Irish and the Picts, by the example of his life, the earnestness of his teaching, the authority with which he administered reproof, and his goodness in distributing whatever he received from the rich. In addition to the vows we have already mentioned, he never ate more than once a day throughout Lent, taking only bread and the thinnest of milk, and even these in great moderation. He used to place the previous day's new milk in a vessel, skim off the cream in the morning, and drink what was left, taking a little bread with it, as we have said. He always practised the same abstinence for forty days before Christmas and for the same number after the solemn feast of the fifty days, that is, Pentecost.

CHAPTER 28

MEANWHILE King Alhfrith sent the priest Wilfrid* to the king of Gaul* to be consecrated bishop for himself and his people. This king sent him to Agilbert* for his consecration, a bishop who has already been mentioned and who, after he left Britain, became bishop of Paris. He was consecrated by him with great splendour in the presence of a number of bishops in the royal town called Compiègne. As Wilfrid lingered abroad for his consecration, King Oswiu, imitating the activities of his son, sent a holy man, modest in his ways, learned in the scriptures, and zealous in carrying out their teachings, to Kent, to be consecrated bishop of the church of York. This was a priest named Chad,* brother of the most reverend Bishop Cedd, who has often been mentioned and abbot of the monastery of Lastingham. The king sent with

him his priest Eadhæd, who was afterwards made bishop of
Ripon during Ecgfrith's reign. When they reached Kent they
found that Deusdedit had died* and no other archbishop had
been appointed in his place. From there they went to the
kingdom of the West Saxons where Wine was bishop. The
latter consecrated Chad with the assistance of two bishops of
the British race who as has repeatedly been said, keep Easter
Sunday, according to their rule, from the fourteenth to the
twentieth day of the moon; but there was not a single bishop
in the whole of Britain except Wine who had been canonically
ordained. So Chad was consecrated bishop and immediately
devoted himself to the task of keeping the Church in truth and
purity, to the practice of humility and temperance, and to
study. He visited cities and country districts, towns, houses,
and strongholds, preaching the gospel, travelling not on
horseback but on foot after the apostolic example. He was one
of Aidan's disciples and sought to instruct his hearers in the
ways and customs of his master and of his brother Cedd.
When Wilfrid returned to Britain after his consecration, he
also introduced many catholic customs into the English
churches so that, as the catholic principles daily gained
strength, all the Irish who had remained among the English
either gave way or returned to their own land.

CHAPTER 29

AT this time the most noble English kings, Oswiu of
Northumbria and Egbert* of Kent, consulted together as to
what ought to be done about the state of the English Church;
for Oswiu, although educated by the Irish, clearly realized
that the Roman Church was both catholic and apostolic; so
with the choice and consent of the holy Church of the English
people, they took a priest named Wigheard, a good man and
well fitted for the office of bishop, one of the clerics of Bishop
Deusdedit, and sent him to Rome to be consecrated bishop so
that, when he had received the rank of archbishop, he could
himself consecrate catholic bishops for the English churches
throughout the whole of Britain. Wigheard duly reached

Rome but died before he could be consecrated; and this is the letter which was sent to King Oswiu in Britain:

To the most excellent lord, our son Oswiu, king of the Saxons, Bishop Vitalian,* servant of the servants of God.

We have received your Highness's welcome letter. As we read it we recognized your most sincere devotion and fervent desire for the life everlasting. We know that, by God's protecting hand, you have been converted to the true and apostolic faith* and we hope that, as you now reign over your people, so in the future you may reign with Christ. That race is indeed blessed which has been found worthy to have so wise a king and one who is a worshipper of God; for you not only worship God yourself but you also labour day and night to bring about the conversion of all your subjects to the catholic and apostolic faith and so save your own soul. Who could fail to be glad over such good news? And who will fail to exult and rejoice over these devoted efforts? For your race has believed in Christ who is God Almighty, as it is written in Isaiah, 'In that day there shall be a root of Jesse, which shall stand for an ensign of the people: to it shall the Gentiles seek.' And again, 'Listen, O isles, unto me, and hearken, ye peoples from afar.' And a little further on, 'It is a light thing that thou shouldest be my servant to raise up the tribes of Jacob and to restore the dregs of Israel. I have given thee for a light to the Gentiles that thou mayest be my salvation unto the end of the earth.' And again, 'Kings shall see, princes also shall arise and worship.' And immediately after, 'I have given thee for a covenant of the people, to establish the earth and possess the scattered heritages; that thou mayest say to the prisoners, Go forth; to them that are in darkness, Show yourselves.' And again, 'I the Lord have called thee in righteousness, and have held thine hand and have kept thee and have given thee for a covenant of the people, for a light of the Gentiles; to open the blind eyes, to bring out the prisoner from the prison and them that sit in darkness out of the prison house.' Most excellent son, as you see, it is clearer than day that it is here foretold that not only you but also all peoples will believe in Christ the Maker of all things. Therefore your Highness must, as a member of Christ, always follow the holy rule of the chief of the apostles in all things, both in the celebration of Easter and in everything delivered by the holy apostles, Peter and Paul, who, like two heavenly lights, illuminate the world, while their teaching daily illuminates the hearts of believers.

After some remarks* about celebrating the true Easter uniformly throughout the whole world, he goes on:

Finally, in view of the length of the journey, we are not at present able to find a man who is entirely suitable and fitted to be your bishop, as you request in your letter. But as soon as a fit person is found, we will send him to your land with full instructions so that he may, by his preaching and with the help of the word of God, entirely root out, with His blessing, the tares sown by the enemy throughout your island.

We have received the gifts sent by your Highness to the blessed chief of the apostles to be a lasting memorial of you. We thank you and will pray continually for your safety and that of the Christian clergy. But the bearer of your gifts has departed this life and is buried in the threshold of the apostles: his death has greatly grieved us. Nevertheless we have directed that the blessings of the saints, in the form of relics of the apostles St Peter and St Paul and of the holy martyrs Laurence, John and Paul, as well as Gregory and Pancras, should be given to your messengers who are the bearers of this letter to be delivered to your Highness. To your wife, our spiritual daughter, we send by the same bearers a cross with a golden key, made from the holy fetters of the apostles St Peter and St Paul: for, hearing of her pious zeal, the whole apostolic see rejoices with us, just as her works of piety smell sweet and blossom in the presence of God. We trust that your Highness will speedily fulfil our desire and dedicate the whole of your island to Christ our God; for you indeed have a Protector in our Lord Jesus Christ, the Redeemer of the human race, who will prosper you in all your efforts to gather together a new people for Christ and establish among them the catholic and apostolic faith. For it is written, 'Seek ye first the kingdom of God and His righteousness and all these things shall be added unto you.' All your islands shall indeed be made subject to Him which is what we both desire. We greet your Excellency with paternal affection and continually pray God in His mercy to assist you and yours in all good works, so that you may reign with Christ in the world to come. May the grace of heaven keep your Excellency in safety.'

The next book will provide a more suitable place for telling who was selected* and consecrated archbishop in place of Wigheard.

CHAPTER 30

ABOUT the same time Kings Sigehere and Sebbi* succeeded Swithhelm, already mentioned, as rulers of the East Saxons, though they were themselves subject to the Mercian King Wulfhere. When this kingdom was suffering from the disastrous plague described above, Sigehere, together with his part of the nation, deserted the sacraments of the Christian faith and apostatized. For the king himself and the majority of both commons and nobles loved this present life, seeking no other and not even believing in any future existence; so they began to restore the derelict temples and to worship images, as if they could protect themselves by such means from the plague. But Sebbi, his colleague and fellow king, held devotedly to the faith which he and his people had accepted and, as we shall see, remained faithful and ended his life happily. As soon as King Wulfhere found that part of the kingdom had apostatized from the faith, he sent Bishop Jaruman, Trumhere's successor, to correct their error and to recall the kingdom to a true belief. A priest who was a companion on his journeys and shared his preaching told me that he acted with great discretion, for he was a religious and good man and, travelling far and wide, he succeeded in bringing back both the people and their King Sigehere to the paths of righteousness. As a result they either abandoned or destroyed the temples and altars they had erected, they reopened their churches, and rejoiced to confess the name of Christ which they had denied, choosing rather to die believing that they would rise again in Him than to live in the filth of unbelief among their idols. When they had accomplished their task, the priests and teachers returned home rejoicing.

BOOK IV

These are the contents of the fourth book of the church of the English people.

13. How Bishop Wilfrid converted the kingdom of the South Saxons to Christ.

14. (16).* How the Isle of Wight received Christian settlers; and how two young princes of the island were put to death immediately after baptism.

15. (17). About a synod held in the plain called Hatfield, Archbishop Theodore presiding.

16. (18). About John, the precentor of the apostolic see, who came to Britain to teach.

17. (19). How Queen Æthelthryth always preserved her virginity and how her body could suffer no corruption in the grave.

18. (20). A hymn about her.

19. (21). How Archbishop Theodore made peace between Kings Ecgfrith and Æthelred.

20. (22). How the bonds of a certain captive were loosed when masses were sung on his behalf.

21. (23). About the life and death of Abbess Hild.

22. (24). How there was a brother in her monastery who received a divine gift of song.

23. (25). How a vision appeared to a certain man of God before the monastery at Coldingham was destroyed by fire.

24. (26). About the deaths of Kings Ecgfrith and Hlothhere.

25. (27). How Cuthbert the man of God was made a bishop; and how up to that time he had lived and taught as a monk.

26. (28). How, when living as a hermit, he produced a fountain of water from dry soil and how he won a crop from seed which he himself had sown out of season with his own hands.

27. (29). How this bishop predicted his own imminent death to Herbert the anchorite.

28. (30). How his body was found free from corruption eleven years after his death; and how, soon afterwards, his successor in the bishopric departed this life.

29. (31). How a certain man was healed of paralysis at his tomb.

30. (32). How another man was lately cured of a disease of the eye at his shrine.

BEGINNING OF BOOK IV

CHAPTER 1

IN the year of the eclipse already mentioned and of the pestilence which quickly followed, Colman, defeated by the unanimous decision of the catholic party, returned to his own people; and Deusdedit, the sixth bishop of the church at Canterbury, died on 14 July. Eorcenberht, king of Kent, died on the same day, leaving his throne to his son Egbert, who held it for nine years. As the see had remained vacant for a considerable time, a priest named Wigheard was sent to Rome by Egbert and also by Oswiu, king of the Northumbrians, with the request that he might be consecrated archbishop of the English Church. This was briefly mentioned in the preceding book. He was a man of English race and very learned in Church affairs. At the same time they sent presents to the pope and no small number of gold and silver vessels. When he arrived in Rome, Vitalian was presiding over the apostolic see; but not long after Wigheard had explained the object of his journey, he and almost all the companions who had travelled with him were carried off by a visitation of the plague.

The pope took advice about the matter and tried very hard to find someone to send out as archbishop of the English Church. Now there was in the monastery of Hiridanum,* not far from Naples in Campania, a certain Abbot Hadrian,* a man of African race and well versed in the holy Scriptures, trained both in monastic and ecclesiastical ways and equally skilled in the Greek and Latin tongues. The pope sent for him and ordered him to accept the bishopric and go to Britain. Hadrian answered that he was unworthy of so exalted a rank, adding that he could point to another who was much better fitted both by age and learning to undertake the office of bishop. He suggested to the pope a certain monk named Andrew, attached to a neighbouring convent of women, who was considered by all who knew him to be worthy of the rank; but his bodily infirmities prevented him from being consecrated bishop. So Hadrian was again urged to accept the bishopric.

Hadrian then asked for a respite to see if he could, in the time, find a man suitable to be consecrated bishop. Just then there was in Rome a monk known to Hadrian whose name was Theodore. He was a native of Tarsus in Cilicia,* a man well trained in secular and divine literature, both Greek and Latin. He was of upright character and of venerable age, being sixty-six years old. Hadrian proposed his name to the pope, who agreed to consecrate him but on one condition, that Hadrian himself should take Theodore to Britain, because he had already travelled twice through Gaul on various missions and was therefore better acquainted with the road and had an adequate number of followers;* also, being a fellow labourer in his teaching work, he would take great care to prevent Theodore from introducing into the church over which he presided any Greek customs* which might be contrary to the true faith. So he was ordained subdeacon, waiting for four months until his hair grew, in order that he might receive the tonsure in the shape of a crown; for he had received the tonsure of the holy apostle Paul, after the Eastern manner. He was consecrated by Pope Vitalian in the year of our Lord 668, on Sunday, 26 March. He was sent to Britain in company with Hadrian on 27 May. They came together by sea to Marseilles and then by land to Arles and handed to John,* the archbishop of that town, the commendatory letters of Pope Vitalian. They were kept back by John until Ebroin,* the king's mayor of the palace, gave them leave to go where they pleased. Thereupon Theodore went to Agilbert, the bishop of Paris, of whom we have spoken before. He was kindly received and entertained by the bishop for a long period. Hadrian went first to Emme,* bishop of Sens, and then to Faro,* bishop of Meaux, and lived comfortably with them for a long time; for the approach of winter compelled them to stay quietly wherever they could. When King Egbert had been told that a bishop, the one they had asked for from the bishop of Rome, was in the kingdom of the Franks, he at once sent his reeve named Rædfrith to bring Theodore to him. When Rædfrith arrived, he took Theodore with the permission of Ebroin and brought him to the port called *Quæntavic.** Here he was delayed for some time owing to sickness, but when he had begun to recover, he sailed to Britain. Ebroin kept Hadrian because he suspected him of having some mission from the emperor* to the kings of Britain, which might be directed against the kingdom over which at that time he held the chief charge. But when he discovered the truth, that Hadrian had never had any such mission at any time, he freed him and allowed him to go after Theodore.* As soon as he arrived, Theodore gave him the monastery of the blessed apostle Peter, where, as I have said, the archbishops of Canterbury are buried. The pope had instructed Theodore at his departure to provide for Hadrian in his province and to give him a suitable place to live with his followers.

CHAPTER 2

THEODORE came to his church on Sunday, 27 May, in the second year after his consecration, and there he spent twenty-one years, three months, and twenty-six days. Soon after he arrived, he visited every part of the island where the English peoples lived and was gladly welcomed and listened to by all. He was accompanied everywhere and assisted by Hadrian, as he gave instruction on the ordering of a holy life and the canonical custom of celebrating Easter. He was the first of the archbishops whom the whole English Church consented to obey. And because both of them were extremely learned in sacred and secular literature, they attracted a crowd of students into whose minds they daily poured the streams of wholesome learning. They gave their hearers instruction not only in the books of holy Scripture but also in the art of metre, astronomy, and ecclesiastical computation. As evidence of this, some of their students still survive who know Latin and Greek just as well as their native tongue. Never had there been such happy times since the English first came to Britain; for having such brave Christian kings, they were a terror to all the barbarian nations, and the desires of all men were set on the joys of the heavenly kingdom of which they had only lately heard; while all who wished for instruction in sacred studies had teachers ready to hand.

From that time also the knowledge of sacred music, which had hitherto been known only in Kent, began to be taught in all the English churches. With the exception of James already mentioned, the first singing master in the Northumbrian churches was Æddi* surnamed Stephen, who was invited from Kent by the most worthy Wilfrid, who was the first bishop* of the English race to introduce the catholic way of life to the English churches.

So Theodore journeyed to every district, consecrating bishops in suitable places and, with their help, correcting whatever he found imperfect. Among these he made it clear to Bishop Chad that his consecration had not been regular, whereupon the latter humbly replied, 'If you believe that my consecration was irregular, I gladly resign from the office; indeed I never believed myself to be worthy of it. But I consented to receive it, however unworthy, in obedience to the commands I received.' When Theodore heard his humble reply, he said that he ought not to give up his office; but he completed his consecration a second time after the catholic manner. At the same time, when Deusdedit was dead and while a bishop for the church at Canterbury was being sought for, consecrated, and sent, Wilfrid was also sent to Gaul from Britain to be consecrated and, since he returned before Theodore's arrival, he ordained priests and deacons even in Kent until such time as the archbishop arrived at his own see. When Theodore came soon afterwards to the city of Rochester, where the bishopric had long been vacant after the death of Damian, he consecrated a man whose name was Putta.* The latter was very learned in ecclesiastical matters but showed little interest in secular affairs and was content with a simple life. He was especially skilled in liturgical chanting after the Roman manner, which he had learned from the disciples of the blessed Pope Gregory.

CHAPTER 3

AT this time King Wulfhere was ruling over the kingdom of
Mercia and, since Jaruman was dead, he asked Theodore to
provide him and his people with a bishop; as Theodore did
not wish to consecrate a new bishop for them, he asked King
Oswiu to give them Bishop Chad, who was then living in
retirement* in his own monastery of Lastingham. Wilfrid was
administering the see of the church at York and of all the
Northumbrians and Picts, as far as Oswiu's power extended.
And because it was the custom of the reverend Bishop Chad
to carry out his evangelistic work on foot rather than on
horseback, Theodore ordered him to ride whenever he was
faced with too long a journey; but Chad showed much hesitation, for he was deeply devoted to this religious exercise, so
the archbishop lifted him on to the horse with his own hands
since he knew him to be a man of great sanctity and he
determined to compel him to ride a horse when necessity
arose. Chad accepted the position of bishop of the Mercian
race and of the people of Lindsey and, following the example
of the early fathers, he administered the diocese in great
holiness of life. King Wulfhere gave him fifty hides of land to
build a monastery, in a place called *Adbaruae*, that is At the
Grove (Barrow),* in the province of Lindsey, where up to the
present day traces of the monastic Rule which he established
still survive.

He had his episcopal seat at a place called Lichfield, where
he also died and was buried, and where the succeeding bishops of the kingdom have their see to this day. He built himself
a more retired dwelling-place not far from the church, in
which he could read and pray privately with a few of his
brothers, that is to say, seven or eight of them; this he did as
often as he was free from his labours and from the ministration of the word. After he had ruled the Church in that
kingdom with great success for two and a half years, divine
providence ordained a time such as Ecclesiastes speaks of, 'a
time for scattering stones and a time for gathering them
together'. A plague sent from heaven came upon them which,

through the death of the body, translated the living stones* of
the church from their earthly sites to the heavenly building.
After many from the church of this most reverend bishop had
been taken from the flesh, his own hour was at hand when
he must pass from this world to be with the Lord. Now
it happened one day that he was in the dwelling already
mentioned, with one brother only, whose name was Owine,
since their other companions had had occasion to return to
the church. This Owine was a monk of great merit who had
left the world with the sole object of winning a heavenly
reward, and therefore in every respect a fit person to receive a
special revelation of the mysteries of the Lord and worthy too
of being believed by such as heard his story. He had come
with Queen Æthelthryth* from the kingdom of the East
Angles, being the chief of her officers and the head of her
household. As his faith and zeal increased, he decided to
renounce the world and this he did in no half-hearted way: he
stripped himself so completely of his worldly possessions that
he left all that he had and, dressed only in a plain garment and
carrying an axe and an adze in his hands, he came to the most
reverend father's monastery at Lastingham. He did this to
show that he was not entering the monastery for the sake of
ease, as some did, but to work hard. This he also proved by
his deeds; for as he was less capable of the study of the
Scriptures, he applied himself more earnestly to manual
labour. In fact, although because he was so reverent and
devout he was received into the company of the bishop and
the brothers and into their house, yet when they were engaged
in reading inside the house, he used to work outside at whatever seemed necessary. To resume my narrative: on one such
day he was occupied with some task outside and his brothers
had gone to the church, while the bishop was engaged alone
in the oratory in reading or prayer; suddenly, as Owine afterwards related, he heard the sound of sweet and joyful singing
descend from the sky to the earth. He said he heard the sound
first of all from the south-east, that is, from the highest point
of the rising of the winter sun; from there it gradually approached him until it reached the roof of the oratory where
the bishop was; it entered in, filling it and all its surroundings.

He listened with close attention to what he heard and then, after the space of half an hour, he heard the same joyful song ascend from the roof of the oratory and return with unspeakable sweetness to the sky in the same way as it had come. He had been standing for some time amazed and earnestly considering what this could mean, when the bishop opened the window of the oratory, clapping his hands to make a signal as he was accustomed to do, to call the attention of anyone outside, and told him to come in. As Owine hurried in, the bishop said to him, 'Go at once to the church and bid those seven brothers come here and you also come with them.' When they had come, he first of all urged them to live virtuously in love and peace with each other and with all the faithful; also to follow with unwearied constancy the Rule of life which he had taught them and which they had seen him carry out, or had learned from the words and deeds of the fathers who had gone before. Then he added that the day of his death was close at hand. 'For', he said, 'the beloved guest* who has been in the habit of visiting our brothers has deigned to come today to me also, to summon me from this world. So return to the church and tell the brothers to commend my departure to the Lord by their prayers and that they also remember to prepare for their own departure, the hour of which is uncertain, by fasting and prayers and good works.' When he had said this and much more in the same strain and when they had received his blessing and gone away in great sorrow, the man who had heard the heavenly song returned alone, threw himself to the ground, and said, 'Father, I beg you to let me ask you something.' 'Ask what you wish', Chad replied. Then Owine said, 'I pray you tell me what was the song of joyful voices which I heard descending from heaven upon the oratory and, after a time, returning to heaven again.' He answered, 'If you heard the sound of singing and saw a heavenly company come down, I command you in the name of the Lord to tell no one before my death. They were indeed angel spirits come to summon me to the heavenly joys which I have always loved and longed for; and they have promised to return in seven days and take me with them.' This was fulfilled just as he had been told, for he was immediately afflicted with bodily weakness which daily grew worse until, on the seventh day as he had been promised, after he had prepared for death by receiving the body and blood of the Lord, his holy soul was released from the prison-house of the body and in the company of angels, as one may rightly believe, sought the joys of heaven.

Nor is it any wonder that he joyfully beheld the day of his death or rather the day of the Lord, whose coming he had always anxiously awaited. For in addition to all his merits of temperance, humility, zeal in teaching, prayers, and voluntary poverty and other virtues too, he was greatly filled with the fear of the Lord and mindful of his last end in all he did. One of his brothers named Trumberht, a monk educated in his monastery and under his Rule and one of those who taught me the Scriptures, used to tell me this about him: if he happened to be reading or doing something else and suddenly a high wind arose, he would at once invoke the mercy of the Lord and beg Him to have pity upon the human race. If the wind increased in violence he would shut his book, fall on his face, and devote himself still more earnestly to prayer. But if there were a violent storm of wind and rain or if lightning and thunder brought terror to earth and sky, he would enter the church and, with still deeper concentration, earnestly devote himself to prayers and psalms until the sky cleared. When his people asked him why he did it he replied, 'Have you not read, "The Lord also thundered in the heavens and the Highest gave His voice. Yea, He sent out His arrows and scattered them and He shot out lightnings and discomfited them"? For the Lord moves the air, raises the winds, hurls the lightnings, and thunders forth from heaven so as to rouse the inhabitants of the world to fear Him, to call them to remember the future judgement in order that He may scatter their pride and confound their boldness by bringing to their minds that dread time when He will come in the clouds in great power and majesty, to judge the living and the dead, while the heavens and the earth are aflame. And so', said he, 'we ought to respond to His heavenly warning with due fear and love; so that as often as He disturbs the sky and raises His hand as if about to strike, yet spares us still, we should implore His mercy, examining the innermost recesses of our hearts and purging out the dregs of our sins, and behave with such caution that we may never deserve to be struck down.'

This brother's account of the bishop's death also agrees with the story of a vision related by the most reverend father Egbert already mentioned, who had lived the monastic life with Chad, when they were both youths in Ireland, diligently engaged in prayer and fasting and meditating on the divine Scriptures. But while Chad returned to his native land, Egbert remained there until the end of his life, an exile for the Lord's sake. A long time afterwards, a very holy and abstemious man named Higebald, who was abbot in the province of Lindsey, came to visit him. As was fitting for holy men they were talking about the lives of the early fathers and saying how gladly they would imitate them, when mention was made of the revered Bishop Chad; whereupon Egbert said, 'I know a man in this island, still in the flesh, who saw the soul of Chad's brother Cedd descend from the sky with a host of angels and return to the heavenly kingdom, taking Chad's soul with him.' Whether he was speaking of himself or of another is uncertain, but what cannot be uncertain is that whatever such a man said must be true.

Chad died on 2 March and was first of all buried close to the church of St Mary; but when the church of St Peter, the most blessed chief of the apostles, was later built, his bones were translated there. In each place frequent miracles of healing occur as a sign of his virtue. For example, quite recently a madman, who had been wandering from one place to another, came there one evening unknown to or unregarded by the guardians of the church, and spent the whole night there. The next morning he came out in his right mind and, to the amazement and joy of all, demonstrated how he had regained his health there through the goodness of God. Chad's place of burial is a wooden coffin in the shape of a little house, having an aperture in its side, through which those who visit it out of devotion can insert their hands and take out a little of the dust. When it is put in water and given either to cattle or men who are ailing, they get their wish and are at once freed from their ailments and rejoice in health restored.

In Chad's place Theodore consecrated Winfrith, a good and discreet man, who, like his predecessors, presided as bishop over the kingdoms of Mercia, the Middle Angles, and Lindsey, over all which King Wulfhere, who was still alive, held sway. Winfrith was one of the clergy of the bishop and had been his deacon for some considerable time.

CHAPTER 4

MEANWHILE Colman, who was a bishop from Ireland, left Britain and took with him all the Irish whom he had gathered together on the island of Lindisfarne. He also took about thirty men of English race, both companies having been instructed in the duties of monastic life. Leaving some of the brothers in the church at Lindisfarne, he went first to the island of Iona, from which he had been sent to preach the word to the English. From there he went on to a small island some distance off the west coast of Ireland, called in Irish Inisboufinde (Inishbofin), the island of the white heifer. When he reached this island, he built a monastery and placed in it monks whom he had brought from both nations. But they could not agree together because the Irish, in summer time when the harvest had to be gathered in, left the monastery and wandered about, scattering into various places with which they were familiar; then when winter came, they returned and expected to have a share in the things which the English had provided. Colman sought to put an end to this dispute and at last, having travelled about far and near, he found a place suitable for building a monastery on the Irish mainland called in the Irish tongue *Mag éo* (Mayo). He bought a small part of the land from the chief to whom it belonged, on condition that the monks who settled there were to pray to the Lord for him as he had provided them with the land. A monastery was forthwith built with the help of the chief and all the neighbours and in it he placed the English monks, leaving the Irishmen on the island. This monastery is still occupied by Englishmen; from small beginnings it has now become very large and is commonly known as *Muig éo* (Mayo). All these monks have adopted a better Rule and it now contains a remarkable company gathered there from England, living after the example of the venerable fathers under a Rule, having an abbot elected canonically, in great devotion and austerity and supporting themselves by the labour of their own hands.

CHAPTER 5

IN the year of the incarnation of our Lord 670, the second year after Theodore came to Britain, Oswiu, king of the Northumbrians, was struck down by a sickness from which he died, being fifty-eight years of age. By this time he was so greatly attached to the Roman and apostolic customs that he had intended, if he recovered from his illness, to go to Rome* and end his life there among the holy places. He had asked Bishop Wilfrid to act as his guide, promising him no small gift of money. He died on 15 February, leaving his son Ecgfrith* as heir to the kingdom.

In the third year of Ecgfrith's reign, Theodore summoned a council of bishops together with many teachers of the church who knew and loved the canonical institutions of the fathers. When they were assembled he began, as befitted an archbishop, by charging them to observe diligently all those things which were conducive to the unity and peace of the church. The text of the decisions of the synod is as follows:

In the name of our Lord God and Saviour Jesus Christ. Under the perpetual reign and governance over His Church of that sovereign, the Lord Jesus Christ: it was thought proper that we should assemble in accordance with the custom laid down by our venerated canon law, to deal with the necessary business of the Church. We met on 24 September, in the first indiction, at a place called Hertford: I, Theodore, though unworthy, appointed bishop of the Church at Canterbury by the apostolic see, and our fellow bishop and brother the worthy Bisi,* bishop of the East Angles; while our brother and fellow bishop Wilfrid, bishop of the Northumbrian race, was represented by his proctors. There were also present our brothers and fellow priests Putta, bishop of the Kentish town* known as Rochester, Leuthere, bishop of the West Saxons, and Winfrith, bishop of the Mercian kingdom. When we had all met together and had sat down each in his own place, I said: 'Beloved brethren, I beseech you, for the fear and love of our Redeemer, that we should all deliberate in common for the benefit of the faith; so that whatever has been decreed and defined by holy fathers of proved worth may be preserved incorrupt by us all.' This and much more I added on the need to preserve charity and unity in the Church. When I had completed my preliminary discourse, I asked each of them in turn if they were willing to keep the canonical decrees which had been laid down by the fathers in ancient times. All our fellow bishops answered, 'Most gladly and readily do we all agree to keep such canons as were laid down by the holy fathers.' I produced forthwith the said book of canons and from this book I put before them ten chapters which I had marked in certain places as being specially necessary for us to know and I asked them all to devote particular attention to them.

Chapter I.* That we all keep Easter Day at the same time, namely on the Sunday after the fourteenth day of the moon of the first month.

Chapter II. That no bishop intrude into the diocese of another bishop, but that he should be content with the government of the people committed to his charge.

Chapter III. That no bishop shall in any way interfere with any monasteries dedicated to God nor take away forcibly any part of their property.

Chapter IV. That monks shall not wander from place to place, that is, from monastery to monastery, unless they have letters dimissory from their own abbot; but they are to remain under that obedience which they promised at the time of their profession.

Chapter V. That no clergy shall leave their own bishop nor wander about at will; nor shall one be received anywhere without letters commendatory from his own bishop. If he has once been received and is unwilling to return when summoned, both the receiver and the received shall suffer excommunication.

Chapter VI. That both bishops and clergy when travelling shall be content with the hospitality afforded them. Nor shall they exercise any priestly function without the permission of the bishop in whose diocese they are known to be.

Chapter VII. That a synod shall be summoned twice yearly. (But on account of various hindrances, it was unanimously decided that we should meet once a year on 1 August at the place known as *Clofæshoh*.*)

Chapter VIII. That no bishop claim precedence over another bishop out of ambition; but all shall take rank according to the time and the order of their consecration.

Chapter IX. That more bishops shall be created as the number of the faithful increases. (This chapter received general discussion, but at the time we came to no decision on the matter.)

Chapter X. On marriage. That nothing be allowed but lawful wedlock. Let none be guilty of incest, and let none leave his own wife except for fornication, as the holy gospel teaches. If anyone puts away his own wife who is joined to him by lawful matrimony, he may not take another if he wishes to be a true Christian; but he must either remain as he is or be reconciled to his own wife.

After these chapters had been discussed in common and resolved upon, and in order that no scandalous controversy should arise among us or any matter be inaccurately published abroad, it was decided that each one should ratify our decisions by attaching his own signature. I dictated to Titill the notary the wording of the decisions for him to write down. This was done in the month and indiction above mentioned. If anyone therefore shall attempt in any way to oppose or disobey the decisions confirmed by our consent and ratified by our signatures, according to the canonical decrees, let him know that he is excluded from exercising any priestly office and from our fellowship. May the grace of God preserve us all who live in the unity of His holy Church.

This synod took place in the year of our Lord 673, the year in which Egbert king of Kent died, in the month of July. He was succeeded by his brother Hlothhere* who reigned for eleven years and seven months. Bisi, bishop of the East Angles, who is known to have been present at this synod, was the successor of Boniface already mentioned, and a man of great sanctity and devotion. When Boniface died after being bishop for seventeen years, Bisi was made bishop in his place and consecrated by Theodore. He was prevented from administering his diocese by a serious illness so, while he was still alive, two bishops were chosen and consecrated in his place, namely Æcci and Baduwine;* and from then until this day the kingdom has had two bishops.

CHAPTER 6

NOT long afterwards, Archbishop Theodore, displeased by some act of disobedience of Winfrith, bishop of the Mercians, deposed him* from the bishopric which he had held only a few years. In his place he consecrated Seaxwulf as bishop, the founder and abbot of the monastery known as *Medeshamstede* (Peterborough) in the land of the Gyrwe. Winfrith after his deposition retired to his own monastery of Barrow and there lived a very holy life until his death.

Theodore then appointed Erconwald* bishop in London, for the East Saxons. Sebbi and Sighere, already mentioned, were the reigning monarchs. Both before and after his consecration, Eorcenwold lived so holy a life that even now miracles bear witness to it. To this day the horse-litter in which he used to be carried when ill is preserved by his followers and continues to cure many people afflicted with fevers and other complaints. Not only are people cured who are placed in or near the litter but splinters cut from it and taken to the sick bring speedy relief.

Before he was made bishop, he founded two famous monasteries, one for himself and the other for his sister Æthelburh, and established an excellent form of monastic Rule and discipline* in both. His own was in the kingdom of

Surrey near the river Thames at a place called Chertsey,* that is, the island of *Ceorot*. His sister's monastery he established at a place called Barking in the kingdom of the East Saxons where she was to live as mother and nurse of a company of women devoted to God. When she had undertaken the rule of this monastery, she proved herself worthy in all things of her brother the bishop, both by her own holy life and by her sound and devoted care for those who were under her rule; and of this heavenly miracles were the witness.

CHAPTER 7

IN this monastery many signs and miracles* were performed which have been written down by those who were acquainted with them as an edifying memorial for succeeding generations and copies are in the possession of many people. Some of these we have taken care to insert in this *History*. The plague which has been so often referred to and which was ravaging the country far and wide had also attacked that part of the monastery occupied by the men, and they were daily being carried away into the presence of the Lord. The mother of the congregation was anxiously concerned as to when the plague would strike that part of the monastery, separated from the men's community, in which dwelt the company of the handmaidens of the Lord. So when the sisters met together, she took to asking in what part of the monastery they would like their bodies to be buried and where they desired a cemetery to be made when they were snatched away from the world by the same catastrophe as the rest. Although she often inquired she received no definite answer from the sisters, but she and all of them received a most definite reply from the divine providence. On a certain night when the servants of Christ had finished their mattin psalms, they went out of the oratory to the tombs of the brothers who had already died. While they were singing their accustomed praises to the Lord, suddenly a light appeared from heaven like a great sheet and came upon them all, striking such terror into them that they broke off the chant they were singing in alarm. This resplendent light, in comparison with which the noonday sun seemed dark, soon afterwards rose from the place and moved to the south side of the monastery, that is, to the west of the oratory. There it remained for some time, covering that area until it was withdrawn from their sight into the heavenly heights. So no doubt remained in their minds that this light was not only intended to guide and receive the souls of Christ's handmaidens into heaven, but was also pointing out the spot where the bodies were to rest, awaiting the resurrection day. This beam of light was so brilliant that one of the older brothers, who was in the oratory at the time with another younger brother, declared in the morning that the rays of light which penetrated the cracks of the doors and windows seemed brighter than the brightest daylight.

CHAPTER 8

IN the same monastery there was a boy named Æsica, not more than three years of age, who, because of his extreme youth, was being looked after and was learning his lessons in the dwelling of the maidens dedicated to God. He was attacked by the plague and, when at the point of death, he called out three times for one of the maidens consecrated to Christ, calling her by name as though she were present, 'Edith, Edith, Edith!' And so he ended this temporal life and passed to the life eternal. The maiden whom he called upon as he died was, on that very day, attacked by the same sickness in the place where she was and carried from this world, following him who had called her to the kingdom of heaven.

Another of these handmaidens of God, when attacked by the same disease and approaching her end, suddenly began about midnight to call out to those who were attending on her, asking them to put out the light which was burning in the room. She repeated her request frequently and, as no one attended to her, she said at last, 'I know that you think I am raving when I ask this; but I assure you that it is not so. I tell you the truth: I see this house filled with a light so bright that that lamp of yours seems to me to be utterly dark.' But still no one replied or did her bidding, so she said again, 'Let your lamp burn then as long as you like; but be sure of this, it gives me no light; when dawn breaks, my light will come to me.' She went on to describe how a certain man of God who had died that year had appeared to her, telling her that at daybreak she would depart to the eternal light. Her vision was speedily proved to be true for the maiden died as day dawned.

CHAPTER 9

WHEN Æthelburh, the devout mother of that devoted community, was herself about to be taken from the world, a marvellous vision appeared to one of the sisters whose name was Torhtgyth. She had lived for many years in the monastery, always seeking to serve God herself in all humility and sincerity and endeavouring to help the mother to keep the discipline of the Rule by teaching or reproving the younger ones. Now in order that her strength, like the apostle's, might be made perfect in weakness, she was suddenly afflicted with a most serious bodily disease and for nine years was sorely tried, under the good providence of our Redeemer, so that any traces of sin remaining among her virtues through ignorance or carelessness might be burnt away by the fires of prolonged suffering. One evening, at dusk, as she left the little cell in which she lived, she saw distinctly what seemed to be a human body, wrapped in a shroud and brighter than the sun, being apparently raised up from within the house in which the sisters used to sleep. She looked closely to see how this glorious visionary body was raised up and saw that it was lifted as it were by cords, brighter than gold, until it was drawn up into the open heavens and she could see it no longer. As she thought over the vision there remained no doubt in her mind that some member of their community was about to die whose soul would be drawn up to the skies by the good deeds she had done, as though by golden cords. And so it came to pass. Not many days afterwards the mother of the congregation, Æthelburh, beloved of God, was taken from the prison-house of the flesh; and such was her record that none who knew her can doubt that, as she departed this life, the gates of her heavenly country were opened for her.

In the same monastery there was a certain nun, of noble family in this world and still nobler in her love for the world to come; for many years her whole body had been so disabled that she could not move a single limb. When she learned that the body of the venerable abbess had been borne into the church to await burial, she asked to be carried in and placed leaning up against it in the attitude of prayer. When this was done she asked Æthelburh, as though she were addressing a living person, to plead on her behalf with the merciful and pitiful Creator that she might be delivered from the cruel tortures which she had endured so long. Nor was it long before her prayers were heard; for twelve days afterwards she too was taken from the body and exchanged her temporal afflictions for an eternal reward.

For three years after the death of the lady abbess Torhtgyth, the handmaid of Christ, remained alive but was so wasted away by the infirmities already described that 'her bones scarcely held together'; at last when the time of her release approached, she lost the use not only of her limbs but also of her tongue. She continued in this state for three days and nights when she was suddenly restored by a spiritual vision and her eyes and mouth were opened. Looking up to heaven she began to speak to the vision she beheld: 'Your coming', she said, 'is most acceptable to me and you are indeed welcome.' When she had said this she was silent for a short time as if she were waiting for an answer from the one whom she saw and was addressing. Again she added as if slightly displeased: 'I cannot be happy to hear this.' Then after another short silence she said for the third time: 'If it cannot be today I beg that there may not be a long delay.' After this there was again a short silence as before, and then she uttered these final words: 'If this is definitely fixed and the decree is unalterable, then I pray that it may not be put off beyond the following night.' When she had finished speaking, those who were sitting around asked her with whom she had been talking. She answered: 'With my beloved mother* Æthelburh.' Thus they realized that Æthelburh had come to announce to her that the time of her departure was near. As she requested, after a night and a day, she was loosed from the bonds of the flesh and her infirmities and entered upon the joys of eternal salvation.

CHAPTER 10

A DEVOTED servant of God named Hildelith* succeeded Æthelburh in the office of abbess and presided over the monastery for many years until she was extremely old. She was most energetic in the observance of the discipline of the Rule and in the provision of all such things as were necessary for the common use. As the site on which the monastery was built was very limited, she decided that the bones of the servants and handmaidens of Christ which had been buried there should all be taken up and transferred to the church of the blessed Mother of God and buried there in one place. How often the brightness of a heavenly light, how often a wonderful fragrance and other signs also appeared—all these things the reader will find in the book from which I have made these extracts.

I think, however, that it would be far from fitting to pass over a miracle of healing which the book describes as having taken place at the cemetery of this congregation dedicated to God. There lived in the neighbourhood a certain *gesith* whose wife was attacked by a sudden dimness of the eyes; her affliction increased so greatly from day to day that she could not see the faintest glimmer of light. After remaining for some time wrapt in the darkness of night, it suddenly occurred to her that, if she were taken to the monastery of the holy virgins and prayed before the relics of the saints, she might recover her lost sight. She carried out her plan forthwith. Her maidens led her to the monastery, which was close at hand, and there she was taken to the cemetery, declaring how complete was her assurance that she would be healed. After she had prayed at length on bended knees, she earned a speedy answer to her prayers; as she rose she received the gift of sight which she was seeking, even before she left the place. Though her maids had

188

led her thither by hand, she joyfully returned home without help. It seemed as if she had lost the light of this world in order to show by her recovery how bright is the light and how great the grace of healing with which the saints of Christ in heaven are endowed.

CHAPTER 11

AT this time, as this book relates, there ruled over the kingdom of the East Saxons a very devout man named Sebbi,* already mentioned. He was given to religious exercises, constant prayers, and the holy joys of almsgiving. He would long before have given up his throne, preferring a private life in a monastery to all the riches and honours of a kingdom, had not his wife obstinately refused to be separated from him. For this reason, many people thought and often said that a man of his disposition ought to have been a bishop rather than a king. After a reign of thirty years, this soldier of the kingdom of heaven was afflicted by a very serious bodily infirmity from which he eventually died. He therefore urged his wife that since neither of them could enjoy or serve the world any longer, they should devote themselves to the service of God. Having obtained her reluctant consent, he came to Waldhere,* bishop of London, Erconwald's successor, and received with his blessing the religious habit which he had long desired. He brought the bishop no small sum of money to be given to the poor, keeping nothing for himself but desiring to remain poor in spirit for the sake of the kingdom of heaven.

As his sickness increased he felt that the day of his death was approaching; and his disposition being such as befitted a king, he feared that, if he felt great pain in the hour of death, he might by his words or his gestures act in a way unworthy of his character. So summoning the bishop of London, the city in which the king was then living, he asked him that there should be no others present at his deathbed except the bishop and two of his servants. This the bishop gladly promised; but not long afterwards, while sleeping, the king saw a comforting vision which removed all his uneasiness on this score and also made known to him on what day he was to die. He saw, as he later described, three men approaching clad in shining robes; one of them sat down by his bed while his companions, standing by, inquired after the condition of the sick man whom they had come to visit. The man who was seated said that his soul would leave his body without any pain and in a great splendour of light; he also declared that the king would die in three days' time. Both these things were fulfilled just as he had learned from the vision. For he died three days afterwards, at three in the afternoon, when he seemed to fall suddenly into a light sleep and breathed his last without feeling any pain. They had prepared a stone sarcophagus* for his burial, but when they came to lay his body in it they found that it was longer than the sarcophagus by a hand's breadth. So they chipped the stone so far as they could, adding about two inches, space. But still it would not take the body. So in view of the difficulty of burying him they debated whether they should look for another coffin or by bending the knees shorten the body so that it would fit the coffin. But an amazing thing happened, certainly the work of heaven which made both of these alternatives unnecessary. Suddenly as the bishop stood by, together with Sigeheard (who reigned after Sebbi with his brother Swæfred* and was the son of the royal monk) as well as a large crowd of men, the sarcophagus was found to be of the right length to fit the body, so that a pillow could even be put in behind the head while, at the feet, the coffin was four inches longer than the body. He was buried in the church of the blessed doctor of the Gentiles, through whose teachings he had learned to aspire to heavenly things.

CHAPTER 12

THE fourth bishop of the West Saxons was Leuthere.* The first was Birinus, the second Agilbert, and the third Wine. When Cenwealh* was dead, during whose reign Leuthere had been made bishop, subkings took upon themselves the government of the kingdom, dividing it up and ruling for about ten years. While they were reigning Leuthere died and was succeeded by Hædde,* who had been consecrated in London by Theodore. During his episcopate the sub-kings were conquered and removed and Cædwalla* became king. After he had reigned two years he renounced the throne, while the same bishop was still in the see, urged on by his love for the kingdom of heaven. He went to Rome and died there, as will be told more fully later on.

In the year of our Lord 676 Æthelred,* king of the Mercians, at the head of a cruel army, devastated Kent, profaning churches and monasteries without respect for religion or fear of God. In the general devastation he also destroyed Rochester, Putta's see, though the bishop was absent at the time. When Putta found that his church was destroyed and all its contents removed, he went to Seaxwulf, bishop of the Mercians, who granted him a church and a small estate, where he ended his life in peace, making no attempt whatever to re-establish his bishopric; for, as was said before, he was more concerned with ecclesiastical than with worldly affairs. So he served God in this church and went round wherever he was invited, teaching church music. Instead of him Theodore consecrated Cwichelm as bishop of Rochester. But when the latter left the bishopric soon afterwards for lack of means and went elsewhere, Theodore appointed Gefmund* in his place.

In the year of our Lord 678, the eighth year of the reign of King Ecgfrith, there appeared during the month of August a star which is known as a comet.* It remained for three months, rising in the early hours of each morning and emitting a kind of lofty column of bright flame. In the same year there arose a dissension* between King Ecgfrith and the most reverend bishop Wilfrid with the result that the bishop was driven from his see while two bishops were put in his place to rule over the Northumbrian race; one was Bosa, who administered the kingdom of Deira, and the other Eata, who presided over Bernicia. The former had his episcopal see in York and the latter at Hexham or else in Lindisfarne; both of them were promoted to the rank of bishop from a monastic community. In addition Eadhæd was consecrated bishop of the kingdom of Lindsey,* which King Ecgfrith had recently won by conquering Wulfhere and putting him to flight. This was the first bishop of its own which the kingdom had had, the second one being Æthelwine, the third Edgar, and the fourth Cyneberht, the present bishop. Before Eadhæd, Seaxwulf was its bishop, being at the same time bishop of the Mercians and the Middle Angles; when he was driven out of Lindsey he continued to administer these provinces. Eadhæd, Bosa, and Eata were consecrated at York by Archbishop Theodore. Three years after Wilfrid's departure he added two more* to their number, Tunberht to the church at Hexham—Eata remaining at Lindisfarne—and Trumwine to the kingdom of the Picts, which at that time was subject to the English. When Æthelred had recovered the kingdom of Lindsey, Eadhæd returned and was placed by Theodore over the church at Ripon.

CHAPTER 13

WHEN Wilfrid had been expelled from his see he spent a long time travelling in many lands, going to Rome and afterwards returning to Britain. Though he could not be received back into his own native land and his diocese, owing to the hostility of King Ecgfrith, yet nothing could hinder him from the ministry of preaching the gospel. So he turned to the kingdom of the South Saxons, which stretches south and west from Kent as far as the land of the West Saxons and contains 7,000 hides. At that time it was still in the bonds of heathen practices. Here Wilfrid taught them the faith and administered the baptism of salvation. The king of this people was Æthelwealh,* who not long before had been baptized in the kingdom of Mercia at the suggestion and in the presence of Wulfhere, who, when Æthelwealh came forth from the font, received him as a son. As a token of his adoption Wulfhere gave him two provinces, namely the Isle of Wight and the province of the Meonware* in the land of the West Saxons. So the bishop, with the king's consent and indeed to his great joy, cleansed his ealdormen and his *gesiths* in the holy fount of baptism; the priests Eappa and Padda, Burghelm and Eddi baptized the rest of the common people either then or later on. The queen, whose name was Eafe, had been baptized in her own country, the kingdom of the Hwicce. She was the daughter of Eanfrith, Eanhere's brother, both of whom were Christians, as were their people. Apart from her, all the South Saxons were ignorant of the divine name and of the faith.

There was, however, in their midst a certain Irish monk named Dícuill who had a very small monastery in a place called Bosham surrounded by woods and sea, in which five or six brothers served the Lord in humility and poverty; but none of the natives cared to follow their way of life or listen to their preaching.

In evangelizing this nation, Bishop Wilfrid rescued them not only from the misery of everlasting damnation but also from temporal death and cruel destruction. For three years before his coming into the kingdom no rain had fallen in those parts, so that a most terrible famine assailed the populace and pitilessly destroyed them. For example it is said that forty or fifty men, wasted with hunger, would go together to some precipice or to the seashore where in their misery they would join hands and leap into the sea, perishing wretchedly either by the fall or by drowning. But on the very day on which the people received the baptism of faith, a gentle but ample rain fell; the earth revived, the fields once more became green, and a happy and fruitful season followed. So, casting off their ancient superstitions and renouncing their idolatry, 'the heart and flesh of all rejoiced in the living God'; for they realized that He who is the true God had, by His heavenly grace, endowed them with both outward and inward blessings. When the bishop first came into the kingdom and saw the suffering and famine there, he taught them how to get their food by fishing: for both the sea and the rivers abounded in fish but the people had no knowledge of fishing except for eels alone. So the bishop's men collected eel-nets from every quarter and cast them into the sea so that, with the help of divine grace, they quickly captured 300 fish of all kinds. These were divided up into three parts: a hundred were given to the poor, a hundred to those who had supplied the nets, while they kept the other hundred for their own use. By this good turn the bishop won the hearts of all and they had the greater hope of heavenly blessings from the preaching of one by whose aid they had gained temporal blessings.

At this time King Æthelwealh gave the most reverend bishop Wilfrid eighty-seven hides of land to maintain his exiled followers. The land was called Selsey, that is, the island of the seal. This place is surrounded on all sides by the sea except on the west where it is approached by a piece of land about a sling's throw in width. Such a place is called in Latin *peninsula* and in Greek *cherronesos*. When Bishop Wilfrid had received this land he founded a monastery there, consisting chiefly of the brothers he had brought with him, and established a Rule of life; his successors, as is well known, occupy the place to this day. For five years, that is, until the death of King Ecgfrith, he carried out the duties of a bishop in those parts both in words and works, being deservedly honoured by all. Since the king had given them the land together with all the stock on it, along with fields and men, he instructed them all in the faith of Christ and washed them in the waters of baptism; among these were 250 male and female slaves,* all of whom he released from the slavery of the devil, at the same time releasing them from the yoke of human slavery by granting them their liberty.

CHAPTER 14*

IT is related that about this time certain special manifestations of heavenly grace were revealed in this monastery; for the tyranny of the devil had been recently overthrown and the reign of Christ had now begun. I have thought it fitting to preserve the memory of one of these manifestations often related to me by the most reverend Bishop Acca,* who declared that it had been told him by some trustworthy brothers from the very monastery.

Almost at the same time that this kingdom had accepted the name of Christ, many of the kingdoms of Britain were attacked by a virulent plague. By divine dispensation and will it reached this monastery which was at the time ruled over by a most devoted priest of Christ named Eappa; many of those who had come with the bishop as well as those who had been recently called to the faith from the South Saxon kingdom were indiscriminately snatched away from this world. So it seemed right to the brothers to observe a three-day fast and humbly implore God in His mercy to show pity on them, either by delivering those who were threatened by this disease from instant death or by preserving the souls of those who died from everlasting damnation.

At this time there was a little boy of the Saxon race in the monastery who had been lately converted to the faith and who had been afflicted by the disease and confined to his bed for a long time. On the second day of fasting and prayer it chanced that the boy was left alone at the second hour of the day in the place where he was lying sick. Suddenly, by divine dispensation, the most blessed chiefs of the apostles deigned to appear to him. Now he was a boy of very simple and gentle disposition and sincerely devoted to the mysteries of the faith which he had received. The apostles greeted him with holy words and said, 'Son, do not let the fear of death trouble you, for we are going to take you today to the heavenly kingdom. But you will first have to wait until mass has been celebrated and then when you have received the viaticum of the body and blood of Christ, you will be taken to the everlasting joys of heaven and set free from sickness and death. Call the priest Eappa and say to him, "The Lord has heard your prayers and has looked favourably upon your devotions and your fasts; therefore not one more from this monastery nor from the adjacent lands nor any of its possessions shall die of the plague. But all those people who are now suffering from the sickness shall be raised up from their sickbeds and restored to their former health—all except you alone, for you will today be freed by death and taken to heaven to behold the Lord Christ whom you have faithfully served. This the divine mercy has deigned to grant the brethren by the intercession of the saintly King Oswald,* beloved of God, who once reigned gloriously over the Northumbrian people with the authority of a temporal kingship and with the devotion and Christian virtue which brought him to the everlasting kingdom. It was on this very day that the king was slain in battle by the heathen and was forthwith carried to the everlasting joys of the souls in heaven, joining the ranks of the elect. Let them seek in their books in which the deposition of the dead is noted down and they will find that it was on this day that he was taken from the world. So let them celebrate masses in all the chapels of this monastery, both in thankfulness for answered prayers and in memory of King Oswald, who once ruled over this people and who prayed to the Lord for them as if of his own race though strangers; let all the brethren come to the church and join in offering the heavenly sacrifices; then let them end their fast and refresh their bodies with the food they need." '

The boy asked for the priest and told him all these things. The priest questioned him carefully about the dress and the looks of the men who had appeared to him. He answered, 'Their robes were magnificent and their faces joyful and beautiful, such as I have never seen before; nor did I think that any men could have such grace and beauty. One was tonsured* like a cleric and the other had a flowing beard. They told me that one was named Peter and the other Paul and that they were the servants of our Lord and Saviour Jesus Christ sent by Him from heaven to watch over our monastery.' The priest believed the boy's words and went out at once to search in his calendar and found that King Oswald had been slain on that very day. So he called the brothers and ordered a meal to be prepared and masses to be said, and all to communicate in their accustomed way. At the same time he ordered a small portion of the sacrifice and oblation of the Lord to be carried to the sick boy.

Soon after this, on the same day, the boy died, proving by his own death the truth of what he had heard from Christ's apostles. As further confirmation of his words no one except himself was carried off at that time from the monastery. Many who heard of the vision were wonderfully encouraged to pray to the divine mercy in times of adversity and to submit to the wholesome remedy of fasting. From that time, not only in this monastery but in many other places, the heavenly birthday of this king and soldier of Christ began to be observed yearly by the celebration of masses.

CHAPTER 15

MEANWHILE Cædwalla, a young and vigorous prince of the Gewisse, being an exile from his own land, came with an army and slew King Æthelwealh, wasting the kingdom with fierce slaughter and devastation. But he was quickly driven out by two of the king's ealdormen, Berhthun and Andhun, who from that time held the kingdom. The former was afterwards killed by Cædwalla when he was king of the Gewisse and the kingdom reduced to a worse state of slavery. Ine,* who ruled after Cædwalla, also oppressed the country in the same harsh way for many years. So it came about that during all this time it could have no bishop of its own. When Wilfrid its first bishop was called home they became subject to the bishop of the Gewisse, that is, the West Saxons, whose see was in the city of Winchester.

CHAPTER 16 (14)

AFTER Cædwalla had gained possession of the kingdom of the Gewisse he also captured the Isle of Wight, which until then had been entirely given up to idolatry, and endeavoured to wipe out all the natives* by merciless slaughter and to replace them by inhabitants from his own kingdom, binding himself, or so it is said, by a vow, though he was not yet Christian, that if he captured the island he would give a fourth part of it and of the booty to the Lord. He fulfilled his vow by giving it for the service of the Lord to Bishop Wilfrid, who happened to have come there from his own people at that time. The size of the island is 1,200 hides according to the English way of reckoning, so the bishop was given 300 hides. Wilfrid entrusted the portion he had received to one of his clergy named Beornwine, who was his sister's son, assigning to him a priest called Hiddila, to teach the word and administer baptism to all who sought salvation.

I think that I must not pass over in silence the fact that among the first fruits of the island who believed and were saved were two young princes, brothers of Arwald, king of the island, who were specially crowned with God's grace. When the enemy was approaching the island they escaped by flight and crossed over into the neighbouring realm of the Jutes. They were taken to a place called *Ad Lapidem* (Stoneham?)* where they thought they could remain concealed from the victorious king; but they were betrayed and condemned to death. On hearing this, Cyneberht,* an abbot and priest whose monastery was not far away at a place called *Hreutford*, that is, the ford of the reed (Redbridge), came to the king', who was living secretly in those parts while he recovered from the wounds which he had received during the fighting on the Isle of Wight. The abbot asked the king whether, if the boys must needs be killed, they might first be instructed in the mysteries of the Christian faith. The king agreed, so Cyneberht instructed them in the word of truth and baptized them in the fount of salvation and thus made sure of their entry into the eternal kingdom. When the executioner arrived, they gladly submitted to temporal death through which they were assured that they would pass to the eternal life of the soul. In this way after all the kingdoms of Britain had received the faith of Christ, the Isle of Wight received it too, yet because it was suffering under the affliction of alien rule, it had no bishop nor see until the time of Daniel, who is now bishop of the West Saxons.

The Isle of Wight lies opposite the borders of the South Saxons and of the Gewisse, with three miles of sea between, which is called the Solent. In this sea the two ocean tides which break upon Britain from the boundless northern ocean meet daily in conflict beyond the mouth of the river Hamble, which enters the same sea, flowing through those Jutish lands which belong to the kingdom of the Gewisse. When their conflict is over they flow back into the ocean whence they came.

CHAPTER 17 (15)

ABOUT this time Theodore heard that the faith of the church at Constantinople had been greatly shaken by the heresy of Eutyches.* As he wished to keep the English churches over which he presided free from any such taint, he convened an assembly of venerable bishops and many learned men and carefully inquired of each of them as to their belief. He discovered that they were all united in the catholic faith. So he took care to have this recorded in a synodal book to serve as a guide and a record to their successors. This is the beginning of the synodal book:

In the name of the Lord Jesus Christ our Saviour, and in the reign of our most religious lords, namely Ecgfrith, king of the Northumbrians, in the tenth year of his reign—17 September and the eighth indiction*—in the sixth year of the reign of Æthelred, king of the Mercians: in the seventeenth year of the reign of Ealdwulf,* king of the East Angles; and in the seventh year of the reign of Hlothhere, king of Kent; Theodore, by the grace of God archbishop of the island of Britain and of the city of Canterbury presiding; and sitting with him the other reverend bishops of the island of Britain, having the most holy gospels before us in the place which in the Saxon tongue is called *Hæthfelth* (Hatfield)*; we united in declaring the true and orthodox faith as our Lord Jesus Christ delivered it in the flesh to the disciples who saw Him face to face and heard His words, and as it was handed down in the creed of the holy fathers and by all the holy and universal councils* in general and the whole body of the accredited fathers of the catholic Church. Following these in all devotion and orthodoxy, we likewise believe and confess their divinely inspired doctrines and confess the Father and the Son and the Holy Spirit to be rightly and truly a Trinity consubstantial in Unity and the Unity in Trinity, that is, one God in three substances or consubstantial persons equal in glory and honour.

After much more to this effect concerning the confession of the true faith, the holy synod added this to its synodal book:

We acknowledge the five holy and universal councils of the blessed fathers who were acceptable to God: that is, of the 318 who met at Nicaea to condemn the impious Arius and his teachings; and of the

199

150 in Constantinople who condemned the madness of Macedonius and Eudoxius and their teachings; of the 200, in the first council at Ephesus, who condemned the worthless Nestorius and his teachings; and of the 630 in Chalcedon who condemned Eutyches and Nestorius and their teachings; and again the fifth council which met in Constantinople in the time of Justinian the second to condemn Theodore and the letters of Theodoret and Ibas and their teachings in opposition to Cyril.

And a little further on it reads:

And we acknowledge the council which was held in the city of Rome in the time of the blessed Pope Martin,* in the eighth indiction, in the ninth year of the reign of the most religious Emperor Constantine. We glorify our Lord Jesus Christ as they glorified Him, adding and subtracting nothing: we anathematize with heart and lips those whom they anathematized and we accept those whom they accepted, glorifying God the Father, who is without beginning, and His only begotten Son, begotten of the Father before all worlds, and the Holy Spirit, ineffably proceeding from the Father and the Son, as proclaimed by all whom we have mentioned above, holy apostles and prophets and doctors. And all we who with Archbishop Theodore have thus set forth the catholic faith subscribe our names to it.

CHAPTER 18 (16)

AMONG those who were present at the synod and assented to the decrees of the catholic faith was the esteemed John, precentor* of the church of the holy apostle Peter and abbot of the monastery of the blessed Martin, who had lately come from Rome at the command of Pope Agatho and under the guidance of the most reverend abbot Biscop,* surnamed Benedict, who has already been mentioned.* After Benedict had built a monastery in Britain, in honour of the blessed chief of the apostles, near the mouth of the river Wear, he visited Rome as he had often done before, this time with Ceolfrith* his companion and fellow worker, who became abbot of the same monastery after him. Benedict was honourably received by Pope Agatho of blessed memory, from whom he asked and obtained a letter of privileges confirmed by the apostolic authority, protecting the liberty of the monastery he had founded; for he knew that Ecgfrith, who had given permission and granted land for the founding of the monastery, desired and approved of this.

Benedict received this Abbot John and brought him to Britain in order that he might teach the monks of his monastery the mode of chanting throughout the year as it was practised at St Peter's in Rome. Abbot John carried out the pope's instructions and taught the cantors of the monastery the order and manner of singing and reading aloud and also committed to writing all things necessary for the celebration of festal days throughout the whole year; these writings have been preserved to this day in the monastery and copies have now been made by many others elsewhere. Not only did John instruct the brothers in this monastery, but all who had any skill in singing flocked in from almost all the monasteries in the kingdom to hear him, and he had many invitations to teach elsewhere.

In addition to his task of teaching chanting and reading, he had also been commissioned by the pope to inquire carefully into the beliefs of the English church, and report on them on his return to Rome. He had also brought with him the decision made by the synod called by the blessed Pope Martin which had recently* been held in Rome and at which 105 bishops were present. It was chiefly directed against those who declared that only one will operated in Christ. He arranged for a copy* of the decree to be made in the monastery of the holy Abbot Benedict. Those who held this belief had greatly disturbed the faith of the church at Constantinople at that time, but by the grace of God they were exposed and overwhelmed. Pope Agatho therefore, wishing to know what was the state of the church in England as well as in other kingdoms, and how far it was free from heretical contagion, entrusted the task to the reverend Abbot John who had already been appointed to go to Great Britain. When the synod we have mentioned was called in Britain for this purpose, it was found, as we have said, that all held the catholic faith untainted and a copy of the proceedings was given to John to take back to Rome.

As he was returning to his own land, not long after he had crossed the Ocean, he was attacked by illness and died. Because of his great affection for St Martin over whose monastery he presided, his body was taken by his friends to Tours and honourably buried there. He had been hospitably entertained by the church in that place on his way to Britain and had been earnestly asked by the brothers to take that road on his return to Rome and to stay at the same church. In fact they provided him with men to accompany him on his journey and to assist him in his appointed task. Though he died on the way, nevertheless the testimony of the English to the catholic faith was carried to Rome and most gladly received by the pope and by all those who heard it or read it.

CHAPTER 19 (17)

KING ECGFRITH married a wife named Æthelthryth, the daughter of Anna, king of the East Angles, who has often been referred to, a very religious man and noble both in mind and deed. She had previously been married to an ealdorman* of the South Gyrwe, named Tondberht. But he died shortly after the marriage and on his death she was given to King Ecgfrith. Though she lived with him for twelve years she still preserved the glory of perfect virginity. When I asked Bishop Wilfrid of blessed memory whether this was true, because certain people doubted it, he told me that he had the most perfect proof of her virginity; in fact Ecgfrith had promised to give him estates and money if he could persuade the queen to consummate their marriage, because he knew that there was none whom she loved more than Wilfrid himself. Nor need we doubt that this which often happened in days gone by, as we learn from trustworthy accounts, could happen in our time too through the help of the Lord, who has promised to be with us even to the end of the age. And the divine miracle whereby her flesh would not corrupt after she was buried was token and proof that she had remained uncorrupted by contact with any man.

For a long time she had been asking the king to allow her to relinquish the affairs of this world and to serve Christ, the only true King, in a monastery; when at length and with difficulty she gained his permission, she entered the monastery of the Abbess Æbbe,* Ecgfrith's aunt, which is situated in a place called Coldingham, receiving the veil and habit of a nun from Bishop Wilfrid. A year afterwards she was herself appointed abbess in the district called Ely,* where she built a monastery and became, by the example of her heavenly life and teaching, the virgin mother of many virgins dedicated to God. It is related of her that, from the time she entered the monastery, she would never wear linen but only woollen garments and would seldom take a hot bath except just before the greater feasts, such as Easter, Pentecost, and Epiphany, and then last of all, after the other handmaidens of Christ who were present had washed themselves, assisted by herself and her attendants. She rarely ate more than once a day except at the greater festivals or because of urgent necessity; she always remained in the church at prayer from the time of the office of mattins until dawn, unless prevented by serious illness. There are indeed some who say that, by the spirit of prophecy, she not only foretold the plague that was to be the cause of her death but also openly declared, in the presence of all, the number of those of the monastery who were to be taken from the world by the same pestilence. She was taken to the Lord in the midst of her people, after holding the rank of abbess for seven years. When she died she was buried by her own command in a wooden coffin, in the ranks of the other nuns, as her turn came.

She was succeeded in the office of abbess by her sister Seaxburh, who had been the wife of Eorcenberht, king of Kent. After Æthelthryth had been buried for sixteen years, the abbess decided that her bones should be raised and placed in the church in a new coffin; she therefore ordered some of the brothers to look for some blocks of stone from which to make a coffin for this purpose. So they got into a boat (for the district of Ely is surrounded on all sides by waters and marshes and has no large stones) and came to a small deserted fortress not far away which is called *Grantacæstir*

(Grantchester) in English, and near the walls of the fortress they soon found a coffin beautifully made of white marble, with a close-fitting lid of the same stone. Realizing that the Lord had prospered their journey, they brought it back to the monastery.

When the tomb of the sacred virgin and bride of Christ was opened and the body brought to light, it was found to be as uncorrupt as if she had died and been buried that very day. Bishop Wilfrid and many others who knew about it testify to this; but more certain proof is given by a doctor named Cynefrith, who was present at her deathbed and at her elevation from the tomb. He used to relate how, during her illness, she had a very large tumour beneath her jaw. 'I was ordered', he said, 'to cut this tumour so as to drain out the poisonous matter within it. After I had done this she seemed to be easier for about two days and many thought that she would recover from her sickness. But on the third day she was attacked by her former pains and was soon taken from the world, exchanging pain and death for everlasting health and life. When, some years later, her bones were to be taken out of the sepulchre, a tent was erected over it and the whole congregation stood round singing, the brothers on one side and the sisters on the other. The abbess herself had gone inside with a few others, for the purpose of raising and washing the bones, when we suddenly heard the abbess cry out from within in a loud voice, "Glory be to the name of the Lord!" Shortly afterwards they called me in, lifting the entrance to the tent; then I saw the body of God's holy virgin raised from the tomb and laid on a bed like one asleep. They drew back the cloth which covered her face and showed me the wound I had made by my incision, now healed, so that instead of the open gaping wound which she had when she was buried, there now appeared, marvellous to relate, only the slightest traces of a scar. Besides this, all the linen clothes in which her body was wrapped appeared as whole and fresh as on the very day when they had been put around her chaste limbs.' It is also related that when she was afflicted with this tumour and by the pain in her neck and jaw, she gladly welcomed this sort of pain and used to say, 'I know well enough that I deserve to bear the weight of this affliction in my neck, for I remember that when I was a young girl I used to wear an unnecessary weight of necklaces; I believe that God in His goodness would have me endure this pain in my neck in order that I may thus be absolved from the guilt of my needless vanity. So, instead of gold and pearls, a fiery red tumour now stands out upon my neck.' It happened also that, by the touch of the linen clothes, devils were expelled from the bodies of those who were possessed by them, and other diseases were healed from time to time. The coffin also in which she was first buried is said to have healed some who suffered from eye troubles; after they had prayed with their heads resting on the coffin, they were quickly relieved of the pain and dimness of their eyes. So the maidens washed her body, wrapped it in new robes, carried it into the church, and placed it in the sarcophagus which they had brought, where it is held in great veneration to this day. This sarcophagus was found to fit the virgin's body in a wonderful way, as if it had been specially prepared for her; and the place for the head, which was cut out separately, seemed to be exactly shaped to its size.

Ely is a district of about 600 hides in the kingdom of the East Angles and, as has already been said, resembles an island in that it is surrounded by marshes or by water. It derives its name from the large number of eels which are caught in the marshes. This servant of Christ wished to have her monastery here because, as has also been said, she sprang from the race of the East Angles.

CHAPTER 20 (18)

IT seems fitting to insert in this history a hymn on the subject of virginity which I composed many years ago in elegiac metre in honour of this queen and bride of Christ, and therefore truly a queen because the bride of Christ; imitating the method of holy Scripture in which many songs are inserted into the history and, as is well known, these are composed in metre and verse.

All-bounteous Three in One, Lord of all time,
  Bless mine emprise, all-bounteous Three in One.
Battle be Maro's* theme, sweet peace be mine;
  Christ's gifts for me, battle be Maro's theme.
Chaste is my song, not wanton Helen's rape.
  Leave lewdness to the lewd! Chaste is my song.
Divine the gifts I tell, not Troy's sad siege;
  Source of earth's joys, divine the gifts I tell.
Eternal God comes down to Virgin's womb;
  To set men free eternal God comes down.
From Virgin-mother springs (God's wicket-gate)
  The Sire of all, from Virgin-mother springs.
Glad the bright virgin-choir to know God born
  Of Virgin's womb, glad the bright virgin-choir.
Her glory made it grow, that holy plant;
  Those virgin flowers, her glory made them grow.
In furnace fierce stood virgin Agatha,
  Eulalia stands firm in furnace fierce.
Keen lions yield to Thecla's spirit high,
  To chaste Euphemia keen lions yield.
Laughs at the sword (of finer temper she)
  Agnes, and Cecily laughs at the sword.
Many the laurels won by holy hearts
  O'er the wide world many the laurels won.
Nor lacks our age its ÆTHELTHRYTH as well;
  Its virgin wonderful nor lacks our age.
Of royal blood she sprang, but nobler far
  God's service found than pride of royal blood.
Proud is she, queening it on earthly throne;
  In heaven established far more proud is she.
Queen, wherefore seek a mate, with Christ thy groom?
  To Him betrothed, queen, wherefore seek a mate?
Royal Mother of Heaven's King your leader now;
  You too, maybe, a mother of Heaven's King.
She, pledged to God her spouse, twelve years had reigned,
  When in the cloister was she pledged to God.
To heaven devoted, there she won new fame,
  And breathed her last, to heaven devoted there.
Veiled in the tomb sixteen Novembers lay,
  Nor rots her virgin flesh veiled in the tomb.
XT, Thine the power! even in the sepulchre
  Her vesture spotless gleams. XT, Thine the power!
Yields to those holy weeds each frightful plague;

Disease aghast yields to those holy weeds.
Zeal frenzied tears the foe that conquered Eve;
    Triumphs the saint, zeal frenzied tears the foe.
Affianced to the Lamb, now famed on earth!
    Soon famed in heaven, affianced to the Lamb!
Many thy wedding gifts while torches blaze.
    The Bridegroom comes; many thy wedding gifts.
Ever on sweetest harp thou sing'st new songs.
    Hymning thy Spouse ever on sweetest harp;
Ne'er parted from the Lamb's high company,
    Whom earthly love ne'er parted from the Lamb.

CHAPTER 21 (19)

IN the ninth year of King Ecgfrith's reign a great battle* was
fought between him and Æthelred, king of the Mercians, near
the river Trent, and Ælfwine,* brother of King Ecgfrith, was
killed, a young man of about eighteen years of age and much
beloved in both kingdoms; for King Æthelred had married his
sister whose name was Osthryth. Although there was good
reason for fiercer fighting and prolonged hostilities between
the kings and between these warlike peoples, Archbishop
Theodore, beloved of God, trusting in God's help, completely extinguished this great and dangerous fire by his
wholesome advice. As a result, peace was restored between
the two kings and between their peoples and no further lives
were demanded for the death of the king's brother, but only
the usual money compensation which was paid to the king
to whom the duty of vengeance belonged. So peace was
maintained for a long period between these kings and their
respective kingdoms.

CHAPTER 22 (20)

IN this battle in which King Ælfwine was killed, a remarkable
incident is known to have happened which in my opinion
should certainly not be passed over in silence, since the story
may lead to the salvation of many. During the battle one of

the king's retainers, a young man named Imma* was struck down amongst others; he lay all that day and the following night as though dead, amongst the bodies of the slain, but at last he recovered consciousness, sat up, and bandaged his wounds as best he could; then, having rested for a short time, he rose and set out to find friends to take care of him. But as he was doing so, he was found and captured by men of the enemy army and taken to their lord, who was a *gesith* of King Æthelred. On being asked who he was, he was afraid to admit that he was a thegn; but he answered instead that he was a poor peasant and married; and he declared that he had come to the army in company with other peasants to bring food to the soldiers. The *gesith* took him and had his wounds attended to. But when Imma began to get better, he ordered him to be bound at night to prevent his escape. However, it proved impossible to bind him, for no sooner had those who chained him gone, than his fetters were loosed.

Now he had a brother whose name was Tunna, a priest and abbot of a monastery in a city which is still called *Tunnacæstir* after him. When Tunna heard that his brother had perished in the fight, he went to see if he could find his body; having found another very like him in all respects, he concluded that it must be his brother's body. So he carried it to the monastery, buried it with honour, and took care to offer many masses* for the absolution of his soul. It was on account of these celebrations that, as I have said, no one could bind Imma because his fetters were at once loosed. Meanwhile the *gesith* who kept him captive grew amazed and asked him why he could not be bound and whether he had about him any loosing spells such as are described in stories. But Imma answered that he knew nothing of such arts. 'However,' said he, 'I have a brother in my country who is a priest and I know he believes me to be dead and offers frequent masses on my behalf; so if I had now been in another world, my soul would have been loosed from its punishment by his intercessions.' When he had been a prisoner with the *gesith* for some time, those who watched him closely realized by his appearance, his bearing, and his speech that he was not of common stock as he had said, but of noble family. Then the *gesith* called him aside and asked him very earnestly to declare his origin, promising that no harm should come to him, provided that he told him plainly who he was. The prisoner did so, revealing that he had been one of the king's thegns. The *gesith* answered, 'I realized by every one of your answers that you were not a peasant, and now you ought to die because all my brothers and kinsmen were killed in the battle: but I will not kill you for I do not intend to break my promise.'

As soon as Imma had recovered, the *gesith* sold him to a Frisian in London;* but he could neither be bound on his way there nor by the Frisian. So after his enemies had put every kind of bond on him and as his new master realized that he could not be bound, he gave him leave to ransom himself if he could. Now the bonds were most frequently loosed from about nine in the morning, the time when masses were usually said. So having sworn that he would either return or send his master the money for his ransom, he went to King Hlothhere of Kent, who was the son of Queen Æthelthryth's sister* already mentioned, because he had once been one of Æthelthryth's thegns; he asked for and received the money from him for his ransom and sent it to his master as he had promised.

He afterwards returned to his own country, where he met his brother and gave him a full account of all his troubles and the comfort that had come to him in those adversities; and from what his brother told him, he realized that his bonds had generally been loosed at the time when masses were being celebrated on his behalf; so he perceived that the other comforts and blessings which he had experienced during his time of danger had been bestowed by heaven, through the intercession of his brother and the offering up of the saving Victim. Many who heard about this from Imma were inspired to greater faith and devotion, to prayer and almsgiving and to the offering up of sacrifices to God in the holy oblation, for the deliverance of their kinsfolk who had departed from the world; for they realized that the saving sacrifice availed for the everlasting redemption of both body and soul.

This story was told me by some of those who heard it from the very man to whom these things happened; therefore since

I had so clear an account of the incident, I thought that it should undoubtedly be inserted into this *History*.

CHAPTER 23 (21)

IN the following year, that is, the year of our Lord 680, Hild* who, as previously stated, was abbess at the monastery called Whitby and a most devoted servant of Christ, departed on 17 November, after having done many heavenly deeds on earth, to receive the rewards of the heavenly life, at the age of sixty-six. Her career falls into two equal parts, for she spent her first thirty-three years very nobly in the secular habit, while she dedicated an equal number of years still more nobly to the Lord, in the monastic life. She was of noble birth, being the daughter of Hereric, King Edwin's nephew. It was in company with Edwin that she received the faith and the mysteries of Christ through the teaching of Paulinus of blessed memory, the first bishop of the Northumbrians, and she preserved that faith inviolate until she was counted worthy to behold Him.

When she had decided to give up the secular habit and serve the Lord alone, she withdrew to the kingdom of the East Angles, for she was a relation of a king of that land. It was her wish, if possible, to cross over to Gaul, leaving her home and all that she had, to live as a stranger for the Lord's sake in the monastery of Chelles,* so that she might the more easily attain to her eternal home in heaven. Her sister Hereswith,* mother of Ealdwulf, king of the East Angles, was at that time living in the monastery under the discipline of the Rule and awaiting her heavenly crown. Inspired by her sister's example, Hild continued a whole year in the kingdom of the East Angles with the intention of going abroad; but then Bishop Aidan called her home and she received a hide* of land on the north side of the river Wear, where, for another year, she lived the monastic life with a small band of companions.

After this she was made abbess in the monastery called *Heruteu* (Hartlepool) which had been founded not long before

by Heiu, a devoted handmaid of Christ, who is said to have
been the first woman in the Northumbrian kingdom to take
the vows and habit of a nun, having been ordained by Bishop
Aidan. But soon after she founded the monastery, she retired
to the town of *Calcaria* which the English call *Kælcacæstir*
(Tadcaster?)* and there she made her dwelling. Hild, the
handmaiden of Christ, was appointed to rule the monastery
and at once set about establishing there a Rule of life in all
respects like that which she had been taught by many learned
men; for Bishop Aidan and other devout men who knew her
visited her frequently, instructed her assiduously, and loved
her heartily for her innate wisdom and her devotion to the
service of God.

When she had ruled over the monastery for some years,*
wholly occupied in establishing a Rule of life there, it happened that she undertook either to found or to set in order a
monastery at a place called *Streanæshalch* (Whitby), a task
imposed upon her which she carried out with great industry.
She established the same Rule of life as in the other monastery, teaching them to observe strictly the virtues of justice,
devotion, and chastity and other virtues too, but above all
things to continue in peace and charity. After the example of
the primitive church, no one was rich, no one was in need, for
they had all things in common and none had any private
property. So great was her prudence that not only ordinary
people but also kings and princes sometimes sought and
received her counsel when in difficulties. She compelled those
under her direction to devote so much time to the study of the
holy Scriptures and so much time to the performance of good
works, that there might be no difficulty in finding many there
who were fitted for holy orders, that is, for the service of the
altar.

We have in fact seen five from this monastery who afterwards became bishops, all of them men of singular merit and
holiness; their names are Bosa,* Ætla,* Oftfor,* John,* and
Wilfrid.* The first, as already related, was consecrated bishop
of York: of the second it may be briefly stated that he was
consecrated bishop of Dorchester: of the last two it will later
be told that John became bishop of Hexham and Wilfrid,

bishop of York. Of Oftfor it may be said that after he had devoted himself to the reading and observance of the Scriptures in both of Hild's monasteries, being anxious to reach still greater heights, he went to Kent to join Archbishop Theodore of blessed memory. After he had spent some further time in sacred studies there, he decided to go to Rome too, which in those days was considered to be an act of great merit. After his return to Britain he went to the kingdom of the Hwicce of which Osric was then king; there he remained for a long time, preaching the word of faith and setting an example of holy life to all who saw and heard him. At that time the bishop of the kingdom, whose name was Bosel,* was greatly troubled by ill-health so that he could not carry out his episcopal duties himself; so Oftfor was appointed bishop in his place with universal approval and was consecrated at Æthelred's command by Bishop Wilfrid of blessed memory, who was at that time acting as bishop of the Middle Angles; for Archbishop Theodore was now dead* and no one had been appointed bishop in his place. Shortly before Bosel became bishop, a most energetic and learned man of great ability named Tatfrith, who was also from Hild's monastery, had been appointed to the see; but he was carried off before his consecration by an untimely death.

All who knew Hild, the handmaiden of Christ and abbess, used to call her mother because of her outstanding devotion and grace. She was not only an example of holy life to all who were in the monastery but she also provided an opportunity for salvation and repentance to many who lived far away and who heard the happy story of her industry and virtue. This was bound to happen in fulfilment of the dream which her mother Breguswith had during the child's infancy. While her husband Hereric was living in exile under the British king Cerdic,* where he was poisoned, Breguswith had a dream that he was suddenly taken away, and though she searched most earnestly for him, no trace of him could be found anywhere. But suddenly, in the midst of her search, she found a most precious necklace under her garment and, as she gazed closely at it, it seemed to spread such a blaze of light that it filled all Britain with its gracious splendour. This dream was truly fulfilled in her daughter Hild; for her life was an example of the works of light, blessed not only to herself but to many who desired to live uprightly.

After she had presided over the monastery for many years, it pleased the blessed Author of our salvation to subject her holy soul to the trial of a long bodily sickness so that, like the apostle, her strength might be made perfect in weakness. She was attacked by a fever which tortured her with its burning heat, and for six years the sickness afflicted her continually; yet during all this time she never ceased to give thanks to her Maker and to instruct the flock committed to her charge both in public and private. Taught by her own experience she warned them all, when health of body was granted to them, to serve the Lord dutifully and, when in adversity or sickness, always to return thanks to the Lord faithfully. In the seventh year of her illness she began to suffer internal pain and her last day came. About cockcrow she received the viaticum of the most holy communion and, summoning the handmaidens of Christ who were in the monastery, she urged them to preserve the gospel peace among themselves and towards all others; even while she was still exhorting them, she joyfully saw death approach or rather, to use the words of the Lord, she 'passed from death into life'.

One the same night it pleased Almighty God by a vision to reveal her death in another monastery some distance away called Hackness,* which she had built that very year. In this monastery there was a nun named Begu who for thirty or more years had been dedicated to the Lord in virginity and had served Him in the monastic life. As she was resting in the sisters' dormitory, she suddenly heard in the air the well-known sound of the bell with which they used to be aroused to their prayers or called together when one of them had been summoned from the world. On opening her eyes she seemed to see the roof of the house rolled back, while a light which poured in from above filled the whole place. As she watched the light intently, she saw the soul of the handmaiden of the Lord being borne to Heaven in the midst of that light, attended and guided by angels. Then awaking and seeing the other sisters lying around her, she realized that what she had seen had been revealed to her either in a dream or in a vision. Greatly afraid, she rose at once and ran to the maiden named Frigyth, who was then presiding over the monastery in place of the abbess. With many tears and lamentations and sighing deeply, she announced that the Abbess Hild, mother of them all, had departed from this world and that she had seen her ascend in the midst of a great light and escorted by angels to the abode of eternal light, to join the company of the citizens of heaven. When Frigyth heard this, she aroused all the sisters, called them to church and ordered them to devote themselves to prayer and psalm-singing on behalf of the soul of their mother. This they did diligently for the rest of the night and, at early dawn, there came brothers from the place where she had died to announce her death. The maidens answered that they already knew of it and, when they explained in detail how and when they had heard of it, it was found that her death had been revealed to them in a vision at the very hour at which the brothers said that she had died. By a beautiful harmony of events, it was divinely ordained that while some of them watched her departure from this life, others watched her entrance into the everlasting life of the spirit. Now these two monasteries are nearly thirteen miles apart.

It is also related that, on the same night and in the same monastery in which this servant of God died, her death was seen in a vision by one of the devoted virgins of God, who had been deeply attached to her. She saw Hild's soul ascend to heaven in the company of angels. She related this openly to the servants of Christ who were with her at the very hour it happened and aroused them to pray for her soul, and this before the rest of the congregation knew of her death, for it was only made known to them as soon as they met next morning. This nun was at the time with some other handmaidens of Christ in the remotest part of the monastery, where the women who had lately entered the monastic life used to spend their time of probation until they were fully instructed and admitted into the fellowship of the community.

CHAPTER 24 (22)

In the monastery of this abbess there was a certain brother who was specially marked out by the grace of God, so that he used to compose godly and religious songs; thus, whatever he learned from the holy Scriptures by means of interpreters, he quickly turned into extremely delightful and moving poetry, in English, which was his own tongue. By his songs the minds of many were often inspired to despise the world and to long for the heavenly life. It is true that after him other Englishmen attempted to compose religious poems, but none could compare with him. For he did not learn the art of poetry from men nor through a man but he received the gift of song freely by the grace of God. Hence he could never compose any foolish or trivial poem but only those which were concerned with devotion and so were fitting for his devout tongue to utter. He had lived in the secular habit until he was well advanced in years and had never learned any songs. Hence sometimes at a feast, when for the sake of providing entertainment, it had been decided that they should all sing in turn, when he saw the harp approaching him, he would rise up in the middle of the feasting, go out, and return home.

On one such occasion when he did so, he left the place of feasting and went to the cattle byre, as it was his turn to take charge of them that night. In due time he stretched himself out and went to sleep, whereupon he dreamt that someone stood by him, saluted him, and called him by name: 'Cædmon,' he said, 'sing me something.' Cædmon answered, 'I cannot sing; that is why I left the feast and came here because I could not sing.' Once again the speaker said, 'Nevertheless you must sing to me.' 'What must I sing?' said Cædmon. 'Sing', he said, 'about the beginning of created things.' Thereupon Cædmon began to sing verses which he had never heard before in praise of God the Creator, of which this is the general sense: 'Now we must praise* the Maker of the heavenly kingdom, the power of the Creator and his counsel, the deeds of the Father of glory and how He, since he is the eternal God, was the Author of all marvels and first created the heavens as a roof for the children of men and then, the almighty Guardian of the human race, created the earth.' This is the sense but not the order of the words which he sang as he slept. For it is not possible to translate verse, however well composed, literally from one language to another without some loss of beauty and dignity. When he awoke, he remembered all that he had sung while asleep and soon added more verses in the same manner, praising God in fitting style.

In the morning he went to the reeve who was his master, telling him of the gift he had received, and the reeve took him to the abbess. He was then bidden to describe his dream in the presence of a number of the more learned men and also to recite his song so that they might all examine him and decide upon the nature and origin of the gift of which he spoke; and it seemed clear to all of them that the Lord had granted him heavenly grace. They then read to him a passage of sacred history or doctrine, bidding him make a song out of it, if he could, in metrical form. He undertook the task and went away; on returning next morning he repeated the passage he had been given, which he had put into excellent verse. The abbess, who recognized the grace of God which the man had received, instructed him to renounce his secular habit and to take monastic vows. She and all her people received him into the community of the brothers and ordered that he should be instructed in the whole course of sacred history. He learned all he could by listening to them and then, memorizing it and ruminating over it, like some clean animal chewing the cud, he turned it into the most melodious verse: and it sounded so sweet as he recited it that his teachers became in turn his audience. He sang about the creation of the world, the origin of the human race, and the whole history of Genesis, of the departure of Israel from Egypt and the entry into the promised land and of many other of the stories taken from the sacred Scriptures: of the incarnation, passion, and resurrection of the Lord, of His ascension into heaven, of the coming of the Holy Spirit and the teaching of the apostles. He also made songs about the terrors of future judgement, the horrors of the pains of hell, and the joys of the heavenly kingdom. In addition he composed many other songs about the divine mercies and judgements, in all of which he sought to turn his hearers away from delight in sin and arouse in them the love and practice of good works. He was a most religious man, humbly submitting himself to the discipline of the Rule; and he opposed all those who wished to act otherwise with a flaming and fervent zeal. It was for this reason that his life had a beautiful ending.

When the hour of his departure drew near he was afflicted, fourteen days before, by bodily weakness, yet so slight that he was able to walk about and talk the whole time. There was close by a building to which they used to take those who were infirm or who seemed to be at the point of death. On the night on which he was to die, as evening fell, he asked his attendant to prepare a place in this building where he could rest. The attendant did as Cædmon said though he wondered why he asked, for he did not seem to be by any means at the point of death. They had settled down in the house and were talking and joking cheerfully with each of those who were already there and it was past midnight, when he asked whether they had the Eucharist in the house. They answered, 'What need have you of the Eucharist? You are not likely to die, since you are talking as cheerfully with us as if you were in perfect health.' 'Nevertheless,' he repeated, 'bring me the Eucharist.' When he had taken it in his hand he asked if they were all charitably disposed towards him and had no complaint nor any quarrel nor grudge against him. They answered that they were all in charity with him and without the slightest feeling of anger; then they asked him in turn whether he was charitably disposed towards them. He answered at once, 'My sons, I am in charity with all the servants of God.' So, fortifying himself with the heavenly viaticum, he prepared for his entrance into the next life. Thereupon he asked them how near it was to the time when the brothers had to awake to sing their nightly praises to God. They answered, 'It will not be long.' And he answered, 'Good, let us wait until then.' And so, signing himself with the sign of the holy cross, he laid his head on the pillow, fell asleep for a little while, and so ended his life quietly. Thus it came about that, as he had served the Lord with a simple and pure mind and with quiet devotion, so he departed into His presence and left the world by a quiet death; and his tongue which had uttered so many good words in praise of the Creator also uttered its last words in His praise, as he signed himself with the sign of the cross and commended his spirit into God's hands; and from what has been said, it would seem that he had foreknowledge of his death.

CHAPTER 25 (23)

ABOUT this time, the monastery of virgins at Coldingham, which has previously been mentioned, was burned down through carelessness. However, all who knew the truth were easily able to judge that it happened because of the wickedness of those who dwelt there and especially of those who were supposed to be its leaders. But God in His mercy did not fail to give warning of approaching punishment so that they might have been led to amend their ways and, by fasting, tears, and prayers, to have averted the wrath of the just Judge from themselves as did the people of Nineveh.

Now in this monastery there was an Irishman named Adamnan who led a life so devoted to God in austerity and prayer that he never took food or drink except on Sundays and Thursdays and often spent whole nights in vigils and prayers. He had first adopted this strict and austere way of life because of the necessity of atoning for the evil he had committed, but in course of time what he was once compelled to do as a penance became a habit.

In his youth he had been guilty of a certain sin but when he came to his senses he was utterly horrified and feared that he would be punished for it by the righteous Judge. So he went to a priest who, he hoped, could show him the way of salvation. He confessed his guilt and asked for advice as to how he could flee from the wrath to come. When the priest heard his offence he said, 'A severe wound calls for an even more severe remedy: so give yourself up to fastings, psalmody, and prayer to the utmost of your ability, so that, when you come before the presence of the Lord with your confession, you may deserve to find mercy.' But as he was in great grief because of his guilty conscience, and because he longed to get free as quickly as possible from the inward bonds of sin which weighed him down, he said, 'I am still young in years and strong in body; so I can easily endure whatever penance you place upon me, if only I may be saved in the day of the Lord, even though you bid me remain standing in prayer all night or fast for a whole week.' The priest said, 'It is too much to endure a whole week without food:* it is enough to fast for two or three days. Do this until I return to you in a short time, when I will show you more fully what you must do and how long you must persevere in your penance.' So with these words the priest went away, having prescribed the measure of his penance, and for some reason he suddenly went to Ireland, which was his native country, and did not come back again to keep his appointment. The man who remembered his injunction as well as his own promise, gave himself up entirely to penitential tears and holy vigils and austerity. So, as has been said, he ate only on Thursdays and Sundays and remained fasting all the rest of the week. When he heard that the priest had gone to Ireland and had died there, he ever afterwards, in accordance with his promise, maintained this same standard of austerity; and though he had begun this way of life in the fear of God and in penitence for his guilt, he now continued it unweariedly for the love of God and because he delighted in its rewards.

When he had practised this diligently for a long time he happened to go one day on a journey of some distance from the monastery, accompanied by one of the brothers. On the return journey, as they approached the monastery and beheld its lofty buildings, the man of God burst into tears, while his face betrayed the sorrow of his heart. When his companion saw this, he asked Adamnan the reason and he replied, 'All these buildings which you now see, both communal and private, will shortly be burnt to ashes.' Thereupon the other monk made it his business, as soon as they entered the monastery, to tell Æbbe,* the mother of the congregation. She was naturally disturbed by this prophecy, summoned

Adamnan to her, and carefully questioned him about this matter and how he came to know of it. He answered, 'I was recently occupied in vigils and singing psalms when I suddenly saw someone standing by me whom I did not recognize. I was greatly startled at his presence, but he told me not to be afraid and added in a friendly kind of manner, "You do well to choose to employ the night hours of rest in vigil and prayer instead of indulging in sleep." I answered, "I know that I have great need to employ my time in salutary vigils and in praying earnestly to the Lord to pardon my sins." "You speak truly," he replied, "but many besides yourself need to atone for their sins by good works and, by setting themselves free from worldly occupations, to labour more eagerly to cultivate a desire for their eternal welfare; yet there are very few who do this. I have just visited every part of this monastery in turn: I have examined their cells and their beds, and I have found no one except you concerned with his soul's welfare; but all of them, men and women alike, are sunk in slothful slumbers or else they remain awake for the purposes of sin. And the cells that were built for praying and for reading have become haunts of feasting, drinking, gossip, and other delights; even the virgins who are dedicated to God put aside all respect for their profession and, whenever they have leisure, spend their time weaving elaborate garments with which to adorn themselves as if they were brides, so imperilling their virginity, or else to make friends with strange men. So it is only right that a heavy vengeance from heaven should be preparing for this place and for its inhabitants in the form of raging fire."' The abbess said, 'Why were you unwilling to reveal these facts to me earlier?' He answered, 'I was afraid to do so out of respect for you, fearing you would be too greatly perturbed; nevertheless you may have this consolation that the calamity will not happen in your time.' When this vision became known, those who lived in the monastery were somewhat afraid for a few days and began to give up their sins and do penance. But after the death of the abbess, they returned to their old defilement and committed even worse crimes; and when they said 'peace and safety', suddenly the predicted punishment and vengeance fell upon them.

It was my revered fellow priest Eadgisl, who then lived in the monastery, who told me of all these happenings. After most of the inhabitants had left Coldingham because it was in ruins, he lived a long time in our monastery and died here. It seemed desirable to include this story in our *History* so as to warn the reader about the workings of the Lord and how terrible He is in His dealings with the children of men, in order that we should not at any time indulge in fleshly delights nor pay so little heed to the judgement of God that His wrath should come suddenly upon us and He should in His righteous anger afflict us with temporal loss or, it may be, judge us still more sternly and bear us away to everlasting perdition.

CHAPTER 26 (24)

IN the year of our Lord 684 Ecgfrith, king of Northumbria, sent an army to Ireland* under his ealdorman Berht, who wretchedly devastated a harmless race that had always been most friendly to the English, and his hostile bands spared neither churches nor monasteries. The islanders resisted force by force so far as they were able, imploring the merciful aid of God and invoking His vengeance with unceasing imprecations. And although those who curse cannot inherit the kingdom of God, yet one may believe that those who were justly cursed for their wickedness quickly suffered the penalty of their guilt at the avenging hand of God. Indeed the very next year the king rashly took an army to ravage the kingdom of the Picts, against the urgent advice of his friends and particularly of Cuthbert,* of blessed memory, who had recently been made bishop. The enemy feigned flight and lured the king into some narrow passes in the midst of inaccessible mountains; there he was killed* with the greater part of the forces he had taken with him, on 20 May, in the fortieth year of his age and the fifteenth of his reign. As I have said, his friends urged him not to undertake this campaign; but in the previous year he had refused to listen to the holy father Egbert, who had urged him not to attack the Irish who had done him no harm; and the punishment for his sin was that he would not now listen to those who sought to save him from his own destruction.

From this time the hopes and strength of the English kingdom began to 'ebb and fall away'.* For the Picts recovered their own land which the English had formerly held, while the Irish who lived in Britain and some part of the British nation recovered their independence, which they have now enjoyed for about forty-six years. Many of the English were either slain by the sword or enslaved or escaped by flight from Pictish territory; among these latter was Trumwine, a reverend man of God who had been made bishop over them and who retired with his companions from the monastery of Abercorn, which was in English territory but close to the firth which divides the lands of the English from that of the Picts. He commended his own people to his friends in such monasteries as he could find and chose his own place of retirement in the monastery, so often mentioned, of the servants and handmaidens of God which is called Whitby. There, with a few of his own people, he lived for many years a life of austerity in the monastery to the benefit of many others besides himself. When he died he was buried in the church of the blessed Apostle Peter, with the honours due to his life and rank. At that time the royal virgin Ælfflæd* presided over the monastery with her mother Eanflæd, both of whom have been mentioned before. But when the bishop came, that devout teacher Ælfflæd found him a very great help in the government of the monastery as well as a comfort in her own life. Aldfrith* succeeded Ecgfrith on the throne; he was a man most learned in the Scriptures, who was said to be the brother of Ecgfrith and son of King Oswiu. He ably restored the shattered state of the kingdom although within narrower bounds.

On 6 February in this year of our Lord 685 Hlothhere, king of Kent, died after a reign of twelve years, having succeeded his brother Egbert, who had reigned nine years. He was wounded in battle with the South Saxons whom Eadric, son of Egbert, had raised against him. He died while his wounds were being attended to. Eadric ruled for a year and a half after Hlothhere and, when Eadric died, various usurpers or foreign kings* plundered the kingdom for a certain space of time until the rightful king, Wihtred,* son of Egbert, established himself on the throne and freed the nation from foreign invasion by his devotion and zeal.

CHAPTER 27 (25)

KING ECGFRITH, in the year that he died, caused the holy and venerable Cuthbert* to be consecrated bishop of Lindisfarne as we have said. Cuthbert had for many years been living a solitary life, in great austerity of mind and body, on a small island called Farne which is in the Ocean, about nine miles away from the church of Lindisfarne. From his earliest years he had always longed for life under a Rule, and it was as a young man that he assumed both the name and the habit of a monk. He first of all entered the monastery of Melrose which is on the banks of the Tweed and was then ruled over by the Abbot Eata, the gentlest and simplest of men who, as has already been mentioned, was afterwards made bishop of Hexham or rather of Lindisfarne. The prior at that time was Boisil, a priest of great virtue and endowed with a spirit of prophecy. Cuthbert humbly submitted himself to Boisil's instruction and received from him a knowledge of the Scriptures and the example of a life of good works.

After Boisil died, Cuthbert was made prior of the monastery and trained many in life under a Rule, both in his capacity as teacher and by his own example. Not only did he teach those in the monastery how to live under the Rule and show them an example of it at the same time, but he also sought to convert the neighbouring people far and wide from a life of foolish customs to a love of heavenly joys. For many of them profaned the creed they held by wicked deeds and some of them too, in times of plague, would forget the sacred mysteries of the faith into which they had been initiated and take to the false remedies of idolatry, as though they could ward off a blow inflicted by God the Creator by means of incantations or amulets or any other mysteries of devilish art. So he frequently went forth from the monastery to correct the

errors of those who sinned in both these ways, sometimes on
horseback but more often on foot; he came to the neighbouring villages and preached the way of truth to those who had
gone astray, just as Boisil had been accustomed to do in his
time. Now it was the custom amongst the English people at
that time, when a clerk or a priest came to a village, for all to
gather at his command to hear the Word, gladly listening to
what was said and still more gladly carrying out in their lives
whatever they heard and could understand. So great was
Cuthbert's eloquence, so keen his desire to drive home what
he had begun to teach, so bright the light of his angelic
countenance, that none of those present would presume to
hide from him the secrets of their hearts, but they all made
open confession of their sins because they realized that these
things could certainly never be hidden from him; and they
cleansed themselves from the sins they had confessed by fruits
worthy of repentance, as he bade them do. Now he used
especially to make for those places and preach in those
villages that were far away on steep and rugged mountains,
which others dreaded to visit and whose poverty and ignorance kept other teachers away. Giving himself up gladly to
this devoted labour, he attended to their instruction with such
industry that he would leave the monastery and often not
return home for a whole week, sometimes even for two or
three weeks and even occasionally for a whole month; but he
would linger among the hill folk, calling the peasants to
heavenly things both by the words he said and by his virtuous
deeds.

So when the venerable servant of the Lord had passed
many years in the monastery at Melrose and had distinguished himself by great tokens of his spiritual powers, the
worthy Abbot Eata transferred him to the island of Lindisfarne so that there also, by his authority as prior, he might
teach the brothers how to keep the discipline of the Rule and
illustrate it by his own behaviour; for the reverend father Eata
ruled this place also as abbot at the time. In fact in this
monastery, even from ancient times, the bishop had been
accustomed to live with his clergy and the abbot to live with
the monks, who none the less belonged to the bishop's house-

hold, because Aidan who was the first bishop of this place came as a monk and established monastic life there. This also, still earlier, the blessed Father Augustine is known to have done in Kent, when the most reverend Pope Gregory wrote to him as has been related above: 'You, my brother, being conversant with monastic rules, ought not to live apart from your clergy in the English Church, which, by the guidance of God, has lately been converted to the faith; but you ought to institute that manner of life which our fathers followed in the earliest beginning of the Church: none of them said that anything he possessed was his own but they had all things in common.'

CHAPTER 28 (26)

LATER on, as Cuthbert grew in merit and in the intensity of his devotion, as has been said before, he attained also to the silence and secrecy of the hermit's life of contemplation. But since I wrote some years ago at length about his life and virtues, both in heroic verse and also in prose, it is enough here merely to mention that when he was about to go to the island, he made this declaration to his brothers: 'If by divine grace it is permitted to me to be able to support myself in this place by the work of my hands, I will gladly stay there; but if matters turn out otherwise, I intend, God willing, to return to you forthwith.' Now this place was utterly lacking in water, corn and trees; and as it was frequented by evil spirits, it was ill suited for human habitation; but it became in all respects habitable as the man of God wished, since at his coming the evil spirits departed. Having driven out the foe, with the help of the brothers he built a small dwelling-place surrounded by a rampart which contained the necessary buildings, namely an oratory and a living-room for common use. He asked the brothers to dig a well in the floor of the living-room, though as the ground was hard and rocky, there seemed to be no hope whatever of a spring. They did so relying upon the faith and prayers of the servant of God, and the next day it was found to be full of water, so that to this day it provides an abundance of its heavenly bounty to all who come there. He also asked for agricultural implements to be brought as well as wheat, and when he had prepared the ground he sowed it at the proper time. But by summer not a single blade, not to mention ears, had sprouted from it. So when the brothers were making their accustomed visit, he ordered them to bring barley to see if perhaps the nature of the soil or the will of the heavenly Giver demanded rather that a crop of this kind should grow there. Though the barley was brought long after the proper time of sowing, he put it in the same ground, when there seemed no hope of any harvest, yet an abundant crop quickly appeared, providing the man of God with the means of supporting himself by his own labour.

He served God in solitude for many years on this island and so high was the rampart that surrounded his dwelling that he could see nothing else but the heavens which he longed to enter. It happened that a synod of no small size was gathered together in the presence of King Ecgfrith near the river Aln in a place called *Adtuifyrdi** (which means 'at the two fords') over which Archbishop Theodore of blessed memory presided, and there Cuthbert was elected to the bishopric of the church of Lindisfarne by the unanimous consent of all. But he could by no means be dragged from his monastery, though many messengers and letters were sent to him. Finally the king himself sailed to the island together with the holy Bishop Trumwine, as well as many other religious and powerful men. Many of the brothers from the island of Lindisfarne came too for the same purpose. They all knelt down and adjured him in the name of the Lord, with tears and prayers, until at last they drew him, also in tears, from his sweet retirement and dragged him to the synod. When he arrived there, he was reluctantly overcome by their unanimous desire and compelled to submit his neck to the yoke of the bishopric. But he was chiefly prevailed upon by the words of Boisil the servant of God, who with prophetic insight had foretold all that was to happen to him and had predicted that he would become a bishop. His consecration, however, was not arranged immediately but only after winter, which was then just beginning. It took place at York, at the Easter festival, in the presence of

King Ecgfrith; seven bishops attended the consecration, among whom Theodore of blessed memory held precedence. Cuthbert was first of all elected to the bishopric of the church at Hexham in the place of Tunberht, who had been deposed from the episcopate; but because Cuthbert preferred to rule over the church of Lindisfarne in which he had lived, it was arranged that Eata should return to the church at Hexham to which he had originally been consecrated and Cuthbert was to undertake the government of the church at Lindisfarne.

After Cuthbert had been consecrated bishop, his works of virtue, like those of the apostles, became an ornament to his episcopal rank. He protected the people who had been committed to his charge with his constant prayers and summoned them to heavenly things by his most wholesome admonitions. He taught them what should be done but first showed them how to do it by his own example, as it is most helpful for a teacher to do. He was before all things fired with divine love, sober-minded and patient, diligent and urgent in devotion and prayer, and friendly to all who came to him for comfort. He held that to give the weak brethren help and advice was a fit substitute for prayer, for he knew that He who said, 'Thou shalt love the Lord thy God', also said, 'Thou shalt love thy neighbour'. He was outstanding in his use of penitential abstinence and, through the grace of contrition, he was always intent on heavenly things. For example, when he offered up the saving Victim as a sacrifice to God, he offered his prayer to the Lord not by raising his voice but by shedding tears which sprang from the depths of his heart.

CHAPTER 29 (27)

AFTER he had spent two years in the bishopric, he returned to his island monastery, for he had been warned by a divine oracle that the day of his death was approaching or rather the day of his entrance into that life which alone can be called life. This he made known to certain people with his usual candour but in obscure language which they only clearly understood at a later time; to others, however, he revealed it openly.

Now there was a priest of holy life named Herbert,* who had long been bound to Cuthbert, the man of God, by the bonds of spiritual friendship. He had been living a solitary life in an island of that large mere from which spring the sources of the river Derwent.* He used to come to Cuthbert every year and listen to his teaching concerning everlasting salvation. When he heard that Cuthbert was visiting the city of Lugubalia (Carlisle), he went there according to his custom, hoping to be inspired more and more to heavenly desires by his helpful advice.* While they were refreshing each other with draughts of heavenly living waters, Cuthbert said, 'Brother Herbert, remember to ask me now whatever you need to know and to discuss with me, because after we have parted we shall never again see each other in this world with the eyes of the flesh. For I am certain that the time of my departure and of laying aside my earthly tabernacle is at hand.' When Herbert heard this, he fell at his feet and with sighs and tears he said, 'I beseech you by the Lord not to desert me but to remember your most faithful companion and ask the merciful Lord that, as we served Him together on earth, we may journey together to the skies to behold His grace in heaven. For you know that I have always sought to live in accordance with your spoken commands and whatever I have done amiss through ignorance and weakness, I have taken equal care to amend at once according to your judgement and will.' The bishop gave himself up to prayer and forthwith, having learned in spirit that he had gained what he sought from the Lord, he said, 'Rise up, brother, and do not weep but be very glad because the Lord in His mercy has granted what we asked of Him.'

The issue of events confirmed the truth of the prophecy for, after they had separated, they did not see each other in the flesh but their spirits left their bodies on one and the same day, namely 20 March; together they beheld the beatific vision and together they were borne to the heavenly kingdom by ministering spirits. But Herbert was first wasted by a long illness, as we may well believe, by the decree of the divine grace, so that if in any way he had less merit than the blessed Cuthbert, the punishment and pain of a long illness might make up for it; and being made equal in grace to his intercessor, he might be counted worthy to depart from the body with him at one and the same hour, and also to be received into one and the same dwelling of perpetual bliss.

The most reverend father died on the island of Farne, having urgently prayed his brothers that he might be buried in the place where he had fought for the Lord for no small space of time. At length, however, he yielded to their entreaties and consented to be carried back to the island of Lindisfarne and buried in the church there. After this was done the reverend Bishop Wilfrid* held the bishopric at that church for a year until the consecration of Cuthbert's successor.

Afterwards Eadberht* was consecrated, a man renowned as well for his knowledge of the divine Scriptures as for his observance of the heavenly commands, especially in alms-giving: in accordance with the law he gave to the poor every year a tenth part, not only of his beasts but also of his corn and fruit and his garments as well.

CHAPTER 30

BUT the divine providence wished to show still further in what glory Saint Cuthbert lived after his death, whose sublime life had been attested before his death by frequent signs and miracles; so He put it into the heart of the brothers, eleven years after his burial, to take his bones—which they expected to find quite dry, the rest of the body, as is usual with the dead, having decayed away and turned to dust—and to put them in a new coffin in the same place, but above the floor, so that they might be worthily venerated. When they reported their decision to Eadberht their bishop, he consented to their plan and ordered them to carry it out on the anniversary of his burial. They did so and, opening the grave, they found the body intact* and whole as if it were still alive, the joints of the limbs flexible and much more like a sleeping than a dead man. Moreover all his garments in which his limbs had been clothed were not only undefiled but seemed to be perfectly new and wonderfully bright. When the brothers saw this, they were struck with great fear and hastened to tell the bishop what they had found. He happened to be alone in a place remote from the church, surrounded on every side by the sea at flood-tide. Here he always used to spend the season of Lent as well as the forty days before the Lord's birthday, in deep devotion, with abstinence, prayers, and tears. In this place his venerable predecessor Cuthbert fought for a while for the Lord in solitude before he went to Farne Island.

So they brought him part of the clothes which had wrapped the holy body. He joyfully received these gifts and gladly listened to the story of the miracle, kissing the garments with great affection as though they were still wrapped round the father's body, and he said, 'Put fresh garments around the body instead of those you have brought and replace it thus in the coffin* which you have prepared. I know most assuredly that the place which has been consecrated by so great a miracle of heavenly grace will not long remain empty. And greatly blessed is he to whom the Lord, the Author and Giver of all blessings, shall deign to grant the right to rest therein.' When the bishop had finished saying these words with many tears and great emotion and trembling voice, the brothers did as he commanded; they wrapped the body in a new garment, put it in a new coffin and placed it on the floor of the sanctuary.

Very soon Bishop Eadberht, beloved of God, was attacked by a dire disease and the violence of the illness increased from day to day. Not long afterwards, that is on 6 May, he too went to be with the Lord. His body was placed in the sepulchre of the blessed Father Cuthbert and they put over it the coffin in which they had laid the incorrupt limbs of the father. It is related that miracles of healing often happened in this place, bearing testimony to the merits of them both. Some of these I have recorded in my book about his life; but I have judged it convenient to add to this book some which I have recently chanced to hear.

CHAPTER 31* (29)

THERE was in the same monastery a brother named Baduthegn, who is still alive and who for a long time had acted as guest-master. It is the testimony of all the brothers and the guests who visited there that he was a man of great piety and devotion, who carried out his appointed duties solely for the sake of his heavenly reward. One day, after he had been down to the sea, washing the blankets and coverings which were used in the guest-house, he was seized on the way back with a sudden pain so that he fell to the ground and lay there prone for a long time, only rising again with difficulty. As he rose, he felt that one side of his body was afflicted with paralysis from head to foot and it was only with a great effort that he reached home, leaning on a stick. The disease gradually increased and, by nightfall, it had become still worse, so that on the next day he could scarcely rise or walk by himself. In his affliction he conceived the wise plan of going to the church as best he could, making his way to the tomb of the reverend Father Cuthbert; there, on bended knees, he intended humbly to beseech the mercy of the Lord so that he might either be delivered from his disease, if this were good for him, or if the divine grace decreed that he must endure so great an affliction still longer, that he might bear the pain that was laid upon him with patience and a quiet mind. He did as he had planned and, supporting his weak limbs with a staff, he entered the church and prostrated himself before the body of the man of God, praying with devout fervour that the Lord, through Cuthbert's intercession, would be propitious to him. While he was praying he seemed to fall into a deep sleep and, as he afterwards used to relate, he felt a great broad hand touch his head where the pain lay; the touch also passed over all that part of his body which had been afflicted by the disease, right down to his feet; slowly the pain fled and health was restored. After this he quickly awoke and rose up completely cured. He gave thanks to God for his recovery and told his brothers what had happened to him; to the joy of them all he returned to the office which he had been accustomed to fulfil so faithfully, yet still more purified and chastened as though by a scourge. The garments too, which had covered the dedicated body of Cuthbert while he was alive and after his death, did not lack the grace of healing, as anyone who reads may find in the book of his life and miracles.

CHAPTER 32 (30)

NOR must I pass over in silence a cure which took place three years ago through his relics and was told me recently by the very brother to whom it happened. It occurred in a monastery built near the river Dacre* from which it received its name, over which the religious man Swithberht then ruled as abbot. In it there was a certain young man whose eyelid was disfigured by an unsightly tumour, which grew daily larger until it threatened the loss of the eye. Though the doctors sought to reduce it by applying fomentations and ointments, they could do nothing. Some thought it should be cut away, while others opposed this course for fear of doing greater harm. The brother had been suffering from this affliction for a long time, and no human aid could cure it; the trouble increased daily and the loss of his eye was imminent, when it happened that he was suddenly healed, thanks to the mercy of the Lord, by the relics of the holy father Cuthbert. When the brothers had found his body uncorrupt after being buried many years, they had taken part of the hair either to give as relics to their friends who asked for them or to show as a proof of the miracle.

One of the priests of the monastery named Thrythred who is now abbot there, had at that time a small part of these relics in his possession. As he entered the church one day and was opening the casket of relics to give part of them to a friend who had asked for some, the young man with the diseased eye happened to be within. The priest gave his friend as much as he wanted and then handed over the rest to the youth to put back in the casket. The latter received the hairs of the holy head and, moved by a timely impulse, applied them to his diseased eyelid, trying for some time to reduce and soften the swelling by their application. Having done this, he replaced the relics in the casket as he had been bidden, believing that his eye would soon be healed by the hair of the man of God which had touched it. Nor was his faith in vain. It was then, as he used to relate, about eight in the morning. After being occupied in mind and body with the duties of the day, he suddenly touched his eye about midday and found that the eyelid was as sound as if there had never been any deformity or tumour on it.

END OF THE FOURTH BOOK

BOOK V*

BEGINNING OF BOOK V GOOD LUCK TO THE READER!

CHAPTER 1

CUTHBERT, the man of God, was succeeded in the solitary life which he lived on Farne Island before he became a bishop by the venerable Oethelwald. The latter, after he had been ordained priest, sanctified his office for many years in the monastery at Ripon by deeds worthy of that rank. In order to illustrate his merits* and the kind of life he lived, I will relate a miracle which was told me by one of the brothers for whose benefit and among whom it was performed, a venerable servant and priest of Christ named Guthfrith, who afterwards presided as abbot over the brothers of the church at Lindisfarne where he had been brought up.

'I came', he said, 'with two other brothers to Farne Island, wishing to talk to the venerable father Oethelwald. After we had been refreshed by his words and had asked his blessing, we were returning home, when suddenly, while we were in the midst of the sea, the calm weather which had accompanied us was broken, and so fierce a wintry tempest arose that we could make no progress either by sailing or rowing and expected nothing but death. After we had struggled for a long time in vain against wind and sea, we looked back to see if perhaps we could, by any effort, at least return to the island we had left. But we found that we were shut in by the storm on every hand, and there was no hope of safety by our own efforts. However, looking into the distance, we saw Oethelwald, the beloved of God, had emerged from his retreat on Farne Island and was watching our progress; for he had heard the crashing of the storm and the boiling ocean and had come out to see what was happening to us. When he saw our desperate plight, he bowed his knees and prayed to the Father of our Lord Jesus Christ for our life and safety. No sooner was his prayer ended than he had calmed the swelling main;* so that the fierce tempest ceased on all sides and favourable winds carried us over a smooth sea to land. As soon as we had landed and carried our little vessel up from the sea, the tempest, which had been calmed for our sakes for a short time, returned and continued to rage furiously all that day; so it was plain to see that the short interval of calm which had occurred was granted by heaven for our escape, in answer to the prayers of the man of God.

Oethelwald remained on Farne Island for twelve years and died there; but he was buried in the church of St Peter the apostle on the island of Lindisfarne, near the bodies of the bishops mentioned above. These incidents took place in the time of King Aldfrith, who succeeded his brother Ecgfrith and ruled over the Northumbrians for nineteen years.

CHAPTER 2

AT the beginning of Aldfrith's reign, Bishop Eata died and was succeeded as bishop of the church at Hexham by a holy man named John.* Many miracles were told of him by those who knew him well and especially by the most reverend and truthful Berhthun, once his deacon but now abbot of the monastery called *Inderauuda* (Beverley), that is, 'in the wood of the men of Deira'. We have thought it fitting to preserve the memory of some of these miracles.

There is a remote dwelling, enclosed by a rampart and amid scattered trees, not far from the church at Hexham, about a mile and a half away, and separated from it by the river Tyne. It has an oratory* dedicated to St Michael the archangel in which the man of God with a few others very often used to devote himself to prayer and reading when a favourable opportunity occurred, and especially in Lent. On one occasion, when he had come there to stay at the beginning of Lent, he told his followers to seek out some poor man who was afflicted by a serious illness or in dire need, to have with them during these days and to benefit from their charity; for this was his constant custom. There was in a village not far away a dumb youth known to the bishop, who often used to come to him to receive alms and had never been able to utter a single word. Besides this, he had so much scabbiness and scurf on his head that no hair could grow on the crown save for a few rough hairs which stuck out around it. The bishop had this young man brought and ordered a little hut to be built for him in the enclosure of their dwelling, in which he could stay and receive his daily allowance. On the second Sunday in Lent, he ordered the poor man to come in to him and then he told him to put out his tongue and show it him. Thereupon he took him by the chin and made the sign of the holy cross on his tongue; after this he told him to put his tongue in again and say something. 'Say some word,' he said, 'say *gæ*', which in English is the word of assent and agreement, that is, yes. He said at once what the bishop told him to say, the bonds of his tongue being unloosed. The bishop then added the names of the letters: 'Say A', and he said it. 'Say B', and he said that too. When he had repeated the names of the letters after the bishop, the latter added syllables and words for the youth to repeat after him. When he had repeated them all, one after the other, the bishop taught him to say longer sentences, which he did. After that those who were present relate that he never ceased all that day and night, as long as he could keep awake, to talk and to reveal the secrets of his thoughts and wishes to others which he could never do before. He was like the man who had long been lame, who, when healed by the Apostles Peter and John, stood up, leapt and walked, entering the Temple with them, walking and leaping and praising God, rejoicing to have the use of his feet of which he had so long been deprived. The bishop rejoiced with him at his cure and ordered the physician to undertake to heal his scabby head. He did as he was bidden and, with the help of the bishop's blessing and prayers, his skin was healed and he grew a beautiful head of hair. So the youth gained a clear complexion, ready speech, and beautiful curly hair, whereas he had once been ugly, destitute, and dumb. So rejoicing in his new-found health he returned home, which he preferred to do though the bishop offered him a permanent place in his own household.

CHAPTER 3

BERHTHUN told another miracle which the bishop performed. The reverend Wilfrid was restored to the bishopric of the church at Hexham after a long exile, and the same John, upon the death of Bosa,* a man of great holiness and humility, was made bishop of York in his place. He went on a certain occasion to a monastery of nuns in a place called *Wetadun** (Watton), over which Abbess Hereburh was at that time presiding. 'After we had arrived,' he said, 'and had been joyfully received by them all, the abbess told us that one of the nuns, who was her own daughter, was afflicted by a grievous illness. She had recently been bled in the arm and, while still under treatment, was seized with a sudden pain which rapidly increased. Her wounded arm grew worse and became so much swollen that it could hardly be encircled by both hands. She was lying in bed and seemed likely to die through the violence of the pain. The abbess asked the bishop to deign to visit her and give her his blessing, believing that she would greatly improve if he blessed or touched her. Then he asked when the girl had been bled and, on hearing that it was on the fourth day of the moon, he exclaimed, "You have acted foolishly and ignorantly to bleed her on the fourth day of the moon; I remember how Archbishop Theodore of blessed memory used to say that it was very dangerous to bleed a patient when the moon is waxing and the Ocean tide flowing. And what can I do for the girl if she is at the point of death?" but the abbess entreated him still more urgently on behalf of her daughter, whom she loved greatly and had planned to make abbess in her place. At last she persuaded him to visit the sick girl. So, taking me with him, he went in to where the maiden was lying, suffering great pain as I have said, and with her arm so swollen that she could not bend her elbow. He stood by her, said a prayer over her, blessed her, and went out. Afterwards, when we were sitting at the table at the usual hour, someone came and called me out saying, "Cwenburh"—that was the girl's name—"asks you to come back to her at once." I did so and as I went in I found her looking much more cheerful and apparently healed. As I sat by her she said, "Shall we ask for something to drink?" I answered, "Yes, indeed, and if you can drink I shall be delighted." A vessel was brought and when we had both drunk she said to me, "After the bishop had prayed for me, given me his blessing, and gone away, I felt better at once, and though I have not yet recovered my full strength, all the pain has entirely gone from my arm where it was most violent and from my whole body, just as if the bishop himself had carried it away, although the swelling still seems to persist in my arm." After we had gone the dreadful swelling departed as the pain had done and the maiden, saved from suffering and death, gave thanks to her Saviour and Lord, with all the other servants of His who were there.'

CHAPTER 4

ABBOT BERHTHUN also used to relate another miracle not unlike this one, which the bishop performed; he said, 'Not far from our monastery, less than two miles away, was the dwelling of a certain *gesith* named Puch, whose wife had been suffering for nearly forty days from a severe disease, so that for three weeks it had not been possible to carry her out of the room in which she lay. Now, at that time, it happened that the man of God was called by the *gesith* to dedicate a church and, after the dedication, the man invited the bishop to dine at his house. The bishop refused, saying that he must return to the monastery which was close by. But the *gesith* was most insistent in his request, vowing that he would give alms to the poor, if only the bishop would deign to come in and break his fast with him that day. I also added my entreaties, promising that I too would give alms for the relief of the poor if he would dine at the *gesith's* house and give him his blessing. When at length and with difficulty we had persuaded him, we went in to dinner. Now the bishop had sent one of the brothers who had come with me to take some holy water, which he had consecrated for the dedication of the church, to the woman who lay ill. He told him to give her some to drink, also instructing him to wash the place where the pain was worst with the water. When this was done, the woman at once rose cured, realizing that she was not only free from her protracted illness but had also recovered her long-lost strength; she brought the cup to the bishop and to the rest of us and continued to serve us all with drink until dinner was finished. In this she imitated the mother-in-law of St Peter,* who had been sick of a fever, but rose and ministered to them, having regained her health and strength at the touch of the Lord's hand.

CHAPTER 5

AT another time he was called by a *gesith* named Addi* to dedicate a church, and when he had completed the task, he was asked by the *gesith* to come and visit one of his servants who lay dangerously ill, so that he had lost all the use of his limbs and seemed to be at the point of death. In fact a coffin had already been made in which he was to be buried. The *gesith* urgently besought him with tears to go in and pray for his servant,* because his life was of great concern to him; and he believed that, if the bishop were willing to lay his hands on him and bless him, he would soon mend. So the bishop went in and found him at the point of death, surrounded by mourners, while the coffin in which he was to be buried was lying beside him. He said a prayer, blessed him, and went out, adding the usual words of comfort, 'I wish you a quick recovery.' Later when they were sitting at the table the boy sent to his master, asking him to let him have a cup of wine because he was thirsty. His master was extremely glad that the servant could drink and sent him a cup of wine blessed by the bishop. He drank it and then, shaking off his lethargy and weakness, he got up and put on his clothes, left his room, and went in to greet the bishop and his fellow guests, saying that he would much like to eat and drink with them. They bade him sit down with them to dinner, greatly rejoicing at his recovery. He sat down, ate, drank, and made merry, behaving like one of the guests; and he lived for many years afterwards enjoying the good health which he had at that time recovered. The abbot recounted the miracle, though he was not himself present when it happened, but it was told him by some who were there.

CHAPTER 6

NOR must I pass over in silence a miracle which Herebald, a servant of Christ, tells as having been performed upon him by the bishop. At the time he was one of the bishop's clergy, but is now ruling as abbot over the monastery which is at the mouth of the Tyne (Tynemouth). 'Living with him,' he said, 'and knowing his way of life extremely well, I considered that it was worthy of a bishop in every particular so far as it is lawful for a man to judge; but I have also discovered, by the experience of others and particularly my own, what his merits were in the eyes of Him who sees the heart; for I was recalled from the threshold of death, so to speak, to the path of life by his prayers and benediction. In my early youth, I was living among his clergy and engaged in the study of reading and song, but I had not yet entirely withdrawn my heart from youthful pleasures. It happened one day, as we were on a journey with him, that we came upon a level and dry road suitable for galloping our horses. The young men who were with him, mostly laymen, began to ask the bishop for leave to gallop and try out their horses against one another. At first he refused, saying that it was an idle request; but at last he gave way to their unanimous pressure and said, "Do as you like, but let Herebald have absolutely no part in the game." Thereupon I earnestly begged him to give me leave to compete with them, for I had great faith in the splendid horse which he himself had given me; but I was unable to gain his consent.

'While the bishop and I were watching, and the horses were galloping back and forth along the course, I was so overcome by a spirit of wantonness that I could hold back no longer; so in spite of his command, I mingled among the contestants and began to race with them. As I did so, I heard him behind my back, saying with a sigh, "Oh, how you grieve me by riding in such a way!" I heard, yet I went on against his orders; immediately, as my fiery horse took a great leap over a hollow in the road, I fell and at once lost all feeling and power of movement just as if I were dead. For in that place there was a stone, level with the ground and covered by a thin layer of turf, and no other stone was to be found over the whole plain. Thus it happened by chance, or rather by divine intervention in order to punish my disobedience, that I hit it with my head and with the hand which I had put under my head as I fell; so my thumb was broken and my skull fractured and, as I said, I lay like a corpse. As I could not be moved, they put up a tent for me to lie in. Now it was about one o'clock in the afternoon and I lay as quiet as if I were dead until evening, when I revived a little and was carried home by my companions. I lay speechless all night, now vomiting blood because some internal organs had been ruptured in my fall. The bishop was deeply grieved by my accident and by the disaster, because he had a special affection for me. So he would not sleep that night with his clergy, as was his custom, but spent the whole night alone in vigil and prayer, imploring, as I suppose, God's mercy for my recovery. In the early morning he came in to me, said a prayer over me, and called me by name. I awoke as though from a heavy sleep and he asked me if I knew who it was who was talking to me. I opened my eyes and said, "Yes, you are my beloved bishop." He answered, "Can you live?" I said, "I can, with the help of your prayers, if it is the Lord's will." Then, placing his hand on my head with words of blessing, he returned to his prayers; when he came back very soon afterwards, he found me sitting up and able to speak; and, urged as it soon appeared by a divine instinct, he began to ask me whether I was perfectly certain that I had been baptized. I answered that I knew without any doubt that I had been washed in the fountain of salvation for the remission of sins, and I told him the name of the priest who had baptized me. The bishop answered, "If you were baptized by that priest you were not perfectly baptized, for I know that, when he was ordained priest, he was so slow-witted that he was unable to learn the office of catechism or baptism; and for this reason I ordered him not to presume to exercise this ministry because he could not perform it properly." Saying this, he made it his business to catechize me forthwith; as he did so and breathed upon my face,* I immediately felt better. Then he called a doctor and ordered him to set and bind up my fractured skull. As soon as I had received his blessing, I was so much better that on the next day I mounted my horse and journeyed with him to another place; and very soon after I had fully recovered, I was washed in the water of life.'

He continued in the bishopric for thirty-three years and then he ascended to the heavenly kingdom and was buried in the chapel of St Peter in his monastery called Beverley,* in the year of our Lord 721. When, owing to advancing years, he was unable to administer his bishopric, he consecrated his priest Wilfrid to the see of York and retired to his monastery, where he ended his days in a way of life honouring to God.

CHAPTER 7

IN the third year of Aldfrith's reign, Cædwalla,* king of the West Saxons, after ruling his people most ably for two years, gave up his throne for the sake of the Lord and to win an everlasting kingdom, and went to Rome. He was anxious to gain the special privilege of being washed in the fountain of baptism within the threshold of the apostles; for he had learned that by the way of baptism alone can the human race attain entrance to the heavenly life; at the same time he hoped that, soon after his baptism, he might be loosed from the bonds of the flesh and pass, cleansed as he was, to eternal joy; and both these things came to pass with God's help just as he had intended. He arrived in Rome while Sergius was pope and was baptized on the holy Saturday before Easter Day in the year of our Lord 689; while still in his white robes, he was attacked by an illness and, on 20 April, he was freed from the bonds of the flesh and joined the company of the blessed in heaven. At his baptism Pope Sergius* had given him the name of Peter, so that he might be united in name also with the blessed chief of the apostles, to whose most sacred body he had come from the very ends of the earth, inspired by loving devotion. He was also buried in St Peter's church and, by order of the pope, an epitaph was placed on his tomb, so that the memory of his devotion might be preserved for ever and those who read it or heard it read might be kindled to religious zeal by his example. This is how it runs:

His high estate, wealth, kin, a mighty crown,
His strongholds, chieftains, spoils, his own renown,
And that of all his sires, Caedwal forsook,
Inspired by love of Heaven, that he might look,
A pilgrim king, on Peter and his shrine,
There taste at his pure fount the streams divine
Whence flows a quickening glory through the earth.
So when with eager soul he sought new birth,
He laid aside his barbarous rage and shame
And, with changed heart, to Peter changed his name
As Sergius bade, who took a father's place
For this his son, reborn by heavenly grace;
And that same grace soon bore him clothed in white,
Up through the skies into the realms of light.
Great the king's faith, Christ's mercy greater still,
Whose counsels far surpass all mortal skill.
From earth's remotest end, from Britain's isle,
To Romulus's town, o'er many a weary mile,
Bearing his gifts by devious ways he passed
Until he gazed on Peter's shrine at last.
Now while within the tomb his body lies,
His soul, washed white, joins Christ's flock in the skies.
'Twould seem he laid his earthly sceptre down
Only to change it for Christ's lasting crown.

Here was buried Cædwalla, otherwise Peter, king of the Saxons, on 20 April, in the second indiction, being thirty years of age more or less, in the reign of the most religious ruler the Emperor Justinian, in the fourth year of his consulship; and in the second year of the papacy of the apostolic ruler, Pope Sergius.

When Cædwalla left for Rome, Ine,* who was of the royal stock, succeeded to the throne. After he had ruled over the West Saxons for thirty-seven years, he also left his kingdom to younger men and went to the threshold of the apostles, while Gregory* was pope, to spend some of his time upon earth as a pilgrim in the neighbourhood of the holy places, so that he might be thought worthy to receive a greater welcome from the saints in heaven. At this time many Englishmen, nobles and commons, layfolk and clergy, men and women, were eager to do the same thing.

CHAPTER 8

THE year after Cædwalla died in Rome, that is, in the year of
our Lord 690, Archbishop Theodore of blessed memory died
at the age of eighty-eight, being old and full of years. He had
long been in the habit of prophesying to his friends that he
would live so long, for it had been revealed to him in a dream.
He remained bishop for twenty-two years and was buried
in the church of St Peter in which the bodies of all the
archbishops of Canterbury are interred. Of him and of all his
fellow archbishops it can rightly and truly be said that their
'bodies are buried in peace* but their name liveth throughout
all generations'. To put it briefly, the English Churches made
more spiritual progress while he was archbishop than ever
before. The epitaph on his tomb, consisting of thirty-four
heroic verses, openly and clearly describes to all comers his
character, his life, his age, and his death. These are the first
lines:

> Here lies a holy bishop's mortal frame;
> In Grecian tongue is THEODORE his name.
> A great high priest was he, the church's head,
> Who in sound doctrine his disciples fed.

and these are the last:

> September was the month, the nineteenth day,
> When from the flesh his spirit took its way,
> Climbing in bliss to share new life and love
> With angel-citizens of heaven above.

Berhtwald* succeeded him, having been abbot of the monastery at Reculver,* which is to the north of the mouth of the
river Yant.* He was a man with a deep knowledge of the
Scriptures and well versed in ecclesiastical and monastic
teaching, but not to be compared with his predecessor. He
was elected to the bishopric in the year of our Lord 692, on 1
July, while Wihtred and Swæfheard* were ruling in Kent. He
was consecrated in the following year on Sunday, 29 June, by
Godwin,* metropolitan of the Gaulish church, and was en-
throned on Sunday, 31 August. Among the many bishops he

consecrated was Tobias* to be bishop of Rochester after the death of Gefmund. Tobias was a man of great learning and was familiar with the Latin, Greek, and English languages.

CHAPTER 9

AT that time the venerable servant of Christ and priest Egbert, a man to be named with all honour, was living a life of exile in Ireland, as has been said before, so that he might reach his heavenly fatherland. He planned to bring blessing to many peoples by undertaking the apostolic task of carrying the word of God, through the preaching of the gospel, to some of those nations who had not yet heard it. He knew that there were very many peoples in Germany from whom the Angles and Saxons, who now live in Britain, derive their origin; hence even to this day they are by a corruption called *Garmani** by their neighbours the Britons. Now these people are the Frisians,* Rugians, Danes, Huns, Old Saxons, and *Boruhtware* (Bructeri);* there are also many other nations in the same land who are still practising heathen rites to whom this soldier of Christ proposed to go, after sailing round Britain,* to try if he could deliver any of them from Satan and bring them to Christ. But if he could not do this, he intended to go to Rome, there to visit and worship at the shrines of the blessed apostles and martyrs of Christ.

But divine revelations and interventions prevented him from carrying out any of these plans. He had already chosen the most vigorous of his companions and those who were outstanding both by their lives and learning and so most suitable for preaching the Word; and everything that was necessary for the voyage was prepared. Then early one morning one of the brothers came to him who had once lived in Britain and been a servant* of Boisil, the beloved priest of God, when this Boisil was prior in the monastery at Melrose under the abbot Eata, as has already been said. The man related to Egbert a vision which he had seen during the night; he said, 'When the mattin hymns* were finished and I had lain down on my bed, I fell into a light sleep and there appeared to me my late master and much loved tutor Boisil who asked me if I recognized him. I answered, "Yes, you are Boisil." He then went on, "I have come to bring to Egbert the reply of his Lord and Saviour which you must deliver to him. Tell him that he cannot perform this proposed journey. But it is God's will that he should go instead and give instruction in the monasteries of Columba." ' Now Columba was the first teacher of the faith to the Picts who lived beyond the hills to the north, and the first founder of the monastery in the island of Iona, which has long been greatly honoured by many of the tribes of Picts and Irish. Columba is now called Columcill by some, which is a compound of the word *cella* and the name Columba. When Egbert heard the story of the vision, he told the brother who related it not to repeat it to anyone else, for fear the vision should be an illusion. He himself silently considered the matter and feared it might be true; but, nevertheless, he was unwilling to cease his preparations for the journey to those people whom he intended to instruct.

A few days afterwards the same brother came back to him and said that on that very night, immediately mattins were finished, Boisil had again appeared to him in a vision saying, 'Why have you delivered the message I gave you to Egbert in so careless and lukewarm a manner? Now go and say to him that, whether he likes it or not, he must go to Columba's monasteries, for they are cutting a crooked furrow and he must call them back to the true line.' On hearing this Egbert again charged the brother to tell no one. Though he was now sure of the vision, he nevertheless attempted to start on his intended voyage with the brothers. But after they had placed all the necessities for such a voyage on board and had waited several days for favourable winds, one night there arose a fierce tempest in which some of the goods in the ship were lost and it was left lying on its side in the water. Nevertheless, everything that belonged to Egbert and his companions was saved. Then, quoting the words of the prophet,* 'For my sake this great tempest is upon you', he withdrew from the undertaking and resigned himself to staying at home.

There was one of his companions named Wihtberht* who was remarkable both for his contempt of this world and for his

learning. He had spent many years in exile in Ireland, living as
a hermit in great perfection of life. He took ship and, after
reaching Frisia, spent two whole years preaching the word of
life to that nation and to its king Radbod, but he reaped no
fruit for all this labour among the barbarians who heard him.
So he returned to his beloved place of exile and began again
to give himself up to the Lord, in his accustomed life of
silence; and although he failed to help strangers to the faith,
yet he took care to help his own people more, by the example
of his virtues.

CHAPTER 10

So Egbert, the man of the Lord, saw that he was not permitted to go and preach to the nations himself, but was retained
to be of some other use to the holy Church, as he had been
forewarned by a prophecy; and even though Wihtberht had
made no headway when he went into those parts, yet Egbert
still attempted to send holy and industrious men to the task of
preaching the Word; among these Willibrord was outstandingly eminent as a priest both in rank and merit. When they
arrived, twelve in number, they went to visit Pippin,* duke of
the Franks, by whom they were graciously received; and as he
had just driven King Radbod* out of nearer Frisia and had
taken it over, he sent them to preach there; at the same time
he gave them the support of his royal authority so that none
should molest them as they preached; he also bestowed many
favours on those who were willing to receive the faith. So it
came about that, aided by divine grace, they converted many
in a short time from idolatry to faith in Christ.

Following their example, two English priests who had long
lived in exile in Ireland for the sake of their eternal fatherland,
came to the kingdom of the Old Saxons in the hope of
winning some in that land to Christ by their preaching. They
both shared the same devotion and also the same name, for
they were both named Hewald, but with this distinction that
because of the different colour of their hair one was called
Black Hewald and the other White Hewald; both were full of

religious devotion, but Black Hewald was more learned in the holy Scriptures. When they reached the land, they went into the guest-house of a certain reeve, asking him to give them safe conduct to the viceroy who was over him because they had a message of importance which they had to deliver to him. The Old Saxons have no king but only a number of viceroys* who are set over the people and, when at any time war is about to break out, they cast lots impartially and all follow and obey the one on whom the lot falls, for the duration of the war. When the war is over, they all become viceroys of equal rank again. So the reeve* received them and though he promised to send them to the viceroy who was over him, as they requested, yet he kept them several days.

When the barbarians saw them continually engaged in psalms and prayers and daily offering up the sacrifice of the saving Victim to God—for they had sacred vessels with them and a consecrated board instead of an altar*—they realized that these men were of a different religion. They began to suspect that, if the Hewalds came to the viceroy and talked to him, they might turn him away from their gods and bring him to a new faith, the Christian religion, and so gradually the whole land would be compelled to change its old religion for a new one. So they seized them suddenly and put them to death. They slew White Hewald quickly with a sword but Black Hewald was put to lingering torture and was torn limb from limb in a horrible fashion; their bodies were thrown into the Rhine. When the viceroy whom they wished to see heard of it, he was extremely angry that the pilgrims had not been permitted to see him as they wished. So he sent and slew all those villagers and burned their village. These priests and servants of Christ suffered on 3 October.

Heavenly miracles were not lacking at their martyrdom. When the heathen threw their dead bodies into the river, as I described, they were carried for nearly forty miles against the current to the place where their companions were. A great ray of light reaching to heaven shone every night upon the spot where they chanced to be and even the heathen who had slain them saw it. One of the brothers appeared by night in a vision to one of their companions whose name was Tilmon, a distinguished man and noble also in the worldly sense, who had been a soldier and become a monk. The vision pointed out to him that the bodies could be found in the place where he saw a light shining from heaven to earth. And so it befell; their bodies were found and buried with the honour due to martyrs, while the day of their passion and also of the finding of their bodies was fittingly observed in those places. In fact, that most glorious duke of the Franks, Pippin, on learning what had happened, sent and had their bodies brought to him and buried with much splendour in the church of the city of Cologne,* on the Rhine. It is said that a spring burst forth in the spot where they were killed which to this day provides the place with an abundant supply of water.

CHAPTER 11

On their first arrival in Frisia, Willibrord,* as soon as he heard that the king had given him permission to preach, hurried to Rome while Pope Sergius was ruling over the apostolic see, in order to begin the missionary task he wished to undertake with the pope's permission and approval. At the same time he hoped to receive some relics of the blessed apostles and martyrs of Christ in order that, when he had destroyed their idols and founded churches in the nation to which he was preaching, he might have relics of the saints ready to put into them, dedicating each church in honour of the saint whose relics they were. He also wished both to learn about and obtain many other things necessary for so great a task. And when he had all that he wanted, he returned to his preaching.

At this time, the brothers who were engaged in the ministry of the Word in Frisia chose one of their number, a meek-hearted man of sober ways named Swithberht,* to be consecrated bishop over them. They sent him to Britain, where at their request he was consecrated by the most reverend Bishop Wilfrid, who was at that time an exile in Mercia, having been driven out of his own land. For at the time Kent had no bishop, since Theodore was dead and Berhtwald, his successor who had crossed the sea to be consecrated, had not yet returned to his episcopal see.

When Swithberht had received the rank of bishop and had returned from Britain, he left soon afterwards to go to the nation of the *Boruhtware* (Bructeri) and led many of them into the way of truth by his teaching. But soon afterwards the *Boruhtware* were defeated by the Old Saxons and those who had accepted the Word were scattered here and there. So the bishop and certain others went to Pippin who, at the request of his wife Bliththryth (Plectrudis), gave him a dwelling-place on an island in the Rhine which in their language is called 'On the Shore' (Kaiserswerth). Here he built a monastery which his heirs still occupy, in which he dwelt for a time, living a life of great austerity; and there he died.

When those who had come from Britain had spent some time in Frisia teaching, Pippin, with the consent of them all, sent the venerable Willibrord to Rome while Sergius was still pope, asking for him to be consecrated archbishop of the Frisians. This was duly performed as Pippin requested, in the year of our Lord 696.* He was consecrated in the church of the holy martyr Cecilia, on the day of her festival, and the pope gave him the name of Clement. He was sent back to the bishopric fourteen days after his arrival in the city.

Pippin gave him* a place for his episcopal see in his famous fortress which, in the ancient language of the people, is called *Wiltaburg*, that is the town of the Wilti, but in the Gallic tongue is called *Traiectum* (Utrecht). The reverend bishop built a church here and preached the word of faith far and wide, recalling many from their errors. He also built a number of churches throughout those districts and established several monasteries. Not long afterwards he appointed in those parts a number of bishops from among the brothers who had come with him or had followed him there for the purpose of preaching. Some of these have now fallen asleep in the Lord, but Willibrord himself, surnamed Clement,* is still alive and honoured for his great age, having been thirty-six years a bishop. After fighting many a battle in the heavenly warfare, he now longs with all his heart for the prize of a heavenly reward.

CHAPTER 12

ABOUT this time a memorable miracle occurred in Britain like those of ancient times. In order to arouse the living from spiritual death, a certain man already dead came back to life and related many memorable things that he had seen, and I think that some of them ought to be briefly mentioned here. There was a man, the father of a family, who lived a religious life together with his household in a district of Northumbria which is called *Incuneningum* (Cunningham).* He was stricken down by an illness which grew worse from day to day until he reached his end and died in the early hours of the night. But at dawn he came to life again and suddenly sat up, so that all who were sitting mourning round his corpse were terrified beyond measure and fled, except his wife, who loved him dearly and remained with him, though trembling with fear. The man comforted her, saying, 'Do not be afraid, for I have indeed risen from death which held me in its bonds, and I have been permitted to live again amongst mankind; nevertheless after this I must not live as I used to, but in a very different way.' He rose and went to the oratory in the village and continued in prayer until daylight came. He thereupon divided everything he possessed into three parts; he gave one part to his wife, another to his sons, and the third part he reserved for himself but immediately distributed it to the poor. Soon afterwards he freed himself from the cares of this world and went to the monastery at Melrose, which is almost encircled by a bend in the river Tweed. He received the tonsure and retired to a secret retreat provided by the abbot. There, until the day of his death, he lived a life of such penance of mind and body that even if he had kept silence, his life would have declared that he had seen many things to be dreaded or desired which had been hidden from other men.

He described what he had seen in this way: 'I was guided by a man of shining countenance and wearing bright robes. We went in silence in what appeared to me to be the direction of the rising of the sun at the summer solstice. As we walked we came to a very deep and broad valley of infinite length. It lay on our left and one side of it was exceedingly terrible with raging fire, while the other was no less intolerable on account of the violent hail and icy snow which was drifting and blowing everywhere. Both sides were full of the souls of men which were apparently tossed from one side to the other in turn, as if by the fury of the tempest. When the wretched souls could no longer endure the fierceness of the terrific heat, they leapt into the midst of the deadly cold; and when they could find no respite there, they jumped back only to burn once again in the midst of the unquenchable flames. Since a countless multitude of misshapen spirits, far and wide, was being tortured in this alternation of misery as far as I could see, and without any interval of respite, I began to think that this might be hell, of whose intolerable torments I had often heard tell. But my guide who went before me answered my thoughts, "Do not believe it," he said, "this is not hell as you think."

'When he had gradually led me further on, utterly terrified by this awful spectacle, I suddenly saw that the places in front of us began to grow dimmer until darkness covered everything. As we entered this darkness, it quickly grew so thick that I could see nothing else except the shape and the garment of my guide. As we went on "through the shades in the lone night",* there suddenly appeared before us masses of noisome flame, constantly rising up as if from a great pit and falling into it again. When my guide had brought me to this place, he suddenly disappeared and left me alone in the midst of the darkness and of the horrible scene. I saw, as the globes of fire now shot up and now fell back again ceaselessly into the bottom of the pit, that the tips of the flames as they ascended, were full of human souls which, like sparks flying upward with the smoke, were now tossed on high and now, as the vaporous flames fell back, were sucked down into the depths. Furthermore, an indescribable stench which rose up with these vapours filled all these abodes of darkness. When I had stood there a long time in great terror, uncertain what to do or where to turn or what end awaited me, I suddenly heard behind my back the sound of wild and desperate lamentation, accompanied by harsh laughter as though a rude mob were insulting their captured foes. As the noise grew clearer and finally reached me, I beheld a crowd of evil spirits, amid jeers and laughter, dragging five human souls, wailing and shrieking, into the midst of the darkness. I could see* that one was tonsured like a clerk, one a layman, and one a woman. The evil spirits dragged them down into the midst of the burning pit; and it came about that, as they descended deeper, I was unable to discern clearly between human lamentations and devilish laughter, but there was a confused noise in my ears. Meanwhile some of the gloomy spirits rose from the flaming abyss and rushed at me, surrounding me with burning eyes and tormenting me with the noisome flame which issued from their mouths and nostrils. They also threatened to seize me with the fiery tongs which they held in their hands, but although they ventured to terrify me, they did not dare to touch me. Being thus surrounded on all sides by foes and black darkness, I cast my eyes in every direction to see if there was any help or way of escape anywhere; and then there appeared behind me, on the road by which I had come, something like a bright star glimmering in the darkness which gradually grew and came rapidly towards me. On its approach all the hostile spirits who were seeking to seize me with their tongs scattered and fled.

'It was the one who had guided me before, whose coming put them to flight; turning to the right he began to lead me in the direction of the rising of the winter sun and quickly brought me out of the darkness into a serene and bright atmosphere. As he led me on in open light, I saw a very great wall in front of us which seemed to be endlessly long and endlessly high everywhere. I began to wonder why we were approaching this wall, since I could nowhere see any gate or window or steps to it. When we had reached the wall we suddenly found ourselves on top of it, by what means I know not. There was a very broad and pleasant plain, full of such a fragrance of growing flowers that the marvellous sweetness of the scent quickly dispelled the foul stench of the gloomy furnace which had hung around me. So great was the light that flooded all this place that it seemed to be clearer than the brightness of daylight or the rays of the noontide sun. In this meadow there were innumerable bands of men in white robes, and many companies of happy people sat around; as he led me through the midst of the troops of joyful inhabitants, I began to think that this might perhaps be the kingdom of heaven of which I had often heard tell. But he answered my thoughts: "No," he said, "this is not the kingdom of heaven as you imagine."

'When we had passed through these abodes of the blessed spirits, I saw in front of us a much more gracious light than before; and amidst it I heard the sweetest sound of people singing. So wonderful was the fragrance which spread from this place that the scent which I had thought superlative before, when I savoured it, now seemed to me a very ordinary fragrance; and the wondrous light which shone over the flowery field, in comparison with the light which now appeared, seemed feeble and weak. When I began to hope that we should enter this delightful place, my guide suddenly stood still; and turning round immediately, he led me back by the way we had come.

'When we had reached the joyful mansions of the white-robed spirits, he said to me, "Do you know what all these things are,* which you have seen?" I answered. "No!" Then he said, "The valley that you saw, with its awful flaming fire and freezing cold, is the place in which those souls have to be tried and chastened who delayed to confess and make restitution for the sins they had committed until they were on the point of death; and so they died. But because they did repent and confess, even though on their deathbed, they will all come to the kingdom of heaven on judgement day; and the prayers of those who are still alive, their alms and fastings and specially the celebration of masses, help many of them to get free even before the day of judgement. Furthermore, the fiery noisome pit which you saw is the very mouth of hell, into which whoever once falls will never be released from it through all eternity. This flowery place in which you see a fair and youthful company, so joyous and bright, is where the souls are received of those who depart from the body practising good works; but they are not in such a state of perfection that they deserve to be received immediately into the kingdom of heaven; nevertheless all of them at the day of judgement will enter into the presence of Christ and the joys of the heavenly kingdom. But any who are perfect in every word and deed and thought, as soon as they leave the body, come to the kingdom of heaven. This kingdom is near the place where you heard the sound of sweet singing, amid delightful fragrance and glorious light. You must now return to the body and live among men again; but if you seek to watch your actions with greater care and keep your ways and words righteous in singleness of heart, you yourself will receive a place after your death among the joyous band of the blessed spirits whom you see. When I left you for a time, I did so in order to find out what your future would be." When he had finished speaking I returned to the body with much distaste, for I was greatly delighted with the sweetness and grace of the place I had seen and with the company of those whom I saw in it. I did not dare to ask any questions of my guide; but meanwhile I suddenly found myself, by what means I know not, alive and in the world of men.'

The man of God was unwilling to relate these and other things he had seen to any who were living a slothful or a careless life, but only to those who were terrified by fear of the torments or delighted with the hope of eternal joys and were ready to make his words a means of spiritual advancement. For instance, in the neighbourhood of his cell there lived a monk named Hæmgisl,* who was an eminent priest and whose good works were worthy of his rank. He is still alive, living in solitude in Ireland and supporting his declining years on a scanty supply of bread and cold water. He would often visit this man and learn from him, by repeated questionings, what sort of things he saw when he was out of the body; it is from his account that these particulars which we have briefly described came to our knowledge. He also told his visions to King Aldfrith, a most learned man in all respects, who listened to them gladly and attentively; at the king's request he was admitted to the monastery already mentioned and was crowned with the monastic tonsure. Whenever the king visited that region, he often went to listen to his story. At that time the abbot and priest Æthelwold, a man of pious and sober life, ruled over the monastery. Now he rules over the episcopal see of Lindisfarne and his deeds are worthy of his rank.

The man was given a more secret retreat in the monastery where he could freely devote himself to the service of his Maker in constant prayer, and as his retreat was on the banks of the river, he often used to enter it in his great longing to chastise his body, frequently immersing himself beneath the water; he would remain thus motionless, reciting prayers and psalms for as long as he could endure it, while the water of the river came up to his loins and sometimes up to his neck. When he came out of the water, he would never trouble to take off his cold, wet garments until the warmth of his body had dried them. When in wintertime the broken pieces of ice were floating round him, which he himself had had to break in order to find a place to stand in the river or immerse himself, those who saw him would say, 'Brother Dryhthelm,'—for that was his name—'however can you bear such bitter cold?' He answered them simply, for he was a man of simple wit and few words, 'I have known it colder.' And when they said, 'It is marvellous that you are willing to endure such a hard and austere life', he replied, 'I have seen it harder.' And so until the day he was called away, in his unwearied longing for heavenly bliss, he subdued his aged body with daily fasts and led many to salvation by his words and life.

CHAPTER 13

ON the other hand, there was a man in the Mercian kingdom whose visions and words, but not his way of life, profited many but not himself. He lived in the time of Cenred,* Æthelred's successor, and was a layman, holding military rank; but however much he pleased the king by his outward industry, he displeased him by his inward negligence. The king warned him constantly to make confession, mend his ways, and give up his sins, before sudden death robbed him of all opportunity of repentance and amendment. But though he was frequently warned, he spurned this salutary advice, always promising that he would repent at some future time. Meanwhile he fell sick and took to his bed, suffering cruel pains. The king who loved him greatly went in to him and urged him to repent of his wickedness even then, before he died. He answered that he did not wish to confess his sins then, but only when he had recovered from his illness, lest his companions should accuse him of doing, for fear of death, something which he would not do when he was in good health; he imagined that he was speaking brave words but, as was afterwards apparent, he had been miserably deceived by the wiles of the devil.

As his disease grew worse, the king came again to see him and reason with him. But he called out at once in wretched tones, 'What do you want now? Why have you come? You can do nothing to help or save me now.' The king answered, 'Do not talk like that; behave like a sane man.' 'I am not mad,' he said, 'but I know the worst and I have seen it clearly.' 'And what is that?' the king asked. 'A short time ago,' he said, 'two most handsome youths came into my home and sat down near me, one at my head and one at my feet. One of them drew out a very beautiful but exceedingly small book and gave it me to read. On looking into it, I found all the good deeds I had ever done written down, but they were very few and trifling. They took the volume back but said nothing to me. Then suddenly there appeared an army of evil spirits with horrible faces; they surrounded the outside of the house, also filling almost the whole of the interior, and they too sat down. Then the one who seemed to be chief among them, judging by his dark and gloomy face and by the fact that he occupied the chief seat, took a volume of enormous size and almost unbearable weight, horrible to behold, and ordered one of his followers to bring it to me to read. On reading it I found all my sins written down very clearly but in hideous handwriting: not only my sins of word and deed but even my slightest thoughts. He said to the glorious white-robed men who sat by me, "Why do you sit here since you know that this man is certainly ours?" They said, "You speak the truth; take him away to help make up the number of the damned." With these words they immediately disappeared. Then two very wicked spirits who had daggers* in their hands struck me, one on the head and one on the foot. These daggers are now creeping into the interior of my body with great torment and, as soon as they meet, I shall die and, as the devils are all ready to seize me, I shall be dragged down into the dungeons of hell.'

Thus spoke the wretched man in his despair and, not long afterwards, he died. Now he suffers everlasting and fruitless punishment in torment because he failed to submit for a brief spell to the penance which would have brought him the fruit of pardon. From this it is clear, as the blessed Pope Gregory writes* about certain people, that he saw this vision not for his own benefit, because it did not profit him, but for the sake of others; so that they, hearing of his fate, may fear to put off their time of repentance while they still have the opportunity, and not be cut off by sudden death and die impenitent. As for the various books he saw offered him by good and evil spirits, this was done by divine providence, so that we may remember that our thoughts and deeds are not scattered to the breeze but are all kept to be examined by the great Judge, and will be shown us at our end either by friendly angels or by our foes. First the angels offered a white book and then the devils offered a black book, the angels a very small one, the devils an enormous one: and it should be noted that in his early years he did some good deeds which he completely obscured by doing evil in his early maturity. If, on the other hand, he had troubled to correct the errors of childhood in his youth, hiding them from God's eyes by well-doing, he might have been able to associate himself with the company of those of whom the psalmist says, 'Blessed are those whose iniquities are forgiven and whose sins are covered.'

I thought I ought to tell this story simply, just as I learned it from the venerable Bishop Pehthelm,* for the benefit of those who read or hear it.

CHAPTER 14

I MYSELF knew a brother, and I would that I had not known him, whose name I could mention if it were any use. He himself belonged to a noble monastery but lived an ignoble life. He was often rebuked by the brothers and the elders there and warned to turn to a more chastened way of life. But although he would not listen to them, yet they bore with him patiently for the sake of his outward service, for he was an exceptionally skilled craftsman. But he was much addicted to drunkenness and the other pleasures of a loose life; he used to remain in his workshop day and night, rather than go to the church with the brothers to sing psalms and pray and listen to the word of life. It happened to him as people say, that he who is not willing to enter the church gate humbly of his own accord, is bound to be carried against his will to the gates of hell, a damned soul. He was attacked by an illness and, when he was in extremity, he called his brothers; lamenting like one already damned, he began to describe how he had seen hell opened and Satan in its infernal depths, with Caiaphas and the others who slew the Lord, close by him in the avenging flames: 'and near them', he said, 'I see a place of everlasting damnation prepared, alas, for me, wretched man that I am.' When the brothers heard this, they began to urge him earnestly to repent even then, seeing that he was still in the body; but he answered despairingly, 'There is no time now for me to change my way of life, since I have already myself seen judgement passed upon me.'

As he uttered these words, he died without receiving the saving viaticum and his body was buried in the furthest corner of the monastery; nor did anyone venture to say masses or sing psalms or even pray for him. Oh, how far asunder has God divided light from darkness! The blessed protomartyr Stephen, when he was about to suffer death for the sake of the truth, saw the heavens opened and the glory of God, and Jesus standing at the right hand of God. The eyes of his mind were fixed before his death upon the place where he was to be after death, so that he might die more happily. But on the other hand this smith, a man of dark mind and dark deeds, when he was at the point of death, saw hell opened and the damnation of the devil and his followers. The unhappy man also saw his own place of imprisonment among them, so that he might perish the more miserably in despair himself, and yet might leave behind him a reason why those who were still alive and knew of this, should seek their own salvation by his own perdition. This happened lately in the kingdom of Bernicia. The story spread far and wide and roused many people to do penance for their sins without delay. And may the reading of this account of ours have the same effect!

CHAPTER 15

AT this time, by the grace of God, the greater part of the Irish in Ireland and some of the Britons in Britain* adopted the reasonable and canonical date for keeping Easter. The priest Adamnan,* abbot of the monks on the island of Iona, was sent by his people on a mission to Aldfrith, king of the Angles, and stayed for some time in his kingdom to see the canonical rites of the church. He was earnestly advised by many who were better instructed than himself that he, in company with a very small band of followers, living in the remotest corner of the world, should not presume to go against the universal custom of the church in the matter of keeping Easter and in various other ordinances. He altered his opinion so greatly that he readily preferred the customs which he saw and heard in the English churches to those of himself and his followers. He was a good and wise man with an excellent knowledge of the Scriptures.

On his return home he sought to bring his own people in Iona and those who were in houses subject to his monastery, into the way of truth which he had himself recognized and accepted with his whole heart; but he was unable to do so. So he sailed to Ireland and preached to the people there, modestly explaining to them the true date of Easter. He corrected their traditional error and restored nearly all who were not under the dominion of Iona to catholic unity, teaching them to observe Easter at the proper time. After he had celebrated Easter in Ireland canonically, he returned to his own island and earnestly put before his own monastery the catholic observance of the date of Easter, but he was unable to achieve his end; and it happened that before the year was over he had departed from the world. Thus by the interposition of divine grace, it came about that a man who greatly loved unity and peace was called to life eternal so that he was not compelled, when Eastertime returned, to have a still graver controversy with those who would not follow him in the truth.

This man wrote a book on the holy places which has proved useful to many readers; his work was based upon information dictated to him by Arculf,* a bishop of Gaul who had visited Jerusalem to see the holy places. He had wandered all over the promised land and had been to Damascus, Constantinople, Alexandria, and many islands of the sea. But as he was returning to his native land by sea, he was cast by the violence of the tempest on to the west coasts of Britain. After many adventures he came to the servant of Christ Adamnan who found him to be learned in the Scriptures and well acquainted with the holy places. Adamnan received him very gladly and eagerly listened to his words; he quickly committed to writing everything which Arculf had seen in the holy places which seemed to be worthy of remembrance. From this he made a book, as I said, which is useful to many and especially to those who live very far from the places where the patriarchs and apostles dwelt, and only know about them what they have learned from books. He gave this book to King Aldfrith and, through his kindness, it was circulated for lesser folk to read. The writer was sent back to his own country laden with many gifts. I think that it will be useful to readers to make some extracts and put them into this *History*.

CHAPTER 16

HE wrote thus* about the Lord's birthplace:

Bethlehem, the city of David, is situated on a narrow ridge, surrounded on all sides by valleys; it is a mile long from west to east, and has a low wall without towers, built around the edge of the plateau. In its eastern corner is a kind of natural half-cave, of which the outer part is said to have been the place of the Lord's birth. The inner part is known as the Lord's manger. The whole of the interior of this cave is covered with precious marble and, over the exact spot where the Lord is said to have been born, stands the great church of St Mary.

He wrote thus about the place of the Lord's passion and resurrection:

Entering the city of Jerusalem from the north end, the first place to be visited, as the layout of the streets demands, is the church of Constantine called the Martyrium. The Emperor Constantine built this in magnificent and royal style, because it was here that his mother Helena found the Lord's cross. Westward from here is the church of Golgotha in which the rock is still visible which once held the cross whereon the Lord's body was nailed. The rock now supports a large silver cross while above it hangs a great circle of bronze with lamps attached. Below the site of the Lord's cross, a crypt has been cut out in the rock and in this is an altar upon which the sacrifice is offered for the honoured dead, while their bodies meanwhile remain outside in the street. To the west of the church is the church of the Anastasis, that is, the Resurrection of the Lord, a round building surrounded by three walls and supported by twelve columns. Between each pair of walls is a broad passage containing three altars fixed in three places in the central wall, namely to the south and north and west. It has eight doors or entrances through the three walls, opposite one another, of which four face south-east and four east. In the centre is the round tomb of the Lord cut out of the rock, and a man standing inside can touch the roof with his hand. It has an entrance to the east and against it that great stone was set; to this day the cave on the inside bears the marks of iron tools. The exterior is completely covered with marble right to the top of the roof. This roof is adorned with gold and bears a great golden cross. On the north side of this tomb is the Lord's sepulchre, cut out of the same rock, being seven feet long and raised about three hand-breadths from the floor. The entrance is on the south side, where twelve lamps burn day and night, four within the sepulchre and eight above it on the right edge. The stone which was placed at the mouth of the sepulchre is now split in two, but the smaller portion stands as an altar of squared stone in front of the tomb itself, while the larger part forms another four-cornered altar, set up at the east end of the church and draped with linen cloths. The colour of the tomb and the sepulchre is white mingled with red.

CHAPTER 17

OUR author writes thus about the place of the Lord's ascension:

The mount of Olives is equal in height to Mount Sion but exceeds it in breadth and length. Except for vines and olives, it has few trees, but it produces much wheat and barley, for the quality of the soil is not marshy but suitable rather for grass and flowers. At the summit, from which the Lord ascended to heaven, there is a great round church which has in its circumference three chapels with vaulted roofs. The interior of the church could not be vaulted or roofed because the Lord's body passed up out of it. To the east it has an altar roofed in with a narrow canopy, and in the centre of the church are to be seen the last footprints of the Lord as He ascended, being open to the sky above. Although the earth is daily carried away by the faithful, yet it still remains and preserves the same appearance of having been marked by the impress of His feet. Around these footprints there is a circular enclosure of bronze, as high as a man's neck, with a great lamp hanging above on pulleys, which shines day and night; it has an entrance from the west. At the west end of the church are eight windows and, opposite them, are as many lamps hanging from cords, whose light can be seen through the glass as far as Jerusalem: and their rays are said to stir the hearts of all who see them to zeal and penitence. Each year on the day of the Lord's ascension, after mass was said, a fierce blast of wind used to come down and throw to the ground all who were in the church.

He writes thus about Hebron and the tombs of the patriarchs:

Hebron, once a city and the capital of David's kingdom, now only shows by its ruins what it once was. A furlong away to the east, in the valley, is a double cave where are the tombs of the patriarchs, their heads facing north, surrounded on four sides by a wall. Each one of these tombs is covered by a single stone, hewn after the shape of a church, those of the three patriarchs being white, while that of Adam is darker and of poorer workmanship; he lies not far from them at the farthest end of the northern wall. There are also some smaller and poorer monuments to their three wives. The hill of Mamre is a mile to the north of these tombs, covered with grass and flowers, with a level plateau on the top. On the north side is Abraham's oak consisting of a trunk only, and twice the height of a man, being enclosed in a church.

I determined to add to this *History* excerpts from these writings for the benefit of readers. They contain the sense of his words but put more briefly and concisely. If anyone wishes to know more of this book, he may find it in the volume itself and in the abridgement of it which I have lately made.

CHAPTER 18

IN the year of our Lord 705 Aldfrith, king of Northumbria, died, having reigned nearly twenty years. His son Osred,* a boy about eight years old, succeeded him and reigned eleven years. At the beginning of his reign Hædde, bishop of the West Saxons, departed to the heavenly life. He was a good and just man, whose life and teaching as a bishop depended more on his innate love of virtue than on what he learned from books. In fact the reverend Bishop Pehthelm (of whom more will be said* in the proper place), who was for a long time deacon and monk with Hædde's successor Aldhelm,* used to relate that many miracles of healing happened on the spot where Hædde died, through the merits of his holiness. He said that the men of that kingdom used to take soil from the place and put it in water for the benefit of the sick, and both sick men and cattle who drank it or were sprinkled with it, were healed. As a result of the constant removal of the sacred soil, a hole of considerable size was made there.

When Hædde died, the bishopric of the kingdom was divided into two dioceses. One was given to Daniel,* who governs it to this day, the other to Aldhelm, who presided over it energetically for four years. Both were fully instructed in ecclesiastical matters and in the knowledge of the Scriptures. For example, Aldhelm, when he was still priest and abbot of the monastery known as Malmesbury, by order of a synod of his own people wrote a remarkable book against the British error of celebrating Easter at the wrong time, and of doing many other things to the detriment of the pure practices and the peace of the Church; by means of this book* he led many of those Britons who were subject to the West Saxons to adopt the catholic celebration of the Easter of the Lord. He also wrote a most excellent book on virginity both in hexameter verse and in prose, producing a twofold* work after the example of Sedulius. He also wrote several other books, for he was a man of wide learning. He had a polished style* and, as we have said, was remarkable for his erudition in both ecclesiastical and in general studies. On his death Forthhere* became bishop in his place; he also was a man most learned in the Scriptures.

While these men administered the see, it was decided by a decree of the synod* that the kingdom of the South Saxons, which had hitherto belonged to the diocese of Winchester, over which Daniel presided, should have an episcopal see and a bishop of its own. Eadberht, who was consecrated first bishop, had been abbot of the monastery of Bishop Wilfrid of blessed memory, which is called Selsey. When he died Eolla succeeded to the bishopric. He departed this life some years ago and the bishopric has remained vacant to this day.

CHAPTER 19

IN the fourth year of the reign of Osred, Cenred, who had ruled the kingdom of Mercia for some time and very nobly, with still greater nobility renounced the throne of his kingdom. He went to Rome while Constantine* was pope, received the tonsure, and became a monk at the shrine of the apostles and remained there until his last days, occupied in prayer, fasting, and almsgiving. He was succeeded by Ceolred,* son of that Æthelred who had been Cenred's predecessor. There came with him also Offa,* son of Sighere, the king of the East Saxons, already referred to; Offa was a youth so lovable and handsome that the whole race longed for him to have and to hold the sceptre of the kingdom. He too, inspired by a like devotion, left his wife, his lands, his kins-men, and his fatherland for Christ and for the gospel in order that he might receive 'a hundredfold in this life* and in the world to come, life everlasting.' He too, when they reached the holy places at Rome, received the tonsure, ended his life in a monk's habit, and so attained to the vision of the blessed apostles in heaven which he had so long desired.

The same year that they left Britain, the famous Bishop Wilfrid* ended his days in the district called Oundle, after he had been bishop for forty-five years. His body was placed in a coffin and carried to the monastery at Ripon, where it was buried in the church of St Peter the Apostle, with the honour befitting so great a bishop. Let us now turn back and briefly relate some of the events of his life. He was a boy of good disposition and virtuous beyond his years. He behaved himself with such modesty and discretion in all things that he was deservedly loved, honoured, and cherished by his elders as though he were one of themselves. After he had reached the age of fourteen, he chose the monastic rather than the secular life. When he told his father this, for his mother was dead, he readily consented to the boy's godly desires and aspirations and bade him persevere in his profitable undertaking. So he came to the island of Lindisfarne and there devoted himself to the service of the monks, diligently striving to learn how to live a life of monastic purity and devotion. Since he was quick-witted he speedily learned the psalms and a number of other books; although he had not yet been tonsured, he was in no small measure distinguished for the virtues of humility and obedience, which are more important than the tonsure; and for this reason he was rightly loved by the older monks as well as by his contemporaries. After he had served God in that monastery for some years, being a youth of shrewd understanding, he gradually came to realize that the traditional way of virtuous life followed by the Irish was by no means perfect; so he resolved to go to Rome to see what ecclesiastical and monastic practices were observed in the apostolic see. When he told the brothers they commended his plan and persuaded him to carry out his purpose. He at once went to Queen Eanflæd because she knew him and because it was through her counsel and at her request that he had been admitted to the monastery. He told her of his desire to visit the shrines of the blessed apostles. She was delighted with the youth's excellent plan and sent him to King Eorcenberht of Kent,

who was her cousin, asking him to send Wilfrid honourably to
Rome. At that time Honorius, one of the disciples of the
blessed Pope Gregory, was archbishop there, a man deeply
versed in ecclesiastical matters. The youth, who was very
active-minded, spent some time in Kent, diligently setting
himself to learn all that he saw, until another young man
came, named Biscop, known also as Benedict, an Anglian of
noble family, who also wished to go to Rome, and who has
already been mentioned.

The king gave Wilfrid to Biscop as a companion and ordered Biscop to take him to Rome with him. When they
reached Lyons, Wilfrid was held back by Dalfinus, the bishop
of the city, while Benedict eagerly continued his journey to
Rome. The bishop was delighted with the youth's prudent
talk, his grace and beauty, his eager activity, and his con-
sistent and mature way of thinking. So as long as he remained,
he supplied him and his companions plentifully with all they
needed; and furthermore he offered Wilfrid, if he would
accept them, a considerable part of Gaul to rule over, his
unmarried niece as his wife, and to adopt him as his son.
Wilfrid thanked him for the kindness he had deigned to show
him, a stranger, but answered that he had resolved upon
another course of life and for that reason had left his native
land and set out for Rome.

When the bishop heard this, he sent him to Rome, providing him with a guide for his journey, supplying him with an
abundance of all things necessary for the road and earnestly
begging that, on his return to his own country, he would come
that way. When Wilfrid arrived in Rome he perseveringly
devoted himself day by day, as he had intended, to constant
prayer and the study of ecclesiastical matters, making friends
with Archdeacon Boniface, a most holy and learned man,
who was also a counsellor to the pope. Under his tuition he
studied each of the four gospels in turn and learned the
correct method of calculating Easter as well as gaining, under
his teacher's guidance, a knowledge of many other matters of
ecclesiastical discipline which were unknown in his own
country. After he had spent some months in these happy
studies, he returned to Dalfinus in Gaul, where he spent three

years, being tonsured by him and so greatly beloved that he proposed to make Wilfrid his successor. But the bishop was cut off by a cruel death and so this was prevented; indeed, Wilfrid was reserved for the task of being a bishop over his own people, the Angles. Queen Baldhild* had sent soldiers and ordered the bishop to be executed; Wilfrid, being one of his clergy, followed him to the place where he was to be beheaded, desiring to perish with him, though the bishop himself firmly opposed it. But when the executioners discovered that he was a foreigner of English race, they spared him and refused to put him to death with his bishop.

On returning to Britain, he made friends with King Alhfrith, who had learned always to obey and love the catholic rules of the church. When he found that Wilfrid was also catholic, he at once gave him ten hides in a place called Stamford, and soon afterwards a monastery with thirty hides in a place called Ripon. He had first offered this site to some who followed the Irish ways, so that they might build a monastery there. But when they were given the choice, they preferred to abandon the place rather than accept the catholic Easter and the other canonical rites of the Roman and apostolic church; so he gave it to one whom he found to be trained in better rules and customs.

At this time he was ordained priest at Ripon, on the command of the king, by Agilbert, bishop of the Gewisse, already mentioned, because the king wished that a man of such learning and devotion should be in special and constant attendance upon him as his priest and teacher. Not long after, as already explained, when the Irish sect had been exposed and banished, Alhfrith sent him to Gaul with the counsel and consent of his father Oswiu, requesting that he should be consecrated as his bishop by that same Agilbert who was now acting as bishop of Paris. Wilfrid was then about thirty years of age. Eleven bishops joined with Agilbert for the consecration, and the ceremony was carried out with great dignity. But since Wilfrid delayed overseas, a holy man named Chad, as already described, was consecrated to the bishopric of York at the command of King Oswiu. He ruled the church outstandingly well for three years and then retired to look after his monastery at Lastingham, while Wilfrid became bishop of the whole Northumbrian kingdom.

Later on, during the reign of Ecgfrith, Wilfrid was driven from the see and other bishops were consecrated in his place, as has already been related. Intending to go to Rome to plead his cause before the pope, he embarked on a ship and was driven by the west wind to Frisia, where he was honourably received by the barbarians and their king Aldgisl.* He preached Christ to them and, after instructing many thousands of them in the word of truth, he washed them from the stains of their sins in the Saviour's font. In this way he first began that work of evangelization which the most reverend bishop of Christ, Willibrord, afterwards completed with great devotion. He spent the winter happily there with these new people of God and then continued his journey to Rome. After his case had been considered in the presence of Pope Agatho and many bishops, it was decided by their unanimous judgement that he had been wrongly accused, and so he was declared worthy to hold his bishopric.

At that time Pope Agatho had called a synod of 125 bishops to Rome to testify against those who declared that there was only one will and operation in our Lord and Saviour. He ordered Wilfrid to be called to sit among the bishops, to declare his own faith and that of the kingdom and the island from which he had come. When it was found that he and his people were catholic in their faith, they decided to insert the following words among the rest of the acts of the synod: 'Wilfrid, beloved of God, bishop of the city of York, appealing to the apostolic see concerning his own case and having been freed by its authority from all charges, specified and unspecified, and being appointed to sit in judgement in the synod with 125 other bishops, has confessed the true and catholic faith on behalf of the whole northern part of Britain and Ireland, together with the islands inhabited by the English and British races, as well as the Irish and Picts, and has confirmed it with his signature.'

After this, Wilfrid returned to Britain and converted the kingdom of the South Saxons from their idolatrous worship to faith in Christ. He also sent ministers of the Word to the Isle of Wight; then during the second year of Aldfrith, Ecgfrith's successor, he was restored to his episcopal seat and his bishopric at the invitation of the king. But five years afterwards he was again accused and driven from the bishopric by the king and several bishops. He went to Rome and was given an opportunity of defending himself in the presence of his accusers, before Pope John and many bishops. It was decided unanimously that his accusers had manufactured false charges against him, at least in part; and the pope wrote to the English kings, Æthelred and Aldfrith, bidding them restore him to his bishopric because he had been unjustly condemned.

His acquittal was greatly assisted by the reading of the acts of the synod of Pope Agatho of blessed memory, which was held when Wilfrid was present in the City and sat in council among the bishops as has already been described. When, as the case required, the acts of this synod were read for some days in the presence of the nobility and a large crowd of people at the command of the pope, they reached the place where it was written: 'Wilfrid, beloved of God, bishop of the city of York, appealing to the apostolic see concerning his own case and having been freed by its authority from all charges, specified and unspecified,' etc., as is stated above. When this was read, amazement fell on those who heard, and, after the reader had finished, they began to ask each other who this Bishop Wilfrid was. Then Boniface, a counsellor of the pope, and several others who had seen him there in the time of Pope Agatho, said that he was the bishop who had been accused by his fellows and had recently come to Rome to be judged by the apostolic see. 'And this man', they said, 'also came here, long ago, on a similar charge; the case and the controversy between the two parties was quickly heard and judgement given by Pope Agatho of blessed memory, who declared that he had been driven unlawfully from his see. The pope held him in such esteem that he ordered him to sit in the assembled council of bishops as being a man of uncorrupt faith and honest mind.' When they heard this, all including the pope declared that a man of such authority, who had been bishop for nearly forty years, ought not to be condemned but should return to his own land with honour, entirely cleared of the charges laid against him.

When he reached Gaul on his way back to Britain, he suddenly fell sick and gradually grew so much worse that he could not ride his horse but had to be carried in a litter by his servants. In this way he reached the city of Meaux in Gaul and there lay as if dead for four days and nights, his faint breathing being the only sound of life apparent. He went for four days and nights without food or drink, without speaking or hearing, and then at last as the fifth day was breaking, he arose and sat up as if he were awaking from a deep sleep. As he opened his eyes, he saw a band of brothers around him singing psalms and weeping; then, sighing gently, he asked where the priest Acca* was. Acca was immediately summoned and, on seeing that he was better and able to speak, fell on his knees and gave thanks to God together with all the brothers who were present. After they had been sitting for a little time conversing, with some trepidation, about the judgements of heaven, the bishop ordered the others to go out for the time being and said to the priest Acca: 'I have just seen an awful vision which I wish you to hear and keep secret until I know what is God's will for me. There stood by me a glorious being in white robes who said that he was the archangel Michael, and added, "I have been sent to recall you from death. For the Lord has granted you life in answer to the prayers and tears of your disciples and brothers and through the intercession of His blessed mother, the ever-virgin Mary. I tell you that you will now be healed of your sickness; but be prepared, for in four years I will visit you again. You will return to your native land and will receive the greater part of the possessions which have been taken from you and will end your days in peace and quiet."'

So the bishop was restored to health, whereupon they all rejoiced and gave thanks to God; he set forward on his journey and arrived in Britain. After they had read the letters sent by the pope, Archbishop Berhtwald and Æthelred, who had once been king and was then abbot, readily took his part. Æthelred summoned Cenred to him, whom he had made king in his place, and urged him to make friends with the bishop, to which the king agreed. Aldfrith, king of Northumbria, scorned to receive him, but he did not long survive; so it came about that, when his son Osred was reigning, a synod was held at the river Nidd and, after some argument on both sides, they all agreed to receive him back into the bishopric of his own church. So he lived in peace for four years, that is, until the day of his death. He died in his own monastery in the district of Oundle, while Abbot Cuthbald was ruling over it; he was carried by the brothers to his first monastery at Ripon and buried in the church of the blessed Apostle Peter close to the altar on the south side, as was mentioned before; his epitaph was inscribed over him as follows:

> Here lie great WILFRID's bones.* In loving zeal
> He built this church, and gave it Peter's name,
> Who bears the keys by gift of Christ the King;
> Clothed it in gold and purple, and set high
> In gleaming ore the trophy of the Cross;
> Golden the Gospels four he made for it,
> Lodged in a shrine of gold, as is their due.
> To the high Paschal feast its order just
> He gave, by doctrine true and catholic,
> As our forefathers held; drove error far,
> And showed his folk sound law and liturgy.
> Within these walls a swarm of monks he hived,
> And in their statutes carefully laid down
> All that the Fathers by their rule command.
> At home, abroad, long time in tempests tossed,
> Thrice fifteen years he bare a bishop's charge,
> Passed to his rest, and gained the joys of Heaven.
> Grant, Lord, his flock may tread their shepherd's path!

CHAPTER 20

IN the year after the death of father Wilfrid, that is in the fifth year of Osred's reign, the most reverend father Hadrian, abbot and fellow labourer in the word of God with Theodore of blessed memory, died and was buried in his monastery in the church of the blessed Mother of God, forty-one years after he was sent by Pope Vitalian with Theodore and thirty-nine years after his arrival in Britain. It is one testimony among many to his learning and to that of Theodore, that his disciple Albinus, who succeeded him as head of the monastery, was so well trained in scriptural studies that he had no small knowledge of the Greek language and that he knew Latin as well as English, his native tongue.

Acca, Wilfrid's priest, became bishop of Hexham in Wilfrid's place. He was a man of great energy and noble in the sight of God and man. He enriched the fabric of his church, dedicated to the blessed apostle Andrew, with all kinds of decoration and works of art. He took great trouble, as he still does, to gather relics of the blessed apostles and martyrs of Christ from all parts and to put up altars for their veneration, establishing various chapels for this purpose within the walls of the church. He has also built up a very large and most noble library, assiduously collecting histories of the passions of the martyrs as well as other ecclesiastical books. He has also zealously provided sacred vessels, lamps, and other objects of the same kind for the adornment of the house of God. Further, he invited a famous singer named Maban, who had been instructed in methods of singing by the successors of the disciples of St Gregory in Kent, to teach him and his people; he kept him for twelve years teaching them such church music as they did not know, while the music which they once knew and which had begun to deteriorate by long use or by neglect was restored to its original form. Bishop Acca was himself a musician of great experience as well as a very learned theologian, untainted in his confession of the catholic faith and thoroughly familiar with the rules of ecclesiastical custom; and he will not cease* to be so until he gains the reward of his piety and devotion. He was brought up from childhood with the clergy of the holy Bosa,* beloved of God, bishop of York, and was instructed by them. Then he came to Bishop Wilfrid in the hope of finding a better way of life and remained in his service all his days until Wilfrid's death; he also went to Rome with him and learned many valuable things about the institutions of the holy Church which he could not have learned in his native land.

CHAPTER 21

AT that time Nechtan,* king of the Picts, who live in the northern parts of Britain, having been convinced by his assiduous study of ecclesiastical writings, renounced the error which he and his race had until then held about the observance of Easter, and led all his people to celebrate with him the catholic time of keeping the Lord's resurrection. In order to make the change more easily and with greater authority, he sought help from the English who, he knew, had long since based their religious practices on the example of the holy Roman and apostolic Church. So he sent messengers to the venerable Ceolfrith, abbot of the monastery of the apostles St Peter and St Paul, one part of which stands at the mouth of the river Wear and the other part near the river Tyne in a place called Jarrow. Ceolfrith ruled illustriously over this monastery* after Benedict already mentioned. The king asked the abbot to send him information by letter to enable him to confute more convincingly those who presumed to celebrate Easter at the wrong time; also about the shape and method of tonsure by which it was fitting that clerics should be distinguished: notwithstanding this request he himself had no small measure of knowledge on these matters. He also asked for builders to be sent to build a church of stone in their country after the Roman fashion, promising that it should be dedicated in honour of the blessed chief of the apostles. He also said that he and all his people would always follow the customs of the holy Roman and apostolic Church, so far as they could learn them, remote though they were from the Roman people and from their language. Abbot Ceolfrith complied with his pious wishes and requests, sending the builders he asked for and also a letter couched in the following terms:

To the most excellent* and glorious Lord, King Nechtan, Abbot Ceolfrith sends greetings in the Lord.

We are most ready and willing to attempt to explain to you the catholic observance of the holy Easter festival as we learned it from the apostolic see, in accordance with your earnest wishes and request, most devout king! For we know that whenever rulers them-selves take trouble to learn and teach and watch over the truth, it is a heaven-sent gift to God's holy Church. Indeed a certain secular writer has said very truly that the world would be in a happy state if kings were philosophers and philosophers were kings. But if a man of this world could speak the truth about the philosophy of this world and judge correctly about the governance of this world, how much more should the citizens of our heavenly home, who are now pilgrims in this world, hope and pray that, the more powerful men grow in this world, the more they may strive to obey the commands of our Judge who is over all things; and by their example and authority induce their subjects to observe these commands as well.

Now there are three rules given in holy Scripture by which the time for keeping Easter has been laid down for us, and these no human authority can alter; of these, two are divinely laid down in the law of Moses, while the third is added in the Gospel as the result of the Passion and Resurrection of the Lord. The law laid down that the Passover should be kept in the first month of the year and in the third week of the month, that is from the fifteenth to the twenty-first day of the month. The apostolic ordinance adds from the Gospel that we are to wait for the Lord's day occurring in that third week and keep the beginning of the Easter season on that day. Whoever then keeps this threefold rule rightly will never make a mistake in fixing the Paschal feast. But if you wish to hear in greater detail and more fully, it is written in Exodus, when the children of Israel were commanded to keep their first Passover, on their liberation from Egypt, 'the Lord said to Moses and Aaron, "This month shall be unto you the begin-ning of months; it shall be the first month of the year to you. Speak to all the congregation of Israel, saying, 'In the tenth day of this month they shall take to them every man a lamb, according to their families and households.'"' And a little further on: 'And ye shall keep it up until the fourteenth day of the same month: and the whole assembly of the congregation of Israel shall kill it in the evening,' From these words it is very clear that in the Paschal observance, though mention is made of the fourteenth day, yet it is not com-manded that the Passover should be kept on that day; but it is commanded that the lamb should be sacrificed on the evening of the fourteenth day, that is on the fifteenth day of the moon, which is the beginning of the third week, when the moon appears in the sky; and because it was on the night of the fifteenth moon that the Egyptians were smitten and Israel redeemed from its long captivity. It says, 'Seven days shall ye eat unleavened bread.' By these words it is directed that the whole of the third week of the first month shall be solemnly observed. But lest we should think that these seven days were to be reckoned from the fourteenth to the twentieth day, it adds forthwith, 'Even the first day ye shall put away leaven out of your house; for whosoever eateth leavened bread from the first until the seventh day, that soul shall be cut off from Israel', and so on up to 'for in this selfsame day I will bring your army out of the land of Egypt'.

So He calls the first day of unleavened bread the day on which He was to bring their army out of Egypt. Now it is evident that they were not brought out of Egypt on the fourteenth day, in the evening of which the lamb was killed and which is rightly called the Passover or Phase, but they were brought out of Egypt on the fifteenth day, as it is clearly stated in the book of Numbers, 'And they departed from Rameses on the fifteenth day of the first month; on the morrow after the Passover, the children of Israel went out with a high hand.' Thus the seven days of unleavened bread, on the first of which the people of the Lord were brought out of Egypt, are to be reckoned, as we have said, from the beginning of the third week, that is, from the fifteenth day of the first month to the end of the twenty-first day of the same month. But the fourteenth day is distinguished from this number by the very title of Passover, as is plainly shown by what follows in Exodus; for when it says, 'In this selfsame day I will bring your army out of the land of Egypt', it immediately continues, 'And ye shall observe this day in your generations for a perpetual ordinance. In the first month, on the fourteenth day of the month, ye shall eat unleavened bread until the one and twentieth day of the month at even. Seven days shall there be no leaven found in your houses.' Now who can fail to see that there are not seven days but eight, from the fourteenth to the twenty-first, if the fourteenth is also reckoned in. But if, as a more diligent study of the scriptural truth shows, we reckon from the evening of the fourteenth day to the evening of the twenty-first, we see at once that while the fourteenth day contributes its evening to the beginning of the Paschal feast, yet the whole solemn festival comprises no more than seven nights and the same number of days. So our definition is shown to be true that the Easter season is to be celebrated in the first month of the year and the third week. It is truly the third week, because it begins on the evening of the fourteenth day and ends on the evening of the twenty-first.

But since it is Christ who is our Passover sacrificed for us, and since He has made the Lord's day (which among the ancients was called the first day of the week) a solemn day because of His Resurrection, it has been included by apostolic tradition in the Paschal festival, which has also decreed that the time of the Passover according to the law must by no means be anticipated or diminished. It ordains instead that according to the precept of the law we must wait for the first month of the year, the fourteenth day of that month and the evening of that day. And when that day should happen to fall on a Saturday, every man must take a lamb according to their families and their houses and sacrifice it at evening, that is, that all churches throughout the world, composing the one catholic Church, should provide bread and wine for the mystery of the body and blood of the spotless 'Lamb that taketh away the sins of the world'; and after the appropriate solemn Easter rite of lessons and prayers and Paschal ceremonies, they should offer it to the Lord in the hope of redemption to come. For it is the night in which the children of Israel were delivered out of Egypt by the blood of the lamb; and also the night in which, by the Resurrection of Christ, all the people of God were freed from eternal death. Then in the morning, at dawn, on the Lord's day, they should celebrate the first day of the Paschal festival. For it is the very day on which the Lord revealed the glory of His Resurrection, while His disciples rejoiced exceedingly at the divine revelation. It is also the first day of unleavened bread about which it is very distinctly written in Leviticus, 'In the fourteenth day of the first month, at even, is the Lord's Passover. And on the fifteenth day of the same month is the feast of unleavened bread unto the Lord. Seven days ye must eat unleavened bread. The first day shall be most solemn and holy.'

If the Lord's day had always fallen on the fifteenth day of the first month, that is, on the fifteenth moon, we could always have celebrated the Passover at the very same time as the ancient people of God: and although the nature of the sacrament is different, yet it would have been with one and the same faith. But because the day of the week does not exactly keep pace with the moon, apostolic tradition (which was established at Rome by St Peter and confirmed at Alexandria by Mark the evangelist, who was his interpreter) has decreed that, when the first month has come and in it the evening of the fourteenth day, we must wait for the Sunday which falls between the fifteenth and the twenty-first day of the month. And Easter is rightly celebrated on whichever of these days it falls, since it is one of the seven days on which the feast of unleavened bread had to be celebrated. So it happens that our Easter never falls outside the third week of the month either before or after, but is observed either throughout the whole of the seven appointed days of unleavened bread or through at least part of them. But even though Easter should only include one of them, that is the seventh, yet that is the day that Scripture commends so highly: 'For the seventh day', it says, 'shall be most solemn and holy; ye shall do no servile work therein.' And none can argue that we do not rightly keep Easter Sunday on the day laid down in the Gospel in the third week of the first month as the law prescribed.

Now that the catholic reason for this observance is clear, it also becomes clear on the other hand how unreasonable is the error of those who presume, without cogent necessity, either to anticipate or overstep the limits set by the law. For those who think that Easter Sunday is to be observed on the fourteenth day of the first month until the twentieth day of the moon unnecessarily anticipate the time prescribed in the law; for when they begin to celebrate the vigils of the holy night from the evening of the thirteenth day, it is clear that they make that day the beginning of their Easter, and they can find no mention of this in the commandment of the law. When they refuse to celebrate the Lord's Easter on the twenty-first day of the month, it is at once clear that they exclude from their solemnity a day which the law often commends as being worthy of commemoration beyond all others. Thus, by a perverse arrangement, they will sometimes keep the whole festival in the second week but they will never put it on the seventh day of the third week. Again, those who think that Easter is to be kept from the sixteenth day of the same month to the twenty-second no less incorrectly turn from the straight path of truth in the opposite direction and, as it were, avoid shipwreck on Scylla, only to fall into the whirlpool of Charybdis and be drowned. For when they teach that Easter is to begin from the rising of the sixteenth moon of the first month, that is, from the evening of the fifteenth day, it is clear that they altogether exclude from their solemnity the fourteenth day of the moon which the law commends first and foremost. Consequently they scarcely touch the evening of the fifteenth day on which the people of God were redeemed from Egyptian bondage, and in which the Lord freed the world with His own blood from the darkness of sin, and in which He was buried and bestowed on us the hope of a blessed rest after death. These people receive in themselves the recompense of their error, when they put Easter Day on the twenty-second day of the moon and openly transgress by violating the legitimate limits of Easter, seeing that they begin Easter on the evening of the day in which the law commanded that it should be finished and completed; and they assign the first day of Easter to a day of which no mention is ever made in the law, namely the first day of the fourth week. And not only are both parties sometimes mistaken in fixing and computing the age of the moon, but they sometimes make mistakes in finding the first month.

This controversy, however, is a greater one than this letter can or ought to deal with. I will only say this that, by reference to the vernal equinox, it can always be decided infallibly which month is first, and which last, according to the lunar computation. Now the equinox, according to the opinion of all eastern nations, and especially of the Egyptians who took the palm from all other learned men in calculations, usually falls on the twenty-first of March, as we can also prove by inspecting a sundial. Now the moon which is at the full before the equinox, that is on the fourteenth or fifteenth day of the moon, belongs to the last month of the preceding year and so is not available for the celebration of Easter. But the moon which is full after the equinox or at the equinox itself belongs to the first month and on that day, as we know without any doubt, they were accustomed to keep the Passover in ancient times and we must celebrate it on the following Sunday. There is a very cogent reason for this for it is written in Genesis, 'And God made two great lights: the greater light to rule the day and the lesser light to rule the night', or as another version has it, 'The greater light to begin the day and the lesser light to begin the night'. As the sun, therefore, rising due east, first indicated the vernal equinox by his point of appearance and then, at sunset that evening, the full moon followed in her turn due east, so year by year the same first lunar month must be observed in the same order, its full moon falling, not before the equinox but either on the day of the equinox as it did in the beginning or after it has passed. But if full moon precedes the time of the equinox even by a single day, the reasons we have given make it clear that this full moon is to be assigned not to the first month of the new year but to the last month of the old year; and, as has been shown, is not available for the Paschal festival.

If you also care to know the mystical reason for this, we are commanded to keep Easter in the first month of the year, which is also called the month of new things; because we ought to celebrate the mysteries of the Lord's Resurrection and of our deliverance when our spirits and minds are renewed to the love of heavenly things. We are commanded to keep it in the third week of that month because Christ Himself who had been promised before the law and under the law came with grace in the third dispensation of the world, to be sacrificed for us as our Passover; and because after the sacrifice of His Passion, He rose from the dead on the third day, He wished this to be called the Lord's day and desired the Paschal feast of His Resurrection to be celebrated each year on the same day; and also because we only celebrate the solemn festival truly if we are careful to keep the Passover with Him, that is, His passing from the world to His

Father, with faith, hope, and love. We are commanded to keep the full moon of the Paschal month after the vernal equinox, the object being that the sun should first make the day longer than the night and then the moon can show to the world her full orb of light, because 'the Sun of righteousness with healing in His wings', that is, the Lord Jesus, overcame all the darkness of death by the triumph of His Resurrection. So, ascending into heaven, he made His Church, which is often typified as the moon, full of the light of inward grace, by sending His Spirit down upon her. This plan of our salvation is what the prophet had in mind when he said, 'The sun was exalted and the moon stood in her order.'

Whoever argues, therefore, that the full Paschal moon can fall before the equinox disagrees with the teaching of the holy Scriptures in the celebration of the greatest mysteries, and agrees with those who trust that they can be saved without the grace of Christ preventing them and who presume to teach that they could have attained to perfect righteousness even though the true Light had never conquered the darkness of the world by dying and rising again. And so after sunrise at the equinox and after the full moon of the first month has followed in due order, that is, after the close of the fourteenth day of the month (all of which we have received as duly to be observed in accordance with the law), we still wait for the Lord's day in the third week as the Gospel directs. So at last we duly celebrate our Easter feast to show that we are not, with the ancients, celebrating the throwing off of the yoke of Egyptian bondage but, with devout faith and love, venerating the redemption of the whole world, which, being prefigured by the liberation of the ancient people of God, is completed in the resurrection of Christ; we also signify that we rejoice in the sure and certain hope of our own resurrection, which we believe will also take place on a Sunday.

Now this computation of Easter which we teach you to follow is contained in a nineteen-year cycle, which was first observed by the Church long ago, that is, in the time of the apostles, especially in Rome and Egypt, as has previously been said. But through the industry of Eusebius, who took his surname from the blessed martyr Pamphylius, it was reduced to a plainer system; so that while up to that time information was sent out annually each year to all the churches from the patriarch of Alexandria, thenceforward it could easily be understood by everyone, a list being made of the dates of the fourteenth moon. Theophilus, patriarch of Alexandria, made an Easter computation for a hundred years for the benefit of the Emperor Theodosius. His successor Cyril drew up a table for ninety-five years, being five cycles of nineteen years each. After this Dionysius

Exiguus added as many more nineteen-year tables employing the same scheme and these extend down to our own day. This table is approaching its end but there are so many mathematicians today that even in our churches here in Britain there are several who have committed to memory these ancient rules of the Egyptians and can easily continue the Easter cycles for an indefinite number of years, even up to 532 years if they wish; after this period all that concerns the succession of the sun, the moon, the month, and the week returns in the same order as before. So we forbear to send you these cycles of times to come because you only asked to be instructed about the reason for the Paschal dating, making it clear that you were provided with catholic Easter tables.

Having said this much about Easter briefly and to the point, as you requested, I would also urge you to be sure that the tonsure, about which also you wished me to write, is in accordance both with the use of the Church and of the Christian faith. We know indeed that the apostles did not all use the same form of tonsure, and the catholic Church nowadays, though it agrees in one faith, one hope, and one charity towards God, does not agree in one and the same form of tonsure throughout the world. For example, to look back to the earlier times, that is, the times of the patriarchs: Job, the pattern of patience, when tribulation came upon him, shaved his head, so proving that in times of prosperity he let his hair grow; but Joseph, who was famous for teaching and practising chastity, humility, piety, and the other virtues, is related to have shaved himself when he was to be freed from slavery, so that it is clear that, during the time he was in prison, he never cut his hair. So each of these men of God differed in outward appearance, though they were alike in having in their inward hearts the same grace and the same virtues.

But though we freely admit that a difference in tonsure is not hurtful to those whose faith in God is untainted and their love for their neighbour sincere (and especially since we never read that there was any conflict among the catholic fathers about differences of tonsure such as there has been about diversity in faith or in the keeping of Easter), nevertheless among all the forms of tonsure which we find either in the Church or among the human race, I would say that none is more worthy to be imitated and adopted by us than the one which that man wore to whose confession the Lord replied, 'Thou art Peter and upon this rock I will build my Church, and the gates of hell shall not prevail against it; and I will give unto thee the keys of the kingdom of heaven.' Nor do I consider any tonsure to be rightly judged more abominable and detestable than that worn by the man who wished to buy the grace of the Holy Spirit, to whom Peter said, 'Thy money perish with thee because thou hast thought that the gift of God may be purchased with money. Thou hast neither part nor lot in the matter.' Nor are we tonsured in the form of a crown simply because Peter was so tonsured, but because Peter wore the tonsure in memory of the Lord's Passion, so we, who desire to be saved by His Passion, wear with Peter the sign of the Passion on our crown, that is to say, on the highest part of the body. See how the whole Church, just because she was made a Church by the death of Him who gave her life, has learnt to bear on her forehead the sign of His holy cross, that, through the constant protection of this symbol, she may be defended from the assaults of evil spirits, and by its constant witness may be reminded that she must crucify her flesh with all its vices and all its lusts: even so it is right for those who, having taken monastic vows or holy orders, must needs bind themselves with stricter bonds of continence for the Lord's sake, to wear upon their heads, by way of tonsure, the likeness of a crown of thorns—that crown of thorns which He in his Passion, bore upon His head, that He might bear (or rather bear off and carry right away) the thorns and briars of our sins. Thus they can show upon their crowns that they are ready to endure all kinds of ridicule and disgrace, gladly and readily, for His sake; thus they can signify that they too are always waiting for the crown of eternal life 'which God hath promised to them that love Him' and, to gain it, they despise both worldly adversity and worldly prosperity. But as for the tonsure which Simon Magus is said to have worn, what believer, I ask you, will not, at the very sight of it, detest and reject it together with his magic? And rightly so. In the front of the forehead it does seem to bear the resemblance to a crown, but when you come to look at the neck, you find that the crown which you expected to see is cut short; so that you recognize this as a fitting fashion for simoniacs but not Christians. For in this present life those whom they deceived thought that they were worthy of the glory of the everlasting crown; but in the life to come they are not only deprived of any hope of a crown but moreover are condemned to eternal punishment.

But do not suppose me to have pursued the argument thus far as one who holds the wearers of this tonsure culpable, those who have upheld catholic unity by faith and works; on the contrary I confidently assert that many of them were holy men and worthy in the sight of God. Among these is Adamnan, a renowned abbot and priest of the company of St Columba, who was sent on a mission from his people to King Aldfrith and wished to see our monastery. He showed wonderful prudence, humility, and devotion, in word and deed. Once when we were talking I said to him, amongst other things,

'Holy brother, you believe that you are going to win the crown of life which knows no end, so why do you wear on your head a form of crown which is incomplete and therefore ill-suited to your belief; and if you are seeking the company of St Peter, why do you copy the form of tonsure which he cursed? And why do you not even now show that you love with all your heart the ways of him with whom you desire to live in bliss for ever?' He replied, 'You know well, my dear brother, that although I wear the tonsure of Simon after the custom of my country, yet I hate and reject with all my heart the wickedness of simony. I long to follow with what little strength I have in the footsteps of the blessed chief of the apostles.' I said, 'I truly believe that it is so; but it would be a sign that you agree in your inmost heart with all that Peter stands for if you also followed his known ways in your outward appearance. I am sure that, in your wisdom, you will readily see that it would be much better for you who are already dedicated to God to let your appearance resemble as little as possible that of the man whom you hate with all your heart and whose horrible face you would shun to look upon. On the other hand, desiring as you do to follow the actions and teachings of him whom you wish to have as an advocate with God, it would be better for you to imitate his outward appearance also.' I said this at the time to Adamnan, who proved how much he had profited by seeing the observances of our churches, because afterwards, when he had returned to Ireland, he led large numbers of that race to the catholic observance of Easter by his preaching; nevertheless he could not bring the monks of Iona, over whom he presided as lawful head, to better ways. If his influence had been sufficient, he would have made it his business to correct their tonsure also.

But I now urge you, O king, in your prudence, to strive in every way to follow these observances which accord with the unity of the catholic and apostolic church, both you and the people over whom the King of Kings and Lord of Lords has set you. Thus it will come to pass that, after you have held sway over this temporal kingdom, the blessed chief of the apostles will gladly open the gates of the heavenly kingdom to you and yours, in company with all the elect. And now, my beloved son in Christ, may the grace of the eternal King keep you in safety to reign for many years and so bring peace to us all.

When this letter had been read in the presence of King Nechtan and many learned men and carefully translated into his own language by those who were able to understand it, it is said that he was greatly delighted by the exhortation; so he rose in the midst of the company of his assembled leaders, and knelt down, thanking God for having made him worthy to receive such a gift from England. 'Indeed,' he said, 'I knew before that this was the true observance of Easter, but I now understand the reasons for observing this date so much more clearly that I seem up to this to have known far too little about it in every respect. So I publicly declare and proclaim in the presence of you all, that I will for ever observe this time of Easter, together with all my people; and I decree that all clerics in my kingdom must accept this form of tonsure which we have heard to be so completely reasonable.' He at once enforced his word by royal authority also. The nineteen-year cycles for Easter were forthwith sent out by public order throughout all the Pictish kingdoms, to be copied, learned, and acted upon, while the erroneous eighty-four-year cycles were everywhere obliterated. All ministers of the altar and monks received the tonsure in the form of a crown; and the reformed nation rejoiced to submit to the newly-found guidance of Peter, the most blessed chief of the apostles, and to be placed under his protection.

CHAPTER 22

NOT long afterwards, those monks of Irish extraction who lived in Iona, together with the monasteries under their rule, were brought by the Lord's guidance to canonical usages in the matter of Easter and of the form of the tonsure. In the year of our Lord 716, when Osred* was killed and Cenred* became ruler of the Northumbrian kingdom, Egbert, beloved of God (a father and priest to be named with all honour and one whom I have often spoken of), came to Iona from Ireland and was most honourably and joyfully received. Being a most gracious teacher and a most devout doer of all that he taught, he was gladly listened to by them all; so by his constant earnest exhortations he converted them from the deep-rooted tradition of their ancestors to whom the apostle's words apply: 'They had a zeal of God but not according to knowledge.' He taught them how to celebrate the chief festival after the catholic and apostolic manner, as has been said, and to wear on their heads the image of the unending crown. It is clear that this happened by a wonderful dispensation of divine mercy, since that race had willingly and ungrudgingly taken pains to communicate its own knowledge and understanding of God to the English nation; and now, through the English nation, they are brought to a more perfect way of life in matters wherein they were lacking. On the other hand the Britons, who would not proclaim to the English the knowledge of the Christian faith which they had, still persist in their errors and stumble in their ways, so that no tonsure is to be seen on their heads and they celebrate Christ's solemn festivals differently from the fellowship of the Church of Christ, while the English are not only believers but are fully instructed in the rules of the catholic faith.

The monks of Iona accepted the catholic ways of life under the teaching of Egbert, while Dúnchad* was abbot, about eighty years after they had sent Bishop Aidan to preach to the English. The man of God, Egbert, remained for thirteen years on the island which he had consecrated to Christ, lighting it once more, as it were, with the gracious light of ecclesiastical fellowship and peace. In the year of our Lord 729, when Easter fell on 24 April, after he had celebrated a solemn mass in memory of the Lord's resurrection, he departed to be with the Lord on the same day. So he began the joyful celebration of the greatest of all festivals with the brothers whom he had converted to the grace of unity, and completed it, or rather continues the endless celebration of it, with the Lord and His apostles and the other citizens of heaven. It was a wonderful dispensation of the divine providence that the venerable man not only passed from this world to the Father on Easter Day, but also when Easter was being celebrated on a date on which it had never before been kept* in those places. The brothers rejoiced in the sure knowledge of the time of Easter according to the catholic rule and were glad to have the protection of the father who had corrected them, as he went to be with the Lord. Egbert was also thankful to have lived to see those to whom he had preached accept and keep with him an Easter Day which they had previously always avoided. So the most reverend father, being assured of their conversion, rejoiced to see the day of the Lord; he saw it and was glad.

CHAPTER 23

IN the year of our Lord 725, being the seventh year of Osric,* king of Northumbria, who was successor to Cenred, Wihtred,* king of Kent, died on 23 April. He was the son of Egbert and left his three sons, Æthelberht, Eadberht, and Alric, heirs of the kingdom which he had governed for thirty-four and a half years. In the following year Tobias, bishop of the church at Rochester, died, a most learned man, as has already been said. He had been a disciple of two masters of blessed memory, Archbishop Theodore and Abbot Hadrian. Besides having a knowledge of both ecclesiastical and general literature, he is also said to have learned Latin and Greek so thoroughly that they were as well known and as familiar to him as his native tongue. He was buried in the chapel of St Paul the Apostle which he had built within the church of St Andrew as his own burial place. Ealdwulf succeeded him as bishop having been consecrated by Archbishop Berhtwald.

In the year of our Lord 729 two comets* appeared around the sun, striking great terror into all beholders. One of them preceded the sun as it rose in the morning and the other followed it as it set at night, seeming to portend dire disaster to east and west alike. One comet was the forerunner of the day and the other of the night, to indicate that mankind was threatened by calamities both by day and by night. They had fiery torch-like trains which faced northwards as if poised to start a fire. They appeared in the month of January and remained for almost a fortnight. At this time* a terrible plague of Saracens ravaged Gaul with cruel bloodshed and not long afterwards* they received the due reward of their treachery* in the same kingdom. In the same year the holy man of God, Egbert, went to be with the Lord on Easter Day as has already been described; and soon after Easter, on 9 May, Osric, king of the Northumbrians, departed this life when he had reigned eleven years, after appointing Ceolwulf,* brother of his predecessor Cenred, as his successor. Both the beginning and the course of his reign have been filled with so many and such serious commotions and setbacks that it is as yet impossible to know what to say about them or to guess what the outcome will be.

In the year of our Lord 731 Archbishop Berhtwald died of old age on 13 January,* having held the see for thirty-seven years, six months, and fourteen days. In the same year Tatwine* was made archbishop in his place. He was from the kingdom of Mercia and had been a priest in the monastery of Breedon. He was consecrated in Canterbury by the venerable bishops Daniel of Winchester, Ingwold* of London, Ealdwine of Lichfield, and Ealdwulf of Rochester on Sunday, 10 June. He was a man renowned for his devotion and wisdom and excellently instructed in the Scriptures.

At the present time Tatwine and Ealdwulf preside over the churches of Kent as bishops; Ingwold is bishop in the kingdom of Essex; Ealdberht and Hathulac are bishops of the East Angles; Daniel and Forthhere are bishops of the West Saxons; Ealdwine is bishop of the Mercian kingdom and Wealhstod is bishop of the people who dwell west of the river Severn; Wilfrid is bishop of the kingdom of the Hwicce and Cyneberht is bishop of the kingdom of Lindsey. The bishopric of the Isle of Wight belongs to Daniel, bishop of Winchester. The kingdom of the South Saxons, having been for several years without a bishop, receives episcopal ministrations from the bishop of the West Saxons. All these kingdoms and the other southern kingdoms which reach right up to the Humber, together with their various kings, are subject to Æthelbald,* king of Mercia. At the present time there are four bishops in the kingdom of Northumbria, over which Ceolwulf rules: Wilfrid* in the church of York, Æthelwold* at Lindisfarne, Acca* at Hexham, Pehthelm* in the place called Whithorn, where the number of believers has so increased that it has lately become an episcopal see with Pehthelm as its first bishop.

The Picts now have a treaty of peace with the English and rejoice to share in the catholic peace and truth of the Church universal. The Irish who live in Britain are content with their own territories and devise no plots or treachery against the English. Though, for the most part, the Britons oppose the English through their inbred hatred, and the whole state of the catholic Church by their incorrect Easter and their evil customs, yet being opposed by the power of God and man alike, they cannot obtain what they want in either respect. For although they are partly their own masters, yet they have also been brought partly under the rule of the English.

In these favourable times of peace and prosperity, many of the Northumbrian race, both noble and simple, have laid aside their weapons and taken the tonsure, preferring that they and their children should take monastic vows rather than train themselves in the art of war. What the result will be, a later generation will discover.

This is the state of the whole of Britain at the present time, about 285 years after the coming of the English to Britain, in the year of our Lord 731. Let the earth rejoice in His perpetual kingdom and let Britain rejoice in His faith and let the multitude of isles be glad and give thanks at the remembrance of His holiness.

CHAPTER 24

IN order to assist the memory, I have thought it well briefly to recapitulate* events already dealt with, each under its particular date.

In the sixtieth year before the incarnation of the Lord, Gaius Julius Caesar was the first Roman to make war on Britain. He was victorious but was unable to obtain control of it.

In the year of our Lord 46 Claudius, the second Roman to come to Britain, brought most of it under his sway and also added the Orkney Islands to the Roman Empire.

167. Eleutherius became bishop of Rome and ruled the church gloriously for fifteen years. Lucius, a king of Britain, sent him a letter, asking to be made a Christian, and gained his request.

189. Severus became emperor and reigned seventeen years. He fortified Britain with a wall from sea to sea.

381. Maximus was made emperor in Britain. He crossed to Gaul and killed Gratianus.

409. Rome was stormed by the Goths, after which the Roman rule in Britain ceased.

430. Palladius was sent by Pope Celestinus to be the first bishop of the Irish Christians.

449. Marcianus and Valentinianus ruled as co-emperors for seven years. In their time the English came to Britain on the invitation of the Britons.

538.* There was an eclipse of the sun on 16 February from six to eight in the morning.

540.* There was an eclipse of the sun on 20 June and the stars appeared at nine in the morning for nearly half an hour.

547. Ida* began to reign, from whom the Northumbrian royal family trace their origin. He reigned for twelve years.

565. The priest Columba came from Ireland to Britain to teach the Picts and established a monastery on Iona.

596. Pope Gregory sent Augustine and some monks to Britain to preach the word of God to the English.

597. These teachers arrived in Britain, roughly 150 years after the coming of the English.

601. Pope Gregory sent the pallium to Britain for Augustine, who had already been consecrated bishop. He also sent several ministers of the Word, among whom was Paulinus.

603. The battle at *Degsastan*.

604. The East Saxons, under King Sæberht, accepted the Christian faith through Bishop Mellitus.

605. Gregory died.

616. Æthelberht, king of Kent, died.

625. Paulinus was consecrated bishop of the Northumbrians by Archbishop Justus.

626. Eanflæd, daughter of King Edwin, was baptized with twelve others on the eve of Whitsunday.

627. King Edwin and his people were baptized on Easter Day.

633. King Edwin was killed and Paulinus returned to Kent.

640. Eadbald, king of Kent, died.

642. King Oswald was killed.

644. Paulinus, once bishop of York and afterwards bishop of Rochester, departed to be with the Lord.

651. King Oswine was murdered and Bishop Aidan died.

653. The Middle Angles under their ruler Peada were initiated into the mysteries of the faith.

655. Penda perished and the Mercians became Christians.

664. There was an eclipse. King Eorcenberht of Kent died and Colman and his Irish returned to their own people. There was a visitation of the pestilence. Chad and Wilfrid were consecrated bishops of the Northumbrians.

668. Theodore was consecrated bishop.

670. Oswiu, king of Northumbria, died.

673. Egbert, king of Kent, died. There was a synod at Hertford in the presence of King Ecgfrith with Theodore presiding. It was most useful and drew up ten canons.

675. Wulfhere, king of Mercia, died after a reign of seventeen years and left his kingdom to his brother Æthelred.

676. Æthelred devastated Kent.

678. A comet appeared. Bishop Wilfrid was driven from his see by King Ecgfrith. In his place Bosa, Eata, and Eadhæd were consecrated bishops.

679. Ælfwine was killed.

680. A synod was held about the catholic faith on the plain of Hatfield, Archbishop Theodore presiding. John, an abbot from Rome was present. In this year the Abbess Hild died at Whitby.

685. Ecgfrith, king of Northumbria, was killed. In the same year Hlothhere, king of Kent, died.

688. Cædwalla, king of the West Saxons, journeyed from Britain to Rome.

690. Archbishop Theodore died.

697.* Queen Osthryth was murdered by her own Mercian nobles.

698.* Berhtred, an ealdorman of the king of Northumbria, was killed by the Picts.

704. Æthelred, after ruling the Mercians for thirty-one years, became a monk and left his kingdom to Cenred.

705. Aldfrith, king of Northumbria, died.

709. Cenred, king of Mercia, after ruling for five years went to Rome.

711. Ealdorman Berhtfrith fought against the Picts.

716. Osred, king of Northumbria, was killed, and Ceolred, king of Mercia, died. Egbert, the man of God, converted the monks of Iona to the catholic Easter and corrected their ecclesiastical tonsure.

725. Wihtred, king of Kent, died.

729. Comets appeared. St Egbert passed away and Osric died.

731. Archbishop Berhtwald died. In the same year Tatwine was consecrated ninth archbishop of the church at Canterbury, during the fifteenth year of the reign of Æthelbald, king of Mercia.

I, Bede,* servant of Christ and priest of the monastery of St Peter and St Paul which is at Wearmouth and Jarrow, have, with the help of God and to the best of my ability, put together this account of the history of the Church of Britain and of the English people in particular, gleaned either from ancient documents or from tradition or from my own knowledge. I was born in the territory of this monastery. When I was seven years of age I was, by the care of my kinsmen, put into the charge of the reverend Abbot Benedict and then of Ceolfrith, to be educated. From then on I have spent all my life in this monastery, applying myself entirely to the study of the Scriptures; and, amid the observance of the discipline of the Rule and the daily task of singing in the church, it has always been my delight to learn or to teach or to write. At the age of nineteen I was ordained deacon and at the age of thirty, priest, both times through the ministration of the reverend Bishop John on the direction of Abbot Ceolfrith. From the time I became a priest until the fifty-ninth year of my life I have made it my business, for my own benefit and that of my brothers, to make brief extracts from the works of the venerable fathers on the holy Scriptures, or to add notes of my own to clarify their sense and interpretation. These are the books:

The beginning of Genesis up to the birth of Isaac and the casting out of Ishmael: four books.

The tabernacle, its vessels, and the priestly vestments: three books.

The First Book of Samuel, to the death of Saul: four books.

On the building of the temple, an allegorical interpretation like the others: two books.

On the book of Kings: thirty questions.

On the Proverbs of Solomon: three books.

On the Song of Songs: seven* books.

On Isaiah, Daniel, the twelve prophets, and part of Jeremiah: chapter divisions taken from the treatise of St Jerome.

On Ezra and Nehemiah: three books.

On the Song of Habakkuk: one book.

On the book of the blessed father Tobias, an allegorical explanation concerning Christ and the Church: one book.

Also, summaries of lessons on the Pentateuch of Moses, on Joshua and Judges, on the books of the Kings and Chronicles, on the book of the blessed father Job, on Proverbs, Ecclesiastes, and the Song of Songs, on the prophets Isaiah, Ezra, and Nehemiah.

On the Gospel of Mark: four books.

On the Gospel of Luke: six books.

Homilies on the Gospel: two books.

On the Apostle (Paul), I have transcribed in order whatever I found in the works of St Augustine.

On the Acts of the Apostles: two books.

On the seven catholic Epistles: one book each.

On the Apocalypse of St John: three books.

Also summaries of lessons on the whole of the New Testament except the Gospels.

Also a book of letters to various people: one of these is on the six ages of the world; one on the resting-places of the children of Israel; one on the words of Isaiah, 'And they shall be shut up in the prison and after many days shall they be visited'; one on the reason for leap year; and one on the equinox, after Anatolius.

Also of the histories of the saints: a book on the life and passion of St Felix the confessor, which I put into prose from the metrical version of Paulinus; a book on the life and passion of St Anastasius* which was badly translated from the Greek by some ignorant person, which I have corrected as best I could, to clarify the meaning. I have also described the life of the holy father Cuthbert, monk and bishop, first in heroic verse and then in prose.

A history of the abbots of the monastery in which it is my joy to serve God, namely Benedict, Ceolfrith, and Hwætberht, in two books.

The history of the Church of our island and race, in five books.

A martyrology of the festivals of the holy martyrs, in which I have diligently tried to note down all that I could find about them, not only on what day, but also by what sort of combat and under what judge they overcame the world.

A book of hymns in various metres and rhythms.

A book of epigrams* in heroic and elegiac metre.

Two books, one on the nature of things and the other on chronology: also a longer book on chronology.

A book about orthography, arranged according to the order of the alphabet.

A book on the art of metre, and to this is added another small book on figures of speech or tropes, that is, concerning the figures and modes of speech with which the holy Scriptures are adorned.

And I pray thee, merciful Jesus, that as Thou hast graciously granted me sweet draughts from the Word which tells of Thee, so wilt Thou, of Thy goodness, grant that I may come at length to Thee, the fount of all wisdom, and stand before Thy face for ever.

Here, with God's help, ends the fifth book of the History of the English Church.

CONTINUATIONS

from the Moore MS (see pp. xxi–ii).

731. King Ceolwulf was captured and tonsured and then restored to his kingdom; Bishop Acca was driven from his see.

732. Egbert* was made bishop of York in place of Wilfrid.

733. An eclipse of the sun occurred on 14 August about nine o'clock in the morning so that its whole orb seemed to be covered with a black and terrifying shield.

734. The moon was suffused with a blood-red hue for about a whole hour around cockcrow on 31 January. Then blackness followed and finally its own light was restored.

Continuation found in MSS. referred to on p. xxiv.

732. Egbert was made bishop of York in place of Wilfrid; Bishop Cyneberht* of Lindsey died.

733. Archbishop Tatwine who had received the pallium from the apostolic authority consecrated Alwih* and Sigeferth* as bishops.

734. Archbishop Tatwine died.

735. Nothhelm was consecrated archbishop and Bishop Egbert, having received the pallium from the apostolic see, became archbishop, the first after Paulinus. He consecrated Frithuberht* and Frithuwold* bishops. The priest Bede died.

737. A great drought rendered the land infertile; and Ceolwulf was tonsured at his own request and resigned the kingdom to Eadberht.*

739. Æthelheard,* king of the West Saxons, and Archbishop Nothhelm died.

740. Cuthbert* was consecrated in place of Nothhelm; Æthelbald, king of the Mercians, treacherously devastated part of Northumbria while Eadberht was occupied with his army fighting against the Picts; Bishop Æthelwold* also died and Cynewulf* was consecrated bishop in his place; Earnwine and Eadberht* were killed.

741. There was a great drought in the land. Charles, king of the Franks,* died and his sons Carloman and Pippin came to the throne.

745. Bishop Wilfrid* and Ingwold, bishop of London, went to be with the Lord.

747. Herefrith,* a man of God, died.

750. Cuthred,* king of the West Saxons, rose against Æthelbald and Angus;* Tewdwr* and Eanred* died; Eadberht added the plain of Kyle* and other lands to his kingdom.

753. In the fifteenth year of King Eadberht's reign an eclipse of the sun took place on 9 January, and very shortly afterwards, in the same year and month, that is 24 January, there was an eclipse of the moon. It was covered with a dreadful black shield, just as the sun had been, shortly before.

754. Boniface,* also known as Winfrith, bishop of the Franks, with fifty-two others won the martyr's crown. Hrethgar* was consecrated archbishop in his place by Pope Stephen.*

757. Æthelbald, king of the Mercians, was treacherously killed at night by his bodyguard in shocking fashion; Beornred* came to the throne; Cynewulf,* king of the West Saxons, died; in the same year Offa* put Beornred to flight and attempted to conquer the Mercian kingdom with sword and bloodshed.

758. Eadberht, king of the Northumbrians, for the love of God and impetuously longing for his heavenly fatherland, received the tonsure of St Peter and resigned his throne to his son Oswulf.

759. Oswulf was treacherously killed by his thegns and in the same year Æthelwold* was elected by his people and began to reign. In his second year a great pestilence occurred and continued for nearly two years. The people were wasted by various kinds of malignant diseases but especially dysentery.

761. Angus, king of the Picts, died. From the beginning of his reign right to the end he perpetrated bloody crimes, like a tyrannical slaughterer; and Oswine* was killed.

765. King Alhred* began to reign.

766. Archbishop Egbert, endowed with royal blood and imbued with divine wisdom, and Frithubert, both truly faithful bishops, departed to be with the Lord.

CUTHBERT'S LETTER
ON THE DEATH OF BEDE

CUTHBERT'S LETTER ON THE DEATH OF BEDE

To his beloved in Christ and fellow teacher Cuthwin,*
greeting in the name of everlasting God from Cuthbert* the
deacon.

The present which you sent me I received with much
gratitude, and it was with great pleasure that I read your
letter, full of religion and sound learning, from which I learnt
that which I chiefly desired to learn, that you are regularly
offering masses and devout prayers for the benefit of God's
chosen servant Bede, our father and our master. I take delight
therefore, more from love of him than through confidence in
my own skill, in sending you a brief account of his passing out
of this world, since I understand that this is just what you have
expressed the wish to receive.

He was taken ill, in particular with frequent attacks of
breathlessness but almost without pain, before Easter, for
about a fortnight; and after it he continued in the same way
cheerful and rejoicing, giving thanks to almighty God day and
night, and indeed almost hour by hour, until Ascension Day,
which was the twenty-sixth of May.* Daily he gave us lessons,
who were his pupils, and spent the rest of his day in chanting
the Psalter, as best he could. The whole of every night he
passed cheerfully in prayer and giving God thanks, except
only when brief slumber intervened; and in the same way,
when he woke up, he would at once take up again the familiar
melodies of Scripture, not ceasing to spread out his hands in
thanksgiving to God. In all truth I can say it: I never saw or
heard of any man so diligent in returning thanks to the living
God. Surely a blessing was upon him! And he used to repeat
that sentence from St Paul 'It is a fearful thing to fall into the
hands of the living God',* and many other verses of Scripture,
urging us thereby to awake from the slumber of the soul by
thinking in good time of our last hour. And in our own
language,—for he was familiar with English poetry,—speaking of the soul's dread departure from the body, he would
repeat:

Facing that enforced journey,* no man can be
More prudent than he has good call to be,
If he consider, before his going hence,
What for his spirit of good hap or of evil
After his day of death shall be determined.

He used to sing antiphons too, for his own comfort and ours, of which one is 'O King of glory,* Lord of might, who didst this day ascend in triumph above all the heavens, leave us not comfortless, but send to us the promise of the Father, even the Spirit of truth. Alleluia.' But when he came to the words 'Leave us not comfortless', he broke down and wept; it was an hour before he tried to repeat what he had left unfinished, and so it was every day. And when we heard it, we shared his sorrow; we read and wept by turns, or rather, we wept continually as we read.

In this exaltation we passed the days between Easter and Pentecost as far as the date I have named; and he was filled with joy, and gave God thanks that he had been found worthy to suffer this sickness. He used to say repeatedly: 'God scourgeth every son whom He receiveth',* and that sentence of St Ambrose: 'I have not so lived, that life among you now would make me ashamed; but I am not afraid to die either, for the God we serve is good.'* During those days there were two pieces of work worthy of record, besides the lessons which he gave us every day and his chanting of the Psalter, which he desired to finish: the gospel of St John,* which he was turning into our mother tongue to the great profit of the Church, from the beginning as far as the words 'But what are they among so many?'* and a selection from Bishop Isidore's* book On the Wonders of Nature;* for he said 'I cannot have my children learning what is not true, and losing their labour on this after I am gone.'

When it came to the Tuesday before Ascension Day, his breathing became very much worse, and a slight swelling had appeared in his feet; but all the same he taught us the whole of that day, and dictated cheerfully, and among other things said several times: 'Learn your lesson quickly now; for I know not how long I may be with you, nor whether after a short time my Maker may not take me from you.'* But it seemed to us that he knew very well when his end should be. So he spent all that night in thanksgiving, without sleep; and when day broke, which was the Wednesday, he gave instructions for the writing, which we had begun, to be finished without delay. We were at it until nine o'clock; at nine o'clock we went in procession with the relics, as the custom of that day required.* One of us stayed with him, and said to him: 'There is still one chapter short of that book you were dictating, but I think it will be hard on you to ask any more questions.' But he replied: 'It is not hard. Take your pen and mend it, and then write fast.' And so he did. At three o'clock he said to me: 'I have a few treasures in my box, some pepper,* and napkins, and some incense. Run quickly and fetch the priests of our monastery, and I will share among them such little presents as God has given me.' I did so, in great agitation; and when they came, he spoke to them and to each one singly, urging and begging them to offer masses and prayers regularly on his behalf, and they promised with a will. But they were very sad, and they all wept, especially because he had said that he thought they would not see his face much longer in this world.* Yet they rejoiced at one thing that he said: 'It is time, if it so please my Maker, that I should be released from the body, and return to Him who formed me out of nothing, when as yet I was not. I have lived a long time, and the righteous Judge has well provided for me all my life long. The time of my departure* is at hand, and my soul longs to see Christ my King in all His beauty.'*

This he said, and other things, to our great profit, and so spent his last day in gladness until the evening. Then the boy of whom I spoke, whose name was Wilberht, said once again: 'There is still one sentence, dear master, that we have not written down.' And he said: 'Write it.' After a little the boy said: 'There! Now it is written.' And he replied: 'Good! It is finished;* you have spoken the truth. Hold my head in your hands, for it is a great delight to me to sit over against my holy place in which I used to pray, that as I sit there I may call upon my Father.' And so upon the floor of his cell, singing 'Glory be to the Father and to the Son and to the Holy Spirit' and the rest, he breathed his last. And well may we believe without hesitation that, inasmuch as he had laboured here always in the praise of God, so his soul was carried by angels to the joys of Heaven which he longed for. So all who heard or saw the death of our saintly father Bede declared that they had never seen a man end his days in such great holiness and peace; for, as I have said, as long as his soul remained in the body, he chanted the 'Gloria Patri' and other songs to the glory of God, and spreading out his hands ceased not to give God thanks.

And of this I assure you, that many more stories could be told or written about him; but tongue untaught cuts my words short. In time, however, I purpose with God's help to write a fuller account* of all that I myself have seen and heard regarding him.

Here ends Cuthbert's letter on the death of the venerable priest, Bede.

THE GREATER CHRONICLE

THE GREATER CHRONICLE

THE SIXTH AGE

3952 THE forty-second year of Caesar Augustus, and the twenty-seventh from the death of Cleopatra and Antonius, when Egypt was turned into a [Roman] province; third year of the one hundred the ninety-third Olympiad;* seven hundred and fifty-second from the foundation of the City [of Rome]; that is to say that year in which all the movements of peoples throughout the world were held in check, and by God's ordaining Caesar established a very real and lasting peace; Jesus Christ the Son of God consecrated the Sixth Age of the world by his coming.

In the forty-seventh year of Augustus, Herod died appropriately awfully: sick with water under the skin and with worms swarming throughout all his body. In his place Augustus established his son Archelaus, who ruled for nine years, up till the end of the reign of Augustus. Then he was exiled to the city of Vienne in Gaul because of the accusations made against him to Augustus concerning his cruelty towards the Jews. To reduce the power of the Jewish kingdom and its insolent behaviour, his four brothers—Herod, Antipater, Lysias, and Philip—were set up as tetrarchs in his place; of these Philip and Herod (previously called Antipas) had already been appointed as tetrarchs while Archelaus was still alive.

3979 Tiberius the stepson of Augustus, that is to say the son of the latter's wife Livia by a previous marriage, ruled for twenty-three years.

In the twelfth year of his reign Pilatus was sent by him to be procurator of Judaea.

Herod the tetrarch, who held the leadership of the Jews for twenty-four years, founded [the cities of] Tiberias and Livias in honour of Tiberius and his mother Livia.

3981 In the fifteenth year of Tiberius, following his baptism which John had predicted, the Lord announced the kingdom

307

of heaven to the world. As Eusebius indicates in his chronicle, this happened in the four thousandth year from the beginning of the world, according to the Hebrew system of years. It should also be noted that the sixteenth year of Tiberius was the eighty-first Jubilee, according to the Hebrews. Why our computation* should make it nineteen years less may easily be discovered by reading the previous parts of this book. According to either version of that chronicle which Eusebius composed, it seemed to him that the years [from Creation] are five thousand two hundred and twenty-eight.

3984 In the eighteenth year of Tiberius the Lord redeemed the world by his passion; and in order to preach throughout the regions of Judaea the Apostles ordained James the brother of the Lord to be bishop of Jerusalem together with seven deacons; after the stoning of Stephen the Church was scattered throughout the regions of Judaea and Samaria.

Agrippa surnamed Herod, son of Aristobulus the son of king Herod, having arrived in Rome as the accuser of the tetrarch Herod, was thrown into prison by Tiberius; where many made friends of him, especially Gaius the son of Germanicus.

3993 Gaius, known as Caligula, ruled for four years, ten months, and eight days.

He released his friend Herod Agrippa from chains and made him king of Judaea, where he ruled for seven years; which is to say until the fourth year of Claudius. Then, having been struck by an angel, he was succeeded on the throne by his son Agrippa, who continued in office for twenty-six years, right up to the destruction of the Jews.

Herod the tetrarch, who also sought the friendship of Gaius, came to Rome on the advice of Herodias. However, being accused by Agrippa he was deprived of his office of tetrarch; fleeing to Spain with Herodias he died there in poverty.

Pilatus, who had spoken the sentence of condemnation on Christ, was so subjected to vexations by Gaius that he killed himself.

Gaius, placing himself amongst the gods, prophaned the holy places of Judaea with the uncleanness of idols.

Matthew, preaching in Judaea, wrote his Gospel.

4007 Claudius [ruled for] thirteen years, seven months, and twenty-eight days.

Having first of all established the Church in Antioch, Peter the Apostle came to Rome, where for twenty-five years he held the episcopal throne; up to the last year of the reign of Nero.

Mark wrote his Gospel at Rome and was sent by Peter to preach in Egypt.

In the fourth year of Claudius a very severe famine occurred, which is recorded by Luke.*

In the same year the emperor conquered Britain, which no one had dared invade before Julius Caesar or since his time. Without battle or bloodshed he brought the greater part of the island under his rule in the course of very few days. He also added the Orkney islands to the empire, and he returned to Rome in the sixth month after he had set out.

In the ninth year of his reign the Jews were expelled from Rome for rioting, as Luke reports.*

The following year a great famine gripped Rome.

4021 Nero [reigned for] thirteen years, seven months, and twenty-eight days.

In his second year Festus took over as procurator of Judaea from Felix, who had sent Paul to Rome. There he had been held in 'free custody' [house arrest] for two years, before being set free to preach; while Nero committed those great crimes that history records of him.

In the seventh year of Nero James the brother of the Lord, having ruled the Church of Jerusalem for thirty years, was stoned to death by the Jews, who revenged themselves on him because they had been prevented from killing Paul.

Albinus Florus succeeded Festus in the governorship of Judaea. Because they could not stand his extravagance and greed and other vices, the Jews rebelled against the Romans. Vespasian was sent against them as Master of the Soldiers and captured many of the towns of Judaea.

On top of his other crimes Nero now persecuted the Christians; of their leaders in Rome he had Peter crucified and Paul killed by the sword.

This emperor attempted nothing of a military kind, and even nearly lost Britain; where two of the finest towns were captured and sacked.

4031 Vespasian [ruled for] nine years, eleven months, and twenty-two days.

He had been declared emperor by his army in Judaea, and leaving the war there to his son Titus, he returned to Rome via Alexandria. In the second year [of the reign] Titus destroyed the kingdom of Judaea and also the temple, one thousand and eighty-nine years after it was first built. This war took four years: two while Nero was still living and two more after him.

Vespasian, amongst other mighty deeds while still a private citizen, was sent by Claudius to Germany and thence to Britain, fighting thirty-two battles. He added two powerful peoples, twenty towns, and the Isle of Wight, near Britain, to the empire.

He erected a Colossus one hundred and seven feet high.

4033 Titus [ruled for] two years and two months.

He was a man so admirable in all forms of virtue that he might have been dedicated to the love of humanity.

He built the amphitheatre in Rome, and in its dedication killed five thousand wild beasts.

4049 Domitian the younger brother of Titus [reigned for] sixteen years and five months.

He, after Nero, was the second emperor to persecute the Christians. Under his rule the Apostle John was exiled to the isle of Patmos, and Flavia Domitilla, niece by his sister of the consul Flavius Clemens, was exiled to the island of Pontia for her proclaiming of the faith.

That same John,* it is said, was placed in a vat of boiling oil, but had attained to such freedom from pain that he remained always immune to corruption of the flesh.

4050 Nerva [ruled for] one year, four months, and eight days.

In his first edict he recalled the exiles; hence the Apostle John, freed in this general pardon, returned to Ephesus. Because he saw that the faith of the Church had been attacked by heretics during his absence, he immediately made it firm by describing the eternal nature of the Word of God in his Gospel.

4069 Trajan [reigned for] nineteen years, six months, and fifteen days.

The Apostle John died peacefully at Ephesus in the sixty-eighth year after the Passion of the Lord and in the ninety-eighth year of his life.

When Trajan started a persecution of the Christians, Simeon (also known as Simon), the son of Cleophas, the bishop of Jerusalem, was crucified.

Ignatius the bishop of Antioch was brought to Rome and thrown to the wild beasts.

Alexander the bishop of Rome was also crowned by martyrdom. He was buried on the Via Nomentana at the seventh milestone from the city, where he was beheaded.

The younger Pliny, the orator and historian from Como, lived at this time; many works of his genius have survived.

The Pantheon at Rome, which Domitian built, was burnt by lightning; it received this name because it was intended to be the dwelling-place of all the gods.

The Jews, plotting a revolt throughout many lands, suffered a much-deserved slaughter.

Trajan extended in all directions the frontiers of the Roman empire, which since Augustus had been defended rather than nobly expanded.

4090 Hadrian the son of Trajan's female cousin [ruled for] twenty-one years.

Because he had read the books composed on the Christian religion, thanks to Quadratus the disciple of the Apostles and to Aristides the Athenian, both men full of faith and wisdom, and to the legate Serenus Granius, he ordered in a letter that the Christians should not be condemned without proper accusation of criminal offences.

He completely vanquished the Jews, in rebellion for the second time, with a final slaughter, and also denied them permission to enter Jerusalem. He restored the walls of the city to their finest state, and ordered it to be called Aelia after himself.

He himself, being most learned in both languages [Latin and Greek], built an extraordinarily fine library in Athens.

Mark was the first non-Jew to be made bishop of Jerusalem, thus ending the line of fifteen Jewish bishops extending for one hundred and seven years from the Passion of the Lord.

4112 Antoninus, called Pius, together with his sons Aurelius and Lucius, [ruled for] twenty-two years and three months.

The philosopher Justin gave Antoninus the book that he had composed on the Christian religion, and made him benevolent towards the Christians. Not long after, being persecuted by Crescens the Cynic [philosopher], he shed his blood for Christ.

In the time of Pius bishop of Rome, Hermes wrote the book called *The Pastor*, in which is contained the command of the Angel that Easter should be celebrated on Sunday.

Polycarp, on coming to Rome, censured for their heretical stain those many people who had recently been corrupted by the teachings of Valentinus and Cerdo.

4131 Marcus Antoninus Verus [ruled] with his brother Lucius Aurelius Commodus for nineteen years and one month.

From the first they administered the empire with equal authority, although until that time there had only ever been single emperors.

They carried on war against the Parthians with great skill and success.

Persecution having broken out in Asia, Polycarp and Pionius were martyred; in Gaul too, many also gloriously shed their blood for Christ.

Not long after a plague, the avenger of evil deeds, devastated many provinces, especially Italy and the city of Rome.

His brother Commodus having died, Antoninus made his own son [also called] Commodus his colleague as emperor.

Melitus of Asia, the bishop of Sardis, gave the emperor Antoninus his *Apology for the Christians*.

Lucius the king of Britain* sent a letter to bishop Eleutherius of Rome, seeking to be made a Christian.

At this time there lived Apollinaris of Asia the bishop of Hierapolis, and Dionysius bishop of Corinth.

4131 Lucius Antoninus Commodus ruled for thirteen years after the death of his father.

He carried out a successful war against the Germans, but otherwise he was given over to all forms of extravagance and obscenity and had none of his father's virtue and piety.

Irenaeus the worthy bishop of Lyons lived at this time.

The emperor Commodus ordered the head of the Colossus removed and replaced it with a copy of his own.

4144 Aelius Pertinax [ruled for] six months.

He was treacherously killed in the palace through the wicked plot of Julian, a lawyer, who seven months after he had begun to rule was [himself] defeated in battle by Severus at the Milvian bridge and killed.

Victor the thirteenth bishop of Rome sent pamphlets everywhere, ordering that Easter should be celebrated on the Sunday falling between the fifteenth and the twenty-first day of the lunar month, as [had been the practice] in the time of his predecessor Eleutherius.

Supporting this decree, Theophilus bishop of Caesarea in Palestine together with other bishops present at the same council, wrote a very useful synodical letter against those who celebrated Easter on the fourteenth day of the lunar month alongside the Jews.

4145 Severus Pertinax [ruled for] seventeen years.

Clement a priest of Alexandria and Panthenus a Stoic philosopher held a very eloquent debate concerning the doctrines of our faith.

Narcissus bishop of Jerusalem, Theophilus bishop of Caesarea, and Polycarp and Bachylus, both bishops of the province of Asia, were all notable at this time.

There were many persecutions of the Christians throughout various provinces; amongst those receiving the crown of martyrdom was Leonidas the father of Origen.

After Clodius Albinus, who had made himself Caesar, was killed at Lyons, Severus campaigned in Britain; where in order to make the provinces more secure from barbarian incursions he built a great ditch and wall,* closely set with watch-towers, that stretched for one hundred and thirty-two miles from sea to sea. He died at York.

Perpetua and Felicitas were thrown to the beasts for Christ in the arena at Carthage in Africa on 7 March.

4163 Antoninus called Caracalla, the son of Severus, [ruled for] seven years.

When Alexander bishop of Cappadocia came to Jerusalem out of desire [to visit] the holy places, at the time that Narcissus, then in extreme old age, was still bishop, he was installed as bishop there, following a revelation from the Lord that this should happen.

Tertullian the African, son of a centurion of [the province of Africa] Proconsularis was praised in the report of all of the churches.

4170 Macrinus [reigned for] one year.

Abgar the holy man ruled at Edessa, as Africanus wanted.

Macrinus together with his son Diadumenian, with whom he had usurped the empire, were killed in a military revolt at Archilaides.

4171 Marcus Aurelius Antoninus [ruled for] four years.

In Palestine the city of Nicopolis, previously called Emmaeus, was [re]founded; Julius Africanus, a writer of that period, was given the commission to do so. This is that Emmaeus which the Lord thought worthy to sanctify by his entry [i.e. presence] after his resurrection, as Luke records.*

Bishop Hippolytus was the author of many works; he brought the *Measure of Time* which he wrote up to the present. His discovering of the sixteen-year Easter cycle gave Eusebius the opportunity to compose a nineteen-year cycle on the basis of it.

4175 Aurelius Alexander [reigned for] thirteen years.

He was devoted to his mother Mammaea and most likeable in all respects.

Urban the bishop of Rome led many to the faith of Christ and to martyrdom.

Origen of Alexandria was renowned throughout the world. Hence Mammaea the mother of Alexander wished to hear him and received him at Antioch with the highest honour.

4191 Maximin [ruled for] three years.

He carried out a persecution of the bishops and clergy of the churches, that is to say of the teachers, largely because the family of Alexander, whom he had succeeded, and of his mother Mammaea, were Christian; above all thanks to the priest Origen.

Pontianus and Antherus, bishops of the city of Rome, were crowned with martyrdom and buried in the cemetery of Calixtus.

4197 Gordian [reigned for] six years.

Julius Africanus was notable amongst the authors of the Church, who in the chronicles that he wrote referred to himself as hastening to Alexandria on account of the very celebrated reputation of Heraclia, who was said to be most learned in divine and philosophical studies and in all Greek learning.

In Caesarea in Palestine Origen taught divine philosophy to the [two] young brothers from Pontus: Theodore (known as Gregory) and Athenodorus, who later became most noble bishops.

4204 Philip together with his son Philip [ruled for] seven years.

He was the first of all emperors to be a Christian,* and the third year of his reign marked the thousandth year from the founding of Rome. Thus, this most august of all anniversaries of past events was celebrated with magnificent games by a Christian emperor.

Origen replied in eight volumes to a certain Epicurean philosopher called Celsus, who had written against our books. He, if I may put it briefly, was so prolific in writing that Jerome somewhere indicates* that five thousand books of his are available for reading.

4205 Decius [ruled for] one year and three months.

He launched a persecution of the Christians out of hatred of the Philips, both father and son, whom he had killed. In this, Fabian the bishop of Rome was crowned with martyrdom. He left his see to Cornelius, who was also martyred. Alexander the bishop of Jerusalem was killed at Caesarea in Palestine and Babylas at Antioch. This persecution, as Dionysius bishop of Alexandria indicates, did not arise from an imperial command, but, as he says, 'A servant of the demons, who in our city was considered to be divine, stirred up the pagan crowds against us for a whole year before the imperial edicts were issued.'

4207 Gallus with his son Volusian [ruled for] two years and four months.

Of this emperor, Dionysius the bishop of Alexandria reported that he was neither able to see or to guard against Decius' mistake, but tripped up over the same stone. Just when his reign was prospering in its opening stages and everything was going according to his will, he persecuted the holy men who were praying to Almighty God for the peace of his rule, and with them both peace and his prosperity took flight.

Origen, not having quite completed the seventieth year of his age, died and was buried in the city of Tyre.

Cornelius the bishop of Rome, at the request of a certain lady called Lucina, moved the bodies of the Apostles from the catacombs at night. On 29 June he reburied the body of Paul on the road to Ostia where he had been beheaded, and that of Peter in the place in which he had been crucified, among the bodies of the holy bishops in the temple of Apollo on Monte Aurelio in the Vatican palace of Nero.

4222 Valerian [ruled] with his son Gallienus [for] fifteen years.

He, having started a persecution of the Christians, was almost immediately captured by Shapur [I] king of the Persians. There, deprived of light, he grew old in miserable slavery. Hence Gallienus, terrified by so clear a sign of divine judgement, restored peace to us [the Christians]. However, thanks to his own libidinous nature and his father's war against God [i.e. the persecution], the Roman empire suffered numerous losses from barbarians and rebels. In that persecution Cyprian the bishop of Carthage, whose writings are most learned, was crowned with martyrdom; his life and passion were recorded by his deacon Pontius, who up to the day of his death had shared his exile.

Theodore, called Gregory, the bishop of Neocaesarea in Pontus, of whom we wrote above, shone in a great glory of miracles. One of these involved his moving of a mountain by his prayers to provide the space needed for the foundation of a church.

Stephen and Sixtus, bishops of Rome, died as martyrs.

4224 Claudius [reigned for] one year and nine months.

He overcame the Goths, who had been ravaging Illyria and Macedonia for the previous fifteen years. For this a golden shield was erected to [honour] him in the Senate house and a golden statue of him set up on the Capitol.

Marcion, a most fluent priest of the church of Antioch, who also taught rhetoric in the same city, argued against Paul of Samosata the bishop of Antioch, who was teaching that Christ had the same nature as man; this dialogue, recorded by notaries, still survives today.

4229 Aurelian [ruled for] five years and six months.

After he had initiated a persecution of us, lightning struck the ground in front of him, to the great terror of the bystanders, and not long after he was killed by some soldiers while travelling on the old road between Constantinople and Heraclea, at a place called Caenofrurium.

Eutychius bishop of Rome was crowned with martyrdom and buried in the cemetery of Calixtus, where he himself had buried three hundred and thirteen martyrs with his own hand.

4230 Tacitus [reigned for] six months.

After he had been killed in Pontus, Florian held the imperial office for eighty-eight days and was killed at Tarsus.

Anatolius, an Alexandrian by birth and bishop of Laodicaea in Syria, who was very learned in the disciplines of philosophy, was widely renowned. The greatness of his genius may most easily be learnt from the book that he wrote on Easter and from his ten books on the principles of mathematics.

The crazy heresy of the Manichees was born at this time.

4236 Probus [ruled for] six years and four months.

Through many severe battles he finally freed the Gallic provinces, which had long been occupied by the barbarians.

The second year of his reign, as we can read in the chronicle of Eusebius, was equivalent to the three hundred and twenty-fifth year of the Antiochenes, the four hundred and second of the Tyrians, the three hundred and twenty-fourth of the Laodicaeans, the five hundred and eighty-eighth of the Edessans, the three hundred the eightieth of the city of

Ascalon, and the beginning of the eighty-sixth Jubilee for the Hebrews, which means their four thousand seven hundred and fiftieth year.

Archelaus bishop of Mesopotamia wrote an account in Syriac of the debate he had with a Manichee who had come from Persia; translated into Greek, this became known to many.

4236 Carus [reigned] with his sons Carinus and Numerian [for] two years.

Gaius, who later died as a martyr under Diocletian, was an illustrious bishop of Rome.

Pierius priest of Alexandria under bishop Theon taught the people with great distinction; so eloquent were his words and his various treatises, which have survived to the present, that he was called 'the younger Origen'. He was very frugal and desirous of personal poverty; after the persecution he spent the rest of his life in Rome.

4258 Diocletian [ruled] with Herculius Maximianus for twenty years.

Carausius, having assumed the purple, took control of the British provinces; Narseh king of the Persians began a war in the East; the 'Five Peoples' invaded Africa; Achilleus seized power in Egypt; for these reasons Constantius and Galerius Maximianus were made co-emperors.

Constantius married Theodora the stepdaughter of Herculius, by whom he had the six half-brothers of Constantine. Galerius married Valeria the daughter of Diocletian.

After ten years the British provinces were regained by the praetorian prefect Asclepiodotus.

In the seventeenth year of their reign Diocletian in the East and Maximian in the West ordered the churches to be destroyed and the Christians killed.

In the second year of the persecution Diocletian abdicated at Nicomedia and Maximian at Milan. However, once begun the persecution did not cease to rage until the seventh year of the reign of Constantine. Constantius, a man of great affability and mildness, died in Britain, at York, in the sixteenth year of his reign.

This persecution was so savage and cruel that in the course of a single month it was found that seventeen thousand had died as martyrs for Christ.

It even crossed the Channel to Britain, where Alban, Aaron, and Julius, together with many other men and women, were condemned to that happy fate.

The priest Pamphilus, a relative of bishop Eusebius of Caesarea, was martyred; the latter wrote a life of him in three books.

4259 In the third year of the persecution, after the death of Constantius, Maximin and Severus were made Caesars by Galerius Maximianus. Of these, Maximin in his malice and debauchery extended the persecution of the Christians.

In this tempest Peter bishop of Alexandria was martyred along with many other Egyptian bishops; as was Lucianus a priest of Antioch, who was outstanding in his character and in his erudition, and Timothy, who was killed at Rome on 22 June.

4290 Constantine, the son of Constantius by his concubine Helena, was made emperor in Britain; he ruled for thirty years and ten months.

In the fourth year from the beginning of the persecution Maxentius, the son of Herculius Maximianus, was made Augustus in Rome.

Licinius, the husband of Constantia the sister of Constantine, was made emperor at Carnuntum.

Constantine turned* from a persecutor into a Christian.

The Catholic faith was set forth at the Council of Nicaea in the six hundred and thirty-sixth year after Alexander, on the nineteenth day of the Greek month of Desi, which is 22 June, in the consulship of Paulinus and Julian, *viri clarissimi*.

Constantine built in Rome, where he was baptized, the basilica of St John the Baptist, which was called the Constantinian basilica. He also built a basilica dedicated to the blessed Peter on the site of the temple of Apollo; and also to the blessed Paul; whose bodies he surrounded with copper five feet thick. He built another [basilica] in the Sosorian Palace, which became known as the basilica of Jerusalem, where he deposited a piece of the wood of the Lord's cross. He built a basilica dedicated to the holy martyr Agnes at the request of his daughter, together with a baptistery in the same place, where his sister Constantia was baptized together with the emperor's daughter. He built another basilica dedicated to the blessed martyr Laurence in the field of Veranus on the Via Tiburtina, and another, between two laurel trees on the Via Levicana, was dedicated to the blessed martyrs Peter and Marcellinus; he also built a mausoleum where he placed his mother in a purple sarcophagus. He built another basilica, dedicated to the holy Apostles Peter and Paul and John the Baptist, in the town of Ostia, next to the port of the city of Rome. He dedicated another basilica in the town of Alba to St John the Baptist, and built another one in the city of Naples.

Constantine, restoring the town of Deprana in Bithynia in honour of the martyr Lucian, who was born there, renamed it Helenopolis after his mother. He also wished to make the city in Thrace which he had given his own name [i.e. Constantinople] the seat of the imperial government and the capital of the East.

He ordered the temples of the pagans to be closed, without any killing.

4314 Constantius ruled for twenty-four years, six months, and thirteen days, with his brothers Constantine and Constans.

James bishop of Nisibis was widely known; by his prayers the city was often saved from disaster.

The Arian heresy, sustained by the leadership of the emperor Constantius, persecuted Athanasius first of all and then all bishops not of its party with exile, imprisonment, and various types of affliction.

Maximinus bishop of the Treveri [of Trier] was outstanding; he received bishop Athanasius of Alexandria with honour at the time that Constantius wished to punish him.

The monk Anthony died as a solitary in his one hundred and fifth year.

The relics of the Apostle Timothy were brought to Constantinople.

After Constantius had visited Rome, the bones of the Apostle Andrew and of Luke the Evangelist were received by the Constantinopolitans with extraordinary excitement.

Bishop Hilary of Poitiers who had been driven from his see by the Arians and exiled to Phrygia, returned to Gaul when a book was presented for him to Constantius in Constantinople.

4316 Julian [reigned] for two years and eight months.

Julian, having converted to the worship of idols, persecuted the Christians.

The pagans broke into the tomb of John the Baptist in the city of Sebaste in Palestine and scattered his bones; after these had been collected up again they burnt them and scattered them more widely. But by the providence of God there were some monks from Jerusalem there, who, gathering together whatever they could, brought them, all mixed together, as an offering to their father [i.e. abbot] Philip. He at once sent them by his deacon Julian to the senior bishop, who was then Athanasius [of Alexandria]. Inspired by the spirit of prophecy he preserved what he had received for future generations by burying the relics in a hole under the sanctuary wall in the presence of a few witnesses.

4317 Jovian [ruled for] eight months.

A synod was held at Antioch by Melitius and his supporters, in which, having rejected *homousion* as a compromise, they upheld the *homoeousion* of the Macedonians.

Jovian, warned by the fall of his predecessor Constantius, in most courteous and respectful letters requested Athanasius to advise him on the nature of his beliefs and on the manner in which the Church should be organized. But an early death put an end to his pious and happy tenure of the imperial throne.

4328 Valentinian [ruled] with his brother Valens for eleven years.

Apollinaris bishop of Laodicaea composed a variety of works on our religion, but later deviating from true belief he created the heresy that bears his name.

Damasus bishop of Rome built the basilica of Saint Laurence next to the theatre, and another in the catacombs where the holy bodies of the Apostles Peter and Paul had lain. In that place he ornamented with verses the tomb covering itself where the holy bodies had lain.

Valens persecuted us, having been baptized by Eudoxius, a bishop of the Arians.

Gratian, the son of Valentinian, was made emperor at Amiens in his third year.

The Martyrium of the Apostles at Constantinople was dedicated.

After the peaceful death of Auxentius, Ambrose was made bishop of Milan; he converted all Italy to the true belief.

Hilary bishop of Poitiers died.

4332 Valens, together with Gratian and with Valentinian, the son of his brother Valentinian, [ruled for] four years.

Valens issued a law that monks should serve in the army; those who refused he ordered to be beaten to death.

The people of the Huns, who had long dwelt secluded in inaccessible mountains, struck by madness, suddenly broke out against the Goths, and scattering them hither and thither expelled them from their ancient settlements. Having crossed the Danube, the Goths were received by Valens as fugitives, without being made to surrender their arms; soon they were driven to rebel because of the greed of duke Maximus, and having defeated Valens' army they spread themselves throughout Thrace with massacres, burnings, and rapine.

4338 Gratian [ruled] with his brother Valentinian [for] six years.

Theodosius was made emperor by Gratian, and in many fierce battles defeated the greatest of those Scythian peoples, that is to say the Alans, the Huns, and the Goths.

Being unable to win his support, the Arians relinquished the churches which they had held by force for forty years.

A synod of one hundred and fifty bishops under bishop Damasus of Rome was held in the Augustan city against Macedonius.

Theodosius made his son Arcadius his colleague as emperor. In the second year of Gratian's reign, in his sixth consulship* [*recte* fifth] and that of Theodosius, Theophilus wrote his paschal *computus*.

Maximus, a most active and upright man, who would have been worthy to be an emperor if he had not broken his oath of allegiance to make himself one by usurpation, was invited to Britain and there made emperor in that fashion by the army. He crossed into Gaul, and there deceived and killed the emperor Gratian at Lyons, and expelled his brother Valentinian from Italy. The latter very justly underwent the penalty of exile together with his mother Justina, because he had polluted himself with the Arian heresy and had harassed Ambrose, the most eminent bulwark of the Catholic faith, by a treacherous siege; not until the relics of the blessed martyrs Gervasius and Protasius were revealed by God and discovered incorrupt did he abandon his wicked undertakings.

4349 Theodosius, who had already ruled the East for six years while Gratian was alive, reigned for eleven years after his death.

He received Valentinian, who had been expelled from Italy, kindly. They killed the usurper Maximus at the third milestone from Aquileia.

He [Maximus] had also despoiled Britain of almost all of its armed youth and military forces, who had followed in the footprints of the tyrant to Gaul. Seeing them not returning, some very savage overseas nations—the Irish from the north-west and the Picts from the north—came into the island thus abandoned by its soldiers and defenders, and oppressed, devastated, and pillaged it.*

Jerome, the interpreter of sacred history, wrote a book about the most illustrious men of the Church, which he brought up to the fourteenth year of Theodosius' reign over the empire.

4362 Arcadius, the son of Theodosius [ruled] with his brother Honorius for thirteen years.

The bodies of the holy prophets Habacuc and Micah were uncovered by divine revelation.

The Goths entered Italy and the Vandals and Alans entered the Gallic provinces.

Innocent bishop of Rome dedicated the basilica of the blessed martyrs Gervasius and Protasius, out of the testamantary bequest of a certain illustrious lady called Vestina.

Pelagius the Briton impugned the grace of God.

4377 Honorius [ruled] with Theodosius the Younger, the son of his brother, for fifteen years.

Alaric the king of the Goths broke into Rome and burnt part of it on 24 August in the one thousand one hundred and sixty-fourth year from its foundation; on the sixth day after his entry he left the looted city.

In the seventh year of the reign of Honorius, God revealed to the priest Lucian the place of burial of the relics of the blessed protomartyr Stephen and of Gamaliel and Nicodemus, about whom it is possible to read in the Gospel and in the Acts of the Apostles. He wrote an account of that discovery in Greek for the whole Church.

The priest Avitus, a man of Spanish birth, translated that account into Latin, and adding a letter of his own sent it to the West by the priest Orosius. That Orosius had been sent by Augustine to Jerome to learn about the nature of the soul; when he came to the holy places he received the relics of the blessed Stephen and returning home was the first to bring them to the West.

The Britons,* unable to put up with the problem of the Irish and the Picts, sent to Rome and, promising their submission, begged for help against the enemy. A legion was immediately sent to them which overthrew the great horde of barbarians and expelled others from the borders of Britain. On preparing to return home it ordered the allies [i.e. the Britons], for the purpose of keeping out the enemy, to build a wall across the island between the two seas. Lacking a master builder, this was built from turf rather than stone and the work was not carried out by trained men. Soon, when the Romans had departed, the former enemy came in ships and trampled on anything that stood in their way, devouring it like ripe corn. Their help having been sought again, the Romans rushed across [the Channel] and defeating the enemy, put them to flight across the seas. From fear of this enemy, they gathered together the Britons and built [another] wall from sea to sea, not as before out of crumbly earth but in solid stone, between the towns that were sited there. But on the southern shores, because they also feared the enemy coming from the sea there, they established towers at intervals overlooking the sea. Then, saying farewell to their allies, they left, not intending to return again.

Boniface bishop of Rome built a chapel in the cemetery of Saint Felicitas, and decorated her sepulchre and that of Saint Silvanus.

The priest Jerome died on 30 September in the twelfth year of Honorius in his ninety-first year.

4403 Theodosius the Younger, the son of Arcadius, [ruled for] twenty-six years.

Valentinian the younger, son of Constantius, was made emperor at Ravenna.

His mother Placidia was entitled Augusta.

The savage race of the Vandals, the Alans, and the Goths, crossing from Spain into Africa, overturned everything with iron, flames, and rapine, and also with the Arian heresy. But, lest he see the ruin of his city, the blessed Augustine, bishop of Hippo and foremost doctor of the Church, went to the Lord on 28 August in the third month of the siege, having lived for seventy-six years and having completed nearly forty years in the clergy and as a bishop. At this time, the Vandals, having captured Carthage, also destroyed Sicily. Paschasinus bishop of Lilybaeum referred to its capture in the letter which he sent to pope Leo about the calculation of Easter.

In the eighth year of Theodosius, Palladius was ordained and sent by pope Celestine to the Irish who believed in Christ, to be their first bishop.

When the Irish and the Picts discovered that the Roman army had left Britain with no intention of returning, they came back again themselves and captured the whole of the island from its indigenous inhabitants, from the far north right up to the wall. Without delay, and with the guardians of the wall defeated, captive, or fugitive and it itself broken, the savage pirates also proceeded through it. In the twenty-third year of the reign of the emperor Theodosius, a letter was sent bearing their [i.e. the Britons'] tears and groans to the most powerful of the Romans, Aetius thrice consul, seeking help. Meanwhile a terrible and very notorious famine attacked the fugitives. Because of this some were forced to surrender to the enemy, but others fought back vigorously from the mountains, caves, and forests, and gave the enemies a defeat. The Irish returned home, though shortly to come back again. The Picts kept hold of the far [i.e. northern] part of the island for the first time and inhabited it thereafter. The above-mentioned hunger was followed by a great opulence of the fruits of the earth, the opulence by luxury and neglect, the neglect by a very severe pestilence, and soon a fiercer plague of new enemies, that is to say the Angles. These they [the Britons] had chosen, by unanimous agreement with their king Vortigern, to invite in as defenders of [their] homeland; but they soon realized that the men they had chosen were attackers and conquerors.

Sixtus the bishop of Rome built the basilica of Saint Mary the mother of the Lord, which the ancients called that of Liberius.

Eudoxia the wife of the emperor Theodosius returned from Jerusalem, bringing with her the relics of the most blessed Stephan the first martyr, that had been placed for veneration in the basilica of Saint Laurence.

The brothers Bleda and Attila, kings of many peoples, depopulated Illyria and Thrace.

4410 Marcian and Valentinian [ruled for] seven years.

The people of the Angles or of the Saxons came to Britain in three longships; as their undertaking prospered, the fame of it was carried back home. They sent for a stronger army, which, joined to the previous one, first of all drove away the enemy that they were seeking [i.e. the Picts and Irish]. Next, turning their arms on their allies, they subjugated virtually the whole of the island by fire or the sword, from the eastern shore as far as the western one, offering as their excuse that the Britons had given them less than sufficient salary for their military services.

John the Baptist revealed [the location of] his head, next to a former dwelling of king Herod, to two eastern monks who had come to Jerusalem to pray. It was then taken to the city of Emesa in Phoenicia and venerated with appropriate honour.

The Pelagian heresy* disturbed the faith of the Britons, who having sought help from the Gallic bishops, received Germanus the bishop of Autun and Lupus, equally by apostolic grace, bishop of Treves as the defenders of the faith. The bishops strengthened the faith by the word of truth and at the same time by miraculous signs. Having gathered some men they checked the campaign of the Saxons and Picts against the Britons by a divine miracle; with Germanus himself as their war-leader, the enemy was forced to flee panic-striken, not by the noise of the tuba but by the crying of Alleluia by the voice of the whole army raised to the stars. He [Germanus] then came to Ravenna, where having been received with the utmost reverence by Valentinian [III] and Placidia, he migrated to Christ. His body was brought to Autun in a procession of honour, accompanied by the working of miracles.

The patrician Aetius, the saviour of the Western empire and the terror of king Attila, was killed by Valentinian; with him fell the Western realm,* and up till today it has not had the strength to be revived.

4427 Leo [ruled for] seventeen years.

He sent individual letters in support of the Chalcedonian *Tome* to all the bishops throughout the world, requesting them to write to him. He received the written agreement of them all concerning the true Incarnation of Christ—as if all had been written at one time and at one command.

Theodoret, bishop of the city called Cyrus, after its founder the Persian king Cyrus, wrote about the true Incarnation of the Saviour against Eutyches and Dioscorus, bishops of Alexandria, who denied the human in the flesh of Christ. He also wrote an *Ecclesiastical History* [covering the period] from the end of Eusebius' work up to his own time; which is to say up to the reign of Leo, under whom he died.

Victorius, at the request of pope Hilarius, wrote a paschal cycle of five hundred and thirty-two years.

4444 Zeno [ruled for] seventeen years.

The body of the Apostle Barnabas and the Gospel of Matthew written by his own hand were found through their own revelation.

Odoacer king of the Goths gained control of Rome, which their kings then held for a long time.

After the death of Theoderic the son of Triarius, another Theoderic, known as Valamer, obtained the kingdom of the Goths, having depopulated both Macedonia and Thessaly. Having set various parts of the royal city [of Constantinople] on fire, he also invaded and occupied Italy.

Huneric the Arian king of the Vandals in Africa exiled or caused to flee more than three hundred and thirty-four Catholic bishops; he closed their churches and afflicted the populace with various torments. Although he cut out innumerable tongues he could not, however, take away the words of the Catholic confession [of faith].

The Britons, under the leadership of Ambrosius Aurelianus (a man of modest means, who alone of the Romans had survived the disaster of the Saxons in which his parents, who had worn the purple, had been killed), provoked the victors to battle and defeated them. From then on first one side then the other had the palm [of victory], until such time as the foreigners [i.e. the Saxons] became the more powerful throughout the whole island, which they have now possessed* for a long while.

4472 Anastasius [ruled for] twenty-eight years.

Trasamund the king of the Vandals closed the Catholic churches and sent two hundred and twenty bishops into exile in Sardinia.

Pope Symmachus, amongst the many acts of the founding or restoring of churches that he performed, constructed a dwelling for the poor, dedicated to Saints Peter, Paul, and Laurence; and each year he sent money and clothes to the bishops who were in exile throughout Africa or in Sardinia.

Anastasius, who supported the heresy of Eutyches, opposed the Catholics, and perished by a divine thunderbolt.*

4480 Justin the Elder [ruled for] eight years.

John bishop of the Roman Church, when he came to Constantinople, met a great crowd that had come out to meet him at the gate called 'golden', and there, in the sight of all, he restored the sight of a blind man who asked [to be cured].

When he returned to Ravenna, Theodoric ordered him and his companions to be imprisoned, out of annoyance that Justin, the defender of Catholic piety, had received him with so much honour.

In that year,* which was that of the consulship of Probus the Younger, he killed the patrician Symmachus at Ravenna. The following year he himself died of a sudden death, and was succeeded in the kingship by his grandson Athalaric.

Hilderic king of the Vandals ordered the bishops to be brought back from exile and the churches to be restored, after seventy-four years of heretical profanation.

Abbot Benedict was outstanding in the glory of his miracles, about which the blessed pope Gregory wrote in his book of *Dialogues*.

4518 Justinian, nephew by a sister of Justin [ruled for] thirty-eight years.

The patrician Belisarius, sent to Africa by Justinian, defeated the Vandals. Carthage was recovered in the ninety-sixth year after its loss; the defeated Vandals were expelled, and their king Gelimer was sent as a captive to Constantinople.

The body of Saint Anthony the monk was found by divine revelation, brought to Alexandria, and buried in the church of the blessed John the Baptist.

Dionysius wrote some paschal tables, beginning in the five hundred and thirty-second year from the Lord's incarnation, which is the two hundred and forty-eighth year of Diocletian [i.e. from his accession in AD 284].

After the consulship of Lampadius and Orestes; in which year the Code of Justinian was promulgated to the world.

Victor bishop of Capua wrote a book about Easter, making clear the errors of Victorius.

4529 Justin the younger [ruled for] eleven years.

The patrician Narses overcame and killed Totila king of the Goths in Italy.

Next, due to the malice of the Romans,* for whom he had long laboured against the Goths, he [Narses] was accused before Justin and his wife Sophia of seeking the enslavement of Italy as his reward. He retired to Naples in Campania, and wrote to the people of the Lombards [telling them] that they should come and possess Italy.

John bishop of the Roman Church completed and dedicated the church of the Apostles Philip and James, which his predecessor Pelagius had begun.

4536 Tiberius Constantine [ruled for] seven years. Gregory, then apocrisarius in Constantinople and later pope, began his books of exegesis on Job. He also showed, in the presence of the emperor Tiberius, that bishop Eutychius of Constantinople had erred in his teaching on resurrection. Thereupon the emperor ordered his book on the subject, which was damaging to Catholic teaching, to be burned. For Eutychius had taught that our human bodies would be impalpable in the glory of resurrection, and would be more subtle than the winds of the air; contrary to that statement of the Lord: 'Touch me and see, because a spirit does not have flesh and bones in the way that you see that I have.'*

The people of the Lombards, accompanied by famine and plague, seized hold of all Italy, and besieged the city of Rome, once herself the devastator; at this time Alboin was their king.

4557 Maurice [ruled for] twenty-one years.

Herminigild, son of Leuvigild the king of the Goths, because of his unshakeable adherence to the Catholic faith, was deprived of his kingdom by his Arian father, and was thrown into prison in chains, until he was struck on the head and killed at the very end of the night of Easter Sunday. He thus exchanged an earthly kingdom for the heavenly one, which he entered as a martyr. His brother soon after took over the kingdom, succeeding their father, and converted all of the Goths under his rule to the Catholic faith, under the direction of Leander bishop of Seville, who had also taught Herminigild.*

In the thirteenth year of the reign of Maurice and the thirteenth year of the indiction Gregory, the bishop of Rome and outstanding teacher, called together a synod of twenty-four bishops around the body of the blessed Apostle Peter, to discuss the needs of the Church.

He also sent to Britain Mellitus, Augustine, and John, and many other God-fearing monks with them, to convert the Angles to Christ. And when Æthelberht was soon converted to the grace of Christ, together with the people of the Cantuarii over whom he ruled, together with those of neighbouring kingdoms, he gave him Augustine to be his bishop and teacher, as well as other holy priests to become bishops. However, the people of the Angles north of the river Humber, under kings Ælle and Æthelfrith, did not hear the Word of life at this time.

Gregory, in the eighteenth year of Maurice and the fourth indiction, writing to Augustine, decreed that the bishops of London and York should receive a pallium from the apostolic see and be metropolitan bishops.

4565 Phocas [ruled for] eight years.

In his second year and the eighth of the indiction, pope Gregory went to the Lord.

At the request of pope Boniface, he [Phocas] proclaimed that the see of the Roman and apostolic Church was the head of all other churches, because the Church of Constantinople was writing about itself as being the first of churches.

The same emperor, also at the request of pope Boniface, ordered that the old temple called the Pantheon, having been cleared of all filthy traces of idolatry, should be converted into a church dedicated to the blessed and ever virgin Mary and all the martyrs; so that where once the cult of all the gods or rather demons was practised, there should thenceforth be a memorial to all the saints.

The Persians in a very severe war against the state overran many Roman provinces, even taking Jerusalem itself. They destroyed churches and profaned the holy furnishings of the places of the saints and of ordinary people, carrying them off; they also stole the standard of the Lord's cross.

4591 Heraclius [ruled for] twenty-five years.

Anastasius the Persian* monk nobly suffered martyrdom for Christ. Born in Persia, he learnt the magic arts from his father when a boy, but when he heard the name of Christ from Christian captives, he soon came to believe in him with all his heart. He left Persia, and came to Chalcedon and then

Hierapolis in search of Christ, going thence to Jerusalem. Having received the grace of baptism, he entered the monastery of abbot Anastasius, at the fourth milestone from the city. There he lived under a monastic rule for seven years, until he came by grace of prayer to Caesarea in Palestine, where he was captured by the Persians. By the sentence of the Marzban, he was kept for a long time among the prisoners, subject to chains and many whippings before being sent back to Persia, to their king Chosroes. By whom over a period of time he was almost whipped to death, suspended by one hand for three hours a day, before he was beheaded and his martyrdom completed, along with seventy others. Soon after, a man possessed by a demon was cured by putting on his tunic; he was amongst those who survived until the emperor Heraclius defeated the Persians with his army and brought the Christian captives back rejoicing. The relics of the blessed martyr Anastasius were first of all venerated in his own monastery, and then after they had been brought to Rome, in the monastery of the blessed Apostle Paul, called 'By the Salvian Waters'.

In the sixteenth year of Heraclius' reign and the fifteenth indiction, also being in the eleventh year of his own reign, and more or less the one hundred and eightieth year from the arrival of the Angles in Britain, Edwin, the most excellent king of the Northumbrian Angles in Britain, received with his people the Word of salvation through the preaching of bishop Paulinus, whom the venerable archbishop Justus had sent from Kent. He established Paulinus' episcopal seat in York. As an auspice of the coming of the faith and of the heavenly kingdom, the power of this king's earthly kingdom was increased: thus, unlike any of the Angles before him, he brought all the bounds of Britain, wherever either the Angles or the Britons dwelt, under his authority. At this time pope Honorius condemned in a letter the Quartodeciman error concerning the observance of Easter, which had appeared amongst the Irish. Also John, who came after Honorius' successor Severinus, wrote to them, while pope-elect, about this same problem of Easter and about the Pelagian heresy, which was coming to life again amongst them.

4593 Heraclonas [ruled] with his mother for two years.

Cyrus of Alexandria, and Sergius and Pyrrhus bishops of the royal city (of Constantinople), instigators of the Acephalite heresy, taught that there was one divine and human operation in Christ and one will. Of these, Pyrrhus came to Rome from Africa in the time of pope Theodore, and displayed what turned out to be a false penitence, when in the presence of the pope and all the clergy and people he presented a signed statement in which he condemned everything that he or his predecessors had done either in their writings or by their actions against the Catholic faith. Hence he was very well received by pope Theodore, as if he really were the bishop of the royal city, but when he had returned home and repeated his former error, the pope, having called together the bishops and clergy in the church of the blessed Peter, Prince of the Apostles, condemned him under the bond of anathema.

4594 Constantine the son of Heraclius [ruled for] six months.

Paul the successor of Pyrrhus showed himself to be not only as committed as his predecessors to their insane beliefs, but also more overt in the persecution of the Catholics. Some of the envoys of the holy Roman Church, who had been sent to correct him, were imprisoned, some were exiled, and some were flogged. He also overturned and destroyed their altar, which had been consecrated in the venerable oratory of the house of Placidia, forbidding them from celebrating mass there. Thus he, like his predecessors, was condemned by the apostolic see by a just sentence of deposition.

4622 Constantine the son of Constantine [ruled for] twenty-seven years.

He was deceived by Paul in the way that his grandfather Heraclius had been misled by Sergius, bishop of that same royal city. He promulgated a *Typos* against the Catholic faith, laying down that neither one nor two wills or operations in Christ should be professed, as if Christ should be believed neither to have willed nor to have acted. In consequence pope Martin convened a synod in Rome of one hundred and five bishops, and under anathema condemned the aforementioned Cyrus, Sergius, Pyrrhus, and Paul as heretics.

Following this, the exarch Theodore was sent by the emperor. He carried off pope Martin from the Constantinian basilica and sent him to Constantinople; afterwards he was exiled to Cherson, where he died, shining in that place in many signs of miracles right up to today. The above-mentioned synod was held in the month of October, in the ninth year of the emperor Constantine, in the eighth indiction.

Soon after the ordination of pope Vitalian the emperor Constantine sent to the blessed Peter a golden Gospel book, decorated on the cover with pearls of great size.

Some years later, in the sixth indiction, he came to Rome and laid on that altar a cloak made of cloth of gold; while all of his army entered the church carrying wax candles.

In the following year there was an eclipse of the sun, which is still remembered in our days, around the fifth hour on 3 May.

Archbishop Theodore and the equally learned abbot Hadrian were sent to Britain by pope Vitalian, and they fertilized many of the churches of the Angles with the fruit of ecclesiastical doctrine.

Constantine, after many and unheard-of raids had been made on the provinces, was killed in his bath in the twelfth indiction. Not long after this, pope Vitalian also sought the heavenly kingdom.

4639 Constantine, the son of the previous Constantine [ruled for] seventeen years.

The Arabs invaded Sicily, and returned to Alexandria with an enormous quantity of loot.

Pope Agatho, at the request of the most pious rulers Constantine, Heraclius, and Tiberius, sent envoys to the royal city, amongst whom was John, then a deacon but who not long after became bishop of Rome, to bring about the reunification of the holy churches of God. They were most benevolently received by Constantine, the most reverend defender of the Catholic faith, and were ordered to put aside all philosophical debates in order to search for the true faith in peaceful discussion, and various works of the Fathers that they were seeking were given to them from the library of Constantinople. One hundred and fifty bishops were present there, under the presidency of the patriarchs George of Constantinople and Macarius of Antioch. And they were convinced that those who asserted that there was one will and one operation in Christ were falsifying very many statements of the Catholic Fathers. With the conflict settled, George was set right, and Macarius with his followers, together with their predecessors Cyrus, Sergius, Honorius, Pyrrhus, Paul, and Peter were anathematized. In Macarius' place Theophanius, an abbot from Sicily, was made bishop of Antioch. So great was the gratitude expressed to the envoys of the Catholic peace, that John bishop of Porto, who was one of them, publicly celebrated mass in Latin in the presence of the emperor and the patriarch in the church of Santa Sophia, on the Sunday of the octave of Easter.

Thus was the sixth universal synod held in Constantinople and [its acts] written in Greek, in the time of pope Agatho, by order of and in the presence of the most pious prince Constantine; in his palace, with the legates of the apostolic see and one hundred and fifty bishops taking part. The first universal synod was held in Nicaea against Arius, with three hundred and eighteen bishops, in the time of pope Julius and under the emperor Constantine. The second was in Constantinople with one hundred and fifty bishops, against Macedonius and Eudoxius in the time of pope Damasus and the emperor Gratian, when Nectarius was ordained bishop of Constantinople. The third was held in Ephesus under the emperor Theodosius the Great and pope Celestine, with two hundred bishops present, against Nestorius, the bishop of the imperial city. The fourth was in Chalcedon, with six hundred and thirty bishops under pope Leo and in the time of the emperor Marcian, against Eutyches the most villainous leader of the monks. The fifth was also in Constantinople in the time of pope Vigilius and under the emperor Justinian, against Theodore and all heretics. The sixth is that of which we have just spoken.

The holy and perpetual virgin of Christ Æthelthryth, daughter of Anna king of the Angles, was given as wife firstly to one great man and then to king Egfrid. After she had preserved the marriage bed uncorrupted for twelve years, having taken the holy veil she was transformed from a queen into a consecrated virgin. Without delay she also became a mother of virgins and the pious nourisher of holy women, and received the place called Ely in order to build a monastery. Her merits while living were also testified to when her body and the clothes in which it had been wrapped were found uncorrupted* sixteen years after her burial.

4649 Justinian the second, the son of Constantine, [ruled for] ten years.

He made a ten-year peace on land and at sea with the Arabs, but the province of Africa that was subject to the Roman empire was assaulted by the Arabs, and Carthage itself was also captured by them and destroyed.

This emperor ordered his protospatharius Zacharias to deport to Constantinople the Roman bishop Sergius, of blessed memory, because he was unwilling to approve of and sign [the acts of] the heretical synod that he was holding in Constantinople. But the militia of the city of Ravenna and of the surrounding regions opposed the evil orders of the emperor and expelled Zacharias from Rome with insults and injuries.

The same pope Sergius ordained the venerable man Willibrord, called Clement, as bishop of the Frisians, where up to the present day he is achieving innumerable daily losses for the devil and gains for the Christian faith, as a pilgrim for the eternal homeland (for he is one of the people of the Angles from Britain).

Justinian was deprived of the glory of his kingdom by the crime of treason, and withdrew to Pontus as an exile.

4652 Leo [ruled for] three years.

By divine revelation, Pope Sergius found a silver box in the sanctuary of the blessed Apostle Peter, where it had long lain hidden in a very dark corner; in it was a cross adorned with many precious stones. Inside this, having removed four metal plates in which the gems were embedded, he discovered a piece, of considerable size, of the life-giving cross of the Lord. From then on each year, on the day of the Exaltation of the Cross, this is kissed and adored by all the people in the basilica of the Saviour, known as the Constantinian.

The most reverend bishop Cuthbert, who from being an anchorite became bishop of the church of Lindisfarne in Britain, spent all his life most worthily, from infancy to old age, as shown by his miracles. His body remained buried but uncorrupted for eleven years, after which it was found, together with the clothes by which he was covered [in the same state] as in the hour of his death, as I have described in the book of his life and miracles; both in the recent prose version and in that which I wrote some years ago in hexameter verse.

4659 Tiberius [ruled for] seven years.

A synod held at Aquileia out of ignorance of the faith was reluctant to accept the [authority of the] fifth universal council, but instructed by the salutary warnings of the blessed pope Sergius it agreed to approve it along with [all] the other churches of Christ.

Gisulf, the duke of the Lombards in Benevento, laid waste Campania with fire and sword and the [taking of] captives. Because there was no one who could resist his advance, the apostolic pope John, who had succeeded Sergius, sent priests to him and very many gifts; he redeemed all of the prisoners and made the enemy return home.

He was succeeded by another John, who amongst many notable deeds, built the oratory of the holy Mother of God inside the church of the blessed Apostle Paul in the most beautiful style.

Aripert,* the king of the Lombards, restored to its possession many farms and estates in the Cottian Alps which had previously belonged to the apostolic see but which had been stolen by the Lombards a long time before; he sent this deed of gift to Rome written in letters of gold.

4665 Justinian [reigned] for a second time, with his son Tiberius for six years.

Receiving help from Terbellius,* the king of the Bulgars, he killed those who had expelled him. These were the patricians Leo, who had usurped his place and also his successor Tiberius, who ejected him [i.e. Leo] from the throne and kept him a captive in Constantinople during all of his reign. He sent the patriarch Callinicus to Rome with his eyes torn out, and gave the bishopric [of Constantinople] to Cyrus, who had been an abbot in Pontus and had supported him when in exile. He ordered pope Constantine to come to him, and received and saw him off him with great honour; requesting him to say mass on Sunday so that he might receive communion from his hand. He prostrated himself on the ground [before the pope] asking intercession for his sins, and renewing all the privileges of the Church [of Rome]. When, against the advice of the apostolic pope, he sent a large army into Pontus in order to apprehend Philip whom he had exiled there, the whole army went over to Philip's side, and made him emperor. Philip returned with the army and fought with Justinian at the twelfth milestone from the city [of Constantinople]. Having defeated and killed Justinian, Philip took over the empire.

4667 Philip [ruled for] one year and six months.

He ejected Cyrus from the bishopric and ordered him to return to being abbot of his monastery in Pontus. The emperor sent letters containing heretical doctrine to pope Constantine, which the latter rejected with the council of the apostolic see; and because of this he set up pictures in the porticus of Saint Peter depicting the acts of the six holy universal synods. For Philip had ordered similar pictures in the royal city [of Constantinople] to be removed. He ordered the people of Rome not to recognize the name of the heretical emperor or his written decrees or gold coins bearing his image. Hence, neither were portaits of him carried into church, nor was his name mentioned in the solemnities of the mass.

4670 Anastasius [ruled for] three years.

He captured Philip and blinded but did not kill him.

He sent letters to pope Constantine in Rome via the patrician Scholasticus, the exarch of Italy, in which he proved himself to be a supporter of the Catholic faith and an upholder of the sixth holy council.

Liutprand, the king of the Lombards, confirmed the gift of the estates in the Cottian Alps, which king Aripert had made and he had repeated, at the request of pope Gregory.

In the seven hundred and sixteenth year from the Incarnation of the Lord, Egbert, a holy man and bishop in monastic life of the people of the Angles, having adopted the life of a pilgrim for the sake of the celestial homeland, converted through his pious preaching many provinces of the Irish to the correct observance of the timing of Easter, from which they had long strayed.

4671 Theodosius [reigned for] one year.

Having been chosen emperor, he defeated Anastasius in a severe battle at the city of Nicaea, and having given him an oath, he forced him to become a cleric and be ordained a priest. In order truly to receive the imperial office, since he was a Catholic, he soon restored to its former position, where it might be venerated, that picture in which six holy synods were depicted, which had been torn down by Philip.

The River Tiber breaking its banks caused many to leave the city of Rome; the flooding was so great that it formed a single broad way, one and a half times the normal height [of the river], extending from the gates of Saint Peter as far as the Milvian bridge. It remained there for seven days, until, with the citizens performing frequent litanies, it at last receded on the eighth day.

At this time many of the people of the Angles, both nobles and commoners, men and women, leaders and led, made a practice of coming from Britain to Rome, by the inspiration of divine love. Amongst these was my abbot Ceolfrid, aged 74 and having been a priest for forty-seven years and an abbot for thirty-five. Having reached Langres, he died and was buried there in the church of the blessed twin martyrs. Amongst other gifts which he had arranged to take with him, he sent to the church of Saint Peter a pandect* of the blessed Jerome's Latin translation [of the Bible] from the Hebrew and the Greek.

4680 Leo [ruled for] eight years.

The Arabs, coming with an immense army, besieged the city of Constantinople for three years; during which time many of the citizens, calling on God on numerous occasions, died of starvation, cold, and disease; until wearied of the siege the Arabs* withdrew. After they had retired, the people of the

Bulgars, from the River Danube, started a war, from which they also withdrew defeated, and returned to their ships. When they were on the high sea, a storm suddenly blew up and many of them were killed by their ships being sunk or being broken up on the shore.

Liutprand,* hearing that the Arabs had depopulated Sardinia and had dug up the place whither the bones of the holy bishop Augustine had once been moved (on account of the ravaging of the barbarians) and where they had been honourably buried, he sent, and paying a great price for them, he received the bones and transported them to Pavia, and reburied them there with the honour due to so great a Father.

BEDE'S LETTER TO EGBERT

BEDE'S LETTER TO EGBERT

To the most dear and most reverend bishop Egbert,* greetings from Bede the servant of Christ. I remember how you said last year, when I was staying for some days in your monastery for purposes of study, that when you came back there again this year you would like to be able to have a talk to me about our common interests in learning. If, by God's will, that could have happened, it would not have been necessary now to send you this letter; as I could have said to you whatever I wanted or was necessary in private conversation. Because this could not be, on account, as you know, of the state of my health, and because of your brotherly affection for me, I have taken the trouble to send you in this letter that which I should have preferred to say in person.* I beg you in the Lord's name not to feel that the intentions of this letter are arrogant, but rather to look upon it as a gift proffered in humility and affection [*pietas*].

I urge your Holiness, my most beloved Father in Christ, to remember to uphold by both holy living and teaching the most sacred office which the Author of all dignities and the bestower of all spiritual gifts has conferred upon you. Neither of these virtues is complete without the other; for the bishop who lives a holy life should not neglect the duty of teaching, and he would be condemned if he gave good instruction but failed to follow it in practice. But he who truly does both is that slave* who joyfully awaits the coming of the Lord, hoping soon to hear the words 'Rejoice you good and faithful slave; because you have been trustworthy over these small matters, I shall place you in charge of greater ones; join in your Master's happiness.'* But if anyone—may it never happen!—receives the office of bishop and does not take care to keep himself free from evil by living well, and does not ensure that the people under his authority are corrected by instruction and punishment, what will happen to him at the hour of the coming of the Lord, the time of which is unknown to him, is made clear in the Gospel; where He says to the useless slave:

'Throw him into the outer darkness, where there will be weeping and gnashing of teeth.'*

I advise you above all, holy father, to avoid all idle chatting and gossiping and other evils of the unrestrained tongue, as being harmful to your episcopal dignity. You should occupy your mind and your tongue in the divine speech* and in meditations on the Scriptures, and above all you should read the Epistles of the blessed Apostle Paul to Timothy and to Titus; also the words of the most holy pope Gregory in which he carefully considered the life and also the vices of those in spiritual authority* [*rectores*] in his *Book of the Pastoral Rule* and in his *Homilies on the Gospels*. In this way your language will be savoured with the salt of wisdom, be elevated above the common speech, and be worthier of the divine ear. For just as it is inappropriate to sully the holy vessels of the altar by ordinary domestic use, so is it unsuitable and demeaning that someone who has been ordained to consecrate the Lord's sacraments on the altar should go out of the church after serving the Lord in the administration of the sacraments and then, with the same mouth and with hands just used for sacred matters, give offence to the Lord by frivolous speech and deeds.

As by the reading of holy texts [*lectio divina*], so can the company of those who are faithful servants of Christ preserve the purity of one's words and actions. Thus, if my speech begins to become lascivious or an improper action suggests itself to me, I am quickly prevented from falling by the hand of my faithful companions. When this is so useful for all of the servants of God, how much more so is it for those of such rank as to have not only the care of their own salvation but also that of the Church entrusted to them. As it is said, 'leaving aside those things which are irrelevant, my daily concern is the care of all the churches. Who is unwell and I am not unwell with him; who is tempted to evil, and I am not burned?'* I do not say this because I think you would act in any other way, but because it is reported of some bishops that they have no men of true religion or self-control around them, but instead are surrounded by those who give themselves up to laughter, jokes, storytelling, eating, drinking, and other seductions of the soft life, and who would prefer each day to fill their stomachs with feasting rather than their minds with heavenly offerings. If you should meet any of these bishops, I should like you to correct them by your holy authority, and to warn them that they ought to have such companions in their day-time and in their night-time activities as might inspire people by actions worthy in the sight of God and by proper teaching; thus they would be able to assist in the spiritual duties of the bishops themselves. Read the Acts of the Apostles, and you will see in blessed Luke's account the sort of companions the Apostles Paul and Barnabas had with them and how they themselves behaved wherever they went. For whenever they entered a city or a synagogue they at once began to preach the word of God and to spread it everywhere. This I should also like you to do, my dearest friend, wherever you can. For you were chosen by the Lord and elected to your high office in order that you might preach the word boldly, with the help of him who is the king of all virtues, our lord Jesus Christ. This you will achieve properly if, whenever you arrive somewhere, you immediately gather together the inhabitants of the place and expound the word to them with moral encouragement, and at the same time set them an example, by living with those companions who came with you as if you were the commander of a heavenly host.

And because the places in the diocese under your authority are so far apart that it would take you more than the whole year on your own to go through them all and preach the word of God in every hamlet and field, it is clearly essential that you appoint others to help you in your holy work; thus priests should be ordained and teachers established who may preach the word of God and consecrate the holy mysteries in every small village, and above all perform the holy rites of baptism wherever the opportunity arises. In this preaching to the populace I consider it most important that you attempt to fix ineradicably in the memory of all those under your rule the beliefs of the Church, as set out in the Apostles' Creed, and also the Lord's Prayer, which a reading of the holy Gospel teaches us. It is most certain that all those who have learned to read Latin will know these well, but the unlearned, that is

345

to say those who only know their own language, must learn to say them in their own tongue and to chant them carefully.* This ought to be done not only by the laity, that is to say those living the ordinary life of the populace, but also by the clergy and the monks, who are experts in Latin. For thus the whole community of the believers may learn of what their faith consists, and how they ought in the strength of that belief to arm and defend themselves against the assaults of evil spirits. Thus they will learn, as a united chorus of supplicants to God, what above all they should seek from the divine clemency. Because of this I have frequently offered an English translation of the Creed and the Lord's Prayer to uneducated priests. For the holy bishop Ambrose advises,* when talking about belief, that the words of the Creed should be chanted by the faithful each morning, as a kind of spiritual antidote to the poison with which the devil tries by day and night to infect them. The custom of frequent prayer and bending of the knee has also taught us to chant the Lord's Prayer very often.

If your pastoral authority can achieve what we have suggested in the ruling over and caring for the flocks of Christ, it is impossible to say how great is the spiritual reward that you will be preparing for yourself in the future with the Shepherd of the shepherds. The fewer the examples you find of this most holy activity amongst the bishops of our people, so much greater will be the prize for your special merit; since in your fatherly affection and care you will be inspiring the people of God through the repetition of the Creed and the chanting of the Lord's Prayer to understanding, love, hope, faith, and the search for those heavenly gifts for which they pray. But on the other hand, if you carry out the task entrusted to you by God less diligently, you will be rewarded in the future alongside the bad and lazy slave who hid his coin;* especially if you demand and receive temporal dues from those whom you have not attempted to repay with the gifts of heavenly support [*beneficium*]. For as the Lord said when he sent his disciples out to preach: 'As you go preach, saying that kingdom of heaven is at hand.' A little later he added: 'Freely you have received, so freely give; do not seek to possess either gold or silver.' If therefore he ordered them to preach the

Gospel freely, and did not permit them to receive gold or silver or any form of worldly recompense from those to whom they preached, what dangers, I ask you, must threaten those who act differently?

You must appreciate what a serious crime is committed by those who most sedulously demand earthly recompense from those who listen to them, but at the same time devote no attention to their eternal salvation by way of preaching, moral exhortation, or rebukes. Be moved by this and weigh it carefully, dearest bishop. For we have heard, and it is indeed well known, that there are many of the villages and hamlets of our people located in inaccessible mountains or in dense forests, where a bishop has never been seen over the course of many years performing his ministry and revealing the divine grace. But not one of these places is immune from paying the taxes that are due to that bishop.* Not only does the bishop never appear in such places, to confirm the baptized by the laying-on of his hand, neither do they have any teacher to instruct them in the truth of the faith or to enable them to distinguish between good and evil deeds. Thus it may come about that not only do the bishops not evangelize freely and confirm the faithful, but also they do something much worse, which is that having received money from their congregations, something the Lord forbade, they neglect the ministry of the word which the Lord ordered. It may be read how the priest Samuel, beloved of God, acted very differently, as testified to by the whole people.

Having dwelt amongst you from my youth up to this very day, behold I stand prepared; speak of me in the presence of the Lord and in the presence of his Anointed one as to whether I have carried off any man's ox or ass, or whether I have falsely accused anyone or have oppressed anyone, or if I have received a bribe from any man's hand; if so today I shall despise it and return it to you. And they said: you have not falsely accused us, nor have you oppressed us nor taken anything from any man.*

Because of his innocence and his justice he was deemed worthy to be numbered amongst the most outstanding of the leaders and priests of the people of God, and he was worthy in his prayers to be heard by and to talk to God; as the Psalmist said: 'Moses and Aaron amongst his priests, and Samuel amongst those who call upon his name; they called upon the Lord and he heard them, and in the column of cloud he spoke to them.'*

If we believe and confess that something useful is conferred on the faithful by the laying-on of hands, through which the Holy Spirit may be received, it follows on the converse, that if the laying-on of hands is deferred, the benefit is denied them. On whom more does this denial of the good reflect than on those bishops who have promised to be their protectors, but who have neglected or have proved unwilling to perform this duty of spiritual leadership? The principle cause of this crime is avarice; against which the Apostle—through whom Christ was speaking—declaimed: 'Greed is the root of all evil',* and again, 'Nor shall the covetous possess the kingdom of God.'* For when a bishop, urged on by a love of money, takes under his authority a larger portion of the population than he could visit and preach to in the course of a year, then it may be shown that he is causing danger both to himself and to those whom he is guiding under the false title of spiritual director.

Dearest bishop, in suggesting these few things about the harm that has been done to our people, I am praying that you may strive zealously to recall to the right way of life any whom you see acting so wickedly. For you have, I believe, in king Ceolwulf* a most active helper in so just an undertaking. From his own love of religion he will be constantly and determinedly anxious to help with anything that relates to the rule of piety, and above all, as you are his dearest and closest relative, he will be keen to assist any good works that you initiate. Therefore, I should like you to advise him wisely, so that in your time you may together put the Church of our people into a better condition than it has been in up to now. Which, it seems to me, could not be better achieved than by consecrating more of our race as bishops;* following the example of the legislator who when he could no longer sustain by himself the problems and contentiousness of the people of Israel, by divine guidance chose and consecrated seventy elders whose aid and counsel might help him bear more lightly the burden placed upon him. For who cannot see how much better it would be for the enormous weight of ecclesiastical government to be divided up amongst many, who could easily take their share, than for one to be oppressed by a load which he cannot carry? For the holy pope Gregory, in a letter* that he sent to the blessed archbishop Augustine about the future and the preservation in Christ of the faith of our people, ordered that twelve bishops should be ordained after all had been converted. Over these the bishop of York, receiving a pallium from the apostolic see, would be the metropolitan. I should like you, holy father, under the protection and guidance of the previously mentioned most pious and God-beloved king, most assiduously to seek to bring about the achieving of that number of bishops; so that by an abundance of office-holders the Church of Christ may be more perfectly governed in all matters that relate to the practice of holy religion. As we are aware, because of the lack of concern on the part of previous kings and the making of unwise donations, it is not easy to find available the kind of place in which a new episcopal see ought be located.

Therefore I would consider it most appropriate for a major council to be held and with its consent and by episcopal and royal decree one of the monasteries* should be considered as a site for an episcopal see. In case either the abbot or the monks should be tempted to oppose or resist this decree they should be given permission to elect one of their own number to be ordained bishop and to exercise episcopal authority over both the monastery itself and over the adjoining regions belonging to that diocese. If it should prove impossible to find anyone in that monastery who should be ordained bishop, then let someone be found to become bishop of the diocese following the rules of canon law. If, with the help of God, you do what we suggest you will very easily achieve, or so we think, metropolitan status* for the church of York, according to the decrees of the apostolic see. If it be felt that, on account of having to support the episcopal dignity, such a monastery should be enlarged by more lands and possessions, there are many such places, as we all know, that only in the most foolish way deserve the name of monastery, having absolutely nothing of real monastic life about them. Some of these I should wish to be turned by the authority of a council from luxury to chastity, from vanity to verity, from indulgence of the stomach and the gullet to continence and heartfelt piety, to help the episcopal see* that now ought to be established.

Such places which are in the common phrase 'useless to God and man', because they neither serve God by following a regular monastic life nor provide soldiers and helpers for the secular powers who might defend our people from the barbarians, are both numerous and large; so whoever establishes episcopal sees in them because of the needs of the times will be judged not to have committed the crime of betraying the divine law but rather to have carried out an act of virtue. For how can it be thought sinful if the illegal decisions of some princes are corrected by the just judgement of better ones, or if the lying pen of evil scribes is destroyed and made as nothing by the discreet sentence of wiser priests, following the example in sacred history, which in describing the times of the kings of Judah from David and Solomon to Zedekiah,* the last of them, shows some of them to have been men of religion but more to have been evil-doers; taking it in turn now for the wicked rulers to alter the decrees of the good ones who had gone before them, and now for the good kings, aided by the spirit of God acting through the holy prophets and priests, to undo the evil deeds of their unjust predecessors; all in accordance with that which Isaiah perceived and said: 'Break the bonds of legal contacts obtained by violence; let the parties thus divided go their own way in freedom, and obliterate every evil document.'* Following this example, your holiness should, together with the most pious king, tear up the irreligious and wicked deeds and documents* of earlier rulers of our people, and should provide in our land those things which are useful either to God or to lay society, lest in our times either religion come to an end, together with the love and fear of Him who sees within us, or with the diminishing of our military forces* those who should defend our borders against barbarian incursions disappear. It is shocking to say how many places that go by the name of monasteries have been taken under the control of men who have no knowledge of true monastic life, with the result that there is nowhere that sons of the nobles or retired soldiers can take possession of. In consequence, wandering and without a spouse, and having passed the age of puberty, they live without a commitment to continence, and in consequence they either leave their homeland for which they ought to be fighting in order to go overseas or, with even greater wickedness and lack of shame, because they lack the intention of being chaste, they give themselves up to indulgence and fornication, not even abstaining from virgins consecrated to God!

There are others, laymen who have no love for the monastic life nor for military service, who commit a graver crime by giving money to the kings and obtaining lands under the pretext of building monasteries, in which they can give freer rein to their libidinous tastes; these lands they have assigned to them in hereditary right through written royal edicts, and these charters, as if to make them really worthy in the sight of God, they arrange to be witnessed in writing* by bishops, abbots, and the most powerful laymen. Thus they have gained unjust rights over fields and villages, free from both divine and human legal obligations; as laymen ruling over monks they serve only their own wishes. Indeed, they do not gather monks there but rather they find those vagrants who have been expelled from monasteries in other places for the sin of disobedience, or whom they have lured away from other monasteries, or, for sure, those of their own followers whom they can persuade to take the tonsure and promise monastic obedience to them. They fill the monastic cells they have built with these cohorts of the deformed, and as a hideous and unheard-of spectacle, those same men occupy themselves with their wives and the children they have engendered, and, rising from their beds, carefully deal with whatever needs to be done within the monastic enclosure. Also with equal shamelessness they obtain places where their wives may construct monasteries, in which with the same stupidity they, although laywomen, permit themselves the role of spiritual guides to the handmaids of Christ. To these it would be appropriate to apply the common proverb: 'Wasps can make honey combs, but use them to store poison rather than honey.'

Thus for about thirty years, from when king Aldfrid was taken from human affairs, our kingdom* [*provincia*] has been made so mad with this insane error that almost everyone of the leading nobles* has bought himself a monastery of this kind during his time in office and has involved his wife in the same wicked offence. With this most evil custom being so prevalent, the kings' ministers and servants have done the same, and thus by this perverse state of affairs a large number of men may be found calling themselves abbots and at the same time leading nobles or ministers or servants of the king; although as laymen they could know something of the monastic life by hearing about it though not experiencing it, they are quite lacking in any share of the character or the training needed to teach it. And such men, as you know, having received the tonsure at their own pleasure, are transformed by their own choice from laymen not into monks but into abbots! But because they have neither knowledge of nor interest in that above-mentioned quality, what applies to them better than that curse in the Gospel: 'If the blind lead the blind, both will fall into the pit'?* Such blindness could certainly be ended at any time, confined by the discipline of regular monastic life* and expelled far beyond the borders of the holy Church by joint episcopal and conciliar authority, if only the bishops did not show themselves to be aiding and abetting in these offences. They not only do not take the trouble to counter unjust decrees with just ones, but instead they prefer to confirm them, as we mentioned above, with their own signatures. They are moved to witness these evil documents by that same love of wealth that impelled the purchasers to buy such monasteries.

Much more could I tell you in this letter about these and other such traitors to the word of God by whom our kingdom is so wretchedly vexed, if I did not know that you yourself have recognized this to be most true. For I have not written what I have as if I were teaching you something about which you did not already know, but in order to warn you by friendly advice that you ought to correct at once, as far as you may, those things which you best of all know to be wrong.

Now I beg and beseech you in the Lord's name that you keep safe the flock entrusted to you from the audacious attacks of the ravening wolves, and that you remember that you have been appointed not as a hireling but as a shepherd; you may show your love for the supreme Shepherd in caring for the sheep of his pasture and in being ready, like the blessed Prince of the Apostles, to lay down your life for those sheep if need be. Take care, I beg you, in case when the same Prince of the Apostles and other leaders of the flocks of the faithful offer to Christ on the Day of Judgement the great achievement of their pastoral care, a group of your sheep deserve to be set amongst the goats on the left hand of the Judge and to go with curses into eternal torment. May you rather deserve at that time to be enrolled in the number of those of whom Isaiah said: 'The least will become a thousand and the smallest a most powerful nation.'* For it is your duty to enquire most carefully into what is done rightly and what wrongly in each monastery of your diocese, in case either an abbot ignorant or contemptuous of the rules of monastic life or an unworthy abbess be put in charge of the servants and handmaidens of Christ; or lest an undisciplined group of contumacious monks rebel against the authority of their spiritual teachers. All the more so, since it is commonly known that you bishops normally say that what happens in individual monasteries is subject to your episcopal investigation and jurisdiction and not that of the king or any other secular lord, unless it turns out that someone in the monastery has offended against those rulers. It is your duty, I say, to ensure that in the places that are consecrated to God the devil does not set up his kingdom, in case conflict replaces peace, discord piety, drunkenness sobriety, and fornication and murder take the throne of charity and chastity; lest there be some found amongst you of whom it needed to be said: 'I saw the evil-doers buried, who, when they were alive, stood in the holy place and were praised in the city as men of good deeds.'*

353

You should also exercise solicitous care for those who remain in the secular life, and remember, as I advised you at the beginning of this letter, to provide them with enough teachers of the life of salvation. Amongst other things you ought to teach them which acts are most pleasing to God and from which sins those who wish to please him ought to abstain; also with what sincerity of heart they should believe in God; with what devotion they ought to pray, begging for divine mercy; how frequently and carefully they need to fortify themselves with the sign of the Lord's cross against the continuous assaults of the evil spirits; how salutary the daily receiving of the Lord's body and blood may be for every sort of Christian, as you know is the custom of the Church of Christ throughout Italy, Gaul, Africa, Greece, and all of the East. It is clear that this kind of religion and sanctification through devotion to God has too long been absent, almost as if it were an alien custom, amongst virtually all the laity of this kingdom because of the lack of care on the part of the instructors; so that even those amongst them who appear to be most religious only receive the holy mysteries at Christmas, Epiphany, and Easter. Meanwhile there are innumerable innocent boys and girls, young men and women, and old people, all of good character, who without any doctrinal worry are able to receive the holy mysteries every Sunday and on the feasts of the holy apostles and martyrs, as you have seen done in the holy Roman and apostolic Church. Also, if someone explains to them the capacity for continence and recommends the virtue of chastity, married people can freely do the same and would gladly wish to do so.

I have sought briefly to express these things, holiest bishop, both in response to your affection and for the good of all, very much wanting and urging you to take care to turn our people away from the old errors and bring them back to the safer and more direct road. If there are some men, of whatever rank or class, who try to restrain or impede your good efforts, you must strive to bring your holy and virtuous undertaking firmly to its end, remembering the heavenly reward. I know indeed that there are some very opposed to what I have been advising, especially those who feel themselves ensnared in those crimes against which I have been warning you, but it is appropriate to remind you of the reply made by the Apostle that 'it is more important to obey God than men'.* It is certainly commanded by God: 'Sell what you own and give alms'* and 'Unless he has renounced all that he possess, he cannot be my disciple.'* But the modern fashion is for those who profess themselves to be the servants of God not only not to sell their possessions but rather to obtain things that are not their own. How does anyone dare enter the service of God, while both retaining those things he had in the secular life and also, under the pretence of a holier life, gathering riches that do not belong to him? That the punishment inflicted by the Apostle on Annanias and Saphira, who were trying to do the same, was not one of penance or correction by means of restitution, but one of instant avenging death and damnation is surely well known? And they had not chosen to acquire other people's goods, merely to retain their own. Hence it is patently obvious how far the spirit of the Apostles stood back from the accepting and amassing of wealth, who served the Lord under his own rule: 'Blessed are the poor, because yours is the kingdom of heaven.'* No less were they instructed by a contrary example: 'Woe to you who are rich, because you have your consolation.' Can we think that by chance the Apostle was wrong or wrote deceptively, when he warned us 'Brothers, do not seek to err', and at once he added: 'Neither the greedy, nor the drunkard, nor the rapacious will possess the kingdom of God'; and again: 'But know this, that no fornicator, nor any debauched, avaricious or rapacious man has any inheritance in the kingdom of Christ and of God, because he is the slave of idols.'* When the Apostle thus clearly labels avarice and rapacity as idolatry, how can those be thought wrong who have withdrawn their hand from signing the documents of a greedy commerce, even when ordered by the king, or who have applied their hand to rooting out harmful documents and their witness lists?

Indeed we ought to wonder at the temerity of the fools, or rather lament the wretchedness of the blind, who, without any thought of the fear of the divine, everywhere and every day are shown to annul and to treat as worthless those things which the Apostles and Prophets have written at the instigation of the Holy Spirit. On the other hand they are terrified of destroying or altering what they or those like them have written out of an instinct for greed and excess, as if it were a holy and divine writ, in the manner—if I am not mistaken—of the heathen, who in defiance of worship of the true God venerate as spirits, fear, cherish, adore, and petition things which they themselves have made and shaped in their own hearts, fully meriting the Lord's rebuke by which He showed the Pharisees to be guilty of preferring their minor regulations to the law of God, saying: 'Why do you disobey the command of God on account of your traditions?'* Even if they offer written documents, witnessed by the signatures of noble people, in defence of their desires, I beg that you will never forget the Lord's decree in which he said: 'Every plant that my heavenly father did not plant will be eradicated.'* This I should certainly like to learn from you, dearest bishop: Our Lord having testified and said that 'wide is the gate and broad the road that leads to damnation, and many are they who enter by it, but slender is the gate and narrow the road that leads to life, and few find it',* what do you believe to be the life and the eternal salvation of those who are known to walk through the wide gate and on the broad highway through all the length of their lives, and who do not care, even in the smallest matters, to resist and struggle against the pleasures of the body and the mind for fear of heavenly retribution? Unless their crimes ought to be believed to have been absolved through the alms that they were seen to give to the poor in the midst of their daily pleasures and indulgences, though the very hand with which an offering is made to God should be as clean and absolved from sin as the conscience. Or perhaps they ought to hope that they may be redeemed after they have died through others offering the holy mysteries, of which they showed themselves unworthy while they lived. Or perhaps the crime of greed seems very small to them? I shall examine it a little further. This is what made Balaam, a man very full of the spirit of prophecy, a stranger to the reward of the saints; Achan the son of Carmi was corrupted by sharing in the curse and was damned; it stripped Saul of the royal insignia; it deprived Gehazi of the power of prophecy and contaminated him and his descendants with a perpetual plague of leprosy; it deposed Judas Iscariot from the glory of the Apostolate; it punished Annanias and Saphira, whom I also allegorized as those unworthy members in a community of monks, with the death of the body; to come to higher matters it both threw the angels out of heaven and expelled our first ancestors from the paradise of perpetual delight. If you wish to know, it is that three-headed dog of the underworld, to whom the stories give the name of Cerberus, from whose rabid teeth the Apostle John protects us when he said 'Dearest, do not love the world, nor those things that are in the world. If anyone loves the world, the love of the Father is not in him. Because everything that is in the world is the longing of the flesh and the longing of the eyes and the pride of life, which are not from the Father but from the world.'* These are brief sayings against the poison of greed. If we wished to deal with drunkenness, gluttony, extravagance, and other such plagues with equal attention, the length of this letter would have to be enormously extended.

May the grace of the supreme Shepherd keep you safe for the healthy pasturing of his sheep, most beloved bishop in Christ. Written on the fifth of November in the third indiction.*

EXPLANATORY NOTES

Details of individuals mentioned more than once will be found at their first occurrence, which may be located by means of the Index. References to Plummer (*Baedae Opera Historica* (Oxford, 1896), vol. ii) and Wallace-Hadrill (*Bede's Ecclesiastical History of the English People: A Historical Commentary* (Oxford, 1988)) indicate that fuller notes may be found for this reference.

ECCLESIASTICAL HISTORY

3 *Ceolwulf*: became king of the Northumbrians in 729 and had to confront unspecified difficulties which were not resolved when Bede wrote two years later (v. 23). Bede's continuator (p. 296) described his capture, tonsure, and later return to his kingdom in 731; in 737 he chose tonsure at Lindisfarne, and seems to have died in 764.

History of the English Church and Nation: properly *Ecclesiastical History of the English People*. Bede stands in the great tradition of ecclesiastical history founded by Eusebius: WH 2–3. His particular field was the bringing of Christianity to the English people: the settlers in the former Roman province of Britain who were politically divided, but lent unity by the mission to them sent by pope Gregory I (590–604) in 596–7.

lately published: after criticism of the rough draft, release of the completed text for general copying.

Should history tell of good men: Bede alludes to the moral purpose of historical writing, a commonplace of the classical form.

sources: in words echoing those of the preface of the *Dialogues* of pope Gregory I, Bede follows the practice of previous writers of ecclesiastical history in delineating his sources, both oral and written, in a section of immense value in establishing his method and evaluating his material.

Albinus: an Englishman, trained by Theodore and Hadrian to succeed the latter as abbot of the monastery of St Peter and St Paul (later known as St Augustine's) in Canterbury. Bede admired his scriptural scholarship (v. 20) and describes him both as the one who had persuaded him to write the *Ecclesias-*

tical History, and as the source of much material on the mission sent by pope Gregory I. The supposed letter from Bede to Albinus, printed by Plummer (i. 3), was first published by Mabillon in his *Vetera Analecta* (Paris, 1723), p. 398, from a manuscript, apparently since lost, which he had not seen; it is unlikely to be genuine.

Theodore: Bede describes in IV. 1 the consecration by pope Vitalian in 668 of this elderly and unlikely archbishop of the English Church. Theodore was a monk from Tarsus, then under Arab rule, and the fourth choice for consecration; nonetheless he was an immensely successful archbishop who for over twenty-one years, until his death, aged 88, in 690, revived Christianity in the English kingdoms and laid the foundations for its institutional development. Book IV gives an account of his activities and their significance.

Hadrian: was from Africa and an abbot of a monastery near Naples who refused Pope Vitalian's offer to consecrate him archbishop of the English Church in 667, but was persuaded to accompany Theodore. He arrived in Canterbury after Theodore, who made him abbot of the monastery of St Peter and St Paul; he spent his time assisting Theodore and instructing students, including his successor Albinus (IV. 2). He probably died in 709 (V. 20).

from written records or from the old traditions: Bede distinguishes oral and written sources. Documents concerning references to Gregory's mission in Canterbury may have included episcopal lists, or Easter tables with marginal notes of events.

disciples of St Gregory: the mission sent to the English people in 596, which arrived in Thanet, in the kingdom of Aethelberht of Kent, in 597, was despatched by pope Gregory I, and was led by Augustine, prior of Gregory's own monastery of St Andrew's in Rome (I. 23–7). In 601 Gregory sent a second group of missionaries, with instructions on the organization of the English Church (V. 29).

4 *Nothhelm*: it seems Nothhelm certainly visited Bede in Wearmouth-Jarrow twice, firstly to bring written materials and oral traditions from Canterbury, and secondly after his visit to the papal archives in Rome, from which he returned with the letters of Gregory I relating to the English mission contained in I. 27–32. See WH 37–8. Bede wrote a series of learned opinions on points in the *Books of Kings* for Nothhelm, who became

archbishop of Canterbury in 735, and died in 739 (Continuations, *sub anno* 735 and 739).

4 *the present Pope Gregory*: pope Gregory II (715–31), previously librarian in charge of the papal archives.

the writings of earlier writers: in his first book Bede made substantial use of the Spanish historian Orosius, *History against the Pagans* (416–18), the British monk Gildas, *On the Ruin of Britain* (c.520–40), the Gallic priest Constantius, *Life of Germanus* (c.475), and of a sixth-century account of the passion of the martyr Alban. The library at Wearmouth-Jarrow was extensive.

Daniel: in 705 Daniel became bishop of Winchester, with jurisdiction over one part of the kingdom of the West Saxons, the other being the diocese of Sherborne, first administered by Aldhelm (v. 18). He also had jurisdiction over the Isle of Wight (IV. 16). Daniel corresponded with Boniface, the distinguished West Saxon missionary to the Continental Saxons, though Bede does not mention him: perhaps an indication of his limited significance in the 720s.

Lastingham: the foundation of this monastery near Whitby by Cedd, on land given by Ethelwald king of the Deirans, is described in III. 23.

Cedd and Chad: of four English brothers from the kingdom of the Northumbrians, all of whom were priests, Cedd and Chad were the two who became bishops and were of great importance in the extension of Christianity in the mid-seventh century. Cedd preached to the Middle Angles after the conversion of Peada (III. 21) and to the East Saxons, of whom he became bishop, after the conversion of Sigeberht (III. 22). After founding the monastery of Lastingham (III. 23) he died in the plague of 664. His brother Chad, who succeeded him as abbot of Lastingham, had studied in Ireland and was a pupil of the Irish missionary to the Northumbrians, Aidan, whose lifestyle and missionary methods he followed closely (III. 28). He became bishop of York in controversial circumstances (III. 28) and later bishop of the Mercians and the people of Lindsey, with his see at Lichfield (IV. 3).

Esi: presumably an abbot of a monastery in the territory of the East Angles: nothing more is known of him. He may have drawn Bede's attention to the *Life of St Fursa*, which he used extensively (III. 19).

Cyneberht: the fourth bishop of the people of Lindsey, and alive when Bede completed his work in 731 (IV. 12). Bede refers to Lindsey as a province, dominated repeatedly during much of the seventh century by the Northumbrians and the Mercians, though it had an ancient royal dynasty of its own.

5 *Cuthbert*: Bede wrote two *Lives of Cuthbert*, one in verse, and the other in prose (*c.*721), based on an earlier anonymous life by a Lindisfarne monk which had not satisfied the community at Lindisfarne. Cuthbert had become a monk at the monastery of Melrose, where he was trained by the prior Boisil, and later became prior himself at Melrose and then at Lindisfarne (IV. 27). After some time as a hermit on Farne Island, he was consecrated bishop of the church of Lindisfarne in 685 (IV. 28), dying two years later (IV. 29). Bede presents Cuthbert as an ideal monk, bishop, and missionary of the kind he recommended for the Church of his own day in his *Letter to Egbert*; he described his growing cult in IV. 30–2.

principles of true history: properly a true law of history. Using a phrase from Jerome which he had already noted in his *Commentary on the Gospel of Luke*, 2, where it is said to be common knowledge that Joseph was the name of the father of the Christ, Bede here defends his inclusion of material based on generally held belief. See WH 5, 207.

9 *Britain*: this geographical introduction is composed of extracts from Pliny the Elder's *Natural History* (AD 77/9), Julius Solinus' *Collections of Memorable Things* (*c.*200), Orosius' *Seven Books of History against the Pagans* (416/18) and Gildas' *On the Ruin of Britain* (*c.*520/40).

4,875 miles: actually 3,600.

St Basil, bishop of Caesarea in Cappadocia (d. 379); the quotation is from his *Hexameron* (4. 6) on the six days of creation, known to Bede in the fifth-century Latin translation by Eustathius.

10 *five languages*: the languages of the four main ethnic groups in Britain: Old English, British (what would now be called Welsh), Irish (Old Irish, the language of Bede's *Scotti*), and Pictish (the nature of which is uncertain due to lack of evidence; it may have been pre-Indo-European). The fifth language, Latin, is included as that of the Western Church, and thus to be found in use alongside all of the other four in Bede's

day. The five languages are compared with the Pentateuch, the first five books of the Old Testament.

10 *Britons*: Bede reports their origin-story, from north-west Gaul, quite simply as a legend. In reality much of western Armorica was resettled by a migration from south-west Britain in the fifth century AD.

Armorica: Roman name for the region of north-western Gaul extending from the Seine to Cape Finisterre and from the Loire to the Channel; it later—by the time of Bede—came to be applied only to the area now known as Brittany.

Pictish race: Bede here reports a legendary origin-story of the Picts, possibly confusing Scythia with 'Scandia', a Roman geographical term for the southern part of the Scandinavian peninsula.

reaching Ireland: Bede gives another legend, concerning the Picts' arrival in Ireland and their settlement in northern Britain, including a rationale for the origin of what he thought was a Pictish practice in his own day, that of female succession to kingship in exceptional circumstances. No such Pictish ruling queens are known; so this was probably a misunderstanding of Pictish matrilineal succession.

11 *Dalreudini*: Bede here describes the origins of the Irish settlement in Argyll and the Western Isles, and the foundation there in the later fifth century of the kingdom of the Dalriada or Dál Riata. The name comes from that of a people living in the north-east of Antrim, who may have been forced into expanding across the sea into Argyll by the growing power in the north of Ireland of the Uí Néill.

Ireland: this description of Ireland evokes that of the land promised to Moses: WH 9.

12 *Now Britain*: almost all of this chapter is taken from Orosius, 6. 7, and 9–10, other than the claim that the very stakes the British set in the Thames were still visible. This information (probably mistaken) must have come from one of Bede's Kentish informants.

year of Rome 693: Bede took the dating of Julius Caesar's first expedition from Orosius; actually it was 699. He then calculated the date from the Incarnation (actually 55 BC); in so doing he was possibly the first person in Britain to follow the example of Dionysius Exiguus in his sixth-century Easter tables in a historical work.

362

13 *year of Rome*: calculated from the traditional date of the foundation of the city, 753 BC. Hereafter Bede uses only 'Year of Our Lord' (i.e. AD) dates.

after: is wrong: Bede and Orosius mean that Claudius (AD 41–54) was the fourth emperor of Rome (i.e. including Augustus).

fourth year: this date Bede took from Eutropius (7. 13—on this author, see note to p. 364), and then calculated an AD date for it; the rest of the narrative of Claudius' campaign comes from Orosius, 7. 6.

14 *Vespasian*: emperor (AD 69–79); for his campaign undertaken in the reign of Nero (54–68) Bede uses Eutropius (7. 19), though he adds the details about the size of the Isle of Wight. The brief reference at the end of the chapter to the revolt of Boudicca, who is not named, comes from Orosius, 7. 14. Cf. the Chronicle, p. 310 above.

Marcus: Marcus Aelius Aurelius Verus (emperor 161–80) and Lucius Aurelius Verus (161–9) were the adopted sons of Antoninus Pius (138–61). The erroneous names used by Bede come from Orosius (7. 15).

Lucius: Bede took this legend from the *Liber Pontificalis*, a collection of short papal biographies initiated in the late fourth century and compiled in the sixth. It appears in the account of pope Eleutherius (*c*.174–89).

Severus: Septimius Severus (193–211); Bede's Incarnation dating is four years out. His account of Severus derives directly from Orosius (7. 17), apart from the discussion of the difference between a wall and a rampart, which derives from the fifth-century military treatise of Vegetius. See W. Goffart, *The Narrators of Barbarian History* (Princeton, NJ, 1988), 301.

15 *In the year*: apart from the Incarnation date and the final sentence, this whole chapter is excerpted from Orosius (7. 25). However, only material relating to Britain is selected. Emperors referred to are Diocletian (285–305), Maximian (286–305, 306–8), Carausius (287–93), and Allectus (293–6).

16 *Fortunatus*: Venantius Fortunatus, an Italian priest and bishop of Poitiers (late 590s); the quotation is of line 155 of his *Carmina*, bk. VIII, no. iii (*MGH AA* iv. 185). Bede changes the word-order. The title he uses is found in only one family of manuscripts.

16 *Alban*: Bede's account comes from a version of the *Passion of St Alban*, first found independently in a manuscript of the tenth century. The earliest known version of the *Passion*, dating to c.500–50, places the martyrdom in the reign of Septimius Severus, and Gildas provides no chronology; but Bede believed, probably rightly, that it should be dated to the time of Diocletian's Persecution (303–5). He was also the first to locate the site of the martyrdom at Verulamium (St Albans). See D. Rollason, *Saints and Relics in Anglo-Saxon England* (Oxford, 1989), pt. II, pp. 23–129.

19 *Aaron and Julius*: Bede took the reference from Gildas, 10. 2 and 11. 2; nothing more is known of them.

When the storm: the first paragraph derives primarily from Gildas, 12. 3, and the second from Orosius, 7. 25.

20 *Arian madness*: theology named after the priest Arius (d. 336), which denied the equality and co-eternity of the three persons of the Trinity. It was very influential in the mid-fourth century, and a letter written on lead and found in Bath in 1880 seems to prove the existence of Arians in Britain at this time. See A. C. Thomas, *Christianity in Roman Britain to AD 500* (London, 1981), 126–7.

Constantius: (I), Caesar—or junior emperor—293–305, then Augustus—senior emperor—305–6; he ruled Britain, Gaul, and Spain.

Constantine: (I), Augustus 306–37, the first Christian emperor, and founder of Constantinople.

Eutropius: Consul in AD 387, he was a pagan and author of a very short history of Rome from the foundation of the city to the year AD 364, called the *Breviarium*.

Council of Nicaea: the first, held in 325; the final theological condemnation of Arianism was not achieved until the Council of Constantinople of 381.

377: Bede is one year out. Gratian ruled from 367 to 383; Valens (364–78) was killed by the Goths in 378, and Theodosius I (379–95) made emperor in January 379. Maximus (383–8) killed Gratian in 383 and took Italy in 387. The text of the chapter, other than the incarnational date, is taken directly from Orosius, 7. 34–5.

21 *Pelagius*: a priest of British origin who became a fashionable spiritual director in Rome before 410. His belief that divine

grace was not a precondition for salvation led to a conflict with the African Church, led by St Augustine of Hippo (d. 430), who was able to secure the condemnation of Pelagius' teaching by both the Roman state and the papacy in 418. He and his followers retained influential backers, and Pelagianism continued to be a contentious theological issue in the West for the rest of the century.

Julianus: bishop of Aeclanum, an Italian who accepted Pelagius' ideas on grace and free will, and who wrote several controversial treatises in support of them. He proved to be Augustine's most formidable intellectual adversary.

Prosper: a minor Gallic aristocrat and author of a chronicle, he championed Augustine's extreme views on the necessity for grace against those in Gaul who would modify them. Under pope Leo I (440–61) he lived in Rome, and may have served in the papal administration.

couplets: epigrams of Prosper: *PL* 51, cols. 149–51.

407: the Alans and others crossed the Rhine on 31 December 406. Constantine III (407–11) ruled over Britain and much of Gaul and Spain. Bede used Orosius, 7. 36 for these events, but the second paragraph is largely his own. The 'from the foundation of the city' dating comes from Orosius (7. 40).

22 *From that time*: Chapters 12–16 derive principally from Bede's reading of the *On the Ruin of Britain* of the British monk Gildas (*fl.* 520–40). Unlike his use of Orosius, from whom he copied almost verbatim the parts that interested him, with Gildas Bede was more selective, intruding phrases, sentences, and whole sections of his own. In general see M. Miller, 'Bede's Use of Gildas', *EHR* 90 (1975), 241–61.

We call: Bede wrongly corrects Gildas here. By his day the 'Irish' (*Scotti*) were long established in western Scotland, in their kingdom of Dalriada. The late fourth- and fifth-century raids to which Gildas was referring did actually come from Ireland.

Giudi: both Stirling and the Roman fort at Cramond have been suggested for this unknown location; WH 210.

23 *the wall*: this erroneous interpretation of the origin of the turf wall, actually built *c.* AD 143 by the Roman governor Quintus Lollius Urbicus, comes from Gildas, 15. 3. Bede would have had no evidence or cause to contradict this. He had, however,

either seen the wall itself or had reports of it, and so added, enthusiastically, the toponymical details concerning its starting and ending points.

24 *rampart*: Bede, following Gildas, 18. 2, is mistakenly implying a fifth-century rebuilding of Hadrian's Wall, which he had already (1. 5) been misled by Orosius into attributing to Septimius Severus. He adds, from first- or second-hand observation, the details concerning the dimensions. These are true for the easternmost sections of Hadrian's Wall as far as the River Irthing.

hooked weapons: 'barbed spears' might be preferred; Gildas, 19. 2. The image of the Picts plucking the Britons off the Wall with hooks, given by the translation here, is picturesque, but not necessarily implied by the Latin.

25 *Theodosius*: Theodosius II (402–50) actually became sole emperor of the Eastern Roman empire in 408, but became the senior ruler of both sections of the empire on the death of his uncle Honorius (393–423).

Palladius: this comes from the entry relating to AD 431 in the mid-fifth century *Chronicle of Prosper*, ed. Mommsen, *MGH AA* ix. 473. Little more is known of Palladius, but his despatch as bishop shows that a Christian community already existed amongst the Irish; one that also predates the missionary labours of St Patrick (late fifth century).

Aetius: Bede makes the correct identification of the 'Agitius' he would have found in the text of Gildas (20. 1) with the Master of the Soldiers Flavius Aetius (d. 454), the military mainstay of the government of the Western emperor Valentinian III (425–55).

third consulship: Aetius held the consulship for the third time in 446.

deadly struggle: Bede supplements Gildas (20. 2) by this brief account of Aetius' other commitments, which derives from the Latin version of the sixth-century *Chronicle of Count Marcellinus*, ed. Mommsen, *MGH AA* xi. 81–2. Bleda was murdered in 445, the famine affected Constantinople in 446, and the collapse of the walls occurred in 447.

Meanwhile: in outline this chapter is drawn mostly from Gildas, 20–3, but Bede omits the abusive epithets his source directs at the Saxons. He is happy to agree with Gildas that the consequences of the arrival of the Saxons represent divine chastisement of the Britons for their vices.

26 *Vortigern*: Vurtigernus; Bede provides a name for the 'proud tyrant' he found in the text of Gildas (23. 1). The source and value of this information remain debatable. He had already used it in the compiling of his Chronicle: see p. 326 above.

Marcian: emperor (450–57) in the East; his Western colleague was Valentinian III (425–55).

27 *At that time*: Bede places the arrival of the first Anglo-Saxons in Britain firmly in the joint reign of Marcian and Valentinian III, i.e. 450–5. Why he does so is not clear, as Gildas provides no chronological guidance here at all.

the enemy: the Picts and Scots; cf. Gildas, 23–5, but apart from a few phrases, Bede uses his own words for most of this chapter.

Saxons, Angles, and Jutes: Bede is the unique source for this threefold division of the Germanic settlers. Their subdivisions that he then lists are those of his own day, and do not represent fifth-century realities. Evidence, both from elsewhere in the *EH* and other texts, such as the eighth-century Mercian *Tribal Hideage* (see D. Hill, *An Atlas of Anglo-Saxon England* (Oxford, 1981), 76–7), proves the existence of numerous small political and ethnic groups, who gradually coalesce into the units known to Bede in the course of the seventh century: see the various contributions to S. Bassett, *The Origins of Anglo-Saxon Kingdoms* (Leicester 1989). Frisians and Franks may also have been involved in the early period of settlement, especially in the south-east, but the once fashionable view that there was also significant Swedish participation is now treated with some scepticism: see the general discussions and the analyses of individual items in R. Farrell and C. Neuman de Vegvar (eds.), *Sutton Hoo: Fifty Years After* (Oxford, Oh., 1992).

people of Kent: called by Bede the Cantuarii, and 'the inhabitants of the Isle of Wight' are the Victuarii; in other words both have Latin names, testifying to greater continuity between late Roman and early Anglo-Saxon society in the south-east than is always allowed for.

Old Saxony: actually Bede calls it 'the region of the Old Saxons'. As with the kingdoms that developed in Britain, he always referred to such political entities by the name of their inhabitants rather than by creating an abstract geographical name: thus he always used 'kingdom of the West Saxons' and not 'Wessex', 'kingdom of the East Angles' and not 'East Anglia', etc. This procedure has been reversed in virtually all modern translations and historical discussions, but this can give a false impression of fixed territorial boundaries and of patriotism tied more to land than to ethnic identity.

27 *Hengist and Horsa*: Bede is the first to mention these, but his information on them is vague. Are they the leaders of all of the peoples he has just mentioned, or only those establishing themselves in Kent? They both appear in *ASC* in the years 449–88, with Horsa being killed in 455. Hengist also features in the Kentish royal genealogy. However, the reality of their existence, and certainly the details of the *ASC* account, should not be relied upon.

Wihtgisl: some of the manuscripts, preferred by P, give 'Wihtgils'. The genealogy needs to be treated with caution. See D. Dumville, 'Kingship, Genealogies, and Regnal Lists', in P. H. Sawyer and I. N. Wood (eds.), *Early Medieval Kingship* (Leeds, 1977), 72–104, on the difficulties of interpreting such texts.

Woden: to be identified with the Norse divinity, Oðin, and found in all of the known Anglo-Saxon royal genealogies other than that of the East Saxons, though not always as the founding figure. For his role in these lists, see E. John, 'The Point of Woden', *ASSAH* 5 (1992), 127–34.

'It was not long': the content of this paragraph, with its apocalyptic language and chronological imprecision, derives from Gildas, 23. 5–25. 1.

28 *When the army*: the content and much of the language of this chapter derives from Gildas, 25–26. 1.

Ambrosius Aurelianus: all that is known of this man, his status, and the siege of 'Mount Badon' (Bath?) comes from the elusive words of Gildas, here quoted almost verbatim by Bede.

29 *fourty-four years*: the same figure is given by Gildas, 26. 1 for the years that have passed since the battle. As Bede lacked any independent chronological indicators by which to date the battle, and the same number is used by him and by Gildas, though for different purposes, it is possible that he misunderstood his source. As he placed the coming of the Saxons in the period 450–5, he would therefore have thought the battle took place *c.*494–9.

A few years: much of this chapter and virtually all of Chapters 18–21 are taken by Bede directly from *The Life of St Germanus, Bishop of Auxerre*. Germanus himself died in either 437 or 442, and this *Life* was written by Constantius of Lyons around the year 475. Despite the relative closeness in date, the reliability of the work as a source of 'hard facts' about the career of Germanus, beyond its basic outlines, has rightly been questioned: see I. Wood, 'The End of Roman Britain: Continental Evidence and Parallels', in M. Lapidge and D. Dumville (eds.), *Gildas: New Approaches* (Woodbridge, 1984), 1–25, esp. 9–17.

Pelagian heresy: see pp. 364–5 above.

Agricola: Bede found this specific context for the story that follows, which comes from the *Life of Germanus*, in the *Chronicle of Prosper* (*MGH AA* ix. 472). However, he ignores Prosper's statement that Germanus was ordered to go to Britain by pope Celestine (422–32). This first visit by Germanus is dated via Prosper's account to 429.

31   *rank of tribune*: is wrong; more accurate is 'holding tribunician power', which was one of the titles of the emperor in the early Roman empire. Constantius, quoted by Bede, is thus classicizing, but thereby implies that the man was a local ruler.

32   *St Alban*: Constantius' narrative precedes all versions of the *Passion of St Alban*, and is the first evidence for the cult. Wood ('The End of Roman Britain'; see note to p. 29 above), 12–14, suggests that Germanus may have indeed developed the veneration of Alban.

33   *Saxons and Picts*: it is hard to see how Bede could have reconciled this story of a Saxon–Pictish alliance with the narrative of the coming of the Saxons that he gives in Chapter 15, and which he obtained from Gildas.

35   *He hastened*: the existence of a second visit has been denied by E. A. Thompson, 'Gildas and the History of Britain', *Britannia*, 10 (1979), 203–26, but if it did occur it would have to be dated *c*.435.

36   *western empire fell*: Bede took these events from the *Chronicle of Marcellinus* (*MGH AA* xi. 86), but diverges from his source by making the death of Valentinian rather than that of Aetius mark the end of the empire. Peculiarly, in the Chronicle (p. 327 above) he follows Marcellinus exactly.

36 *Meanwhile*: this very short chapter is the only link Bede can provide between the events he has just described, dating from the mid-fifth century, and the inception of the papal mission to the kingdom of Kent in 596. It is unlikely that he would have made such a chronological leap if he had any other substantial materials relating to Britain in this period available to him.

unspeakable crimes: Bede here adds a personal note of complaint against the Romano-British; one which also helps explain why he had embraced Gildas' very critical view of their society with such relish, and why his subsequent references to the British Church are so negative.

37 *Maurice*: Tiberius Maurice (582–602); for the history of the empire in this period, see M. Whitby, *The Emperor Maurice and his Historian* (Oxford, 1988).

Gregory: the Great, pope (3 September 590–12 March 604); Maurice's tenth year fell between August 591 and August 592; so Bede's calculations are a full year out, but his statement of the length of Gregory's pontificate is correct.

fourteenth year: August 595 to August 596.

Augustine: prior of the monastery that Gregory founded on his own family property on the Caelian Hill in Rome.

The letter: this and other papal letters quoted by Bede in Chapters 23–32 were brought to him from Rome by the priest Nothhelm, as described in the preface to *EH*. They caused him to modify and expand his previous understanding of the events of the conversion of Kent, as can be seen by contrasting the *EH* version with the way he wrote about it in his Chronicle of 725. His previous knowledge of Gregory and of the mission may have derived primarily from the *Life of Gregory* written *c*.680–704 at Whitby (possibly by a nun); see B. Colgrave, *The Earliest Life of Gregory the Great* (Kansas City, Kan., 1968), for edition and translation.

38 *indiction*: this was a regular cycle of fifteen years, used initially for tax-assessment purposes, but which remained a conventional way of dating documents in the late Roman empire. From its use the years within each indictional cycle can be distinguished, but some additional chronological information is needed to indicate the particular cycle.

Etherius: actually bishop of Lyons (586–602) not of Arles. Bede adopts the term archbishop used in the Anglo-Saxon Church, but the Frankish equivalents were called metropolitan bishops. Similar letters were sent to bishops of Marseilles, Arles, and Tours to secure assistance and safe passage for the mission.

Candidus: was being sent as Rector of the Patrimony, to take charge of the running of the estates owned by the Roman Church in southern France.

39 *Æthelberht*: king in Kent (Cantia) 560–616 (see II. 5). The accuracy of Bede's information on his length of reign should not be assumed, any more than the certainty of the extent of his power. These were the Kentish traditions of the early eighth century and not necessarily the realities of the late sixth.

English: actually 'Anglian'; it is unwise to presume that Bede had a 'national' sense of the various ethnic groups that made up the different kingdoms, transcending their division into Angles, Saxons, Jutes (and others).

hides: see notes to II. 9, p. 379 below.

interpreters: Gregory's instructions about obtaining interpreters are found in book VI of his letters, nos. 49 and 57; Bede does not quote from either of these.

Bertha: daughter of the Merovingian king Charibert I (561–7), whose short-lived realm had been centred on Paris. It has been suggested that such links led the Franks to think of themselves as exercising a political hegemony over at least south-east England in the late sixth and early seventh centuries (see I. Wood, *The Merovingian North Sea* (Alingsås, 1983), and I. Wood, 'The Franks and Sutton Hoo' in id. (ed.), *People and Places in Northern Europe 500–1600* (Woodbridge, 1991), 1–14); but there is no evidence this was ever recognized or was even known in Britain.

Liudhard: also known from a small gold medallion bearing his name, part of the St Martin's treasure, preserved in Liverpool City Museum. That he was a bishop must indicate the previous existence of a Christian community to whom he would minister. The implication of Bede's account is that he was dead by 597.

40 *gesiths*: Bede uses the word *comites*, which could have a technical meaning, 'counts'—in this context royal officials—but could also mean simply 'companions'.

English race: more accurately 'people of the Angles'; it is unlikely that Æthelberht would have used such a term or that anyone, other perhaps than in Rome, thought there was a single dominant ethnic group to be found in lowland Britain at this time.

40 *chief city*: it is significant that Æthelberht's kingdom was centred on a Roman town, as little is now known of early Anglo-Saxon Canterbury. York was probably formally the main royal centre of the Northumbrian kingdom of Deira, at least in the time of Edwin (see II. 14), and London possibly that of the kingdom of the East Saxons. In general, though, all Anglo-Saxon kings will have been peripatetic, except during the winter, and primarily to be found in rural residences.

41 *St Martin*: the western section of the chancel of the extant church of St Martin in Canterbury is thought to have formed part of the church of queen Bertha: see H. M. and J. Taylor, *Anglo-Saxon Architecture* (Cambridge, 1965), i. 143–5. This reference, like that to Liudhard, hints at the survival of Christian worship in post-Roman lowland Britain prior to the arrival of Augustine.

at last: in contrast to the account of the baptism of the Northumbrian king Edwin (II. 14), Bede lacked clear chronological information on the dating of that of Æthelberht, but his words do not necessarily suggest it was long delayed, as this translation implies.

Arles: in fact Augustine was consecrated at Gregory's request by Gallic bishops, possibly including Etherius of Lyons (*not* Arles) on the way to Britain in 596/7. This story of a return to Francia by Augustine after the baptism of Æthelberht appears to be a rationalization by Bede from conflicting data, and has no basis in reality. For him to have gone from Kent to Arles to be consecrated, and then back to Canterbury to send messengers to Rome to announce it, would have been strangely laborious.

Laurence and the monk Peter: both came from Gregory's monastery of St Andrew in Rome. Laurence succeeded Augustine as archbishop in 604, and Peter became first abbot of the monastery of SS Peter and Paul in Canterbury; see II. 4 and I. 33.

42 *answers*: what follows is a short treatise, derived from an exchange of letters between Augustine and Gregory, correlating the questions asked and the replies given. Earlier arguments impugning the authenticity of this text have long been disposed

of; see P. Meyvaert, *Benedict, Gregory, Bede and Others* (London, 1977), item x. This text was known to Bede by 721, when he made use of it in his *PLC*.

43 *grow accustomed*: 'entrust them to the minds of the English as their particular customs' would be better for this phrase.

46 *bishop of Arles*: this is a more peculiar question than usually realized, in that there were several other metropolitan bishops in Francia. However, the bishops of Arles had enjoyed close relations with the papacy for much of the sixth century, and were often treated as Rome's particular link to the Gallic Church (rather in the way that the system of papal legates to individual kingdoms would later develop). It is possible that Gregory envisaged the archbishops of Canterbury as having a similar role, not only in Britain but also acting as deputies to the metropolitan bishops of Arles in the pastoral oversight of the Frankish bishops, especially in the north. There is no evidence that this was ever able to be turned into practice.

54 *Vergilius*: Bede assumes that Vergilius of Arles (588–613?) was Etherius' successor, because he had mistakenly been led to believe that the latter was bishop of Arles rather than of Lyons; see notes to I. 24, p. 370 below.

55 *nineteenth year*: this year ran from August 600 to August 601.

pallium: a thin band of white wool worn by the popes in the performance of the liturgy, the use of which could be conferred on approved metropolitan bishops. Its despatch became a regular feature of archiepiscopal succession in Canterbury, and references to it can be found in *EH* I. 27 (question 7), II. 8, 17, 18, and 20 (for York).

London: Gregory, relying on the former Roman administrative structures, assumed that London (actually in the kingdom of the East Saxons) would be the seat of the new archbishopric; contemporary political realities had already led to Canterbury's taking this role instead.

59 *king of the English*: Gregory never seems to have been informed about the complexities of the ethnic divisions amongst the Anglo-Saxons, and treats them all as Angles. By Bede's account Æthelberht and his people were Jutes.

Constantine: Roman emperor (306–37), who converted to Christianity in 312. In reality the emperor's personal choice did not bring about such a rapid transformation of religious adherence, but for Gregory, as in the parallel case of the conversion of the Visigoths in Spain from Arianism to Catholicism in 587–9, royal decision was the key to conversion of the people.

60 *end of the world approaches*: this was a theme frequently found in Gregory's writings.

a church: on the site of the present cathedral, but no trace survives.

61 *a monastery*: this later became known as St Augustine's. Its church, rather than the archiepiscopal one, became the burial place for most of the seventh-century archbishops and the Kentish kings. See Taylor and Taylor, *Anglo-Saxon Architecture*, i. 134–42.

Æthelfrith: king of the Bernicians (592–616), and also of the Deirans (604–16); for these kingdoms, see notes to III. 1, p. 384 below. Bede saw him as an Anglian Saul, both because of his military successes, which were a crucial part of the establishment of the Northumbrian kingdom, and also because of his eventual replacement by Edwin (see II. 12), who would become the first of its kings to become a Christian; i.e. he took the role of David in this allegory. See J. M. Wallace-Hadrill, *Early Germanic Kingship in England and on the Continent* (Oxford, 1971), 76–8, and J. McClure, 'Bede's Old Testament Kings' in P. Wormald, D. Bullough, and R. Collins (eds.), *Ideal and Reality in Frankish and Anglo-Saxon Society* (Oxford, 1983), esp. 87.

the spoil: The quotation is from Gen. 49: 27.

Aedan: Aidán mac Gabrán, king of Dalriada (574–606: *AU*); on this kingdom and the Irish in western Scotland, see notes to I. 1, p. 362 above.

62 *Degsa*: or Degsastan; often identified with Dawston Rigg in Liddesdale.

Theobald: his role is not clear: he could as easily have been the ally of Aedán as a supporter of Æthelfrith.

Phocas: Roman emperor 602–10, who overthrew Maurice in a military insurrection.

65 *605*: Gregory died on 12 March 604; otherwise Bede is right about the length of his pontificate.

full account: Bede's information may in part derive from the anonymous *Life of Gregory*, written *c*.680–704 in Whitby, poss-

Explanatory Notes

ibly by a nun (see Colgrave, *The Earliest Life of Gregory the Great*). Otherwise, and more certainly, it derives from the *Liber Pontificalis*, a compilation of short papal biographies. See Meyvaert, *Benedict, Gregory, Bede*, item VIII, and Goffart, *The Narrators of Barbarian History*, 303–7. Bede uses this chapter not only to commemorate Gregory but also to present a model of the ideal bishop.

Felix: Felix IV, pope 526–30.

entered a monastery: Gregory turned his own family home on the Caelian Hill in Rome into the monastery of St Andrew. Monastic life there followed rules of his own devising.

67 *thirty-five books*: this work, first delivered as sermons, is known as the *Moralia* and was completed by April 591.

Tiberius Constantine: was made Caesar in 574, when Justin II (565–78) became insane, and was sole emperor from 578 to 582.

69 *Maurice*: (582–602) was overthrown in a military revolt led by Phocas (602–10).

71 *Ælle*: Although not stated by Bede, Ælle, king of the Deirans (c.568/9–c.598/9) was the father of the Northumbrian monarch Edwin (616–33) according to a genealogy preserved in the Moore MS of the *EH*; also *HB* 62 and 63.

this story: For consideration of non-legendary motives for Gregory's despatch of the mission of Augustine, see R. A. Markus, 'Gregory the Great's Europe', *TRHS* 5th series, 31 (1981), 21–36.

borders of the Hwicce: The border between the kingdom of the West Saxons and that of the Hwicce probably ran along the southern edge of the Cotswolds in the early seventh century. The precise location of 'Augustine's Oak' is unknown.

keep Easter Sunday: The British and northern Irish churches had retained older traditions of how to calculate the date of Easter, which had been abandoned by Rome in the fifth century. The effect of applying alternative forms of calculation was that in some years Easter would fall on totally different Sundays according to the system followed.

72 *Bancornaburg*: Bangor Iscoed, located twelve miles south of Chester. Little is known of this monastery, and nothing more of its abbot Dinoot. It has been suggested that this story, which is somewhat critical of Augustine, came to Bede from a British

375

source. He altered the moral of the tale in his account of the subsequent slaughter of the monks of Bangor by the pagan Northumbrian king Æthelfrith, which is used to show that Augustine's prophecy of their destruction was well founded. On the battle see R. Bromwich, *Trioedd Ynys Prydein: The Welsh Triads* (2nd edn., Cardiff, 1978), 163–5.

74 *emporium*: testimony to the commercial importance of London, at least in Bede's day, if not necessarily in Augustine's. No traces are known of Æthelberht's St Paul's. The dedication is rare outside Rome, and must derive from the missionaries' origins in that city.

75 *St Andrew*: the choice of Andrew as patron of the episcopal church of Rochester probably reflects the dedication to him of Gregory's monastery on the Caelian, where Augustine and his companions had been monks. On the remains of this church in Rochester, uncovered in 1889, see Taylor and Taylor *Anglo-Saxon Architecture*, ii. 518–19.

death: the year of Augustine's death is not specified, but falls between 604 and 610. His emphasis on the role of miracle in the validation of his work seems to be made explicit in his epitaph.

during his lifetime: Bede stresses this precedent, as it was uncanonical for a bishop to consecrate or even appoint his own successor.

76 *Bishop Dagan*: unidentified. See P. Grosjean in *Analecta Bollandiana*, 64 (1946), 232–7.

77 *Columbanus*: (d. 615), formerly a monk of Bangor in Ireland, he arrived in Francia in 591 and founded the monastery of Luxeuil in Burgundy under the patronage of king Childebert II (575–96). He was exiled from Francia in 610, and moved to the Lombard kingdom in northern Italy, where he founded the monastery of Bobbio. A monastic rule, a penitential, at least thirteen sermons, five letters, and some verses of his have survived. From this letter Laurentius would seem to have met him in Francia, possibly in 596/7.

Pope Boniface: Boniface IV (15 September 608–8 May 615), was formerly treasurer to Gregory the Great and continued many of his policies. The synod was held in 610, and is known only from Bede.

all the southern kingdoms: this chapter is famous, or notorious, for its account of the five kings who exercised 'rule over all the southern kingdoms'. This has been interpreted as referring to an institutionalized overlordship, but what else is known of the kings named here, not least from other sections of Bede's work, shows that this never existed. Some of these rulers, notably the three Northumbrian ones, did occasionally exercise a military ascendancy over several, though never all, of their neighbours. Oswy (642–70), for example, was only dominant south of the Humber in the years 655–8. Other even more powerful kings, notably Æthelbald of Mercia (716–57), are not included in Bede's list. In the late ninth century one of the authors of the *Anglo-Saxon Chronicle* (*ASC*: Parker MS only) added Egbert of Wessex to Bede's five, and coined the phrase 'Bretwalda' (probably 'Britain-ruler') to describe their status. No such title was ever used in practice. Political influence and military power remained permanently fluid in pre-tenth-century Anglo-Saxon kingdoms. Bede probably did not invent this misleading categorization, as he makes no other reference to either Ælle or Ceawlin. See P. Wormald, 'Bede, the *Bretwaldas* and the Origins of the *Gens Anglorum*', in Wormald *et al.*, *Ideal and Reality*, 99–129, and S. Keynes, 'Rædwald the Bretwalda' in C. B. Kendall and P. S. Wells, *Voyage to the Other World: The Legacy of Sutton Hoo* (Minneapolis, 1992), 103–23.

78 *Ælle*: recorded in the *ASC* as coming to Britain in 477, and taking the fortress of Pevensey (Sussex) in 491. The dates are untrustworthy and the former event, at least, legendary. See M. Welch, 'The Kingdom of the South Saxons: The Origins', in S. Bassett, *The Origins of Anglo-Saxon Kingdoms* (Leicester, 1989), 75–83.

Ceawlin: presented, probably erroneously, by the *ASC* as a king of the West Saxons. Such an ethnic group may not have formed itself in his time. His activities are recorded in entries for the years 556, 560, 568, 571, 584, 592, and 593. The *ASC*'s dates for this period are not secure. See D. Dumville, 'The West Saxon Genealogical Regnal List and the Chronology of Early Wessex', *Peritia*, 4 (1985), 21–66.

gaining the leadership: this phrase is one of the few in Bede in which his meaning is unclear. Various translations have been suggested, each altering its significance. What it seems to be saying is that Rædwald obtained independent rule over his own people, the East Angles, even during the lifetime of Æthelberht of Kent. It is notable that the author of the Anglo-Saxon translation of *EH* was equally perplexed, and omitted the entire phrase.

78 *code of laws*: probably to be identified with the extant code of laws ascribed to him in the *Textus Roffensis*, but this sole manuscript is twelfth-century, and the title there given to the work is not original. See F. L. Attenborough, *The Laws of the Earliest Kings* (Cambridge, 1922), 4–17 and N. R. Ker, *Catalogue of Manuscripts Containing Anglo-Saxon* (Oxford, 1957), no. 373.

   oiscingas: at best this genealogy represents the view of Kentish dynastic succession held in the early eighth century.

79 *three sons*: who may have been Sæward, Seaxread, and Seaxbald. See B. Yorke, *Kings and Kingdoms of Early Anglo-Saxon England* (London, 1990), 46–53.

80 *Gewisse*: an early name for the people who became the West Saxons.

   scourged him hard: for other examples of supernatural floggings see Jerome, *Epistle 22*; *Vitas Patrum Emeretensium*, III. viii. 3–4, and Adomnán's *Life of Columba*, III. v.

81 *entered the heavenly kingdom*: Laurentius probably died in January of 619.

   Pope Boniface: Boniface V (23 December 619–25 October 625).

   Deusdedit: pope (19 October 615–8 November 618); both of these popes were drawn from the ranks of the Roman clergy, and have been seen as being opposed to the monastic enthusiasm of Gregory the Great. If so, this did not affect their interest in the Anglo-Saxon mission.

82 *Four Crowned Martyrs*: this dedication parallels one in the city of Rome, on the Caelian, near Gregory's monastery.

83 *Eadbald*: in the Latin the name given is *Adulluald*, and it has therefore been proposed that two separate kings ruled Kent at this time. However, the name derives from a scribal error on the part of the papal notary who wrote the letter, which was sent prior to Boniface V's death in October 625. Through carelessness he substituted the name of the contemporary Lombard king Adaluald (616–26) for that of the Kentish monarch. The letter contradicts the account of II. 6, which attributes Eadbald's conversion to Laurentius. Letters sent by Boniface V to the Northumbrian rulers in 625 (II. 10, 11) confirm that Eadbald's conversion and baptism were achieved by Justus rather than Laurentius.

84 *Edwin*: king of both parts of Northumbria (616–33). The dating
    of the events described in this chapter is controversial. See
    S. Wood, 'Bede's Northumbrian Dates Again', *EHR* 98 (1983),
    280–96, and D. P. Kirby, *The Earliest English Kings* (London,
    1991), 37–44. If it be accepted that Bede's story of Laurentius
    converting Eadbald is mistaken, then there is no need to place
    that event earlier than 624/5 or to try to modify the chronology
    and narrative of this chapter. The consecration of Paulinus in
    July 625 is associated with the marriage, itself apparently de-
    pendent on Edwin's willingness to convert. In practice, how-
    ever, he failed to do so for several years.

    hides: Bede's phrase is *familiarum mensura*, 'measure of fam-
    ilies'. The probability is that this is a fiscal unit rather than one
    of physical measurement, but it has not been established that
    it is identical to the 'hide', a unit that first appears in the
    eighth-century *Tribal Hideage*; on which see Hill, *An Atlas of
    Anglo-Saxon England*, 76–7.

    became related: N. J. Higham, *The Kingdom of Northumbria
    350–1100* (Cirencester, 1993), 115, suggests the marriage was
    to symbolize an alliance between Edwin and Eadbald, aimed at
    containing the rising power of the West Saxons. This might
    explain the subsequent West Saxon attempt to murder Edwin
    (p. 85).

85 *Cwichelm*: king of the West Saxons (*c.*614–36) *ASC* also
    records Cynegils (611–42?) as king of the West Saxons at this
    time. Although it takes the story of the attempted assassination
    from Bede, no reference is made to the subsequent war. It does,
    however, refer to a conflict between the West Saxons and the
    Mercians in 628.

86 *thegn*: Bede's word is *minister*. This would seem to be a mem-
    ber of the royal household, in personal attendance on the
    monarch or other members of the ruling family.

87 *letter*: this letter and that in II. 11 must predate the death of
    Boniface V in October 625, and follow Edwin's marriage to
    Æthelburh earlier that year. Both letters retain their formal
    titles, something missing from all of the papal letters quoted in
    Book I. It has been suggested that these two reached Bede
    independently of the others, which were brought to him from
    Canterbury by Nothhelm. See Meyvaert, *Benedict, Gregory,
    Bede*, item XI.

91 *Æthelfrith*: ruled 592–616, was initially ruler of the northern Northumbrian kingdom, Bernicia, but conquered Deira from Æthelric (599–604) in 604.

93 *it is related*: another version of this story appears in the Whitby *Life of Gregory the Great*. See Colgrave, *The Earliest Life of Gregory*, ch. 16.

94 *east bank of the river Idle*: in the light of the speed and surprise achieved it is likely that Rædwald's army used the Roman roads. In which case the battle was probably fought in the vicinity of Bawtry.

95 *his council*: this story was much loved by ninteenth-century constitutional historians looking for early evidence of 'the Witan(agemót)', an institutionalized assembly or even 'Parliament' they detected in the later Anglo-Saxon period; e.g. E. A. Freeman, *The Norman Conquest* (Oxford, 1870), i. 98–115.

96 *Goodmanham*: Bede's *Godmunddingaham* has been identified as Goodmanham, near Market Weighton in the East Riding of Yorkshire; see Higham, *The Kingdom of Northumbria*, 67 and 105–9, and D. Wilson, *Anglo-Saxon Paganism* (London, 1993), 30, on the significance of the site in relation to the early history of the kingdom of the Deirans.

97 *holy baptism*: later Welsh traditions, first recorded in the early ninth century, claim that Edwin was baptized by 'Rhun son of Urien': *HB* 63.

church of stone: no traces of these churches have yet been found.

Ceorl: no other reference to him can be found earlier than the twelfth century. Henry of Huntingdon (died *c*.1155) seems to locate his reign *c*.597–607, but this should be considered with caution. See W. Davies, 'Annals and the Origin of Mercia', in A. Dornier, *Mercian Studies* (Leicester, 1977), 17–29.

chrisom: a garment worn by children for a week following their baptism.

Yeavering: for the excavations of this site see B. Hope-Taylor, *Yeavering* (London, 1977). The other palace sites have not been located precisely, but *Maelmin* may be near Millfield, two miles from Yeavering; ibid. 13. The Roman settlement of *Cambodunum* is modern Cleckheaton in the West Riding, and *Loidis* is the modern Leeds. An alternative suggestion for Bede's *Cambodunum*, deriving the name from 'Field of the

Don', is Doncaster: Higham, *The Kingdom of Northumbria*, 85–6.

98 *Elmet*: a British kingdom in southern Yorkshire, probably centred between the River Don and Wharfedale, conquered by the Deirans in the reign of Edwin; see Higham, *The Kingdom of Northumbria*, 84–7.

Eorpwald: king of the East Angles (*fl. c.*627); his conversion probably followed rapidly on from that of Edwin.

Rædwald: king of the East Angles (?–pre-627) has been said to have been buried in Mound One at Sutton Hoo, near Woodbridge, Suffolk; see R. Bruce-Mitford (ed.), *The Sutton Hoo Ship Burial* (London, 1975), i. 683–717. The evidence for such an assumption and for the related belief that the nineteen mounds represent the cemetery of the East Anglian royal dynasty is almost non-existent: see J. Campbell, 'The Impact of the Sutton Hoo Discovery on the Study of Anglo-Saxon History', in Kendall and Wells, *Voyage to the Other World*, 79–101. The recent excavations of the site (on which see M. Carver, *The Age of Sutton Hoo* (Woodbridge, 1992), 343–71) tend to confirm rather than weaken these doubts.

99 *Wuffings*: the lack of relationship between the names of the members of this dynasty is surprising. Attempts to make this family Scandinavian in origin and related to the Scandinavian Wylfingas (from the Anglo-Saxon poem *Beowulf*) are unwise; see R. T. Farrell, 'Beowulf, Swedes and Geats', *Saga Book of the Viking Society*, 18 (1970/3), 220–96; also R. Frank, '*Beowulf* and Sutton Hoo: The Odd Couple', in Kendall and Wells, *Voyage to the Other World*, 47–64, on the unhelpful impact of the Anglo-Saxon epic poem *Beowulf* on the study of Sutton Hoo.

Sigeberht: king of the East Angles (*c.*630/1–?): he has a name also used by the Frankish Merovingian dynasty, and had spent some period of exile in Francia. On problems of chronology of his and related reigns, see I. Wood, 'The Franks and Sutton Hoo', in id. (ed.) *People and Places in Northern Europe* (Woodbridge, 1991), 3–4.

Bishop Felix: was already consecrated bishop when he came to Britain, and was deployed by archbishop Honorius (*c.*627–53) to aid Sigeberht. A bishop Felix held the see of Châlons in 626/7. A political exile, perhaps following the death of Chlotar

II in 629, would explain the otherwise inexplicable phenomenon of a wandering bishop searching for employment.

99 *Dunwich*: a recent refinement to the argument over the identification of *Dommoc* is the suggestion that it was located in a Roman fort that was eroded away by the sea, probably around the middle of the ninth century, near the present site of Dunwich. See J. Haslam, '*Dommoc* and Dunwich: A Reappraisal', *ASSAH* 5 (1992), 41–6.

Lindsey: this 'kingdom' (Bede uses *provincia*) in the north of the later county of Lincoln once had its own ruling dynasty, but was conquered by the Northumbrians prior to these events. On its origins see B. Eagles, 'Lindsey' in Bassett, *The Origins of Anglo-Saxon Kingdoms*, 202–12, and A. Vince (ed.), *Pre-Viking Lindsey* (Lincoln, 1993). It became an area of dispute between the Northumbrians and the Mercians in the later seventh century.

Blæcca: he is called 'praefectus' by Bede, implying substantial regional authority, but in subordination to a monarch, in this case Edwin of Northumbria. He may have been a member of the former royal house of Lindsey; see B. Yorke, 'Lindsey: The Lost Kingdom Found?', in Vince, *Pre-Viking Lindsey*, 141–50.

stone church: on this church see Higham, *The Kingdom of Northumbria*, 121–2.

100 *Partney*: although also referred to in III. 11, Bede gives no account of the origin of this monastery. For its possible structure, see D. A. Stocker, 'The Early Church in Lincolnshire', in Vince, *Pre-Viking Lindsey*, 101–22, esp. 110–12.

man of zeal: WH 80 offers a better translation of this phrase: 'a man at once zealous and noble through Christ and in the Church'.

take no harm: one of a number of points in which Bede's imagery reflected his Old Testament models. See J. McClure, 'Bede's Old Testament Kings', in Wormald *et al.*, *Ideal and Reality*, 76–98.

tufa . . . thuf: the temptation to equate this with the metal object found in Mound One at Sutton Hoo that has tendentiously been called 'the Standard' should be resisted.

Honorius: pope Honorius I (27 October 625–12 October 638), a conscious disciple of Gregory the Great in many aspects of his pontificate.

102 *10 November*: although the exact day of Justus' death is recorded for liturgical commemoration, the year can only be said to be *c.*627.

archbishop of Canterbury or York: Honorius envisaged a structuring of the English Church in which the metropolitan sees of Canterbury and York would be equal and independent. The collapse of Paulinus' mission in 633 (see II. 20) prevented this being put into practice. Although the revived diocese was restored to its metropolitan status in 735, the archbishops of York thereafter remained under the primacy of Canterbury.

103 *Heraclius*: emperor (610–41); he overthrew Phocas in a military revolt. From the *Paschal Chronicle*, composed *c.*630, it is known that he associated his eldest son Heraclius Constantine with him as titular joint ruler on January 613. The regnal year of the latter given in this letter should be the 22nd, not the 23rd. Heraclius Constantine's half-brother Heracleonas was made Caesar in 631, and then joint emperor in 638.

John: pope John IV (24 December 640–12 October 642). This letter was sent in the interval between his election and consecration, while awaiting the imperial mandate permitting the latter. It is notable that the see of Rome was directed during this period by two vicegerents, one of whom signed the letter before the pope-elect.

Severinus: pope Severinus (28 May–2 August 640).

a letter: Bede probably deliberately abridged the central part of the letter, either because he realized that the accusations levelled against the Irish were here wrongly grounded (i.e. they were not following Jewish practices but archaic Christian ones), or because he understood that Rome itself used a different system for calculating the date of Easter (albeit with identical results) from that which he followed. On the greater diversity of such systems than is often appreciated, and the differences between Roman and Anglo-Saxon procedures, see W. Stevens, 'Sidereal Time in Anglo-Saxon England', in Kendall and Wells *Voyage to the Other World*, 125–52.

104 *teachers and abbots*: a council, attended by the bishops and abbots mentioned, was held, perhaps to consider the letter sent by pope Honorius, and its views were then sent to the short-reigned Severinus, leaving his successor to reply in this letter. The individuals named have been identified as the bishop of Armagh, the abbot-bishop of Clonard, the bishops of Nendrum,

Connor, and Bangor (?), the abbots of Moville, Tory Island, and Leighlin, the bishop of Devenish, and the abbot of Iona respectively. The final recipient, Saran (*ob*. 662: *AU*) is not known to have held any office, but is called *sapiens*/wise.

104 *Pelagian heresy*: by a twist of logic, in v.21 the Picts are warned against Irish Easter observances because they are Pelagian. See p. 282, and first note to p. 21.

105 *Cædwalla*: Cadwallon (latinized by Bede as *Caedualla*) son of Cadfan was king of Gwynedd (north-west Wales). Bede is perhaps being tendentious in speaking of this war as a rebellion. Under Edwin's predecessor Æthelfrith Northumbrian power was edging into north Wales, as evidenced by the battle at Chester. The newly emerging kingdom of the Mercians was also threatened by the expansion of Northumbrian dominion.

Penda: the beginning of Penda's rule in Mercia is placed in 626 in the *ASC*. That he was aged 50 at the time of his accession (Parker MS of *ASC*) seems improbable. 'Very strenuous' is inadequate: 'a man exceptionally gifted as a warrior' is suggested in WH 84.

head of King Edwin: the Whitby *Life of Gregory* indicates that Edwin's body was buried beside the altar dedicated to Gregory the Great in the monastery at Whitby. This Bede confirms in III. 24. A separate burial of the head at York is quite probable.

106 *King Dagobert*: Dagobert I (king of Austrasian Francia 623–38/9 and of Neustria and Burgundy 629–38/9) was also a relative, via Æthelburh's Meroyingian mother.

110 *two portions*: the boundary between the Bernicians and the Deirans is thought to be the valley of the Tees or the North York Moors. It has been argued that the concept of a distinct 'Northumbrian race' is due to Bede, but he may only be responsible for the terminology. See WH 87 and 226–8.

Very soon: in the year 634; for discussions of chronology, see M. Miller, 'The Dates of Deira', *Anglo-Saxon England*, 8 (1979), 35–61 and S. Wood, 'Bede's Northumbrian Dates Again', *EHR* 98 (1983), 280–96.

Eanfrith: he probably married a member of the Pictish royal house, and became the father of the later king Talorgen (653–7). See A. P. Smyth, *Warlords and Holy Men* (London, 1984), 61–3.

111 *Denisesburn*: for other references to this battle, see *Annales Cambriae, sub anno* 631; *HB* 64; *Life of Columba*, I. 1: A. O. and M. O. Anderson (eds.), *Adamnán's Life of Columba* (Oxford, 1991), 198–203.

great veneration: Iona tradition claimed that St Columba appeared to Oswald in a vision prior to the battle, and that the king himself revealed it to abbot Ségéne (d. 652). The traditions concerning the battle that were known to Bede probably came from the monastery of Hexham, founded by Wilfrid in the 670s.

just cause: WH 89 offers the preferable translation: 'we fight a just war for the salvation of our people', pointing out that the context is one of a 'victory won through faith' rather than an ethnic conflict. The special role of the cross may be evocative of Constantine's victory at the Milvian bridge in 312 and the vision that preceded it. Bede would have known of this through Rufinus' translation of Eusebius' *Ecclesiastical History*. See R. Cramp, *Early Northumbrian Sculpture* (Jarrow Lecture, 1965), 4–5.

Heavenfield: the Tudor antiquary Leland located the site of the battle at Hallington, eight miles north-east of Hexham. *Itinerary*, v, ed. L. Toulmin Smith (London, 1910), 61.

112 *day before*: 4 August. For the death of Oswald, see III. 9.

113 *the Irish elders*: is strangely vague. From the fact that Aidan, the bishop sent by them, came from Iona, it is possible that this was where Oswald directed his appeal.

Aidan: on his career, see H. Mayr-Harting *The Coming of Christianity to Anglo-Saxon England* (London, 1972), 94–9. He was bishop of Lindisfarne from *c*.634 to 651.

Anatolius: bishop of Laodicea (*fl. c*.280), who devised the first known nineteen-year cycle for the dating of Easter. Bede held that the Irish were mistaken in thinking they were following his system.

114 *ealdormen*: the Latin is *duces*, and may indicate members of the royal court entrusted with specific regional administrative and military functions. See J. Campbell, *Bede's 'Reges' and 'Principes'* (Jarrow Lecture, 1979) and A. Thacker, 'Some Terms for Noblemen in Anglo-Saxon England', *ASSAH* 2 (1981), 201–36.

114 *country of the Irish*: the Latin is *regio Scottorum*, 'region of the Scots', and probably indicates Dalriada rather than Ireland proper.

Justin the second: reigned 14 November 565–78, he was the nephew of Justinian I (527–65).

Columba: (521/2?–9 June 597), a member of the cenel-Conaill branch of the northern Ui Néill, he founded a number of monasteries in Ireland. These included Derry and Durrow. He went into exile in Dalriada in 563, following his judicial condemnation, for reasons that are unclear, at the Synod of Teiltiu. His first monastery in the Inner Hebrides was on the island of Hinba, and in 565 he founded, following a gift of the island from the Pictish king Bruide, the monastery of Iona. A *Life of St Columba* was written *c.*688/92 by abbot Adamnán of Iona (679–704), but it seems certain that Bede did not know it.

Picts: a preliterate society composed of Celtic and pre-Celtic elements, they were the indigenous inhabitants of most of northern and central Scotland in the Roman and post-Roman periods. Politically they were divided into at least two kingdoms, and in this period were subjected to military pressure and territorial expansion on the part of the Irish of the kingdom of Dalriada and the Northumbrians. Their principal surviving monuments are a series of carved symbol-stones, but what little is known of their history and society has to be reconstructed from the literary accounts of non-Pictish observers, such as Bede.

115 *Ninian*: more correctly Nynia; little is known of him beyond this account. His activities have been dated to the early fifth century. No other bishop of Whithorn is known between him and Pehthelm (*c.*731–5). See J. MacQueen, *St Nynia* (Edinburgh, 1991); C. Thomas, *Whithorn's Christian Beginnings* (Whithorn Lecture, 1992).

St Martin: Martin of Tours (d. 397), a Pannonian and former soldier who became a monk in Gaul. He founded the monastery of Ligugé, near Poitiers, and was made bishop of Tours in 372. He was subject of a very influential *Life* by his disciple, the Gallic aristocrat Sulpicius Severus, and his cult became widespread in western Europe, as evidenced not least by the church dedication (and presence of some relics?) at Whithorn.

Whithorn: traces of the early monastery and a Northumbrian settlement have been found close to the south-west of the ruins of the Augustinian priory; see P. Hill and D. Pollock, *The Whithorn Dig* (Whithorn, 1992).

Bridius the son of Malcolm: Bridei son of Maelchon, Pictish king (*AU sub anno* 558 and 560).

even bishops: it has often been thought that such a system applied throughout the Irish Church in this period, but recent suggestions would make of it a peculiarity of the Columban family of monasteries. See R. Sharpe, 'Some Problems Concerning the Organization of the Church in Early Medieval Ireland', *Peritia*, 3 (1984), 230–70.

116 *Egbert*: he spent the years 716 to 729 at Iona; he was a bishop. See also III. 27 and V. 9, and the Chronicle (p. 339 above).

as some believe: Bede was aware that this accusation was ill-grounded. This may have led him to suppress part of the papal letter in II. 19. See D. O'Cróinín, 'New Heresy for Old: Pelagianism in Ireland and the Papal Letter of 640', *Speculum*, 60 (1985), 505–16.

Ségéne: abbot of Iona (c.624–52).

117 *slothfulness*: (*segnitia*) was a vice that Bede thought prevalent in the Church of his own day. In this context it is clear that he meant both spiritual and intellectual indolence. See his *Letter to Egbert* (p. 344 above).

slavery: the role of slavery in early Anglo-Saxon society has been barely noticed, but references such as this and the story in IV. 22 indicate its prevalence; see J. Campbell *Essays in Anglo-Saxon History* (London and Ronceverte, W. Va., 1986), 136–8.

118 *the mother of all virtues*: Bede derives his view of 'discretion', by which is meant spiritual insight, primarily from Gregory the Great, but is the first to make it the source of other virtues. See C. Dagens, *Saint Grégoire le Grand* (Paris, 1977), 117–24.

all the peoples: the real extent of Oswald's power and its basis can not easily be gauged. Both Bede and Adamnán, who calls him 'emperor of all Britain' (*Life of Columba*, I. 1), had ideological reasons of emphasize it. A reference in the *Annals of Ulster* to the siege of Edinburgh in 637/8 has been seen as suggesting that he conquered Lothian. His reign was, however, brief and a conflict with Penda of Mercia in 642 proved fatal.

119 *Bebba*: hence *Bebbanburg*; such links of place-names and people are frequent in the earliest sections of *ASC*, but need to

be regarded with some scepticism. *HB* 63 makes Bebba to be the first wife of the Bernician king Æthelfrith (d. 616).

119 *Acha*: second (?) wife of Æthelfrith, was a daughter of king Ælle of the Deirans. Bede stresses Oswald's role in combining the two rival dynasties of the Bernicians and the Deirans in his person, but here ignores the survival after 633 of a son and of a grandson of Edwin.

Cynegisl: or Cynegils, king of the West Saxons (*c*.611–42).

Birinus: his role is mysterious. Why was a consecrated bishop sent to Britain, apparently on papal authority, quite independent of the hierarchical structure that had been created around Canterbury?

120 *It so happened*: the presence of the Christian Oswald in the West Saxon kingdom at the time that Cynegisl received baptism can hardly have been coincidental.

whose daughter: the twelfth-century *Life of St Oswald* names her as Cyneburh, but this may be only an intelligent guess.

Dorchester: in Oxfordshire, in the Thames valley. The location of the see on the very northern fringes of the West Saxon kingdom is notable. That the baptism took place in Dorchester is no more than an assumption. That both Cynegisl and Oswald are involved in making the grant to Birinus has caused some speculation—see WH 98 and 231. Was Oswald confirming Cynegisl's grant or did he own property in the kingdom, as dowry from his wife? That Oswald merely witnessed his father-in-law's deed of gift is probably the best explanation. See P. Wormald, 'Bede, the *Bretwaldas* and the *Gens Anglorum*', in Wormald *et al.*, *Ideal and Reality*, 112.

Hædde: bishop of the West Saxons (676–705). See v. 18.

Cenwealh: king of the West Saxons (642–73). That he reigned for exactly as long as his father raises some doubts as to dates in the *ASC*. The conflict with Penda is dated to 645 in *ASC*, which also has him restored to his kingdom by 648.

Agilbert: bishop of the West Saxons *c*.650–664/8; bishop of Paris *c*.664/8–*c*.680. He was buried in the crypt of the monastic church of Jouarre, where his sarcophagus is still preserved. His sister Theodechildis was the first abbess of Jouarre, which was founded by their uncle Ado, former treasurer of Dagobert I (623–38/9). Agilbert's episcopal consecration must initially have been to a Gallic see, which he left, voluntarily or otherwise, to go to Ireland. *ASC* dates his succession to Birinus in 650, and his ejection from it in 660. *EH* III. 25 makes him still bishop of the West Saxons at the time of the Synod of Whitby in 664.

121 *barbarous speech*: jolly as is the story of Agilbert's dreadful Frankish accent, it is notable that Cynegisl's plan was to increase the number of episcopal sees in the kingdom, evidence of the expansion of Christianity and of the need for better ecclesiastical organization. Other bishops, notably Wilfrid of York, proved equally irascible when faced with a division of their dioceses. H. P. R. Finberg, *The Early Charters of Wessex* (Leicester, 1964), 215, while doubting the language story, thinks the real reason was the Mercian threat to the northern frontiers of Wessex. If so, why divide the see, instead of just moving it?

Wine: (called Æscwine in *ASC*), bishop of the West Saxons (660?–3?: according to *ASC*) and bishop of London (?–676), was of Saxon origin but consecrated bishop in Francia. Once more Canterbury has no part to play. It is conceivable that the West Saxon kings were linked with a Frankish metropolitan see; if so Rouen, then under Agilbert's relative Audoenus (641–84), would be most probable.

Leuthere: bishop of the West Saxons (670–6). His selection is further proof of the orientation of the West Saxon church towards Neustria, though in this case the consecration was carried out by Theodore of Canterbury.

122 *Eorcenberht*: king of the Cantuarii (640–64), he was probably the son of Eadbald by his second marriage, according to later tradition, to a Frankish wife called Ymma. It has been suggested that she was a daughter of the Neustrian Mayor of the Palace Erchinoald (641/2–*c*.657/9); hence the use of the Eorc/ Erch first element in the king's name. See I. Wood, 'The Franks and Sutton Hoo', 7.

Brie: Faremoutiers-en-Brie, founded in 613 by Burgundofara under the inspiration of the Irish abbot Columbanus.

Chelles: this monastery became famous after its refoundation in 660 by Balthildis, widow of Clovis II (640–57), herself almost certainly of Anglo-Saxon origin. Bede's perspective may be distorted slightly, as it is unlikely that Chelles would have been attractive to a Saxon princess before that date.

122 *Æthelburh*: abbess of Faremoutiers and daughter of the East Anglian king Anna (d. 654). The links by marriage to the family of Erchinoald may help explain how these various members of the Kentish and East Anglian dynasties became abbesses of Frankish monasteries.

Seaxburh: according to a later *Life of Seaxburh* she played an important role alongside her husband in imposing Christian norms on Kentish society. She succeeded her sister Æthelthryth as abbess of Ely in 679.

124 *that year*: Bede is rather undermining the purpose of this *damnatio memoriae* by telling us this, twice indeed. See III. 1.

Maserfelth: from at least the twelfth century this has been identified with Oswestry (when the name was 'Oswald's-tree'); if this is correct, the location of the battle would suggest that it occurred in the course of Northumbrian aggression directed against the Mercians or against the Welsh princes.

126 *Osthryth*: Northumbrian wife of Æthelred of Mercia (675–704), she was murdered by her husband's people in 697 (*ASC*). Æthelred retired to become a monk and abbot of Bardney in 704. He was buried there in 716.

Bardney: for a recent interpretation of the character of this monastery and its wider importance in the kingdom of Lindsey, see D. A. Stocker, 'The Early Church in Lincolnshire' in Vince, *Pre-Viking Lindsey*, 101–22, esp. 107–10.

honoured bones: the translation of Oswald's bones to Bardney took place *c*.679. Where they had been since 642 is unknown.

127 *former hatred*: the hostility of the monks of Bardney to the memory of Oswald may derive from the possible Mercian origin of the monastery. Lindsey became part of the Mercian kingdom during the reign of Penda's son Wulfhere (658–75). This and the murder of Osthryth suggest how sensitive the Mercians remained over earlier attempts of the Northumbrians to dominate them.

Æthelwine: bishop of Lindsey 680–92.

130 *the fame*: for the spread of the cult of Oswald, see P. Clemoes, *The Cult of St Oswald on the Continent* (Jarrow Lecture, 1983).

Acca: bishop of Hexham 709–31.

Willibrord: see notes to V. 10, pp. 413–14 below.

131 *Oswiu*: or Oswy, king of Bernicia 642–70, and of Deira 655–70.

Alhfrith: king of Deira under his father from some point after 655 to some point after 664; Bede never explains how or when he attacked his father or what became of him.

Oethelwald: son of Oswald and king of Deira (651–5); see p. 395.

Ithamar: bishop of Rochester 644– post 655. See III. 20.

132 *Oswine*: although not stated explicitly here, it is clear that Northumbria split into its two component kingdoms on the death of Oswald. Oswiu obtained rule over the Bernicians, while the Deirans reverted to their indigenous dynasty in the person of Oswine (643–51). The latter was the son of Osric (633–4), cousin of Edwin (see III. 1). The *ASC* implies that Oswiu was initially accepted in Deira but lost it in 643.

Wilfare: unidentified, but its proximity to Catterick shows it was on the border between the two kingdoms. The implication would be that Oswine's army disintegrated in face of the superior Bernician forces, and he was forced to hide.

reeve: the Latin is *praefectus*, 'prefect'; although often translated as being equivalent to the later Anglo-Saxon office of reeve (essentially a local official), this was not necessarily what Bede implies. His terminology was mainly either biblical or Roman, and in the later Roman empire a prefect was the principal civil administrator immediately under the emperor; see Campbell, *Essays in Anglo-Saxon History*, 107.

Gilling: Ceolfrith, abbot of Jarrow (682–716) and of Wearmouth (688–716), was a novice at this monastery, and it has been suggested that Bede's information concerning Oswine came through him: WH 107. This personal link would also explain the prominence here given to Oswine, an otherwise minor figure in Northumbrian history. The monastery was built by Oswiu at the request of his wife Eanfled, a relative of Oswine through her father Edwin.

134 *Utta*: later abbot of Gateshead (III. 21).

Eanflæd: for her birth in 626 see II. 9 and V. 24. She later became abbess of Whitby (IV. 26).

135 *royal city*: 'city' (*urbs*) may seem rather grandiose for Bamburgh, but see Campbell, *Essays in Anglo-Saxon History*, 98–108, for Bede's use of this word.

136 *Finan*: bishop of Lindisfarne 651–61.

Explanatory Notes

137 *De Temporibus*: ed. C. W. Jones in *Bedae Opera de Temporibus* (Cambridge, Mass., 1943), 293–303.

138 *Sigeberht*: king of the East Angles (630/1–?). See Wood, 'The Franks and Sutton Hoo', 1–14, for problems of dating his reign.

Eorpwald: his reign has to be placed vaguely in the mid-620s. His father Rædwald was alive in 616, and his (half?) brother Sigeberht's rule has to begin *c*.630/1. The latter obtained the kingdom after a three-year reign by the pagan Ricberht (II. 15). The death of Eorpwald, whose conversion followed that of Edwin in 627, must be placed *c*.627/8.

enmity of Rædwald: why Sigeberht was in fear of Rædwald is not known. Bede indicates in II. 15 that Eorpwald was the son of Rædwald, and here that Sigeberht was brother to Eorpwald. However, he deliberately avoids stating that Sigeberht was Rædwald's son. It is probably sensible to assume that he was Rædwald's stepson; one, moreover, who may have challenged his authority.

Ecgric: Bede's limited information on East Anglia at least enables us to glimpse the existence of various subkingdoms or confederate kingdoms in the region prior to the mid-seventh century. The date of Sigeberht's abdication is incalculable. The *ASC* enters bishop Felix's preaching in East Anglia under the year 636.

139 *Anna, son of Eni*: *ASC* (Laud MS) places his death in 653, but 654 is more likely. In the Anglian genealogies Eni is a son of Tytla, and thus a brother of Rædwald. The extraordinary range of names found in this set of kings may lead to the suspicion that the genealogy is largely a *post factum* rationalization, based on the assumption that there must have been a single ruling dynasty.

Fursa: Bede's information on him seems to derive from the extant anonymous *Life of St Fursa* (*MGH SRM* iv. 423–40), which was probably written in the monastery of Péronne *c*.656.

life of a pilgrim: pilgrimage, which could take the form of perpetual self-imposed exile, was a major feature of Irish spirituality and led to the establishment of several significant monasteries in Britain and Francia by such Irish monks. As in this case, these depended on securing the patronage of local secular lords. Important as several of these foundations became, there has been a tendency to exaggerate the importance of the Irish monastic contribution at this time.

392

139   *Cnobhere*: the identification with Burgh Castle is challenged by J. Campbell, 'Bede's Words for Places', in P. H. Sawyer, (ed.), *Names, Words and Graves: Early Medieval Settlement* (Leeds, 1979), 36 n. 6.

142   *Foillán*: murdered in Francia in 655; he brought the community of *Cnobheresburg* to Francia following the death of Fursa (see below). He became abbot of Fosses *c*.651–5.

     Ultán: abbot of Fosses 655–*c*.680.

     heathen invasions: probably refers to Mercian attacks, such as those in which kings Sigeberht and Anna were killed (III. 17–18).

143   *Clovis*: Clovis II (640–57), son of Dagobert I (623–38/9), was the king of Neustrian Francia and of Burgundy.

     Lagny: Fursa's emigration to Gaul and the foundation of Lagny is probably to be dated to *c*.645, as he died there on 16 January 649 (*AU sub anno* 649; *MGH SRM* iv. 439). Foillán and the entire community of *Cnobheresburg* moved to Francia *c*.650, following Fursa's death. This marks the end of the Irish presence in East Anglia. The monks of *Cnobheresburg* were installed by the Neustrian Mayor of the Palace Erchinoald in his newly created monastery of Péronne, but were rapidly expelled by him. They were then taken under the patronage of the Austrasian Pippinid family, who established them *c*.651 in the monastery of Fosses. See A. Dierkens, 'Prolégomènes à une histoire des relations culturelles entre les îles britanniques et le continent pendant le haut moyen âge', in H. Atsma (ed.), *La Neustrie* (Sigmaringen, 1989), 371–94, esp. 385–8.

     Thomas: bishop of the East Angles 648–53.

     Gyrwe: one of the smaller ethnic groups from which the major Anglo-Saxon kingdoms developed. The North and South Gyrwe are known to have lived on the western edges of the Fens. See D. Dumville, 'Essex, Middle Anglia and the Expansion of Mercia', in Bassett, *The Origins of Anglo-Saxon Kingdoms*, 123–40, esp. 130–1.

     Berhtgisl, also named Boniface: bishop of the East Angles 653–70.

     Deusdedit: archbishop of Canterbury 655–64. He was the first Anglo-Saxon to be made archbishop. Later Canterbury tradition claimed his original name was Frithonas. (Rolls Series edn. of Thomas of Elmham, 192).

143 *Damian*: bishop of Rochester *c*.655–? (late 660s).

144 *the Middle Angles*: had once formed a separate kingdom, but in reality had recently been absorbed politically into the orbit of Mercia. Penda's appointment of his son Peada as their king was a recognition of both of these facts. See Dumville, 'Essex, Middle Anglia and the Expansion of Mercia', 123–40.

brother-in-law and friend: these relationships are not easy to assess, in that Aldfrith later proved a threat to his father Oswiu (III. 14), and Peada collaborated with the Northumbrians after their killing of his father Penda in 655. Certainly, Peada's apparent willingness to contemplate conversion would seem to be drawing him into the Northumbrian political and cultural orbit. The dating is imprecise here, but the ecclesiastical changes of III. 20 would indicate the early 650s, and III. 21 implies 653. Alhflæd later became abbess of the monastery on Coquet Island, and a significant figure in Northumbrian dynastic politics (*PLC* 24, *LW* 43 and 60).

Cyneburh: also recorded as a patron of the monastery of Peterborough in the spurious 664 charter (Laud MS of *ASC* and other copies).

Ad Murum: see notes to III. 22, p. 395 below.

Cedd: later bishop of the East Angles. See III. 22.

Diuma: bishop of the Mercians 655/6–? (pre-658).

Utta: abbot of Gateshead (see III. 15), he was possibly the informant of Bede for this episode as well as for others in which he was directly involved.

145 *Infeppingum*: unidentified region, though later tradition has Diuma buried at Charlbury in Oxfordshire.

Ceollach: bishop of the Mercians. Bede obviously had no precise chronology for the earliest Mercian bishops. In III. 25 he implies that Trumhere was bishop at the accession of king Wulfhere in 658. If so, Ceollach's episcopate was very brief, as indeed must have been that of Diuma.

Sigeberht: king of the East Saxons; his conversion may be dated to *c*.653, and seems to represent another success for the Northumbrian diplomatic offensive, which saw Peada son of Penda of Mercia converted, and also in 653 a nephew of the Northumbrian king made king of the Picts. (See note on p. 396).

145 *Sigeberht the Small*: this name, poor fellow, is all that is known of him.

146 *Ad Murum*: this makes it clear that this estate was located near Hadrian's Wall, and it has been tentatively identified with Wallbottle. It would seem probable that the baptisms of Peada and Sigeberht took place at the same time, as well as in the same place.

Cedd: bishop of the East Saxons c.653/61–4. It is notable that Oswiu was able to summon him from the kingdom of the Middle Angles.

147 *Swithhelm*: died c.664 (III. 30). Yorke, *Kings and Kingdoms*, 48 suggests that he and his brother Swithfrith, who appears to have been a co-ruler with him, may have been the murderers of Sigeberht.

Rendlesham: see J. Newman, 'The Late Roman and Anglo-Saxon Settlement Pattern in the Sandlings of Suffolk', in Carver *The Age of Sutton Hoo*, 36–8, for recent discoveries on this site. No relationship between this and the cemetery at Sutton Hoo should be presumed.

Æthelwold: king of the East Angles 655–63; see Yorke, *Kings and Kingdoms*, 63.

148 *Oethelwald*: king of Deira 651–5? A son of Oswald, he obtained control of Deira, either by appointment from or in opposition to his uncle Oswiu, after the latter's killing of Oswine in 651. He may later have had backing from Penda of Mercia, to whom he was allied prior to the battle of the Winwaed in 655 (III. 24). He is not heard of again after Penda's fall.

In the habitations . . . reeds and rushes: Isa. 35: 7.

149 *whose rules he had established*: should be translated 'having appointed priors': see WH 233–4.

live near the body of their father: such migration of a community so as to relocate itself around the burial place of the founder, as occurred in the case of Fursa and the monks of *Cnobeshere* (III. 19), is a distinctive Irish practice.

150 *the whole people*: Bede is being rhetorical here, drawing on images from the Old Testament. Half of the Northumbrians, Oethelwald's Deirans, are found firstly supporting Penda and then neutral in the conflict. For the influence of the OT on the kind of descriptions Bede thought appropriate for a military

encounter, see J. McClure, 'Bede's Old Testament Kings', in Wormald *et al.*, *Ideal and Reality*, 76–98.

150 *Alhfrith*: his involvements here and in III. 25 would make him too old to be a son of Oswiu by his marriage to Eanflæd. He is probably a full brother of the later king Aldfrith, and thus son of Oswiu by his first marriage to an Irish princess. See H. Moisl, 'The Bernician Royal Dynasty and the Irish in the Seventh Century', *Peritia*, 2 (1983) 103–26; *LW* 7 makes him a co-ruler with his father by the 660s, if not before.

Ecgfrith: later to be king of Northumbria (670–85).

Cynewise: wife of Penda; to judge by the name, of probable West Saxon origin.

Æthelhere: king of the East Angles 654–5. That he is called 'the author of the war' with no further explanation seems uncharacteristically oblique, and the suggestion of J. O. Prestwich, 'King Æthelhere and the Battle of the Winwæd', *EHR* 83 (1968), 89–95, based on a reading of the Leningrad manuscript, is appealing. This allows the controversial phrase to stand at the beginning of a new sentence, and be a reference to Penda, whose responsibility for the war has been heavily underlined earlier in the chapter.

Winwæd: unidentified, but assumed to be one of the tributaries of the Humber. The battle was fought on the southern fringes of Northumbria, hardly allowing Penda to have carried out the extensive ravaging that Bede earlier implies.

Ælflæd: daughter of Oswiu and Eanflæd, joint abbess of Whitby (680–*c*.715) with her mother.

151 *hides*: here Bede's phrase is *possessiones familiarum*, 'properties of families', similar but not identical to his use in II. 9. He uses *possessiones terrarum*, 'properties of lands' (in the diminutive form) for what are here translated as 'estates'.

152 *the Pictish race*: it has been proposed that the contemporary Pictish king Talorgen (653–7), son of Oswiu's brother Eanfrith, was imposed on them by the Northumbrian ruler. See Smyth, *Warlords and Holy Men*, 61–3.

Peada: thus murdered in 656. The reasons were unknown to Bede.

hides: here the phrase used is *terra familiarum*, 'land of families'.

Wulfhere: king of the Mercians 658–75. This successful revolt against Oswiu marked the end of any form of Northumbrian overlordship south of the Humber.

Trumhere: bishop of the Mercians *c.*658–62.

Jaruman: bishop of the Mercians 662–*c.*667.

Chad: bishop of the Mercians 670–3 (see III. 28).

Winfrith: bishop of the Mercians 673–5 (see IV. 3).

Chapter 25: all of this long chapter is missing from the Anglo-Saxon version of *HE*. For the context of the synod described in it, see Mayr-Harting, *The Coming of Christianity*, 103–13.

Theodore: archbishop of Canterbury 668–90; the act of dedication may be datable to 678. See P 188.

Eadberht: bishop of Lindisfarne 687–98.

153 *Ronan*: nothing else is known of him. The Church in the south of Ireland had by this time largely adopted Continental practices with respect to the dating of Easter. See K. Harrison, *The Framework of Anglo-Saxon History to AD 900* (Cambridge, 1976), 61–75.

Finan: bishop of Lindisfarne 651–61.

Colman: bishop of Lindisfarne 661–4.

154 *Dalfinus*: Bede drew some of his information from the *LW*, and was misled by it into confusing Dalfinus, who was the prefect of Lyons with his brother Aunemundus, the archbishop of Lyons (*c.*650–58/60). *LW* 4–6.

Ripon: see D. P. Kirby, 'Bede, Eddius Stephanus and the Life of Wilfrid', *EHR* 98 (1983), 101–14, on the different approaches to the memory of Wilfrid adopted by his monasteries of Ripon and Hexham.

interpreter: this seems to imply that some of their Irish clergy were unable to speak to the Anglo-Saxons in the vernacular. As the subsequent speech of Agilbert shows, this was not just a problem for the Irish; see also J. McClure, 'Bede's *Notes on Genesis* and the Training of the Anglo-Saxon Clergy', in K. Walsh and D. Wood (eds.), *The Bible in the Medieval World* (Oxford, 1985), 17–30, for problems of Latin/Anglo-Saxon communication.

157 *as the history of the Church informs us*: a reference to the account of the First Council of Nicaea of 325 in Rufinus' translation and continuation of Eusebius' *Ecclesiastical History*.

158 *your father Columba*: compare the arguments here put in the mouth of Wilfrid in relation to Columba with Bede's presentation of the same problem in respect of Aidan in III. 17.

160 *tonsure in the form of a crown*: on the dispute over the two shapes of tonsure (the distinctive monastic shaved head), see E. James, 'Bede and the Tonsure Question', *Peritia*, 3 (1984), 85–98.

Eata: abbot of Melrose (located at Old Melrose on the Tweed near the present town) since at least 651, also the first abbot of Ripon before it was given to Wilfrid, he became bishop of Bernicia in 678 (IV. 12). After the subdivision of the see he moved to Hexham in 685, and died in 687.

English: 'Anglian' (i.e. Northumbrian) would be better.

161 *3 May*: it actually occurred on 1 May.

Pægnalæch: unidentified.

in England: the translation is wrong; the text implies there were many English *in Ireland*. WH 237.

162 *Egbert*: on whom see also III. 4, V. 9, and V. 22.

Æthelwine: bishop of Lindsey 680–92, see III. 11.

Rathmelsigi: identified as Clonmelsh (Co. Carlow): see D. O'Cróinín 'Rath Melsigi, Willibrord and the Earliest Echternach Manuscripts', *Peritia*, 3 (1984), 17–42, esp. 23.

163 *Alhfrith sent the priest Wilfrid*: although not stated explicitly here, the intention is that the see of York be revived for Wilfrid. Neither he nor Alhfrith wished him to be consecrated by bishops who either held erroneous views on the Easter question or had themselves been consecrated by such bishops. This was not a necessary position theologically, in that the validity of the sacraments was not affected by the character of the administrator. However, it made a good if aggressive propaganda point, as well as emphasizing Roman and Frankish links.

king of Gaul: Chlotar III (657–73) of Neustria and Burgundy. *LW* 12 makes Oswiu and Alhfrith jointly responsible, and implies that his consecration took place during the holding of a council in Francia, at which fourteen bishops were present. WH 133 wisely suggests that Oswiu decided to forestall his son's unilateral decision to give the see to Wilfrid, by having his own candidate, Chad, consecrated in England (see the rest of this chapter). *LW* is thus being tendentious in emphasizing the unity of the two kings.

sent him to Agilbert: the chronology has to be somewhat elastic. Agilbert attended the Synod of Whitby as bishop of the West Saxons (III. 25) but now appears as bishop of Paris. Similarly, Cedd was present at the Synod but has by now been succeeded as abbot of Lastingham by his brother (see next note).

Chad: he succeeded Cedd as abbot of Lastingham in 664, the latter having died soon after attending the Synod of Whitby, in the plague that swept the island that year. Chad held the see of York from 664 to 669.

164 *Deusdedit had died*: on 14 July 664.

Egbert: reigned 664–73. It seems probable that the two kings consulted one another rather than that Oswiu was in a position to exercise authority in Kent. Bede originally attributed the action exclusively to Egbert (*HA* 3), but augmented his account when he came to write the *EH* because he had obtained a copy of the papal letter quoted here, which shows that Oswiu used Wigheard as a messenger to Rome.

165 *Vitalian*: pope 30 July 657–27 January 672.

true and apostolic faith: this is a reference to the decisions taken at Whitby rather than back to the original conversion.

After some remarks: archbishop Ussher of Armagh found what he thought was part of the section of the papal letter omitted by Bede; Jones, *Bedae Opera*, 104.

166 *Who was selected*: whether Bede was wrong in thinking that Wigheard had been chosen as archbishop or Vitalian misunderstood what Rome was being asked to do cannot be determined. It is not certain that the pope was just seizing an opportunity to intrude an archbishop of his own selection.

Sigehere and Sebbi: again Bede's knowledge of East Saxon chronology is vague. He implies that Sigehere and Sebbi succeeded Swithhelm after Wulfhere became king of Mercia in 658. The plague came in 664, and Jaruman was bishop of the Mercians until *c*.667.

169 *14 (16)*: Chapter 14 is omitted in the *c* class of manuscripts, which also treat the very short text of Chapter 15 as the final part of Chapter 13. See Introd., pp. xx–xxxiii above.

170 *Hiridanum*: location unknown. Some of the early MSS have *Niridanum*, the reading preferred by P.

Hadrian: his ability to read Greek is a rare skill for a western cleric by this period. Bede had a limited working knowledge of it. Little is known of the Church in North Africa in the seventh century, despite its earlier importance, and Hadrian is one of its few products who can be identified.

171   *Cilicia*: (the south-eastern corner of modern Turkey); there was a monastery of Cilician monks called *ad Aquas Salvias* on the road from Rome to Ostia, and it is suggested that this may be where Theodore was living: WH 136. This is where the relics of St Anastasius were venerated: see the Chronicle (p. 332 above), and it would thus have been Theodore who introduced his cult into Britain. Bede wrote a *Life of St Anastasius* (see note to p. 295 below).

had an adequate number of followers: this is a little weak; 'and was well supplied with his own men' gets closer to the sense. In other words he had a powerful body of servants and other dependants, to provide an armed following for the journey.

Greek customs: actually 'in the manner of the Greeks'. Bede is here referring to the danger of theological errors, in particular the Monothelete, or 'one-energy', doctrine that had been promoted by the emperors Heraclius (610–41) and Constans II (642–68). See also the Chronicle (pp. 333–5 above).

John: metropolitan bishop of Arles (by 660–pre-680).

Ebroin: Mayor of the Palace of Neustria *c*.659–73, 675–81.

Emme: or Emmo, bishop of Sens by 660–pre-680.

Faro: or Burgundofaro, bishop of Meaux by 637–?, brother of Fara the founder of Faremoutiers (see III. 7).

172   *Quæntavic*: *Quentovic*, a major Channel port in the Roman and pre-Viking periods; the site is located at the mouth of the River Canche, south of Boulogne.

mission from the emperor: Frankish fear of renewed imperial involvement in the West may have stemmed from Constans II's decision to move his capital from Constantinople to Syracuse in Sicily between 666 and 668. His successor Constantine IV (668–85) reversed this.

Theodore: he arrived in 669, having been consecrated in March 668, and died on 19 September 690.

173   *Æddi*: this is often taken to be the same as Stephanus, the author of *LW*, who is often called Eddius Stephanus in consequence. However, there are no good grounds for such an assumption.

173 *first bishop*: P 206 points out that Bede records five bishops of
English origin earlier than Wilfrid, without suggesting they
were unorthodox or supporters of Celtic traditions: Ithamar,
Thomas, Boniface, Deusdedit, and Damian.

   Putta: bishop of Rochester 669/70–676.

174 *living in retirement*: although reconsecrated by Theodore, Chad
had withdrawn to Lastingham in 669, resolving the dispute
with Wilfrid over the bishopric of the Northumbrians. He
became bishop of the Mercians in 670, and his death occurred
on 2 March 673.

   At the Grove: the standard identification of this place with
Barrow-on-Humber is now doubted; see D. A. Stocker, 'The
Early Church in Lincolnshire', in Vince, *Pre-Viking Lindsey*,
114, with further references.

175 *living stones*: a metaphor from I Pet. 2: 4.

   Æthelthryth: see IV. 19.

176 *beloved guest*: it is revealed later in the chapter that this refers to
Chad's brother Cedd (d. 664).

180 *to go to Rome*: for the growth of the practice of Anglo-Saxon
kings retiring to Rome, see C. Stancliffe, 'Kings Who Opted
Out', in Wormald *et al.*, *Ideal and Reality*, 154–76.

   Ecgfrith: king of (all?) the Northumbrians 670–85; see note to
IV. 21, p. 406 below. There is a chronological problem in that
September 673 would fall in the fourth year of the reign of
Ecgfrith. See S. Wood, 'Bede's Northumbrian Dates Again',
EHR 98 (1983), 284.

181 *Bisi*: bishop of the East Angles, had succeeded Boniface *c.*670.

   of the Kentish town: 'of the fortress (*castellum*) of the Cantuarii
(men of Kent)'.

   Chapter I: this and all the following canons are taken directly or
slightly adapted from the decisions of the great Church councils of the fourth and fifth centuries. These had originally been
written in Greek, but a translation into Latin had been made in
Rome in the early sixth century.

182 *Clofæshoh*: unidentified, but it must have been a location
relatively central for bishops coming from both Kent and
Northumbria.

183 *Hlothhere*: king of Kent 673–85; this is the Anglian form of the
Frankish name Chlotar.

183 *Æcci and Baduwine*: Æcci took over as bishop for 'the South Folk' (i.e. Suffolk), based on *Dummoc*/Dunwich (?), while Baduwine became first bishop for 'the Northern Folk' (i.e. Norfolk), with a church at North Elmham. Some remains of the latter are still visible.

deposed him: this and Theodore's treatment of Chad (IV. 1), without apparent reference to the kings, indicate a more robust attitude to the secular powers than shown by any of his predecessors. This is very much in the tradition of the Roman Church.

Erconwald: bishop of London 675–93; his name might link him with the Kentish royal house. Relics of him were preserved in St Paul's and one of his miracles was the subject of the Middle English poem *St Erkenwald* (*c*.1386).

Rule and discipline: this is misleading: Bede is stating that an ordered monastic life was followed in these monasteries, not that there was a written rule.

184 *Chertsey*: in 672–4 Frithuwold, sub-king of Surrey, granted land by charter to Eorcenwold for this monastery. See J. Blair, 'Frithuwold's kingdom and the origins of Surrey', in Bassett, *The Origins of Anglo-Saxon Kingdoms*, 97–107.

signs and miracles: this and the next three chapters derive from the otherwise lost book of miraculous events connected with the monastery of Barking (itself the subject of recent excavations).

187 *my beloved mother*: cf. the miraculous return of Cedd to summon Chad (IV. 3).

188 *Hildelith*: abbess of Barking and dedicatee of Aldhelm's prose version of his work *On Virginity*; see S. Hollis, *Anglo-Saxon Women and the Church* (Woodbridge, 1992), 109–12. She died after 717.

189 *Sebbi*: king of the East Saxons from post-658–*c*.693/5.

Waldhere: bishop of London 693–705/16.

190 *sarcophagus*: probably the reuse of a Roman one; Sebbi was buried in St Paul's in London, which still remained an East Saxon town.

Sigeheard . . . Swæfred: kings of the East Saxons; not mentioned again in *EH*.

Leuthere: bishop of the West Saxons 670–6.

190　*Cenwealh*: died in 672 (*ASC*, which adds that his wife Seaxburh then ruled for a year).

191　*Hædde*: bishop of the West Saxons 676–705.

Cædwalla: king of the West Saxons 685–8 (*ASC*). Whether he had previously been one of the sub-kings is not known, but probable. His sudden renunciation and rapid death, seven days after his baptism in Rome according to *ASC*, may argue terminal illness, but see Stancliffe, 'Kings Who Opted Out', 170–1.

Æthelred: king of the Mercians 675–704; he retired to the abbey of Bardney, of which he became the abbot (see v. 19 and 24).

Gefmund: (Gebmund): bishop of Rochester *c*.677–post 692 (v. 8).

comet: it actually appeared in 676, but 678 is right for the conflict with Wilfrid.

a dissension: *VW* 24 makes it clear that this dispute was over the plan to split Wilfrid's diocese in two, and that archbishop Theodore was involved. Indeed, he may have instigated it. It is possible that Wilfrid was intended to retain the northern half, based on Hexham where he had founded a monastery, but he refused any compromise. See M. Roper, 'Wilfred's Landholdings in Northumbria', in D. P. Kirby (ed.), *St Wilfrid at Hexham* (Newcastle-Upon-Tyne, 1974), 61–80.

192　*Lindsey*: was conquered by Ecgfrith *c*.673/5 and regained by Mercia in 679. The Northumbrian conquest led to the creation of the new diocese. After the Mercian reconquest the Northumbrian appointee Eadhæd fled and was replaced by Æthelwine (680–92).

two more: the northern section of the former Northumbrian diocese was thus further subdivided in 681. Trumwine's see, in the Pictish territories conquered by Northumbria, was centred on Abercorn on the Forth of Firth.

Æthelwealh: killed by the West Saxon Cædwalla (IV. 15). His reception as godson by Wulfhere must predate the latter's death in 675, i.e. long before Wilfrid's arrival in Sussex. This was a significant political act, involving the two participants in mutual obligations. *HW* 41 ignores this and has Wilfrid convert the king (*c*.681–5). Æthelwealh's wife Eafe was from the royal house of the Hwicce, a subkingdom of Mercia. This may confirm Bede's account. See H. Mayr-Harting, 'St Wilfrid in

Sussex', in M. J. Kitch (ed.), *Studies in Sussex Church History* (London, 1981), 1–17.

192 *Meonware*: a name preserved in that of the Meon valley in south Hampshire.

194 *male and female slaves*: these slaves are the same as the 'men' given with the estates; in other words they were tied to the lands given to Wilfrid by the king.

Chapter XIV: this chapter is missing from the *c* class of the MSS, and may be the product of a late revision of the work by Bede.

Acca: bishop of Hexham 709–31.

195 *King Oswald*: This story would indicate that the Northumbrian cult of Oswald was introduced into Sussex by Wilfrid's followers.

196 *One was tonsured*: the standard medieval images of Peter (tonsured with curly white hair) and Paul (bald with a long brown beard) became fixed iconographically by the early fifth century. The boy is thus describing them in the way his contemporaries would have expected them to have appeared.

197 *Ine*: king of the West Saxons 688–728.

wipe out all the natives: why Cædwalla intended this act of genocide is not clear. It is dated to 686 in *ASC*. *VW* 42 presents a rather different picture of Cædwalla; but the intentions of Bede and of Stephanus were not identical.

198 *Stoneham?*: Stone (Hampshire) is now preferred: WH 156–7.

Cyneberht: nothing more is known of him or of his monastery.

199 *Eutyches*: the most prominent of the early Monophysite theologians, who denied the separation of the human and divine natures in Christ. His teaching was condemned most fully at the Council of Chalcedon in 451, but continued to attract adherents. Attempts to reach a compromise over this issue, which split the Eastern Church, had included the official promotion under the emperor Heraclius (610–41) of the Monothelete doctrine, which propounded the idea of two natures but a single will or 'energy'. A renewed imperial initiative aimed at eliminating both of these doctrines was launched by Constantine IV in 678, culminating in the holding of an oecumenical council (the sixth) in Constantinople in November 680. In preparing Western views pope Agatho (678–81) secured

the holding of a number of provincial councils. Of these Theodore's synod at Hatfield was one. Bede was unaware of the wider purpose of the synod and mistaken as to its significance: there was no chance of Monophysite or Monothelete doctrines establishing themselves in Britain. He based his deductions on the synodal acta, which contained the credal statement given here. This would have been sent to Rome to confirm the orthodoxy of the Church under Theodore's direction and then form part of the papal presentation at the Council of Constantinople. The Neustrian/Burgundian synod of Marly (679/80) was probably similarly motivated.

eighth indiction: there has been argument over the date, but the general consensus, based on Theodore's probable use of an indiction starting on 1 September, would place the synod in 679.

Ealdwulf: king of the East Angles 663–713. It is notable that the Northumbrian king Ecgfrith is not named here. Did none of the bishops of his kingdom attend? An important preparatory document for the synod was certainly produced in Northumbria: see IV. 19 and notes.

Hatfield: contrary to the standard view that locates the site of the synod at Hatfield in Hertfordshire, the meeting almost certainly took place in the region of the former small kingdom of Hatfield, bordered by Deira, Elmet, Mercia, and Lindsey and centred on Hatfield Chase; see Higham, *The Kingdom of Northumbria*, 87–9. As is clear from the battle of the Idle in 616 (note to p. 94), this was a region easily accessible from East Anglia as well as from Northumbria and Mercia.

universal councils: here referring to the first five oecumenical councils, in which in theory the whole Church was represented. These were the councils of Nicaea (325), I Constantinople (381), Ephesus (431), Chalcedon (451) and II Constantinople (553). See the Chronicle (pp. 334–5 above).

200 *Pope Martin*: (5 July 649–17 June 653); he was exiled for his opposition to the Monothelete doctrine promulgated in the *Typos* of the emperor Constans II (642–68)—who, as here, was officially called Constantine. See the Chronicle (p. 334 above).

precentor: John's title was *archicantator* or arch-chanter, in charge of the singing of the liturgical offices in the papal basilica of St Peter. His monastery of St Martin's was adjacent to it.

200 *Biscop*: Benedict Biscop (628?–689), a Northumbrian noble who became a monk. He spent two years at Lérins, and was briefly abbot of St Peter and St Paul in Canterbury, before the arrival of Hadrian (670/1). He was the founder of Wearmouth (674) and Jarrow (681), and made visits to Rome in 678–80 and 685–6 to obtain books, paintings, relics, and other embellishments for them. See P. Wormald, 'Bede and Benedict Biscop' in G. Bonner (ed.), *Famulus Christi: Essays in Commemoration of the Thirteenth Centenary of the Birth of the Venerable Bede* (London, 1976), 141–69 and E. Fletcher, *Benedict Biscop* (Jarrow Lecture, 1981).

who has already been mentioned: he has not, and no satisfactory explanation exists for Bede's error here. WH 239.

Ceolfrid: (642–716); abbot of Jarrow (from 681) and of Wearmouth (from 688). He resigned in 716 and died *en route* to Rome. See the Chronicle (p. 339 above); also J. McClure, 'Bede and the Life of Ceolfrid', *Peritia*, 3 (1984), 71–84.

201 *recently*: this was the Lateran Council of October 649.

a copy: John was clearly in England as much to help in the organization of the provincial synod as to teach chant. A manuscript of the acts of the Lateran Council was written at Jarrow or Wearmouth in preparation for Hatfield, and John was expected to bring the decrees of the synod back with him to Rome.

202 *ealdorman*: *princeps*: see Campbell, *Essays in Anglo-Saxon History*, 88–9.

203 *Æbbe*: sister of Oswiu; see IV. 25.

Ely: it is thought that Bede used a lost *Life of Æthelthryth* (who can also, more conveniently, be called Audrey!) produced in her monastery of Ely. *ASC* dates her foundation of Ely to 673 and her death to 679. On Æthelthryth and the early saints of Ely, see S. J. Ridyard, *The Royal Saints of Anglo-Saxon England* (Cambridge, 1988), 176–81.

206 *Maro's*: the Roman poet Vergil (Vergilius Maro), referring here to the first line of his *Aeneid*: *Arma virumque cano*: '[Of] Arms I sing and the man'.

207 *great battle*: fought in 679, this regained Lindsey for the Mercians.

Ælfwine: *VW* (17 and 24) calls him a king; it has been suggested that he ruled Deira under his brother Ecgfrith. Note that the obligations of feud, and compensation via payment of a *wergild*, can apply as much to death in battle as to murder.

208 *Imma*: on this story, see WH, pp. xxiv–xxvi.

many masses: this link between the masses and the loosening of chains can also be found in a work with which Bede was familiar: Gregory the Great's *Dialogues*, IV. 59.

209 *Frisian in London*: this is further slight testimony to the commercial importance of London in the late seventh century. Little archaeological evidence for the city in this period has yet emerged; see A. Vince, *Saxon London* (London, 1990), 13–17.

Æthelthryth's sister: Seaxburh, daughter of Anna king of the East Angles, and wife of Earconberht of Kent (640–64); see IV. 19.

210 *Hild*: (614–80); see Hollis, *Anglo-Saxon Women*, 243–70, for Bede's treatment of her role, and possible deliberate diminution of it. Of her father Hereric no more is recorded.

Chelles: was not founded/restored by Balthildis until 660, and so this is unlikely to have been Hild's intended destination.

Hereswith: married Æthelric of East Anglia if the ninth-century genealogy of the East Anglian kings in MS BL Cotton Vespasian B 6 be believed.

received a hide: from Aidan? He is also found involved in the establishment of Heiu's monastery.

211 *Kælcacæstir (Tadcaster?)*: E. Ekwall, *Concise Dictionary of English Place Names* (Oxford, 1960), 270, prefers Kelk in the East Riding.

for some years: Bede's chronology implies that the move to Hartlepool occurred in 649. The foundation of Whitby has to be between 651 and 664.

Bosa: bishop of York 678–86, 691–706.

Ætla: bishop of Dorchester (Oxon.)—early 670s.

Oftfor: bishop of the Hwicce c.691–?.

John: of Beverley, bishop of Hexham 687–706 and of York 706–21.

Wilfrid: Wilfrid II, bishop of York 721–32.

212 *Bosel*: bishop of the Hwicce ?–c.690.

now dead: Archbishop Theodore died in 690. His successor Berhtwald was not consecrated until 1 July 692.

212 *Cerdic*: possibly the same as Ceretic king of Elmet: *HB* 63.

213 *Hackness*: Hild had developed a family of monasteries, including Hartlepool, Whitby, and Hackness (13 miles from Whitby).

215 *Now we must praise*: a nine-line Northumbrian poem that corresponds to the description here has been preserved in four MSS, and a version in the West Saxon dialect survives in thirteen others. See D. G. Scragg, 'The Nature of Old English Verse', in M. Godden and M. Lapidge (eds.), *The Cambridge Companion to Old English Literature* (Cambridge, 1991), 55–70, esp. 55–8.

219 *a whole week without food*: by Irish penitential standards a week's fast would be the expiation for a very trivial offence. For example, in the *Penitiential of Cummean* this would be the penance imposed on a layman for being drunk (for which a monk would fast forty days). See L. Bieler, *The Irish Penitentials* (Dublin, 1963).

Æbbe: sister of Oswiu. Her death and the destruction of Coldingham are placed in the mid-680s. See Hollis, *Anglo-Saxon Women*, 101–2.

221 *Ireland*: also recorded in *AU* for AD 685: 'The Saxons lay waste Mag Breg and many churches in the month of June.' Mag Breg is the plain around Tara, south of the river Boyne. Smyth, *Warlords and Holy Men*, 26, thinks British fugitives, notably from the former kingdom of Rheged, were using bases in eastern Ireland to raid Northumbria. This episode is also important evidence for seventh-century Anglo-Saxon maritime power; see J. Haywood, *Dark Age Naval Power* (London, 1991), 54–75.

Cuthbert: see *ALC* III. 6 and IV. 8 and *PLC* 24 and 27 for Cuthbert's prophesies of Ecgfrith's fate. Bede's main treatment of Cuthbert in *EH* follows in IV. 27–32.

he was killed: *AU* for AD 686 locates the battle at Dún Nechtain, thought to be Dunnichen near Forfar in Angus. H. Moisl, 'The Bernician Royal Dynasty and the Irish in the Seventh Century', *Peritia*, 2 (1983), 103–26, esp. 120–4, suggests this was an alliance involving not just the Picts and the Dalriadans, but also the Uí Néill of Ireland, and aimed at replacing Ecgfrith by his half-brother Aldfrith. The latter's mother may have come from the Uí Néill.

222 *'ebb and fall away'*: Virgil, *Aeneid* 2. 169. See notes to V. 1.

222 *Ælfflæd*: daughter of Oswiu and Eanflæd, she became joint abbess of Whitby and its dependencies after the death of Hild in 680. *PLC* 28 indicates that she also ruled over a monastery at Carlisle *c*.685. Trumwine's death occurred prior to the writing of *ALC* (699–705).

Aldfrith: king of the Northumbrians 685–705. Bede was unwilling to be positive that he was the son of Oswiu. He says the same in *PLC* 24, where he also calls him illegitimate. *VLC* makes no mention of him. It should be noted that *PLC* and *EH* were written after this branch of the dynasty had been dethroned in 716, and when the kingdom was being ruled by a rival line.

223 *foreign kings*: *ASC* records the West Saxon king Cædwalla ravaging Kent in 686 and 687; his brother Mul may have tried to make himself king there, but was burned to death in the latter year.

Wihtred: *ASC* (Laud MS) records Wihtred and 'Wæbheard' ruling in Kent in 692, and Wihtred 'succeeding' to the kingdom in 694. He died in 725. A law code was issued in his name at an ecclesiastical council held at Barham in the fifth year of his reign. 'Wæbheard' is probably a corruption of Swæfheard, son of the East Saxon king Sæbbi, who is known from S 10 and 11 to have ruled part of Kent by 690. *EH* v. 8 records him as still ruling in 692. Another king called Oswine is attested to by S 12–14 of 689–90.

Cuthbert: Chapters 27–32 form a brief 'Life of Cuthbert', of which Bede had already written two (*VLC* written by 716; *PLC* by 721). He omits the miraculous stories about Cuthbert which constitute the main part of those works.

226 *Adtuifyrdi*: this synod, held in 684, also deposed bishop Tunberht of Hexham (681–4), whom Cuthbert was initially chosen to replace. Although it is not part of Bede's purpose, this shows the much greater control that Canterbury, in the person of Archbishop Theodore, was trying to exercise over the other English dioceses.

228 *Herbert*: this story is found in *ALC* IV. 9, and *PLC* 28. The text in *EH* is almost a verbatim repetition of the latter, with some minor stylistic variations.

river Derwent: an island, still called St Herbert's, in Derwentwater in the Lake District.

228 *helpful advice*: PLC 28 states that Cuthbert was in Carlisle to ordain priests and to admit king Ecgfrith's widow into monastic life. Why this specific context is here omitted, and why, of all the stories about Cuthbert's life in *PLC*, Bede has repeated this one in *EH*, remain unclear.

229 *Bishop Wilfrid*: his year as bishop would be 687–8. *PLC* 40 hints that this was a difficult time for Lindisfarne: 'so great a blast of trial beat upon that church that many of the brethren chose to depart from the place' (tr. Colgrave, p. 287). Bede omits any suggestion of this in *EH*.

Eadberht: bishop of Lindisfarne 688–98.

body intact: it was this, taken as a clear sign of special spiritual grace, that may have led to the development of the cult of Cuthbert, and certainly to the commissioning of the first account (*ALC*) of miraculous events that could be associated with him.

230 *the coffin*: this has survived, and is still visible in Durham cathedral. For the preservation of this and other burial items associated with Cuthbert, see C. F. Battiscombe (ed.), *The Relics of St Cuthbert* (Oxford, 1956).

Chapter XXXI: these miracle stories and those in Chapter 32 are not found in *PLC* and must represent tales that Bede heard after writing that work (before 721).

232 *Dacre*: in Westmorland. The names of the abbots would suggest this was an Anglo-Saxon not a Celtic foundation.

234 *BOOK V*: the heading to the list of chapters, as found in Books I–IV inclusive, is missing, apparently in all major manuscripts. This book, which is less well structured than the previous ones, may have been awaiting a final revision at the time of Bede's death.

236 *merits*: as elsewhere, Bede deduces the quality of the spiritual life of the subject of his story from the miracles that God performs at his intercession. Why this has been chosen to begin Book V is unclear, as thematically it belongs with the final chapters of Book IV.

swelling main: (*tumida aequora*) is a borrowing from Virgil, *Aeneid* I. 142. For arguments over Bede's direct or indirect knowledge of Virgil, see WH 175 and 241.

237 *John*: John of Beverley, bishop of Hexham 687–706, and of York 706–21.

237 *oratory*: the Latin here is *clymiterium*, which is unique, and
suggests an early corruption in the text. St John's Lee (Acomb)
and Warden, both immediately north of Hexham, have been
suggested as locations for this oratory.

239 *Bosa*: died 706; despite this praise, Bede has virtually nothing
to say of him.

Wetadun: located seven miles north of Beverley in the East
Riding; nothing else is known of this monastery or its abbess.

241 *mother-in-law of St Peter*: Matt. 8: 14–15.

Addi: both he and Puch of v. 4 are seeking to have their own
churches dedicated. As in seventh-century Francia and the
Visigothic kingdom in Spain, noblemen built such churches on
their estates for the use of their family and servants. A possible
surviving English example of such a building is the church
of Escomb near Bishop Auckland, but the lack of any early
documentary record relating to this building makes its original
purpose impossible to determine.

servant: the word used, *puer* ('boy'), and the behaviour ascribed to him at the end of the chapter suggest this was not just
a servant, but a junior member of Addi's military household.

243 *breathed upon my face*: this procedure is advocated by Bede for
the exorcising evil spirits from the body in his *Commentary on
Samuel*, III. xvii. 53: ed. D. Hurst, *CCSL* CXIX. 162.

244 *Beverley*: actually *In Silva Derorum*, 'In the Wood of the
Deirans'; the name Beverley ('Beaver Stream') is first recorded
in the year 1000.

Cædwalla: Bede's view of Cædwalla is strangely positive in the
light of the brevity of his reign and the ferocity of his treatment
of neighbouring realms (IV. 15–16). This must result from the
abdication and pilgrimage described here, also singled out
in v.24. Alternatively, Goffart, *The Narrators of Barbarian History*, 319–20, suggests that Bede's praise of Cædwalla was
ironic.

Sergius: pope 15 December 687–9 September 701. Bede is
unusually well informed on these events in Rome. The highly
tendentious account of Cædwalla in *VW* 42 indicates that he
got on well with Wilfrid, and it may be that Wilfrid's companions on his visit to Rome in 703/4, such as Acca, later bishop of
Hexham, provided the route for these details to come to Bede.

245 *Ine*: king of the West Saxons 688–726.

245   *Gregory*: Gregory II, pope 19 May 715–11 February 731.

246   *bodies are buried in peace*: Eccles. 44: 14.

     Berhtwald: a gap of nearly two years intervenes. *VW* 43 claims, probably mendaciously, that Theodore had told Wilfrid that he wished him to be his successor. The delay and the subsequent Gallic consecration of Berhtwold have been seen as evidence of a dispute over the succession. See N. Brooks, *The Early History of the Church of Canterbury* (Leicester, 1984), 76–8.

     Reculver: *ASC* records the foundation of the monastery by the priest Bass under the patronage of king Egbert of Kent in the year 669. A Saxon church survived on the site until 1805. See Taylor and Taylor, *Anglo-Saxon Architecture*, ii. 503–9.

     river Yant: called the Genlade by Bede. It is the northern arm of the River Wantsum.

     Wihtred and Swæfheard: see notes to iv. 26 above, p. 409.

     Godwin: Godinus, metropolitan bishop of Lyons by 688; died after 701. Bede has anglicized the name. 'Gaulish church' is wrong, as the phrase used by Bede is a synonym for Lyons.

247   *Tobias*: bishop of Rochester after 692; died 726.

     Garmani: K. Jackson, *Language and History in Early Britain* (Edinburgh, 1953), 281, suggests this is a colloquial British Latin form for *Germani*, not otherwise preserved.

     Frisians: this list is either anachronistic or archaic. The Rugians and the Huns were last in contact with northern Europe in the fifth century. This may be taken to represent Egbert's view of the unconverted Continental neighbours of the Anglo-Saxons.

     Bructeri: were located between the Rivers Lippe and Ruhr in northern Germany. Their defeat by the Continental or 'Old' Saxons in the 690s is recorded in v. 11.

     sailing round Britain: Egbert was in *Rathmelsigi*, probably in Co. Carlow in south-east Ireland. He thus planned to sail all round the north of Britain on his way to the Continent; to visit island monasteries, such as Iona, Lindisfarne, etc.? The story of the vision of Boisil that follows indicates that Egbert was, perhaps, more concerned about these than with a missionary venture-cum-pilgrimage to Rome. It should be noted that evangelizing in this period was envisaged as a short-term activity, something that could be undertaken *en route* elsewhere. For examples, see Wilfrid in Sussex and in Frisia: *VW* 41 and 26.

247 *servant*: is misleading. Bede states that this monk was also the disciple of Boisil. The Melrose (and Lindisfarne via Eata) links of this story are notable. Some of Egbert's followers felt there was work to be done closer to home.

the *mattin hymns*: Although not envisaged in the *Rule of Benedict* or other southern monastic rules, a period of sleep after Mattins in certain periods of the summer (when Mattins was celebrated earlier in the day) can be found in the tenth-century *Regularis Concordia* and may reflect earlier rules that made allowances for northern climates.

248 *words of the prophet*: Jonah 1:12.

Wihtbert: also referred to in Alcuin's *Life of Willibrord*, ch. 4, ed. Reischmann, p. 50, and also possibly a signatory to the acts of the Irish Council of Birr of 697 ('Ichtbricht').

249 *Pippin*: Pippin II (d. 714), Mayor of the Palace of Austrasia (the eastern Frankish kingdom) and after 687 the dominant figure in Frankish politics generally.

Radbod: the king of the Frisians (d. 719). This campaign in the 690s is referred to in *The Chronicle of Fredegar*, continuations, ch. 7, ed. J. M. Wallace-Hadrill (London, 1960), 86, which records Pippin's capture of the port of Dorestad.

250 *viceroys*: Bede uses the Biblical 'satrap'. He is the only source for this view of Saxon political life, but it accords with the impression gained from the better documented period of Charlemagne's Saxon wars of the late eighth century. See in general A. Genrich, *Die Altsachsen* (Hildesheim, 1981).

reeve: translating *vilicus*. 'Village headman' may give a clearer impression.

an altar: for a contemporary example, see the one found in the tomb of Cuthbert: C. F. Battiscombe (ed.), *The Relics of St Cuthbert* (Oxford, 1956), 326–36, displayed in Durham cathedral. A chalice from such a set of vessels is preserved in Hexham abbey.

251 *church of the city of Cologne*: the fourth- to eighth-century episcopal church, traces of which have been found under the later medieval cathedral. Pippin's involvement in this may argue greater Frankish backing for the Hewalds' venture than Bede was aware of.

Willibrord: (d. 739); the *Life* written in 796 by his relative Alcuin (d. 804) provides some additional details on his early life. The son of a Northumbrian called Wilgis, who retired to live as a hermit on Spur Head, he was brought up in Wilfrid's monastery at Ripon, before going to study in Ireland in Egbert's monastery of *Rathmelsigi* (see notes to III. 27, p. 398 above). It is worth noting that Wilfrid had himself had a brief involvement with the evangelizing of the Frisians (*VW* 26) and thus Willibrord's debt to both Egbert's missionary interests and the Wilfridan tradition of Ripon may be more fully integrated than is usually believed. See R. Collins, *Early Medieval Europe* (London, 1991), 240–1.

251 *Swithberht*: the consecration must have taken place after Berhtwold's election in July 692 and before his return to England in August 693.

252 *696*: Bede was misinformed. Willibrord's own Calendar indicates that the year was 695. Also St Cecilia's day (21 November) fell on a Sunday, the normal day for consecrating bishops, in 695 and not in 696. On Willibrord and the Frisian mission, see W. Levison, *England and the Continent in the Eighth Century* (Oxford, 1946), 45–69.

Pippin gave him: his establishment of Willibrord in Utrecht should probably be dated to the winter of 703/4.

Clement: according to Alcuin, *Life of Willibrord*, 7, Pope Sergius (687–701) gave this name to Willibrord when consecrating him archbishop in 695. It was probably intended as a reference to the Clement who was one of St Paul's missionary followers (Phil. 4: 3).

253 *Cunningham*: assumed to be the district of Ayrshire of this name.

254 *in the lone night*: Virgil, *Aeneid* 6. 268.

255 *I could see*: it is notable that the 'human souls' envisaged here look like the material bodies of their possessors. Apocalyptic imagery may have been influenced by its artistic depiction, the earliest manifestations of which were to be found in fifth-century Rome.

256 *what all these things are*: the man had been shown four variants of the afterlife, but, while such visions of future reward and punishment become increasingly prevalent in medieval literature (and art) from this period onwards, there is at this stage little or no formal theological underpinning of such details as the two purgatorial states described here.

257 *Hæmgisl*: whose account of this vision was Bede's source. As Bede calls this a *relatio* rather than a *narratio*, a written account is implied.

258 *Cenred*: king of the Mercians 704–9 (See v. 19 and notes, p. 416 below). His role in this story displays aspects of Gregory the Great's ideas on *rectores*, all with responsibility for the spiritual guidance of those under their authority. Normally this would relate to a clerical or monastic context, but Gregory would have wished kings to think of themselves in the same light. In 709 Cenred abdicated to live as a monk in Rome.

260 *daggers*: the word used (*vomeres*) normally means plough-shares, and only appears as a correction added to the two earliest manuscripts (the Moore and the Leningrad MSS—see Introd. pp. xxi–xxii). The Anglo-Saxon translators certainly took the word to mean daggers or knives, but whether it was actually intrinsic to Bede's original text remains questionable. Readers of J. R. R. Tolkien's *The Lord of the Rings*, book ii, ch. 11, will recognize the theme.

Pope Gregory writes: Gregory the Great, *Dialogues*, IV. 40.

Pehthelm: (the Northumbrian form, as used by Bede, is Pecthelm): formerly a monk of Malmesbury (Wilts.) and bishop of Whithorn in Galloway by 731. He died in 735.

262 *Britons in Britain*: this could refer in particular to the kingdom of Cornwall; see v. 18.

Adamnan: abbot of Iona 679–704; born *c*.628 and related to Columba. His visit to Northumbria was to secure the release of Irish prisoners taken by Ecgfrith in 684 (*HE* IV. 26).

263 *Arculf*: his pilgrimage is recounted in greater detail in Adamnán's extant *De Locis Sanctis* ('On the Holy Places'), ed. D. Meehan, *SLH* 3 (1958). His experiences show that Jerusalem and Egypt remained open to western visitors, despite the Arab conquests of the 630s. That he should have been driven off course to the Hebrides on the way home from the Mediterranean suggests he lived in Brittany or the north-west of Francia.

thus: Bede here paraphrases rather than quotes directly from Adamnán. By his own account, at the end of v. 17, he made an abridgement of the whole work. Other than for these extracts, this has been lost.

266 *Osred*: king of the Northumbrians 705–16. In *VLC* ll. 554–5 Bede hailed him as a new Josiah (king of Judah 640–609 BC, who came to the throne aged 8; see 2 Kgs.: 22). Although not mentioned by Bede, a usurper called Eadwulf seized power for about two months between Aldfrith and Osred.

more will be said: there is a brief reference to him in v. 23, but this promises more than is fulfilled; another sign of hasty editing of Book V?

Aldhelm: born *c*.639, a former pupil of abbot Hadrian at Canterbury and from 675 abbot of Malmesbury; he was bishop of Sherborne (or 'bishop to the West of the Wood' in *ASC*) 705–8/9, and after Bede the most prolific of the early Anglo-Saxon ecclesiastical authors in both prose and verse.

Daniel: bishop of Winchester 705–44, he was one of Bede's main informants on West Saxon matters; see Preface, p. 4 above. He was also a mentor and friend of the Anglo-Saxon missionary bishop Boniface; so it often causes surprise that Bede makes no mention of the latter.

by means of this book: the *Letter to Gerontius* (or Geraint, king of Cornwall).

267 *twofold*: what is known as *opus geminatum*, the writing of parallel versions of a work in both prose and verse, as in Bede's two lives of Cuthbert.

polished style: on which see M. Winterbottom, 'Aldhelm's Prose Style and its Origins', *ASE* 6 (1977), 39–76, who shows that he owed more to his Canterbury training than to Irish learning.

Forthhere: bishop of Sherborne 708/9–37/9.

by a decree of the synod: 'by a synodal decree' is better, as it is not clear that Bede is referring here to the West Saxon synod that led Aldhelm to write his *Letter to Gerontius* (see above). The episcopates of the two bishops of Selsey mentioned here can be dated no more precisely than saying both were post-705 and pre-731.

Constantine: pope 25 March 708–9 April 715.

Ceolred: king of the Mercians 709–16, son of the former king Æthelred (675–704).

Offa: probably a sub- or co-king of the East Saxons *c*.700: see Yorke *Kings and Kingdoms*, 49–50, 53–4. That both Cenred and

Offa simultaneously gave up their kingdoms and went to Rome together may imply some political upheaval that is otherwise concealed from us.

267 *a hundredfold in this life*: cf. Mark 10: 29–30.

268 *the famous Bishop Wilfrid*: the account given here is largely a précis of *VW*, but with some omissions, e.g. Wilfrid's period in Mercia, and the failed attempt at a reconciliation with king Aldfrith and archbishop Berhtwald at the Synod of Austerfield in 703 (*VW* 46–9).

270 *Queen Baldhild*: widow of Clovis II (640–57) and regent of Neustria 657–64/5. See J. Nelson, 'Queens as Jezebels', in D. Baker (ed.), *Medieval Women* (Oxford, 1978), 31–77.

271 *Aldgisl*: king of the Frisians *c*.679; otherwise only known from *VW* 26–7.

273 *the priest Acca*: later abbot and bishop of Hexham 709–31; see v. 20. He may have died in 740 (*HR sub anno* 740, p. 32).

274 *Here lie great WILFRID'S bones*: this verse epitaph is not in *VW*, and it has been suggested that it is Bede's own composition. WH 194.

275 *he will not cease*: this was written prior to Acca's expulsion from his see in 731.

Bosa: bishop of York 678–86, 691–706, formerly a monk of Whitby. His death is never mentioned by Bede, who becomes less comprehensive in the recording of episcopal successions in Book V.

276 *Nechtan*: (or Nechton) son of Derile; king of the Picts 706–24/6, 728–9. Bede places his request to Ceolfrith with items dating from around the year 710.

this monastery: following Benedict Biscop's intention, the two foundations were regarded as a single monastery, and from the time of Ceolfrid (d. 716) were ruled by a single abbot.

To the most excellent: this letter is the longest document quoted in *HE* and seems out of proportion to the rest of Book V, but it has been suggested that Bede may himself have contributed to its composition: WH 196. The conclusion of the chapter stresses the theme of adherence to Petrine, i.e. Roman, norms. This is taken up again in v. 22.

286 *Osred*: Bede gives no explanation for his death; the early ninth-century Northumbrian poem by Æthelwulf, *De Abbatibus*, ii

417

(ed. A. Campbell (Oxford, 1967), 4–7) refers to his ill-treatment of his nobles.

286 *Cenred*: king of the Northumbrians 716–18, of a different branch of the dynasty to his immediate predecessors.

287 *Dúnchad*: abbot of Iona 707–17. If Bede is right, Egbert persuaded the monks of Iona to accept these changes almost immediately, something Adamnán had failed to do over several years.

never before been kept: 21 April would have been the latest date possible for Easter under the rules previously used in Iona for the calculation of Easter.

288 *Osric*: king of the Northumbrians 718–29; brother of king Osred.

Wihtred: see notes to IV. 26. His sons Æthelbert II and Eadbert appear to have ruled jointly from 725 until 748 or possibly *c.*762. Alric is not heard of again; see Yorke, *Kings and Kingdoms*, 30–1.

two comets: probably only one comet, approaching and then drawing away from the sun.

At this time: no Arab attacks on Gaul are recorded for 729. Bede, who was best informed about events in the Rhône valley, may be reporting the raid of 725, which penetrated as far north as Autun, or he may be thinking of the very first Arab raid, back in 721.

not long afterwards: the only events this can refer to are the defeat of the first Arab attack on Gaul at Toulouse in 721 or that of another Arab raid at the battle of Poitiers in October (?) of 732 or 733. If it were the latter, this would represent a late revision or posthumous editorial addition to the text of Book V. Bede's lack of contemporary information about Arab attacks on Gaul is also apparent in the Chronicle.

treachery: Bede, like most of his contemporaries, was ignorant of the nature of Islam, and regarded it as a heretical form of Christianity.

Ceolwulf: king of the Northumbrians 729–37, who abdicated to enter a monastery.

289 *13 January*: *c*-class manuscripts are probably correct in making this date 9 January.

Tatwine: archbishop of Canterbury 731–4; a collection of verse riddles and a grammatical treatise by him are extant: *CCSL*

418

cxxxiii. His monastery was at Breedon-on-the-Hill in Leicester-shire, where some fine if damaged eighth-century carvings are still preserved; see A. Dornier, 'The Anglo-Saxon monastery at Breedon-on-the-Hill', and R. Cramp, 'Schools of Mercian Sculpture', in Dornier, *Mercian Studies*, 155–68 and 191–233.

289 *Ingwold*: bishop of London 716–45. Bede makes no reference to his consecration, nor to that of Ealdwine of Lichfield. His interest in or information on episcopal successions is greatly diminished in Book V.

Æthelbald: king of the Mercians 716–57; the descendant of a brother of Penda, he came from a different branch of the Mercian dynasty, one that had previously produced no kings.

Wilfrid: Wilfrid II, bishop of York 721–32, died 745. He was replaced in 732 by Egbert, but the text of *HE* was not corrected here.

Æthelwold: bishop of Lindisfarne 721–40.

Acca: bishop of Hexham 709–31.

Pehthelm: bishop of Whithorn *c*.731–5.

290 *to recapitulate*: the chronology is not always the same as that found in the preceding narrative chapters, nor do the Incarnational dates given here always correspond to the normally accepted dating of some of the events listed.

291 *538, 540*: neither eclipse appears in the text of *EH*.

547. Ida: Ida does not appear elsewhere in *EH*. It has rightly been argued that Bede calculated the date from a list of Northumbrian kings and their lengths of reign. This is not a contemporary source.

292 *697, 698*: these entries are not found in the *c* MSS. Berhtred may be the same as Berht of IV. 26. Berhtfrith of 711 may be his son.

293 *I, Bede*: this brief account of his own life and writings may have been added here by Bede, following the precedent of Gregory of Tours (d. 594) who did the same in concluding his *Ten Books of Histories*.

294 *seven*: manuscripts of the *c* class have *six*, which is the correct number of books for this work: ed. D. Hurst, *CCSL* cxix B.

295 *life and passion of St Anastasius*: this work, long thought lost, has been identified; see C. Vircillo Franklin and P. Meyvaert in *Analecta Bollandiana*, 100 (1982), 373–400.

295 *book of epigrams*: some of these have been found: M. Lapidge, 'Some Remnants of Bede's Lost *Liber Epigrammatum*', *EHR* 90 (1975), 798–820.

CONTINUATIONS

296 *Egbert*: bishop of York 732–66; his see was restored to archiepiscopal dignity in 735. He was a brother of the Northumbrian king Eadberht.

Cyneberht: bishop of Lindsey ?–732.

Alwih: bishop of Lindsey 733–50.

Sigeferth: bishop of Selsey 733–post-747.

Frithuberht: bishop of Hexham 735–66.

Frithuwold: bishop of Whithorn 735–65.

Eadberht: king of the Northumbrians 737–58; a cousin of Ceolwulf.

Æthelheard: king of the West Saxons 728–41 or 726–40.

Cuthbert: archbishop of Canterbury 740–60.

Æthelwold: bishop of Lindisfarne 724–40.

Cynewulf: bishop of Lindisfarne 740–80; he suffered at the hands of king Eadberht in 750, who seized Lindisfarne and imprisoned him, for protecting Offa, son of the former king Aldfrith (d. 705).

Earnwine and Eadberht: unknown.

297 *Charles, king of the Franks*: Charles Martel, Mayor of the Palace of Austrasia (715/6–41) and *de facto* ruler of most of Francia from 721; he did not install a new Merovingian king after the death of Theuderic IV (721–37). His son Pippin III (d. 768) made himself the first king of the Carolingian dynasty in 751.

Wilfrid: the deposed bishop of York (721–732).

Herefrith: possibly the priest used by Boniface as an intermediary with the Mercian king Æthelbald, *c.*746: Boniface, *Ep.* 74, ed. Tangl, *MGH SRG.*

Cuthred: king of the West Saxons 740/1–56.

Angus: Son of Fergus, king of the Picts 727/9–61; how a West Saxon king could be plotting against a Pictish one (see under year 761) is not easy to envisage; some textual corruption might be suspected here.

Tewdwr: Teudubr son of Beli, king of Strathclyde 722–52.

Eanred: unknown.

297 *plain of Kyle*: in Ayrshire.

Boniface: the West Saxon missionary, archbishop of Mainz and founder of the monastery of Fulda. He was murdered in 754 by some pagan Frisians.

Hrethgar: Boniface's successor as bishop of Mainz (archbishop from 781) was Lul (754–86).

Pope Stephen: Stephen II (26 March 752–26 April 757).

Beornred: king of the Mercians (757); his relationship to any of his predecessors is unknown.

Cynewulf: king of the West Saxons 757–86; the continuator's error would seem to derive from the *ASC*, which includes an account of the reign and the death of Cynewulf in its annal for 757 reporting his accession. If so, this text is ninth century or later.

Offa: king of the Mercians 757–96; from another branch of the dynasty.

Æthelwold: king of the Northumbrians 759–65; known as Æthelwold Moll.

Oswine: probably a member of the former Northumbrian royal house, he was killed by Æthelwold Moll at *Edwinesclif* (*ASC*).

298 *Alhred*: king of the Northumbrians 765–74.

CUTHBERT'S LETTER

300 *Cuthwin*: possibly to be identified with an abbot of the same name recorded in the *Liber Vitae* of Durham (a list of the dead who were to be commemorated annually in the liturgy, the earliest part of which was drawn up at Lindisfarne); his monastery is not known.

Cuthbert: became a monk of Wearmouth and Jarrow in 718 and was abbot *c*.764; in his letters to bishop Lul of Mainz (754–86) he described himself as the 'disciple of Bede' and was responsible for sending manuscripts of several of the latter's works to Germany.

twenty-sixth of May: Ascension Day fell on Thursday 26 May in 735; note that from the ensuing description it is clear Bede actually died on 25 May, but as his death came in the evening this fell liturgically into the Feast of the Ascension, which begins with the Vespers of the preceding day.

'*It is a fearful thing . . . living God*': Heb. 10: 31; Vulgate.

301 *Facing that enforced journey*: in the original letter Cuthbert gave only a Latin paraphrase; the earliest manuscript to contain the

Old English text dates to the ninth century, and it is impossible to be sure that Bede himself composed this poem. Of the twenty-nine that contain it, the manuscripts of purely English provenance normally have the poem in the West Saxon dialect, whilst the original Northumbrian form is preserved in manuscripts that circulated on the Continent. These will have derived from a copy sent, perhaps by Cuthbert himself, to one or other of the Anglo-Saxon missionaries working in Germany in the mid-eighth century.

301   *O King of glory*: almost certainly one of the antiphons from the liturgy for Ascension Day, but, as no Anglo-Saxon antiphonal survives from as early a date as this, this can be no more than a reasonable assumption.

'God scourgeth . . . He receiveth': Heb. 12: 6; Vulgate.

'I have not so lived . . . is good': this is attributed to Ambrose in the *Life of Ambrose* by Paulinus, ch. 45: *PL* vol. xiv, col. 43.

gospel of St John: nothing more is known of this translation, which to judge by what is said here had only reached chapter 6 by the beginning of Bede's last day.

'But what are they . . . so many?': John 6: 9; Vulgate.

Bishop Isidore's: Isidore of Seville (d. 636), the foremost scholar of the Spanish Church in the early seventh century, many of whose works enjoyed a rapid transmission to northern Italy and Francia and thence to Ireland and to England.

On the Wonders of Nature: Cuthbert actually refers to it by its unofficial but popular title, the *Libri Rotarum* or 'Books of Wheels'; a name probably deriving from its use of illustrative diagrams in the form of sets of concentric circles. It is clear from the context that Bede disapproved of some of the content, and was preparing an abridged edition of it. See P. Meyvaert, 'Bede the Scholar' in Bonner, *Famulus Christi*, esp. 58–60; on the other hand J. Fontaine, *Isidore de Séville: Traité de la nature* (Bordeaux, 1960), 79 and n. 1, argues instead that Bede was translating excerpts into Old English.

'Learn your lesson . . . take me from you.': Job 32: 22; Vulgate.

custom of that day required: this indicates that the community were here following the Gallic practice of Rogation processions in the days preceding Ascension Day. These developed in southern Gaul in the fifth century and were not followed in

Rome. This shows something of the liturgical influence of the Frankish Church on its Anglo-Saxon neighbour.

302 *pepper*: such spices, which had to be traded via the Indian Ocean and the eastern Mediterranean, were very valuable; as was *incense*, brought from south-east Arabia. *napkins* is an unhelpful translation; these *oraria* were small cloths or veils used in the performance of the liturgy.

in this world: this sentence is a deliberate reminiscence of the sorrow of the elders of the Church of Ephesus at parting from St Paul: Acts 20: 38.

The time of my departure: cf. 2 Tim. 4: 6.

my King in all His beauty: cf. Isa. 33: 17.

It is finished: the last words of Christ: John 29: 30. Was this the sentence that Wilberht was referring to? The ensuing phrase 'you have spoken the truth' implies it was, but this would mean that Bede translated thirteen chapters of the Gospel that day. In reality Cuthbert was probably being more rhetorical than factual.

303 *fuller account*: either never written or lost.

THE GREATER CHRONICLE

307 *Olympiad*: as the Olympic Games had been held once every four years, this provided the basis for a chronological cycle; dating by Olympiad went out of use after the fifth century AD.

308 *Why our computation*: such didactic asides have led to the view that Bede wrote the *DTR*, and with it the Chronicle, primarily for the purposes of teaching in the monastery of Wearmouth-Jarrow.

309 *recorded by Luke*: Acts 11: 28.

as Luke reports: Acts 18: 2.

310 *That same John*: this story comes from Jerome's polemical treatise against Jovinian, 1. 26; and is a good example of Bede's use of non-historical texts in the compiling of the Chronicle.

312 *Lucius the king of Britain*: cf. *EH* I. 4; see notes to p. 4.

313 *a great ditch and wall*: Bede takes this from Orosius, 7. 17. 6–7; cf. *EH* I. 5; he was misled by Gildas into believing that two further walls were built by the Romans, in the fifth century.

314 *as Luke records*: Luke 24: 13–35.

315 *first of all emperors to be a Christian*: this story, which has no factual basis, came to Bede from Orosius, 7. 20. 2.

Jerome somewhere indicates: Bede was probably thinking of one of Jerome's letters; though nothing quite so specific has been found.

319 *Constantine turned*: this is Bede's own deduction from his data, and contradicts the image of Constantine and his father Constantius as non-persecutors, which early fourth-century Christian authors such as Eusebius and Lactantius wished to promote.

322 *in his sixth consulship*: it was actually his fifth and last; the year referred to is AD 380.

323 *devastated, and pillaged it*: the information for this entry comes from Gildas, 13–14, though Bede does not quote him verbatim.

324 *The Britons*: cf. *EH* I. 12; this whole entry derives from Gildas, 15–16, but is largely rewritten.

327 *The Pelagian heresy*: cf. *EH* I. 17: this is a condensation of part of Constantius' *Life of St Germanus of Auxerre*; as with the sections deriving from Gildas, it is clear that the chronology of fifth-century Britain used in *EH* had already been developed by Bede in writing his Chronicle.

with him fell the Western realm: Bede takes this view directly from his source, the Latin version of the sixth-century *Chronicle of Count Marcellinus*. He alters it in *EH*, having the murder of Valentinian III in the following year mark the end of the Western empire.

328 *which they have now possessed*: Bede here takes a long view over the outcome of these struggles; in *EH* I. 16 he follows Gildas more closely in having this see-saw struggle last up till the siege of Mount Badon. See note to p. 28.

perished by a divine thunderbolt: this tale comes from the *Liber Pontificalis*, 54, on the pontificate of Hormisdas (514–23).

329 *In that year*: AD 525.

due to the malice of the Romans: this story, which appears in a number of seventh- and eighth-century sources, is taken by Bede from the *Liber Pontificalis*, 63, on John III (561–74).

330 '*Touch me and see ... that I have.*': Luke 24: 39.

Herminigild: this version of the death of Hermenigild derives from that in Gregory the Great's *Dialogues*, III. 31, but the wording is Bede's own.

331 *Anastasius the Persian*: Bede's own *Life of St Anastasius* has been identified: see notes to p. 295; he claims in *EH* v. 24 to have written it because the previous Latin translation of the Greek original was so bad; the relative length of this account in the Chronicle indicates that Bede was particularly interested in him.

336 *were found uncorrupted*: Bede only includes three of the numerous Anglo-Saxon saints to be found in *EH* in the Chronicle: two of them, Æthelthryth and Cuthbert, are noted because their bodies were found intact when dug up some years after their burial. For Bede this was a special symptom of sanctity. The third one to be included (p. 339) is bishop Egbert, who was responsible for bringing Iona into line on the matter of the dating of Easter.

337 *Aripert*: Aripert II, king of the Lombards (701–12); Bede took this from *Liber Pontificalis*, 88, on pope John VII (705–7), but 'anglicized' the name 'Haripertus' as 'Hereberectus'.

Receiving help from Terbellius: the information comes from *Liber Pontificalis*, 88.

339 *pandect*: the whole Bible in a single volume. This volume, which never reached Rome, was discovered in Milan in 1887. It is written in an uncial script so fine that it long delayed the recognition that this manuscript had been written in Northumbria. See R. Bruce-Mitford, *The Art of the Codex Amiatinus* (Jarrow Lecture, 1967).

the Arabs: the source for Bede's knowledge of this event is not known; the information probably came via Rome and was transmitted orally. It is interesting that Bede, writing in 725, knew nothing of the Arab attacks on southern and western Francia that had commenced in 721. The lateness of the arrival of any such information may explain some of the chronological ambiguities attending the mention of them in *EH* v. 23.

340 *Liutprand*: king of the Lombards (712–44); the story is not recorded elsewhere. Paul the Deacon took it directly from Bede in his *History of the Lombards*, VI. 48.

343 *bishop Egbert*: bishop of York 732–66; he received a papal pallium in 735, becoming the first archbishop of the see since Paulinus (*HE* II. 20). He was the brother of the Northumbrian king Eadbert (737–58). There is a brief eulogy of him in Alcuin's poem *The Bishops, Kings and Saints of York*, ed. P. Godman (Oxford, 1982), lines 1248–87.

in person: while there is no need to doubt the reference to Bede's ill health, this is a rhetorical preface, and it should not be assumed that Bede would have forgone the opportunity of writing what is more of a free-standing moral treatise than a letter.

slave: although habitually translated by the more anodyne 'servant' from the Reformation onwards, this diminishes the full force of the original here in Matt. 25: 21–3 and elsewhere in the New Testament.

'Rejoice you . . . Master's happiness': Matt. 25: 21–3.

344 *'Throw him . . . gnashing of teeth.'*: Matt. 25: 30; Vulgate.

divine speech: Origen (186–254) first developed the idea that the Bible was written in a divine language, infinitely more subtle and profound than any human language, and capable of expressing different levels of meaning simultaneously; see his *De Principibus*, 4. 1–3. Bede is not here implying that Egbert might speak 'in the divine speech', but is encouraging him to biblical reading, which in the Early Middle Ages was normally done aloud.

those in spiritual authority: this is the nearest translation of the word *Rectores*, used by pope Gregory the Great (590–604), not least in his *Pastoral Rule* of 591. See R. Markus, 'Gregory the Great's *Rector* and his Genesis', in J. Fontaine *et al.* (eds.), *Grégoire le Grand* (Paris, 1986), 137–46. Bede took this, and much else of his ideas on spiritual direction and the monastic life, from Gregory.

'leaving aside . . . not burned?': 2 Cor. 11: 28–9; Vulgate.

346 *chant them carefully*: from his vocabulary it is clear that Bede envisaged a chanting recitation of these texts. Later in the paragraph he indicates that this could be accompanied by a series of genuflexions. This was an Irish penitential practice; e.g. L. Bieler (ed.), *The Irish Penitentials* (Dublin, 1963), p. 279, nos. 10–14.

Explanatory Notes

346 *Ambrose advises*: in his *On Virgins*, III. iv. 20.

who hid his coin: cf. Matt. 25: 26–30.

347 *taxes that are due to that bishop*: the earliest Anglo-Saxon reference to a tax payable to the Church by each household appears in clauses 4 and 61 of the law code of king Ine of the West Saxons (688–726), issued *c*.690. See Attenborough, *The Laws of the Earliest English Kings*, 36 and 56. Bede here provides evidence that a similar system applied in Northumbria.

'Having dwelt . . . from any man': 1 Sam. 12: 2–4; Vulgate.

348 *'Moses and Aaron . . . spoke to them'*: Ps. 98: 7–8; Vulgate.

'Greed is the root of all evil.': 1 Tim. 6: 10–11; Vulgate.

'Nor shall the covetous . . . kingdom of God.': 1 Cor. 6: 10; Vulgate.

king Ceolwulf: since the completion of Bede's *EH*, Ceolwulf had been deposed and rapidly restored (in 731). He abdicated and retired to Lindisfarne in 737. The causes of these events are unknown. He was Egbert's cousin.

more of our race as bishops: it is clear from the reference to Gregory's letter later in this paragraph that Bede is talking only about the Northumbrian kingdom. Instead of Gregory's expected twelve bishops under the metropolitan authority of York, the only Northumbrian sees at this time were York, Hexham, Lindisfarne, and Whithorn. Bede's advice was ignored, as no new sees were to be created, nor was the enormous see of York further subdivided.

349 *in a letter*: the text of this is in *EH* I. 29; see p. 55 above.

one of the monasteries: apart from York, all of the Northumbrian bishoprics were centred on monasteries. So Bede's assumption that a new see would do likewise is not surprising.

metropolitan status: this was achieved in 735, when York was made an archbishopric again by pope Gregory III (731–41); this status had lapsed after the flight of Paulinus in 633.

350 *the episcopal see*: although Bede had just talked about bringing the total number of northern sees up to twelve, as envisaged by Gregory, he here restricts the proposal to a single new creation. If he had a particular location in mind, it was probably in Deira, which had no monastic-centred sees and was served only by York.

Zedekiah: all other translations have substituted 'Hezekiah' (king of Judah 716–687 BC), but Bede's text is clear: he wrote and meant Zedekiah (598–587 BC), king of Judah at the time of the Babylonian destruction of the Temple.

350 *'Break the bonds . . . every evil document.'*: Bede here totally distorts the biblical text in the interest of his very idiosyncratic argument. The Jerusalem Bible translation of the Vulgate text of Isa. 58: 6, which is what he claims to be quoting, reads: 'undo the thongs of the yoke, to let the oppressed go free, and break every yoke'.

deeds and documents: Bede is suggesting that written landgrants and deeds of sale should be capable of being overturned if subsequently deemed 'unjust'. Not only does Bede here prove the use of charters (i.e. written legal records of such transactions) in Northumbria, but he is also advancing an argument that undermines their very purpose, which is to perpetuate and provide a legally secure witness to the reality of the sale, grant, or exchange thus recorded. See P. Wormald, *Bede and the Conversion of England: The Charter Evidence* (Jarrow Lecture, 1984).

diminishing of our military forces: Bede implies that estates thus granted to monasteries (whatever their character) are freed from obligation to contribute to the royal army when summoned. Wormald (*Bede and the Conversion of England*, 19–24) argues that what Bede really objected to was the permanent alienation of land that the kings could use to reward and thus augment their military following.

351 *witnessed in writing*: charters normally ended with the signatures or marks of those who had witnessed the making of the grant or sale, who could subsequently be called on to provide oral testimony to support the written record if the reality of the act reported were ever challenged. Bede's approach is legally anarchic, in that all such safeguards would be subverted if the documents could later be annulled on the basis of the—rather subjectively defined—morality of the recipients and their intentions.

352 *kingdom*: here translating *provincia*; that this was Bede's meaning is shown in Campbell, *Essays in Anglo-Saxon History*, 86–7.

leading nobles: here translating *praefecti*, thought to imply the highest level of office-holder under the kings; including, in some of the Anglo-Saxon kingdoms, members of families that had once been royal; see A. Thacker, 'Some Terms for Noblemen in Anglo-Saxon England, *c*.650–850', *ASSAH* 2 (1981), 201–36, esp. 210–13.

'If the blind . . . into the pit?': Matt. 15: 14; Vulgate.

regular monastic life: i.e. following a monastic rule, whether one of the widely known ones, such as those of Benedict and Columbanus, or one specific only to the individual monastery and drawn up by its founder; as, for example, the kind of rule that would have been used at pope Gregory's monastery on the Caelian.

353 *'The least . . . a most powerful nation.'*: Isa. 60: 22; Vulgate.

'I saw the evil-doers . . . men of good deeds.': Eccles. 8: 10; Vulgate.

355 *'it is more important . . . God than men.'*: Acts 5: 29; Vulgate.

'Sell what you own and give alms': Luke 12: 33; Vulgate.

'Unless he has renounced . . . be my disciple.': Luke 14: 33; Bede slightly alters the wording of the Vulgate in the first phrase.

'Blessed are the poor . . . kingdom of heaven.': Luke 6: 21 and 24; Vulgate.

'But know this . . . slave of idols.': Eph. 5: 5; Vulgate.

356 *'Why do you disobey . . . your traditions?'*: Matt. 15: 3; Vulgate.

'Every plant . . . will be eradicated.': Matt. 15: 13; Vulgate.

'wide is the gate . . . few find it.': Matt. 7: 13–14; Vulgate.

357 *'Dearest, do not love the world . . . but from the world.'*: 1 John 2: 15–16; Vulgate, though Bede adds the 'Dearest'.

in the third indiction: this dates the letter to the year 734, as this is the only time this number of the indiction would have appeared in the period between the beginning of Egbert's episcopate in 732 and Bede's death in 735.

INDEX

Aaron of Caerleon 19, 319, 364
Abercorn 23, 222, 403
Abraham 265–6
Acephalite Heresy, *see*
  Monotheletism
Acca, bishop of Hexham xvi,
  130, 194, 273, 275, 289, 296,
  390, 404, 411, 417, 419
Acha, sister of king Edwin 119,
  388
Adam 53
Adamnán of Coldingham
  218–20
Adamnán, abbot of Iona 262–6,
  284, 285, 387, 415
Adda, priest 144
Addi 241, 411
Ad Murum (Wallbottle?) 144,
  146, 395
Adtuifyrdi, synod of 226, 409
Æbbe, abbess of Coldingham
  203, 219–20, 406, 408
Æcci, bishop of *Dummoc* 183,
  402
Æddi, cantor 173, 400
Ælfflæd, abbess, daughter of king
  Oswiu 150–1, 222, 396, 409
Ælfric, uncle of king Edwin 110
Ælfwine, brother of king Ecgfrith
  207, 292, 406–7
Ælle, king of the Deirans 71,
  331, 375, 388
Ælle, king of the South Saxons
  78, 377
Æsica 185
Æthelbald, king of the Mercians
  289, 293, 296, 297, 377, 419
Æthelberht, king of the Cantuarii
  39–40, 58–60, 61, 74–5,
  77–9, 84, 131, 291, 331, 371,
  377; laws of 78, 378
Æthelberht II, joint king of the
  Cantuarii 288, 418

Æthelburh (Tata), daughter of
  king Æthelberht 84, 89–91, 97,
  106, 379
Æthelburh, daughter of king
  Anna 122, 123–4, 390
Æthelburh, sister of bishop
  Erconwald 183, 184, 186–8
Æthelfrith, king of the
  Northumbrians 61–62, 73–4,
  91–4, 110, 331, 374, 376, 380
Æthelheard, king of the West
  Saxons 296, 420
Æthelhere, king of the East
  Angles 150, 396
Æthelhild, abbess 127
Æthelhun, brother of bishop
  Æthelwine 162, 163
Æthelhun, son of king Edwin 97
Æthelred, king of the Mercians
  126, 191, 192, 199, 207, 208,
  212, 258, 267, 272, 273, 292,
  403
Æthelthryth (Audrey), abbess of
  Ely 175, 202–5, 206, 209,
  335–6, 406, 425
Æthelthryth, daughter of king
  Edwin 97
Æthelwealh, king of the South
  Saxons 192, 194, 197, 403–4
Æthelwine, bishop of Lindsey
  127, 162, 192, 390, 398
Æthelwine 132
Æthelwold, bishop of Lindisfarne
  257–8, 289, 296, 419
Æthelwold, king of the East
  Angles 147, 395
Æthelwold Moll, king of the
  Northumbrians 297, 421
Ætla, bishop of Dorchester
  (Oxon.) 211, 407
Áedán, king of Dalriada 61, 374
Aetius, Master of Soldiers 25, 36,
  326, 327, 366, 369

Index

444

The Oxford World's Classics Website

www.worldsclassics.co.uk

- Browse the full range of Oxford World's Classics online

- Sign up for our monthly e-alert to receive information on new titles

- Read extracts from the Introductions

- Listen to our editors and translators talk about the world's greatest literature with our Oxford World's Classics audio guides

- Join the conversation, follow us on Twitter at OWC_Oxford

- Teachers and lecturers can order inspection copies quickly and simply via our website

www.worldsclassics.co.uk

American Literature

British and Irish Literature

Children's Literature

Classics and Ancient Literature

Colonial Literature

Eastern Literature

European Literature

Gothic Literature

History

Medieval Literature

Oxford English Drama

Poetry

Philosophy

Politics

Religion

The Oxford Shakespeare

A complete list of Oxford World's Classics, including Authors in Context, Oxford English Drama, and the Oxford Shakespeare, is available in the UK from the Marketing Services Department, Oxford University Press, Great Clarendon Street, Oxford OX2 6DP, or visit the website at www.oup.com/uk/worldsclassics.

In the USA, visit www.oup.com/us/owc for a complete title list.

Oxford World's Classics are available from all good bookshops. In case of difficulty, customers in the UK should contact Oxford University Press Bookshop, 116 High Street, Oxford OX1 4BR.

Bhagavad Gita

The Bible Authorized King James Version
With Apocrypha

Dhammapada

Dharmasūtras

The Koran

The Pañcatantra

The Sauptikaparvan (from the
Mahabharata)

The Tale of Sinuhe and Other Ancient
Egyptian Poems

Upaniṣads

ANSELM OF CANTERBURY	The Major Works
THOMAS AQUINAS	Selected Philosophical Writings
AUGUSTINE	The Confessions On Christian Teaching
BEDE	The Ecclesiastical History
HEMACANDRA	The Lives of the Jain Elders
KĀLIDĀSA	The Recognition of Śakuntalā
MANJHAN	Madhumalati
ŚĀNTIDEVA	The Bodhicaryàvatàra

The Anglo-Saxon World

Beowulf

Lancelot of the Lake

The Paston Letters

Sir Gawain and the Green Knight

Tales of the Elders of Ireland

York Mystery Plays

GEOFFREY CHAUCER   The Canterbury Tales
                         Troilus and Criseyde

HENRY OF HUNTINGDON   The History of the English People
                         1000–1154

JOCELIN OF BRAKELOND   Chronicle of the Abbey of Bury
                         St Edmunds

GUILLAUME DE LORRIS   The Romance of the Rose
and JEAN DE MEUN

WILLIAM LANGLAND   Piers Plowman

SIR THOMAS MALORY   Le Morte Darthur

JANE AUSTEN	**Emma**
	Mansfield Park
	Persuasion
	Pride and Prejudice
	Sense and Sensibility
MRS BEETON	**Book of Household Management**
LADY ELIZABETH BRADDON	**Lady Audley's Secret**
ANNE BRONTË	**The Tenant of Wildfell Hall**
CHARLOTTE BRONTË	**Jane Eyre**
	Shirley
	Villette
EMILY BRONTË	**Wuthering Heights**
SAMUEL TAYLOR COLERIDGE	**The Major Works**
WILKIE COLLINS	**The Moonstone**
	No Name
	The Woman in White
CHARLES DARWIN	**The Origin of Species**
CHARLES DICKENS	**The Adventures of Oliver Twist**
	Bleak House
	David Copperfield
	Great Expectations
	Nicholas Nickleby
	The Old Curiosity Shop
	Our Mutual Friend
	The Pickwick Papers
	A Tale of Two Cities
GEORGE DU MAURIER	**Trilby**
MARIA EDGEWORTH	**Castle Rackrent**

	Women's Writing 1778–1838
WILLIAM BECKFORD	Vathek
JAMES BOSWELL	Life of Johnson
FRANCES BURNEY	Camilla
	Cecilia
	Evelina
	The Wanderer
LORD CHESTERFIELD	Lord Chesterfield's Letters
JOHN CLELAND	Memoirs of a Woman of Pleasure
DANIEL DEFOE	A Journal of the Plague Year
	Moll Flanders
	Robinson Crusoe
	Roxana
HENRY FIELDING	Joseph Andrews and Shamela
	A Journey from This World to the Next and The Journal of a Voyage to Lisbon
	Tom Jones
WILLIAM GODWIN	Caleb Williams
OLIVER GOLDSMITH	The Vicar of Wakefield
MARY HAYS	Memoirs of Emma Courtney
ELIZABETH HAYWOOD	The History of Miss Betsy Thoughtless
ELIZABETH INCHBALD	A Simple Story
SAMUEL JOHNSON	The History of Rasselas
	The Major Works
CHARLOTTE LENNOX	The Female Quixote
MATTHEW LEWIS	Journal of a West India Proprietor
	The Monk
HENRY MACKENZIE	The Man of Feeling
ALEXANDER POPE	Selected Poetry